AMERICAN ANT

AND

DISCOVERIES IN THE WEST:

BEING AN EXHIBITION OF THE EVIDENCE

THAT AN ANCIENT POPULATION OF PARTIALLY CIVILIZED NATIONS
DIFFERING ENTIRELY FROM THOSE OF THE PRESENT INDIANS PEOPLED
AMERICA MANY CENTURIES BEFORE ITS DISCOVERY BY
COLUMBUS, AND INQUIRIES INTO THEIR ORIGIN,

WITH A

COPIOUS DESCRIPTION

OF MANY OF THEIR STUPENDOUS WORKS, NOW IN RUINS,
WITH CONJECTURES CONCERNING WHAT MAY HAVE
BECOME OF THEM.

Compiled from Travels, Authentic Sources, and the
Researches of Antiquarian Societies.

BY JOSIAH PRIEST.

[Fourth Edition.]

ALBANY:
PRINTED BY HOFFMAN & WHITE.
1834.

NORTHERN DISTRICT OF NEW-YORK, To Wit:

Be it remembered, that on the twenty-first day of March, Anno Domini 1833, Josiah Priest, of the said district, hath deposited in this office a book, the title of which is in the words following, to wit:—" American Antiquities, and Discoveries in the West: being an exhibition of the evidence that an ancient population of partially civilized nations, differing entirely from those of the present Indians, peopled America many centuries before its discovery by Columbus. And inquiries into their origin, with a copious description of many of their stupendous works, now in ruins; with conjectures concerning what may have become of them. Compiled from travels, authentic sources, and the researches of antiquarian societies. By JOSIAH PRIEST,"—the right whereof he claims as author and proprietor, in conformity with an act of Congress, entitled " An Act to amend the several acts respecting copy rights."

RUTGER B. MILLER,
Clerk U. S. D. C. N. D. N. Y.

Published by
Ancient American Archaeology Foundation
P.O. Box 370, Colfax, Wisconsin 54730

ISBN 0-9703985-2-2

Printed by
Hayriver Press
Colfax, Wisconsin

PREFACE.

Although the subject of American antiquities is everywhere surrounded with its mysteries; yet we indulge the hope, that the volume we now present the public, will not be unacceptable, as on the account of its mysteriousness and obscurity, we have been compelled to wander widely in the field of conjecture, from which it is not impossible but we may have produced some original and novel opinions.

We have felt that we are bound by the nature of the subject, to treat wholly on those matters which relate to ages *preceding* the discovery of America by Columbus; as we apprehend no subject connected with the history of the continent *since* that time, can be entitled to the appellation of Antiquities of America.

If we may be permitted to judge from the liberal subscription this work has met with, notwithstanding the universal prejudice which exists against subscribing for books, we should draw the conclusion, that this curious subject has not its *only* admirers within the pales of antiquarian societies.

If it is pleasing as well as useful to know the history of one's country—if to feel a rising interest as its beginnings are unfolded—its sufferings—its wars—its struggles—and its victories, delineated; why not also, when the story of its *antiquities*, though of a graver and more majestic nature, are attempted to be rehearsed.

The traits of the *ancient* nations of the *old* world are every where shown by the fragments of dilapidated cities, pyramids of stone, and walls of wondrous length; but here are the wrecks of empire, whose beginnings, it would seem, are older than *any* of these, which are the mounds and works of the west, towering aloft as if their builders were preparing against another flood.

We have undertaken to elicit arguments, from what we suppose evidence, that the *first* inhabitants who peopled America, came on by land, at certain places, where it is supposed once to have been united with Asia, Europe, and Africa, but has been torn asunder by the force of earthquakes, and the irruptions of the waters, so that what animals had not passed over before this great physical rupture, were forever excluded; but not so with men, as they could resort to the use of boats.

We have gathered such evidence as induces a belief that America was, anciently, inhabited with partially civilized and agricultural nations, surpassing in numbers its present population. This, we imagine, we prove, in the discovery of thousands of the traits of the ancient operations of men over the entire cultivated parts of the continent, in the forms, and under the character of mounds and fortifications, abounding particularly in the western regions.

We have also ventured conjectures respecting what nations, in some few instances, may have settled here; also what may have become of them. We have entered on an examination of some of those works, and of some of the articles found on opening some few of their tumuli; which we have compared with similar articles found in similar works in various parts of the other continents, from which very curious results are ascertained.

As it respects some of the ancient nations who may have found their way hither, we perceive a strong probability that not only Asiatic nations, very soon after the flood, but that also all along the different eras of time, different races of men, as Polynesians, Malays, Australasians, Phœnicians, Egyptians, Greeks, Romans, Israelites, Tartars, Scandinavians, Danes, Norwegians, Welsh, and Scotch, have colonized different parts of the continent.

We have also attempted to show that America was peopled before the flood; that it was the country of Noah, and the place where the ark was erected. The highly interesting subject of American antiquities, we are inclined to believe, is but just commencing to be developed. The immensity of country yet beyond the settlements of men, towards the Pacific, is yet to be explored by cultivation, when other evidences, and wider spread, will come to view, affording, perhaps, more definite conclusion.

As aids in maturing this volume, we have consulted the works of philosophers, historians, travellers, geographers, gazetteers, the researches of antiquarian societies, with miscellaneous notices on this subject, as found in the periodicals of the day. The subject has proved as difficult as mysterious; any disorder and inaccuracies, therefore, in point of inferences which we have made we beg may not become the subjects of the severities of criticism.

If, however, we should succeed in awakening a desire to a farther investigation of this curious subject, and should have the singular happiness of securing any degree of public respect, and of giving the subscriber an equivalent for his patronage, the utmost of the desires of the author will be realized.

JOSIAH PRIEST.

CONTENTS.

	Page.
Location of Mount Ararat,	9
Origin of human complexions, with other curious matter,	14
Respecting the division of the earth by Noah among his sons,	22
Idenity and real name of Mechisedec of the scriptures,	24
Division of the earth in the days of Peleg, and of the spreading out of the nations, with other interesting items,	32
Of the antiquities of the west,	38
Supposed ruins of a Roman fort at Marrietta,	42
Course of the lost ten tribes of Israel, when they left Assyria for Arsareth,	55
Accounts of the convulsions of the globe,	79
Evidences of an ancient population in America different from that of the Indians,	83
Discoveries on the Muskingum, a river in the Ohio,	87
Discoveries of the remains of ancient pottery,	106
A catacomb of embalmed mummies, found in Kentucky,	110
A fac simile of the ancient letters of the Phœnicians,	116
Ancient letters of America and Africa, with a fac simile of the same,	118
A further account of western antiquities, with antediluvian traits,	125
A cavern of the west, containing hieroglyphics cut in a rock by the ancient nations,	139

CONTENTS.

Tracks of men and animals found in the rocks of Tennessee and St. Louis,... 151
Cotubamana the giant chief of one of the islands of the coast of America,.. 154
Still further accounts of discoveries in the west,............ 195
Vast works of the ancient nations on the east side of the Muskingum, Ohio,... 161
Ruins of ancient works at Circleville, Ohio,................. 163
Ancient works on paint creek,.............................. 166
A recent discovery of one of those ancient works among the Alleghany mountains,.. 169
Ancient wells found in the bottom of paint creek,............ 169
A description of western tumuli or mounds,.................. 171
Great works of the ancient nations on the north fork of Paint creek, Ohio,.. 183
Traits of ancient cities on the Mississippi,................. 187
Traditions of the native Mexicans respecting their migrations from the north,... 189
Supposed use of the ancient roads as found connected with some of the western mounds,..................................... 193
Traits of the Mosaic history found among the Azteca Indians, 199
Ceremonies of the fire worshippers as witnessed on the Ozark river, 209
Origin of fire worship,...................................... 212
A further account of western antiquities, and of curious articles, 213
Discovery of America by Europeans before the time of Columbus, 224
Ruins of the city of Otolum, recently discovered in America,.. 239
Discovery of a large stone covered with exquisite engravings, with a fac simile of the same,............................. 247
A further account of Europeans in America before the time of Columbus,... 251
Further accounts of western antiquities,..................... 256
Great stone castle of Iceland,............................... 258

CONTENTS.

Further accounts of instruments found in the tumuli of the west, 260
Great size of the Mexican mounds, 267
Predilection of the ancients to pyramid building, 268
A fac simile of antediluvian letters, 273
Voyages and shipping of the Mongol Tartars, and their settlements on the western coast of America, 276
A further account of western discoveries, 282
Various opinions respecting the original inhabitants of America, 285
Voyages of the ancients from Italy and from Africa to America, and its adjacent islands, 292
Further remarks on the subject of human complexions, 296
Still further remarks on human complexions with other interesting subjects, 298
Cannibalism practised in America, and elsewhere, 303
Ancient languages of the early nations of America, with a fac simile of the glyphs of Otolum the Amercan city, 309, 311
Atlantic nations of America, and of their languages, 313
Primitive origin of the English language, 316
Colonies of the Danes in America, 323
Ancient chronology of the Iroquois Indians, 336
Traits of an ancient colony of Negroes from Africa, in South America, 340
On the disappearance of the ancient lakes of the west, and of the formation of seacoal, 342
Further remarks on the draining of the westren country of its ancient lakes, 358
Supposed causes of the disappearance of the ancient nations of the west, 364
Lake Ontario supposed to have been formed by the crater of a volcano, 367
Remarks on geology, 372

CONTENTS.

Supposed resemblance of the western Indians to the ancient Greeks, ... 378
Supposed traits of the ancient Romans in America, ... 386
Traits of white nations in Georgia and Kentucky, before Columbus's time, and the traditions of the Indians respecting them, ... 390
Description of Mount Ararat on which the ark rested, ... 399

AMERICAN ANTIQUITIES

AND

DISCOVERIES IN THE WEST.

A LOFTY summit on a range of mountains, called Ararat, in Asia, furnished the resting place of the Ark, which contained the progenitors of both man and animals, who have replenished the Globe since the era of the Deluge.

Ararat is a chain of mountains, running partly round the southern end of the Caspian, and is situated between the Caspian and Black Seas; in latitude north, about 38 deg. agreeing with the middle of the United States, and is from London a distance of about two thousand four hundred miles, in a southeasterly course, and from the city of Albany, in the United States, is nearly six thousand, in an exact easterly direction, and the same latitude, except a variation of but three degrees south.

We have been thus particular to describe the exact situation, as generally allowed, of that range of mountains; because from this place, which is nearly on the western end of the Asiatic continent, Noah and his posterity descended, and spread themselves over many parts of the earth, and as we suppose, even to America, renewing the race of man, which well nigh had become extinct from the devastation and ruin of the universal flood.

But that the flood of Noah was *universal*, is gravely doubted; in proof of which, the abettors of this doubt, bring the traditional history of the ancient Chinese. Professor Rafinesque, of the city of Philadelphia, confessedly a learned and most able antiquarian, has recently advanced the following exceedingly interesting and curious matter, which relates to this subject.

"*History of China before the Flood.* The traditions preserved by many ancient nations of the earliest history of the earth and mankind, *before* and after the great geological floods, which have desolated the globe, are highly interesting; they belong at once to geology, archeology, history and many other sciences. They are the only glimpses to guide us where the fossil remains or medals of nature, are silent or unknown.

Ancient China was in the eastern slopes and branches of the mountains of Central Asia, the hoary *Imalaya,* where it is as yet very *doubtful* whether the flood thoroughly extended."

But though this is doubted, we cannot subscribe to the opinion, however great our deference may be for the ability and research of those who have ventured to doubt. We feel by far a greater deference for the statement of the Hebrew author of the book of Genesis; an historian of the highest *accredited* antiquity. This author says plainly, that " *all* the high hills under the *whole heaven* were covered;" and that " fifteen cubits," and upwards, the waters prevailed; and the mountains were covered. But not so, if we are to believe the above suggestion, which would leave a very large tract of country of Central Asia exempt from the flood of Noah, as also a part of South America.

This opinion, which contradicts the Bible account of that flood, is founded on "the traditional history of China, which speaks of two great floods which desolated, but did not overflow the land. They answer, says Mr. Rafinesque, to the two great floods of Noah and Peleg, recorded in the Bible. " The latter, the flood of Peleg, or Yao, was caused, he says, by volcanic paroxysms all over the earth;" but " much less fatal than the flood of Noah, or Yu-ti, in China."

Respecting this flood, " the following details are taken chiefly from the Chinese historians, Liu-yu and Lo-pi, whose works are called Y-tse, and Uai-ki, as partly translated by Leroux." These say, that " the first flood happened under the 8th Kɪ, or period called Yu-ti, and the first emperor of it," was " *Chin-sang*, about 3170 years before Christ," 826, before the flood.

But neither can this be true, as the flood of Noah took place 1656 years from the creation, which would be but 2,344 years *before* Christ; being a mistake of about 826 years. Wherefore, if there is any truth in the Chinese history at all, those histories must allude to some flood *before* that of Noah; an account of which may have been received from Noah himself, and preserved in the Chinese histories written after the flood.

The flood alluded to, by the above named historians, did not, it is true, according to their account, overflow the whole earth, but was such as that the waters did not return to their usual channels for a long time; "the misery of mankind was extreme; the beasts and serpents were very numerous;" being driven together by the pursuit of the waters, and also "storms and cold" had greatly increased. Chin-sang collected the wandering men to unite against the wild beasts, to dress their skins for clothing, and to weave their fur into webs and caps. This emperor was venerated for these benefits, and began a SHI, or dynasty, that lasted 350 years."

This account would suit very well to the character of Nimrod the founder of the first monarchy after the flood, whom we are much inclined to think the Chinese historians point out, instead of any king before the era of the flood of Noah.

But to the research of the highly gifted antiquarian, Rafinesque, we are greatly indebted in *one important* respect: It is well known that persons in the learned world have greatly admired the boasted antiquity of the *Chinese* nations, who, by their records, make the earth much older than the account given by Moses. But this philosopher on this subject writes as follows: "The two Chinese words, *Ki* and *Shi*, translated *period* and *dynasty*, or family, are of some importance. As they now stand translated, they would make the world very old; since no less than ten Ki, or periods, are enumerated, (we are in the 10th;) wherein 232 SHI, or dynasties of emperors, are said to have ruled in China, during a course of 276,480 years before Christ, at the *lowest* computation; and 96,962,220 before Christ, at the *highest;* with many intermediary calculations, by various authors.

But if Ki, he says, may also mean a *dynasty*, or division, or people, as it appears to do in some instances, and SHI, an *age*, or a *tribe*, or reign, the whole preposterous computation will prove false, or be easily reduced to agree with those of the Hindoos, Persians and Egyptians;" and come within the age of the earth as given in the Scriptures.

If the central region of Asia, and parts of South America, may have been exempted from that flood, we may then safely inquire, whether other parts of the globe may not also have been exempt; where men and animals were preserved; and thus the account of the ark, in which, as related by Moses, both men and animals were saved, is completely overturned. But the universal traditions of *all nations*, contradict this, while the earth, every where, shows signs of the operations of the waters, in agreement with this universal tradition. If such a flood never took place, which *rushed* over the earth with extraordinary violence, how, it may be inquired, are there found in Siberia, in north latitude 60 and 70 deg. great masses of the bones of the elephant and rhinoceros—animals of the hot regions of the equator. From this it is evident that the flood which wafted the bodies of those animals, rolled exactly over all China and the Hindoo regions. In all parts of the earth, even on the highest regions and mountains, are found oceanic remains. Whales have been found in the mountains of Greenland, and also in other parts, as in America, far from the ocean.

Chinese history, it is true, gives an account of many floods, which have ruined whole tracts of that country, as many as sixty-five, one of which, in the year 185 before Christ, it is said, formed that body of water called the Yellow Sea, situated between Corea and China.

But were the history of American floods written, occasioned by similar causes; such as rivers rupturing their mountain barriers; and the shocks of earthquakes, since the time of Noah's flood; who could say there would not be as many. We shall have occasion to speak of this subject before we close this volume.

It is said that the history of China gives an account of the state of mankind before the flood of Yuti, or Noah, and represents them as having been happy, ruled by benevolent monarchs, who took nothing and gave much; the world submitted to their virtues and good laws; they wore no crowns, but long hair; never made war, and put no one to death. But this is also contrary to the account of Moses; who says the earth before the flood was corrupt before God, and was *filled* with violence. But they carry their description of the happiness of men so high, as to represent perfect harmony as having existed between men and animals; when men lived on roots and the fruits of the earth; that they did not follow hunting; property was common, and universal concord prevailed. From this high wrought account of the pristine happiness of man, we are at once referred to the original state of Adam in Paradise, and to his patriarchal government after his fall; and it is likely also to that of his successors, till men had multiplied in the earth; so as to form conflicting interests, when the rapine and violence commenced, as spoken of by Moses, which it seems grew worse and worse, till the flood came and took them all away.

That the central parts of Asia were not overflown by the deluge, appears of vast importance to some philosophers of the present day to be established. For *if so*, we see, say they, at once, how both men and animals were preserved from that flood; and yet this does not, they say, militate against the Mosaic account; for the very word *ark* is, in the original language, *theba*, and signifies *refuge*, and is the country of Thibet. So that when Moses talked about an ark, he only meant the central part of Asia, or Thibet, in which men and animals were saved, instead of a vessel.

Theba, or *Thibet*, situated in what is called Central Asia, and in size equal to three-fourths of the area of the United States, is indeed the highest part of that continent, and produces mountains higher than any other part of the earth: yet Moses says, that the flood prevailed fifteen cubits and upwards above the *highest* mountains.

Thibet is situated in latitude 30 degrees north, exactly between Farther India, Hindostan and Siberia, where banks of the bones of equatorial animals are found, as we have noticed; by which we assertain that the deluge rolled over this very *Theba*, the country supposed to have been left dry at the time of Noah's flood.

But that opinion will not do; for the Mosaic account plainly says, that God said to Noah, "*make thee an ark of gopher wood.*" Surely Noah did not *make* the central part of Asia, called Theba, or Thibet; neither was he called upon to do so, as it would have taken *much gopher wood* to have formed the whole, or a part of so large a country. But respecting the word which is translated *ark* in the scriptures, it is said by Adam Clarke to be, in the original, *Tebath*, and not *Theba*.

The word *Tebath*, he says, signifies *vessel*, and means no more nor less than a vessel, in its most common acceptation, a hollow place, capable of containing persons, goods, &c. The idea, therefore, that the word *ark* signified the central parts of Asia, called

Theba, or Thibet, falls to the ground; while the history, as given by Moses, respecting the flood of Noah, remains unshaken.

The same author has also discovered that a race of ancient people, in South America, called the *Zapotecas*, boast of being *antediluvian* in America, and to have built the city of Coat-lan, so named because this city was founded at a place which swarmed with serpents; therefore named Snake-city, or Coat-lan, built 327 years before the flood; and that, at the time of the flood, a remnant of them, together with their king, named Pet-ela, (or dog,) saved themselves on a mountain of the same name, Coat-lan.

But we consider this tradition to relate *only* to the *first* efforts at architecture *after* the flood of Noah, round about the region of Ararat, and on the plains of Shinar. The very circumstance of this tribe being still designated by that of the *Dog* tribe, is an evidence that they originated not before the flood as a nation, but in Asia, since that era; for in Asia, as in America, tribes of men have also been thus designated, and called after the various animals of the woods. The Snake Indians are well known to the western explorers in America, as also many other tribes, who are named after various wild animals. And the circumstance of their city being built at a place where there were many serpents, shows the allusion to point to the same time and place spoken of on page 11, where the Chinese historians, *Liu-yu* and *Lo-pi*, say the serpents were driven together by the waters, where, according to the Zapotecas, the city of Snakes, or Coat-lan, was built.

Supposed Origin of Human Complexions, with the ancient signification of the Names of the three Sons of Noah, and other curious matter.

The sons of Noah were three, as stated in the book of Genesis; between whose descendants the whole earth, in process of time, became divided. This division appears to have taken place in the earliest ages of the *first* nations after the flood, in such manner as to suit, or correspond with the several constitutions of those nations, in a physical sense, as well as with a reference to the various complexions of the descendants of these three heads of the human race.

This preparation of the nations, respecting animal constitution and color, at the fountain head, must have been directed by the hand of the Creator, in an arbitrary manner; by which not only his sovereignty, as the Governor of the earth, with all its tribes, is manifest, but also his wisdom; because the *same* physical constitutions which are suited to the temperate and frigid zones of the globe, could not endure the burning climates of the torrid; so neither are the constitutions of the equatorial nations so tempered as to enjoy the snowy and ice-bound regions in the high latitudes north and south of the equator.

The very names, or words, Shem, Ham and Japheth, were, in the language of Noah, (which was probably the pure Hebrew,) in some sense, significant of their future national character. We proceed to show in what sense their names were descriptive, prospectively, of their several destinies in the earth, as well also as that *Ham* was the very *name* of his color, or complexion.

The word *Shem*, says Dr. Clarke, signifies *renown*, in the language of Noah; which, as that great man, now no more, remarks, has been wonderfully fulfilled, both in a temporal and spiritual sense. In a temporal sense, first, as follows: His posterity spread themselves over the finest regions of Upper and Middle Asia, Armenia, Mesopotamia, Assyria, Media, Persia, and the Indus, Ganges, and possibly to China, still more eastward.

The word *Japheth*, which was the name of Noah's third son, has also its meaning, and signifies, according to the same author, that which may be exceedingly enlarged, and capable of spreading to a vast extent.

His posterity diverged eastward and westward from Ararat, throughout the whole extent of Asia, north of the great range of the Taurus and Ararat mountains, as far as the Eastern ocean; whence, as he supposes, they crossed over to America, at the straits of Behring, and in the opposite direction from those mountains, throughout Europe, to the Mediterranean sea, south from Ararat; and to the Atlantic ocean west from that region; whence also they might have passed over to America, by the way of Iceland, Greenland, and so on to the continent, along the coast of Labrador, where traces of early settlements remain, in parts now desert. Thus did Japheth enlarge himself, till his posterity literally encompassed the earth, from latitude 35 degrees north and upward, toward the pole.

The word *Ham* signified that which was burnt or *black*. The posterity of this son of Noah peopled the hot regions of the earth, on either side the equator.

But as it respects the complexions of these *heads* of the nations of the earth, we remark as follows: Shem was undoubtedly a red or copper colored man, which was the complexion of all the antediluvians.

This conclusion is drawn from the fact, that the nations inhabiting the countries named as being settled or peopled by the descendants of *Shem* have always been, and now are, of that cast. We deem this fact as conclusive, that such was also their progenitor, *Shem*, as that the great and distinguishing features and complexion of nations change not, so as to disappear. Shem was the father of the Jewish race, who are of the same hue, varying, it is true, some being of a darker, and some of a lighter shade, arising from secret and undefinable principles, placed beyond the research of man; and also, from amalgamation by marriage with white, and with the darker nations, as the African. But to corroborate our opinion that the antediluvians were of a *red*, or copper complexion, we bring the well-known statement of Josephus, that ADAM, the *first* of men, was a red man, made of red earth, called virgin earth, because of its beauty and pureness. The word *Adam*, he also says, signifies that color which is *red*. To this account the tradition of the Jews corresponds, who, as they are the people most concerned, should be allowed to know most about it.

Shem, therefore, must have been a red man, derived from the complexion of the first man, Adam. And his posterity, as above described, are accordingly of the same complexion; this is well known of all the Jews, unmixed with those nations that are fairer, as attested by history, and the traveller of every age, in the countries they inhabit.

The word *Ham*, which was the name of the second son of Noah, is the word which was descriptive of the color which is *black*, or burnt. This we show from the testimony of Dr. Hales, of England, who was a celebrated natural philosopher and mathematician of the 17th century, who is quoted by Adam Clarke, to show that the *word* Ham, in the language of Noah, which was that of the antediluvians, was the term for that which was *black*.

It is not possible, from authority so high and respectable, that doubts can exist respecting the legitimacy of this word, and of its ancient application. Accordingly, as best suited to the *complexion* of the descendants of *Ham*, the hot regions of the equator were allotted to those nations.

To the Cushites, the southern climes of Asia, along the coast of the Persian gulf, Susiane, or Cushistan, Arabia, Canaan, Palestine, Syria, and Egypt and Lybia in Africa. These countries were settled by the posterity of Ham, who were, and now are, of a glossy black.

But the vast variety of shades and hues of the human face, are derived from amalgamations of the *three* original complexions, red, black, and white. This was the act of God, giving to the three persons, upon whom the earth's population depended, by way of perpetuity, such complexions, and animal constitutions, as should be best suited to the several climates, which he intended, in the progress of his providence, they should inhabit.

The people of these countries, inhabited respectively by these heads of nations, the immediate descendants of Shem, Ham and Japheth, *still* retain, in full force, the ancient, pristine red, white, and black complexions, except where each have intruded upon the other, and become scattered, and mingled, in some degree, over the earth. Accordingly, among the African nations, in their *own* proper countries, now and then a colony of whites have fixed their dwellings. Among the *red* nations are found, here and there, as in some of the islands of the Pacific, the *pure* African; and both the black and the red are found among the white nations; but *now*, much more than in the earliest ages, a general amalgamation of the three *original* colors exists.

When we speak of the original, or pristine complexions, we do not mean *before* the flood, except in the family of Noah, as it is our opinion that neither the *black* or the *white* was the complexion of Adam and all the nations before the flood, but that they have been produced by the power and providence of the Creator in the family of Noah only.

Much has been written to establish the doctrine of the influence of *climate* and *food*, in producing the vast extremes between a fair and ruddy white, and a jet black. But this mode of reasoning, to establish the origin of the human complexion, we imagine very inconclusive and unsatisfactory; as it is found that no distance of space, lapse of ages, change of diet, or of countries, can possibly "remove the leopard's spots, or change the Ethiopian's skin." No lapse of ages has been known to change a white man and his posterity to the hue or shape of an African, although the hottest rays of the burning clime of Lybia, may have scorched him ages unnumbered, and its soil have fed him with its roots and berries, an equal length of time. It is granted, however, that a white man with his posterity, will *tan* very dark by the heat of the sun; but it can never alter, as it *never* has materially altered, the shape of his face from that which was characteristic of his nation or people, nor the form of his limbs, nor his curled hair, turning it to a *wool*, provided, always, the blood be kept pure and unmixed.

Power in the decomposition of food, by the human stomach, does not exist of sufficient force to overturn the deep foundation of *causes* established in the very germ of being, by the Creator. The circumstance of what a man may eat, or where he may chance to breathe, cannot derange the economy of *first* principles. Were it so, it were not a hard matter for the poor African, if he did but know this choice trait of philosophy, to take hope and shake off entirely his unfortunate skin, in process of time, and no longer be exposed, solely on that account, to slavery, chains, and wretchedness.

But the inveteracy of complexion against the operation of climate, is evinced by the following, as related by Morse. On the eastern coast of Africa, in latitude 5 deg. north, are found jet black, tawny, olive, and *white* inhabitants, all speaking the same language, which is the Arabic. This particular part of Africa is called the Magadoxo kingdom: the inhabitants are a stout, warlike nation, of the Mahometan religion. Here, it appears, is permanent evidence that climate or food have no effect in materially changing the hues of the complexion, each retaining their own original tincture; even the *white* is found as stubborn in this torrid sky, as the black in the northern countries.

The whites found there are the descendants of the ancient Romans, Vandals and Goths, who were, it is asserted by John Leo, the African, who wrote a description of Africa in Arabic, all anciently comprehended under the general name of *Mauri*, or *Moors*, as well as the black Moors themselves.—(*Morse's Universal Geography*, vol. ii., pp. 754, 781.)

PROCOPIUS, a Greek historian of the 6th century, speaks of a race of fair complexioned people, with ruddy countenances and yellow hair, who dwelt far within the desert of Lybia, which is in Africa. The same race was found by Dr. Thomas Shaw, the antiquary, who was born in the 17th century, who speaks of them as retaining their fair complexion and yellow hair, although a lapse of years no less than twelve hundred had transpired, from the time of Procopius till the time of Dr. Shaw. The latitude of their country is between 10 and 12 degrees south.—(*Encyclopedia*, vol. vi., part 2, p. 668, American edition.)

Shem, according to the commonly received opinion, was the eldest son of Noah; and as the complexion of this child did not differ from that of other children born before the flood, all of whom are supposed to have been red, or of the copper hue, on the ground of Adam's complexion; Noah did not, therefore, name the child at first sight, from any extraordinary impulse arising from any singular appearance in the complexion, but rather, as it was his *first* born son, he called him Shem, that is, *renown*, which name agrees, in a surprising manner, with what we have hereafter to relate, respecting this character.

The impulse in the mind of Noah, which moved him to call this *first* son of his *Shem*, or *renown*, may have been similar to that of the patriarch Jacob respecting his *first* born son. He says, *Reuben*, thou art my *first* born, my might, and the beginning of my strength, the excellency of dignity, and the excellency of power. The ideas are similar, both leading to the same consequence; in one case it is *renown*, in the other the excellency of power, which is equivalent to renown: and, in both cases, arise from the mere circumstance of those children being the *first* born.

It is not unusual for parents to feel this sensation, on the birth of a *first* child, especially if it be a son; however, it is not impossible but the prophetic spirit moved Noah so to name *this* son by the extraordinary appellation, *renown*, or Shem; and the chief trait of celebrity which was to attach itself to the character of Shem, was to arise out of the fact of his being the type of the Messiah; and the time was to come when this person, after the flood should have passed away, would be the *only* antediluvian survivor; on which account, all mankind must, of necessity, by natural and mutual consent, look up to this man with extraordinary veneration.

By examining the chronological account of the Jewish records, we find the man Shem lived five hundred years *after* the flood, and that he over-lived Abraham about forty years. So that he was not only the oldest man on the earth at that time, but also the only surviving antediluvian, as well as the great typical progenitor of the adorable Messiah.

Here was a foundation for *renown*, of sufficient solidity to justify the prophetic spirit in moving Noah to call him *Shem*, a name full of import, full of meaning, pointing its signification, in a blaze of light, to him whose birth and works of righteousness were to be of consequences the *highest* in degree to the whole race of Adam, in the atonement.

But at the birth of HAM, it was different. When this child was born, we may suppose the house or *tent* to have been in an uproar, on the account of his *strange* complexion; the news of which, we may suppose, soon reached the ear of the father, who, on beholding it, at once, in the form of an exclamation, cried out, HAM! that is, it is *black!* and *this* word became *his* name.

It is believed, that in the first ages of the world, things were named from their supposed qualities; and their supposed qualities arose from *first* appearances. In this way, it is imagined, Adam named all the animals at first sight; as the Lord God caused them to pass before him, a *sudden* impulse arising in his mind, from the appearance of each creature; so that a suitable name was given.

This was natural; but not more so than it was for Noah to call his second son *Ham*, because he was *black;* being struck by this uncommon, unheard of, complexion of his own child, which impelled him at once to name him as he looked.

We suppose the same influence governed at the birth of JAPHETH, and that at the birth of this child, greater surprise still must have pervaded the household of Noah, as *white* was a cast of complexion still more wonderful than either *red* or *black*, as these two last named complexions bear a stronger affinity to each other than to that of white.

No sooner, therefore, as we may suppose, was the news of the birth of this third son carried to Noah, than, being anxious to embrace him, saw with amazement, that it was diverse from the other two, and from all mankind; having not the least affinity of complexion with any of the human race; and being in an ecstacy, at the sight of so fair and ruddy an infant, beautifully white and transparent of complexion, cried out, while under the influence of his joy and surprise, JAPHETH! which word became his name; to this, however, he added afterwards, God shall greatly enlarge Japheth, and he shall dwell in the tents of Shem and Canaan; that is, Ham shall be his servant; so that, in a political sense, he was higher than the other two.

But if our opinion on this subject is esteemed not well supported, we would add one other circumstance, which would seem to amount to demonstration, in proving Ham and his posterity to have been black at the outset.

The circumstance is as follows: At two particular times, it appears from Genesis, that Noah declared, Ham, with his posterity, should serve or become servants to both the posterity of Shem and Japheth. If one were to inquire whether this has been fulfilled or not, what would be the universal answer? It would be—it has been fulfilled. But in what way? Who are the people? The universal answer is, the African race are the people. But how is this proved, unless we allow them to be the descendants of Ham?

If, then, they are his descendants, they have been such in every age, from the very beginning; and the same criterion, which is their color, has distinguished them. This proves their progenitor, Ham, to have been black; or otherwise, it had been impossible to distinguish them from the posterity of the other two, Shem and Japheth; and whether the denunciation of Noah has been fulfilled or not, would be unknown. But as it is known, the subject is clear; the distinguishing trait by which Ham's posterity were known at *first*, must of necessity have been, as it is now, black.

We have dwelt thus far upon the subject of human complexions, because there are those who imagine the variety now found among men, to have originated *purely* from climate, food, and manner of living; while others suppose a *plurality* of fathers to have been the cause, in contradiction of the account in Genesis, where one man is said to have been the father all mankind. But on this curious subject, respecting the variety of complexions see, toward the close of this volume, the remarks of Professor Mitchell, late of New-York.

Respecting a division of the Earth, by Noah, among his Sons.

It cannot be denied but the whole earth, at the time the ark rested on mount Ararat, belonged to Noah, he being the prince, patriarch, or head and ruler of his own family; consequently, of all the inhabitants of the earth, as there were *none* but his own house. This is more than can be said of any other man since the world began, except of the man Adam. Accordingly, in the true character of a Patriarchal Prince, as related by Eusebius, an ecclesiastical writer of the fourth century, and by others, that Noah, being commanded of God, proceeded to make his *will*, dividing the *whole* earth between his three sons, and their respective heirs or descendants.

To Shem he gave all the East; to Ham, all *Africa;* to Japheth, the continent of *Europe*, with its *isles*, and the northern parts of *Asia*, as before pointed out. And may we not add America, which, in the course of Divine Providence, is *now* in the possession of the posterity of Japheth, and it is not impossible but this quarter of the earth may have been known even to Noah, as we are led to suspect from the statement of Eusebius.

This idea, or information, is brought forward by Adam Clarke, from whose commentary on the Scriptures, we have derived it. That a knowledge of not only Africa, Asia, and Europe, was in the possession of Noah, but even the *islands* of Europe, is probable, or how could he have given them to the posterity of his son *Japheth*, as written by Eusebius.

It may be questioned, possibly, whether these countries, at so early a period, had yet been explored, so as to furnish Noah with *any* degree of knowledge respecting them. To this it may be replied, that he lived *three hundred and fifty years* after the flood, and more than a hundred and fifty after the building of the tower of Babel and the dispersion of the first inhabitants, by means of the confusion of the ancient language.

This was a lapse of time quite sufficient to have enabled explorers to have traversed them, or even the whole earth, if companies had been sent out in different directions, for that express purpose, and to return again with their accounts to Noah. If the supposition of Adam Clarke, and others, be correct; which is, that at that time the *whole* land of the globe was so situated that no continent was quite separate from the others by water, as they are now; so that men could traverse by land the whole globe at their will: if so, even America may have been known to the first nations, as well as other parts of the earth.

This doctrine of the union of continents, is favored, or rather founded on a passage in the book of Genesis, 10th chap. 20th ver., where it is stated that one of the sons of Eber was PELEG, so named, because, in *his days*, the *earth* was divided; the word *Peleg*, probably signifying *division*, in the Noetic language.

The *birth* of Peleg was about an hundred years after the flood, the very time when Babel was being built. But we do not imagine this great convulsionary division of the several quarters of the globe took place till perhaps an hundred years after the birth of Peleg, on account of the peculiar latitude of the expression, " in the days of Peleg." Or, it may have been even two hundred years after the birth of Peleg, as this person's whole life was but two hundred and thirty-nine years, so that Noah over-lived him eleven years.

" In the days of Peleg," therefore, may as well be argued to mean, near the close of his life, as at any other period; this would give time for a very considerable knowledge of the earth's countries to have been obtained; so that Noah could have made a judicious division of it among the posterity of his sons.

This grand division of the earth, is supposed by some, to have been only a *political* division; but by others, a physical or geographical one. This latter opinion is favored by Adam Clarke. See his comment on the 25th verse of the 10th chapter of Genesis, as follows:—" A separation of *Continents* and islands from the main land, the earthy parts having been united in one great continent, previous to the days of Peleg." But at this era, when men and animals had found their way to the several quarters of the earth, it seemed good to the Creator to *break down* those uniting portions of land, by bringing into action the winds, the billows, and subterranean fires, which soon, by their repeated and united forces, removed each isthmus, throwing them along the coasts of the several continents, and forming them into islands; thus destroying, for wise purposes, those primeval highways of the nations. This subject continued on page 32.

Supposed identity and real name of Melchisedec, of the Scriptures.

This is indeed an interesting problem, the solution of which has perplexed its thousands; most of whom suppose him to have been the Son of God, some angelic, or mysterious supernatural personage, rather than a mere man. This general opinion proceeds on the ground of the Scripture account of him, as commonly understood, being expressed as follows:—"Without father, without mother, without descent, having neither beginning of days, nor end of life, but made like unto the Son of God, abideth a priest continually."—(*Hebrews vii. 3.*)

But, without further circumlocution, we will at once disclose our opinion, by stating that we believe him to have been SHEM, the eldest son of Noah, the immediate progenitor of Abraham, Isaac, Jacob, and the Jews, and none other than SHEM, "the man of name, or renown."

We derive this conclusion from the research, and critical commentary of the learned and pious Adam Clake, who gives us this information from the tradition of the Jewish Rabbins, which, without hesitation, gives this honor to Shem.

The particular part of that commentary to which we allude as being the origin of *our* belief, on this subject, is the preface of that author to the book of Job, on page 716, as follows: "SHEM lived five hundred and two years after the deluge; being still alive, and in the three hundred and ninety-third year of his life, *when* Abraham was born; *therefore,* the Jewish tradition, that *Shem was* the Melchisedec, or my righteous king of Salem," which *word* Melchisedec, was "an epithet, or title of *honor* and respect, *not* a proper name, and therefore, as the *head* and *father* of his race, Abraham paid tithes to him. This seems to be *well* founded, and the idea is confirmed by these remarkable words: (*Psalms* cx.) Jehovah hath sworn, and will not repent or change, *at tah cohenleolam al dibarte Malkitsedek.* As if he had said: Thou, my only begotten son, first born of many brethren, not according to the *substituted* priesthood of the sons of Levi, who, after the sin of the golden calf, stood up in lieu of all the first born of Israel, invested with their forfeited rights of primogeniture of king and priest: the Lord hath sworn and will not repent, (change.) *Thou* art a priest for ever, after the (my order of Melchisedec, my own original primitive) order of primogeniture: even as *Shem,* the *man* of *name,* the *Shem* that stands the first and foremost of the sons of Noah. The *righteous Prince, and Priest of the Most High God,* meets his descendant, ABRAHAM, after the slaughter of the kings, with refreshments; and blessed him, as the head and father of his race; the Jews in particular; and, as such, he received from Abraham the tithe of all the spoil.

How beautifully does Paul of Tarsus, writing to the Hebrews, point, through Melchisedec, (or Shem, the head and father of their race,) invested in all the original rights of primogeniture, Priest of the most high God, blessing Abraham as such, before Levi had existence, and as such, receiving tithes from Abraham, and *in* him *from* Levi, yet in the loins of his forefathers: Moses, on this great and solemn occasion, records simply this: Melchisedec, king of SALEM, Priest of the most high God, *sine genealogie;* his pedigree not mentioned, but standing as *Adam* in St. Luke's genealogy without father and without mother, *Adam of God.*—(*Luke* iii., 38.) How beautifully, I say, doth St. Paul point, through Melchisedec, to Jehoshua, our great High Priest and King, Jesus Christ, whose eternal generation who shall declare! *Ha Mashiach,* the Lord's annointed High Priest and King, after the order of Melchisedec; only begotten, first born son.

Thus far for the preface on the subject of Melchisedec, showing that he was none other than Shem, the son of Noah. We shall now give the same author's views of the same *supposed* mysterious *character,* Melchisedec, as found in his notes on the 7th Hebrews, commencing at the third verse.

Without father, without mother, without descent, having neither beginning of days, nor end of life. "The object of the Apostle, in thus producing the example of Melchisedec, was to show, 1st.

That Jesus was the person prophesied of in the 110th Psalm; which Psalm the Jews uniformly understood as predicting the Messiah. 2d. To answer the objections of the Jews against the legitimacy of the priesthood of Christ, arising from the stock from which he proceeded. The objection is this: If the Messiah is a *true priest*, he *must* come from a legitimate stock, as all the priests under the law have regularly done; otherwise we cannot acknowledge him to be a priest.

"But Jesus of Nazareth has not proceeded from such a stock; therefore we cannot acknowledge him for a priest, the antetype of Aaron. To this objection the Apostle answers, that it was not necessary for the priest to come from a particular stock; for Melchisedec was a priest of the most high God, and yet was not of the stock either of Abraham (for Melchisedec was before Abraham,) or Aaron, but was a *Canaanite*.

"It is well known that the ancient Jews, or Hebrews, were exceedingly scrupulous in choosing their *high priest*; partly by divine command, and partly from the tradition of their common ancestors, who always considered this office to be of the highest dignity. 1st God commanded, (*Leviticus* xxi. 10,) that the high priest should be chosen from among their brethren; that is, from the family of Aaron. 2d. That he should marry a virgin. 3d. He must not marry a widow. 4th. Nor a divorced person. 5th. Nor a harlot. 6th. Nor one of another nation. He who was found to have acted contrary to these requisitions, was, *jure divino*, excluded from the pontificate, or eligibility to hold that office.

"On the contrary, it was necessary that he who desired this honor should be able to prove his descent from the family of Aaron; and if he could not, though even in the priesthood, he was cast out; as we find from Ezra, ii. 62, and Nehemiah vii. 63. To these divine ordinances the Jews have added, 1st. That no *proselyte* could be a priest. 2d. Nor a slave. 3d. Nor a bastard. 4th. Nor the son of a Nithinnim; these were a class of men who were *servants* to the priests and Levites, (not of their tribe,) to draw water, and to hew wood. 5th. Nor one whose father exercised any *base trade*.

"And that they might be *well* assured of all this, they took the utmost care to preserve their genealogies, which were regularly kept in the archives of the temple. When, if any person aspired to the sacerdotal function, his geneological table was carefully inspected, and if any of the above blemishes was found in him he was rejected."

But here the matter comes to a point as it respects our inquiry respecting Melchisedec's having no father or mother.

"*He who could not* support his pretensions by just genealogical evidences, was said to be *without father*. Thus in *Bereshith Rabba*, sec. xviii. fol. 18, are these words: *For this cause shall a man leave father and mother.* It is said, if a proselyte to the Jewish religion have married his own sister, whether by the same father or by the same mother, they cast her out, according to Rabbi Meir. But the wise men say, if she be of the *same mother*, they cast her out; but if of the same father, they retain her, *shein ab la gai,* for a Gentile *has no father*, that is, his father is *not* reckoned in the Jewish genealogies."

In this way, both Christ and Melchisedec were without father, and without mother, had neither beginning of days, descent of lineage, nor end of life in *their* books of genealogies, which gave a man a right to the priesthood, as derived from Aaron; that is, were not descended from the original Jewish *sacerdotal* stock. Yet Melchisedec, who was a Canaanite, was a priest of the most high God. This sense SUIDAS* confirms, under the word Melchisedec, where, after stating that he reigned a prince in Salem, (that is Jerusalem,) 113 years, he died a righteous man. To this he adds: "He is, therefore, said to be without *descent* or *genealogy*, because he was not of the seed of Abraham (for Abraham was *his* seed,) but of Canaanitish origin."

We think this sufficient to show the reason why he is said to have had no father or mother, beginning of days, nor end of life, as stated in Hebrews. But this is not said of him in the book of Genesis, where we first become acquainted with this truly wonderful character.

It should be recollected that the Jewish genealogies went no farther back, for the qualifications of their priestly credentials, or eligibility to the pontifical office, than to the time and family of Aaron, which was more than four hundred years after that of

---

* Suidas, a Greek scholar of eminence, who flourished A. D. 975, and was an ecclesiastical writer of that age.

Abraham and Melchisedec. No wonder, then, that Christ's genealogy was not found in their records, so as to give him a claim to that office, such as they might approve.

But inasmuch as Melchisedec was greater than Abraham, from whom the Jewish race immediately originated, he argues from the authority of the 110th Psalm, where Melchisedec is spoken of, which the Jews allowed to be spoken of Christ, or the Messiah, who was to come, and was, therefore, a priest after the order of that extraordinary Prince of Peace, and King of Salem; because, neither had he such a claim on the Jewish genealogies, as required by the Jews, so as to make him eligible to *their* priesthood, for they knew, or might have known, that Christ did not come of the Aaronic race, but of the line or tribe of Judah.

That he was a man, a mere man, born of a woman, and came into the world after the ordinary manner, is attested by St. Paul's own extraordinary expression. (*See Hebrews*, vii. 4.) "Now consider how great this MAN was, unto whom Abraham gave the tenth of the spoils." However wonderfully elevated among men, and in the sight of God; however powerful and rich, wise, holy, and happy; he was, nevertheless, a mere *man*, or the tenth of the spoils he would not have received.

But the question is, what man was he, and what was his name? "Now consider how *great* this man was," are words which may possibly lead us to the *same* conclusion, which we have quoted from the preface of the book of Job.

There are not wanting circumstances to elevate this man, on the supposition that he was Shem, in the scale of society, far above a common level with the rest of the inhabitants of his country, of sufficient importance to justify St. Paul in saying, "now consider how great this man was."

We shall recount some of the circumstances; and first, at the time he met Abraham, when he was returning from the slaughter of the kings who had carried away Lot, the half brother of Abraham, with all his goods, his wife and children, and *blessed* him; he was the *oldest* man then on the earth. This circumstance alone was of no small amount, and highly calculated to elevate Shem in the eyes of mankind; for he was then more than five hundred and fifty years old.

Second: He was then the only man on the earth who had lived before the flood; and had been conversant with the nations, the institutions, the state of agriculture and the arts, as understood and practised by the antediluvians.

Third: He was the only man who could tell them about the location of the garden of Eden; a question, no doubt, of great curiosity and moment to those early nations, so near the flood; the manner in which the fall of Adam and Eve took place. He could tell them what sort of fruit it was, and how the tree looked on which it grew; and from Shem, it is more than probable, the Jews received the idea that the forbidden fruit was that of the *grape vine*, as found in their traditions.

SHEM could tell them what sort of serpent it was, whether an orang-outang, as believed by some, that the evil spirit made use of to deceive the woman; he could tell them about the former beauty of the earth, before it had become ruined by the commotion of the waters of the flood; the form and situation of countries, and of the extent and amount of human population. He could tell them how the nations who filled the earth with their violence and rapine, used to go about the situation of the happy garden to which no man was allowed to approach nor enter, on account of the dreadful Cherubim and the flaming sword; and how they blasphemed against the judgments of the Most High on that account.

Fourth: Shem could inform them about the progress of the ark, where it was built, and what opposition and ridicule his father Noah met with while it was being builded; he could tell respecting the violent manners of the antediluvians, and what their peculiar aggravated sins chiefly consisted in—what God meant when he said, that "*all flesh* had corrupted its way before Him," except the single family of Noah. There are those who imagine, from that *peculiar* phraseology, "*all flesh* hath corrupted its way on the earth," that the human *form* had become mingled with that of animals. If so, it was high time they were drowned, both man and beast, for reasons too obvious to need illustration here; it was high time that the soil was purged by water, and torn to fragments and buried beneath the earthy matter thrown up from depths not so polluted.

It is not at all improbable but from this strange and most horrible practice, the *first* ideas of the ancient statuaries were derive of delineating sculpture which represents monsters, half human and half animal. This kind of sculpture, and also paintings, abounded among the Egyptians, the Greeks, and the Romans, as well as other nations of the early ages. Of these shapes were many of their gods; being half lion, half eagle, and half fish; according to the denomination of paganism who adored these images.

Fifth: Shem was the only man in the days of Abraham, who could tell them of the promised Messiah, of whom he was the *most* glorious and expressive type afforded to men, before his coming, as attested by St. Paul. It is extremely probable, that with this man, Abraham had enjoyed long and close acquaintance, for he was descended of his loins, from whom he learned the knowledge of the *true God*, in all probability, in the midst of his Chaldean, idolatrous nation, and became a convert to the faith of Melchisedec. From the familiar manner with which Melchisedec, or Shem, who, we are compelled to believe, was indeed Melchisedec, met Abraham, and blessed him, in reference to the great *Messiah*, we are strongly inclined to believe them old acquaintance.

Sixth: It appears that Shem, or Melchisedec, had gotten great possessions and influence among men, as he had become king of *Salem*, or ancient *Jebus*, where Jerusalem was afterwards built, and where mount Zion reared her towers, and was the only temple, in which the true God was understandingly worshipped, then on the earth. It is not impossible but the mountainous region about Mount Horeb, and the mountains round about Jerusalem, were, before the flood, the base or foundation of the country, and exact location of the region of the garden called Eden, the place where Adam was created. But when the waters of the deluge came, they tore away all the earthy matter, and left standing those tremendous pinnacles and overhanging mountains of the region of Jerusalem and Mount Horeb.

By examining the map on an artificial globe, it will be seen, the region of country situated between the eastern end of the Mediterranean sea, the Black and Caspian seas, and the Persian gulf, the country now called Turkey, there are many rivers running into these several waters, all heading toward each other; among which is the Euphrates, one of the rivers mentioned by Moses, as deriving its origin in the garden, or country of Eden. Mountainous countries are the natural sources of rivers. From which we argue that Eden must have been a high region of country, as intimated in Genesis, entirely inaccessible on all sides, but the east; at which point the sword of the Cherubim was placed to guard the way of the tree of life. Some have imagined the Persian gulf to be the spot where the garden was situated. But this is impossible, as that the river Euphrates runs *into* that gulf, from toward Jerusalem, or from north of Jerusalem And as the region of Eden was the source of *four* large rivers, running in different directions, so also, now the region round about the present head waters of the Euphrates, is the source of many rivers, as said above; on which account, there can be but little doubt, but *here* the Paradise of Adam was situated, before the deluge. If the Euphrates is one of the rivers having its source in the garden or country of Eden, as Moses has recorded, it is then proved, to a demonstration, that the region as above described, is the ancient and primeval site of the literal Paradise of Adam.

The latitude of this region is between 20 and 30 degrees north, and running through near the middle of this country, from east to west, is the range of mountains known by that of *Mount Taurus* and *Mount Ararat*. So that we perceive this part of the globe is not only the ancient Eden, from where the human race sprang forth, at first but that also it was renewed probably near the same spot, in the family of Noah, after the flood.

Thus far we have treated on the subject of Melchisedec, showing reasons why he is supposed to have been *Shem*, the son of Noah, and reasons why St. Paul should say, " Now consider how great this *man* was." We will only add, that the word *Melchisedec* is *not* the name of that man so called, but is only a *term*, or appellation, used in relation *to* him, by God himself, which is the same as to say, *my righteous king*. So that Melchisedec was not the *name* he received at his birth, but was *Shem*, as the Jews inform us in their traditions.

Division of the Earth in the days of Peleg, and of the spreading out of the nations, with other curious matter.

But to return to the subject (left on page 23,) respecting the division of the earth in the days of Peleg. If, then, the division of the earth was a physical one, consequently such as had settled on its several parts before this division became forever separated towards the four quarters of the globe. If this position be true, the mystery is at once unriddled, how men and animals are found on all the earth, not excepting the islands, however far removed from other lands by intervening seas.

But of this matter we shall speak again towards the close of this work, when we hope to throw some degree of light upon this obscure, yet exceedingly interesting subject.

We here take the opportunity to inform the reader, that as soon as we have given an account of the dispersion of the inhabitants of the earth, immediately after the flood, from whom sprang the several nations mentioned in sacred and profane ancient history, we shall then come to our main subject, namely, that of the antiquities of America.

In order to give an account of those nations, we follow the Commentary of Adam Clarke, on the 10th chapter of the Book of Genesis; which is the *only* book to which we can resort for information of the kind; all other works which touch this point, are only illustrative and corroboratory. Even the boasted antiquity of the Chinese, going back millions of ages, as often quoted by the sceptic, is found, when rightly understood, to come quite within the account given by Moses of the creation.

This is asserted by Baron Humboldt, a historian of the *first* order, whose mind was embellished with a universal knowledge of the manners, customs, and traits of science, of the nations of the earth, rarely acquired by any man.

The Chinese account of their *first* knowledge of the *oldest* of their *gods*, shows their antiquity of origin to be no higher than the creation, as related in Genesis. Their *Shastrus*, a book which gives an account the incarnation of the god *Vishnoo*, states, that his first incarnation was for the purpose of bringing up the Vedas, (sacred books) from the deep. This appearance of Vishnoo, they say, was in the form of a fish. The books, the fish, and the deep, are all derived from Noah, whose account of the creation has furnished the ground of this Chinese tradition. In his second incarnation, he took the newly created world on his back, as he assumed the form of a tortoise, to make it stable. This alludes to the Mosaic account, which says, God separated the water from the dry land, and assigned them each their place. In his third incarnation he took the form of a *wild boar*, and drew the earth out of the sea, into which it had sunk during a periodical destruction of the world. This is a tradition of the deluge, and of the subsiding of the waters, when the tops of the mountains first appeared. A fourth incarnation of this god was for the rescue of a son, whose father was about to slay him. What else is this but the account of Abraham's going to slay his son Isaac, but was rescued by the appearance of an angel, forbidding the transaction. In a fifth incarnation he destroyed a giant, who despised the gods, and committed violence in the earth. This *giant* was none other than Nimrod, the author of idolatry, the founder of Babel, who is called, even by the Jews, in their traditions, a *giant*.

The inhabitants of the Tonga islands, in the South Pacific ocean, have a similar opinion respecting the first appearance of land, which evidently points to the flood of Noah.

They say, that at a certain time, the god Tangaloa, who was reputed to preside over arts and inventions, went forth to fish in the *great* ocean, and having from the sky let down his hook and line into the sea, on a sudden he felt that something had fastened to his hook, and believing he had caught an immense fish, he exerted all his strength, and presently there appeared above the surface several points of rocks and mountains, which increased in number and extent, the more he strained at his line to pull it up.

It was now evident that his hook had fastened to the very bottom of the ocean, and that he was fast emerging a vast continent; when, unfortunately, the line broke, having brought up only the Tonga islands, which remain to this day.

The story of this fishing god, *Tangaloa*, we imagine is a very clear allusion to the summits of Ararat, which first appeared above the waters of the flood in Asia.

"Now these are the generations of the sons of Noah, Shem, Ham and Japheth; and unto them were sons born after the flood." (*Genesis* x. 1, and onward.)

The sons of Japheth: "Japheth is supposed to be the same with Japetus of the Greeks, from whom, in an extreme remote antiquity, that people were supposed to have derived their origin. On this point most chronologists are pretty well agreed. Gomer is supposed to have peopled Galatia; this was a son of Japheth. So Josephus, who says that the Galatians, (or French people, derived from the ancient Belgaic tribes,) were *anciently* named Gomerites. From him the Cimmerians, or Cimbrians, are supposed to have derived their origin. Bochart, a learned French protestant, born at Rouen, in Normandy, in the 16th century, has no doubt that the Phrygians sprung from this person; and some of our principal commentators are of this opinion.

Madai, one of the sons of Japheth, is supposed to be the progenitor of the ancient Medes. JAVAN was another of his sons, from whom, it is almost universally believed, sprung the Ionians of Asia Minor. TUBAL is supposed to be the father of the Iberians, and that a part, at least of Spain was peopled by him and his descendants; and that Meschech, who is generally in Scripture joined with him, was the founder of the Cappadocians, from whom proceeded the Muscovites or Russians.

TIRAS. From this person, according to general consent, the Thracians derived their origin.

ASHKENAZ. From this person was derived the name *Sacagena*, a province of Armenia. Pliny, one of the most learned of the ancient Romans, who lived immediately after the commencement of the Christian era, mentions a people called Ascanticos, who dwelt about *Tannis*, or Palus Mæoticus; and some suppose, that from Ashkenaz the Euxine or Black sea derived its name; but others suppose, that from him the Germans derived their origin.

RIPHATH. The founder of the Paphlagonians, which were anciently called Riphatoel.

TOGARMA. The inhabitants of *Sauromates*, or of Turcomania.

ELISHAH. As Javan peopled a considerable part of Greece, it is in that region we must look for the settlements of his descendants. Elishah probably was the first who settled at Elis, in Peloponesus.

TARSHIS. He first inhabited *Cilicia*, whose capital, anciently, was the city of Tarsus, where St. Paul was born.

KITTIM. Some think by this name is meant Cyprus; others, the isle of Chios; others, the Romans; and others, the Macedonians.

DODANIM, or RHODANIM. Some suppose, that this family settled at Dodana; others, at the Rhone, in France; the ancient name of which was Rhodanus, from the Scripture Rhodanim:—"By these, were the *isles* of the *Gentiles* divided in their lands." EUROPE, of which this is allowed to be a general epithet, and comprehends all those countries to which the Hebrews were obliged to go by sea; such as Spain, Gaul or France, Italy, Greece, and Asia Minor.

Thus far we have noticed the spreading out over many countries, and the origin of many nations, arising out or from Japheth, *one* of the sons of Noah; all of whom were white, or at least come under that class of complexions.

The descendants of HAM, another of the sons of Noah, and some of the nations springing from him, we shall next bring to view.

CUSH, who peopled the Arabic *nome*, or province, near the Red sea, in Lower Egypt. Some think the Ethiopians sprung from him.

MIZRAIM. This family certainly peopled Egypt; and both in the east and west Egypt is called Mizraim.

PHUT. Who first peopled an Egyptian nome, or district, bordering on Lybia.

CANAAN. He who *first* peopled the land so called; known also by the name of the *Promised Land*. These were the nations which the Jews, who descended from Shem, cast out from the land of Canaan, as directed by God, because of the enormity and *brutal* nature of their crimes; which were such as *no* man of the present age, blessed with a Christian education, would excuse on a jury, under the terrors of an oath, from the punishment of death. They practised, as did the antediluvians and Sodomites, those things which were calculated to mingle the human with the brute. Surely, when this is understood, no man, not even a disbeliever in the inspiration of the Bible, will blame Moses for his seeming severity, in cutting off those nations with the besom of entire extermination.

"SEBA. The founder of the *Sabeans*. There seems to be three different people of this name, mentioned in the tenth chapter of Genesis, and a fourth in the twenty-fifth chapter of the same book." The queen of Sheba was of this race, who came, as it is said, from the uttermost parts of the earth, to Jerusalem, to know the wisdom of Solomon and the Hebrew religion; she was therefore, being a descendant of Ham's posterity, a black woman.

HAVILLAH, Sabtah, Ramah, Sabtechah, Sheba, Dedan. These are names belonging to the race of Ham, but the nations to whom they gave rise, is not interesting to our subject.

NIMROD, however, should not be omitted, who was of the race of Ham, and was his grandson. Of whom it is said, he was a mighty hunter before the Lord; meaning not only his skill and courage, and amazing strength and ferocity, in the destruction of wild animals, which infested the vast wilds of the earth at that time, but a destroyer of men's lives, and the originator of idolatry.

It was this Nimrod who opposed the righteous Melchisedec; and taught, or rather compelled, men to forsake the religion of Shem, or Melchisedec, and to follow the institutes of Nimrod.

" The beginning of his kingdom was *Babel, Erech, Acad,* and *Calneh,* in the land of Shinar.—(*Genesis* x. 10.)

The tower of Babel and the city of Babylon were both built on the Euphrates. Babel, however, was first built by Nimrod's agency, whose influence, it appears, arose much from the fierceness of his disposition, and from his stature and great muscular powers; qualifications which ignorant and savage nations, in every age, have been found apt to revere. The Septuagint version of the Scriptures speaks of Nimrod as being a surly giant. This was a colored man, and the first monarch of the human race since the flood.

But whether monarchical or republican forms of goverment obtained before the flood is uncertain. Probability would seem to favor neither; but rather that the patriarchal government should then have ruled. Every father, to the fourth and fifth generation, must have been, in those days, the *natural* king or chief of his clan.

These, after a while, spreading abroad, would clash with each other's interest, whence petty wars would arise, till many tribes being, by the fortune of war, weakened, that which had been most fortunate, would at once seize upon a wider empire. Hence monarchies arose. But whether it so fell out before the flood, cannot now be ascertained. A state, however, of fearful anarchy seems to be alluded to in the Scriptures; where it is said, that the earth was "*filled with violence.*" This, however, was near the time of the flood.

Popular forms of government, or those called republican or democratical, had their origin when a number of distant tribes or clans invaded a district or country so situated as that the interests of different tribes were *naturally* somewhat blended; these, in order to repel a distant or strange enemy's encroachments, would naturally unite under their respective chiefs or patriarchs. Experience would soon show the advantage of union. Hence arose republics.

The grand confederacy of the five nations, which took place among the American Indians, before their acquaintance with the white man, shows that such even among the most savage of our race, may have often thus united their strength—out of which civilization has sometimes, as well as monarchies and republics, arisen.

Since the flood, however, it is found that the descendants of Japheth originated the popular forms of government in the earth; as among the Greeks, the Romans, and more perfectly among the Americans, who are the descendants of Japheth.

We shall omit an account of the nations arising out of the descendants of SHEM, (for we need not mention the Jews, of whom all men know they descended from him;) for the same reasons assigned for the omission of a part of the posterity of Ham, because they chiefly settled in those regions of Asia, too remote to answer our subject any valuable purpose.

"In confirmation, however, that all men have been derived from one family, let it be observed, that there are many usages, both sacred and civil, which have prevailed in *all* parts of the world, which could owe their own origin to nothing but a general institution, which could not have existed, had not mankind been of the same blood originally, and instructed in the same common notions before they were dispersed" from the mountains of Ararat, and the family of Noah. Traits of this description, which argue to this conclusion, will, in the course of this work, be made to appear; which to such as believe the Bible, will afford peculiar pleasure and surprise.

Antiquities of the West.

There are no parts of the kingdoms or countries of the old world, but have celebrated in poetry and sober history, the mighty relics and antiquities of ancient empires, as Rome, Babylon, Greece, Egypt, Hindostan, Tartary, Africa, China, Persia, Europe, Russia, and many of the islands of the sea. It yet remains for America to awake her story from its oblivious sleep, and tell the tale of her antiquities—the traits of nations, coeval, perhaps, with the eldest works of man this side of the flood, and even before.

This curious subject, although it is obscured beneath the gloom of past ages, of which but small record remains; beside that which is written in the dust, in the form of mighty mounds, tumuli, strange skeletons, and aboriginal fortifications; and in some few instances, the bodies of preserved persons, as sometimes found in the nitrous caves of Kentucky, and the west, yet affords abundant premises to prompt investigation and rational conjecture. The mounds and tumuli of the west, are to be ranked among the most wonderful antiquities of the world, on the account of their number, magnitude, and obscurity of origin.

"They generally are found on fertile bottoms and near the rivers. Several hundreds have been discovered along the valley of the Mississippi; the largest of which stands not far from Wheeling, on the Ohio. This mound is fifty rods in circumference, and ninety feet in perpendicular height.

This is found filled with thousands of human skeletons, and was doubtless a place of general deposite of the dead for ages; which must have been contiguous to some large city, where the dead were placed in gradation, one layer above another, till it reached a natural climax, agreeing with the slope commenced at its base or foundation.

It is not credible, that this mound was made by the ancestors of the modern Indians. Its magnitude, and the vast numbers of dead deposited there, denote a population too great to have been supported by mere fishing and hunting, as the manner of Indians has always been. A population sufficient to raise such a mound as this, of earth, by the gradual interment of the deceased inhabitants, would necessarily be too far spread, to make it convenient for the living to transport their dead to *one single* place of repository. The modern Indians have ever been known, since the acquaintance of white men with them, to live only in *small* towns; which refutes the idea of its having been made by any other people than such as differed exceedingly from the improvident and indolent native; and must, therefore, have been erected by a people *more* ancient than what is commonly meant by the Indian aborigines, or wandering tribes, and more industrious.

Some of these mounds have been opened, when, not only vast quantities of human bones have been found, but also instruments of warfare, broken earthen vases, and trinkets. From the trees growing on them, it is supposed, they have already existed at least six hundred years; and whether these trees were the first, second, or third crop, is unknown; if the second only, which, from the old and decayed timber, partly buried in the vegetable mould and leaves, seems to favor, then it is all of twelve hundred years since they were abandoned, if not more.

Foreign travellers complain, that America presents nothing like *ruins* within her boundaries; no ivy mantled towers, nor moss covered turrets, as in the other quarters of the earth. Old Fort Warren, on the Hudson, rearing its lofty decayed sides high above West-Point; or the venerable remains of two wars, at Ticonderoga, upon Lake Champlain, they say, afford something of the kind. But what are mouldering castles, falling turrets, or crumbling abbeys, in comparison with those ancient and artificial aboriginal hills, which have outlived generations, and even all tradition; the workmanship of altogether unknown hands.

Place these monuments and secret repositories of the dead, together with the innumerable mounds and monstrous fortifications, which are scattered over America, in England, and on the continent of Europe, how would their virtuosi examine, and their antiquarians fill volumes with their probable histories. How would their fame be conveyed from learned bodies, and though literary volumes, inquiring who were the builders, of what age of the world, whence came they, and their descendants; if any, what has become of them; these would be the themes of constant speculation and inquiry.

At Marietta, a place not only celebrated as being the first settlement on the Ohio, but has also acquired much celebrity, from the existence of those extensive and supposed fortifications, which are situated near the town. They consist of walls and mounds of earth, running in straight lines, from six to ten feet high, and nearly forty broad at their base; but originally must have been much higher. There is also, at this place, one fort of this ancient description, which encloses nearly fifty acres of land.

There are openings in *this* fortification, which are supposed to have been, when thronged with its own busy multitude, "used as gateways, with a passage from one of them, formed by two parallel walls of earth, leading towards the river.

This contrivance was undoubtedly for a defence against surprise by an enemy, while the inhabitants dwelling within should fetch water from the river, or descend thither to wash, as in the Ganges, among the Hindoos. Also the greatness of this fort is evidence not only of the power of its builders, but also of those they feared. Who can tell but that they may have, by intestine feuds and wars, exterminated themselves? Such instances are not unfrequent among petty tribes of the earth. Witness the war between Benjamin and his brother tribes, when but a mere handful of their number remained to redeem them from complete annihilation. Many nations, an account of whom as once existing, is found on the page of history, now have not a trace left behind. More than sixty tribes which once traversed the woods of the west, and who were known to the first settlers of the New-England states, are now extinct.

The French of the Mississippi have an account, that an exterminating battle was fought in the beginning of the 17th century, about two hundred and thirty years ago, on the ground where Fort Harrison *now* stands; between the Indians living on the Mississippi, and those of the Wabash. The bone of contention was, the lands lying between those rivers, which both parties claimed. There were about 1000 warriors on each side. The condition of the fight was, that the victors should possess the lands in dispute. The grandeur of the prize was peculiarly calculated to inflame the ardor of savage minds. The contest commenced about sunrise. Both parties fought desperately. The Wabash warriors came off conquerors, having *seven* men left alive at sunset, and their adversaries, the Mississipians, but *five*. This battle was fought nearly fifty years before their acquaintance with white men."—*Webster's Gazetteer*, 1817, p. 69.

It is possible, whoever the authors of these great works were, or however long they may have lived on the continent, that they may have, in the same way, by intestine feuds and wars, weakened themselves, so that when the Tartars, Scythians, and descendants of the *ten* lost tribes, came across the straits of Bhering, that they fell an easy prey, to those fierce and savage northern hordes.

It is not likely, that the vast warlike preparations which extend over the whole continent, south of certain places in Canada, were thrown up, all of a sudden, on a *first* discovery of a *strange* enemy; for it might be inquired, how should they know such a mode of defence, unless they had acquired it in the course of ages, arising from necessity or caprice? but it is probable, they were constructed to defend against the invasions of each other; being of various origin and separate interests, as was much the situation of the ancient nations in every part of the world.

Petty tribes of the same origin, over the whole earth, have been found to wage perpetual war against each other, from motives of avarice, power, or hatred. In the most *ancient* eras of the history of man, little *walled* towns, which were raised for the security of a few families, under a chief, king, or patriarch, are known to have existed; which is evidence of the disjointed and unharmonious state of human society; out of which, wars, rapine, and plunder, arose: such may have been the state of man in America, before the Indians found their way here; the evidence of which is, the innumerable fortifications, found every where in the western regions.

Within this fort, of which we have been speaking, found at Marietta, are elevated *squares*, situated at the corners; some one hundred and eighty feet long, by one hundred and thirty broad, nine feet high, and level on the top. On these squares, erected at the corners of *this* great enclosure, were doubtless, placed some modes of annoyance to a beseiging enemy; such as engines to sling stones with, or to throw the dart and spear, or whatever might have been their modes of defence.

Outside of this fort, is a most singular mound, differing in form from their general configuration: its shape is that of a sugar loaf, the base of which is more than a hundred feet in circumference;

its height thirty, encompassed by a ditch, and defended by a parapet, or wall beyond the ditch, about breast high, through which is a way toward the main fort. Human bones have been taken from many of these mounds, and *charcoal*, with fragments of pottery; and what is more strange than all the rest, in one place, a skeleton of a man, buried *east* and *west* after the manner of enlightened nations was found, as if they understood the cardinal points of the compass. On the breast of *this* skeleton was found a quantity of isinglass, a substance sometimes used by the *ancient* Russians, for the purposes that glass is now used.

Ruins of a Roman Fort at Marietta.

But respecting this fort, as above, we imagine, that even the Romans may have built it, however strange this may appear. The reader will be so kind as to have patience till we have advanced all our reasons for this strange conjecture, before he casts it from him as impossible.

Our reasons for this idea, arise out of the great similarity there is between its form and fortifications, or camps, built by the ancient Romans. And in order to show the similarity, we have quoted the account of the forms of Roman camps from Josephus's description of their military works. See his works, Book v. chap. 5, page 219, as follows:

"Nor can their enemies easily surprise them with the suddenness of their incursions, for as soon as they have marched into an enemy's land, they do not begin to fight till they have *walled* their *camp* about; nor is the fence they raise, rashly made, or uneven; nor do they all abide in it; nor do those that are in it, take their place at random: but if it happens that the ground is uneven, it is first levelled."

"Their camps are also *four square* by measure; as for what space is within the camp, it is set apart for tents, but the outward circumference hath the resemblance to a wall; and is adorned with *towers* at equal distances, where, between the towers stand the engines for throwing arrows and darts, and for slinging stones, where they lay all other engines that can annoy the enemy, ready for their several operations.

"They also erect four gates, one in the middle of each side of the circumference, or square, and those large enough for the entrance of beasts, and wide enough for making excursions, if occasion should require. They divide the camp within into streets, very conveniently, and place the tents of the commanders in the middle; in the very midst of all, is the general's own tent, in the nature and form of a temple, insomuch that it appears to be a city, built on the sudden, with its market place, and places for handicraft trades, and with seats for the officers, superior and inferior, where if any differences arise, their causes are heard and determined.

"The camp and all that is in it, is encompassed with a *wall* round about, and that sooner than one would imagine, and this by the multitude and skill of the laborers. And if occasion require, a trench is drawn round the whole, whose depth is four cubits, and its breadth equal," which is a trifle more than six feet in depth and width.

The similarity between the Roman camps and the one near Marietta, consists as follows: They are both four square; the one standing near the great fort, and is connected by two parallel walls, as described; has also a ditch surrounding it, as the Romans sometimes encircled theirs; and doubtless, when first constructed, had a fence of timber (as Josephus says, the Romans had,) all round it, and all other forts of that description; but time has destroyed them.

If the Roman camp had its elevated squares at its corners, for the purposes of overlooking the foe and of shooting stones, darts, and arrows; so had the fort at Marietta, of more than a hundred feet square, on an average, of their forms, and nine feet high. Its parapets and gateways are similar; also the probable extent of the Roman encampments agrees well with the one at Marietta, which embraces near fifty acres within its enclosure; a space sufficient to have contained a great army; with streets and elevated squares at its corners, like the Romans. Dr. Morse, the geographer, says, the war camps of the ancient Danes, Belgæ, and Saxons, as found in England, were universally of the *circular*, while those of the Romans, in the same country, are distinguished by the *square* form;

is not this, therefore, a trait of the same people's work in America as in England?

Who can tell but during the *four hundred* years the Romans had all the west of Europe attached to their empire, but they may have found their way to America, as well as other nations, the Welch, and Scandinavians, in after ages, as we shall show, before we end the volume.

Rome, it must be remembered, was mistress of the known world, as *they* supposed, and were in the possession of the arts and sciences; with a knowledge of navigation sufficient to traverse the oceans of the globe, even without the compass, by means of the stars by night, and the sun by day.

The history of England informs us, that as early as fifty-five years before the Christian era, the Romans invaded the island of Britain, and that their ships were so large and heavy, and drew such a depth of water, that their soldiers were obliged to leap into the sea, and fight their way to the shore, struggling with the waves and the enemy, both at once, because they could not bring their vessels near the shore, on account of their size.

America has not yet been peopled from Europe so long, by a hundred years, as the Romans were in possession of the island of Britain. Now what has not America effected in enterprise, during this time; and although her advantages are superior to those of the Romans, when they held England as a province, yet, we are not to suppose they were idle, especially when their character at that time, was a martial and a *maritime* one. In this character, therefore, were they not exactly fitted to make discoveries about in the northern and western parts of the Atlantic, and may, therefore, have found America; made partial settlements in various places; may have coasted along down the shores of this country, they came to the mouth of the Mississippi, and thence up that stream, making here and there a settlement. This supposition is as natural, and as possible, for the Romans to have done, as that *Hudson* should find the mouth of the North river, and explore it as far north as to where the city of Albany is now standing. It was equally in their power to have found this coast by chance, as the Scandinavians in the year 1000 or thereabouts, who made a settlement at the mouth of the St. Lawrence; but more of this in due time.

To show that the Romans did actually go on voyages of *discovery*, while in possession of Britain, we quote from the history of England, that when Julius Agricola was governor of South Britain, he sailed quite round it, and ascertained it to be an island.

This was about one hundred years after their first subduing the country, or fifty-two years after Christ.

But they may have had a knowledge of the existence of America prior to their invasion of Britain. And lest the reader may be alarmed at such a position, we hasten to show in what manner they might have attained it, by relating a late discovery of a planter in South America.

"In the month of December, 1827, a planter discovered in a field, a short distance from Mont-Video, a sort of tomb stone, upon which strange, and to him unknown, signs or characters were engraved. He caused this stone, which covered a small excavation formed with masonry, to be raised, when he found two exceedingly ancient *swords*, a *helmet* and *shield*, which had suffered much from rust; also an *earthen* vessel of large capacity.

The planter caused the swords, the helmet and earthen *amphora*, together with the stone slab, which covered the whole, to be removed to Mont-Video, where, in spite of the effect of time, *Greek* words were easily made out, which, when translated, read as follows: " During the dominion of *Alexander*, the son of *Philip*, king of Macedon, in the sixty-third Olympiad, Ptolemaios"—it was impossible to decipher the rest, on account of the ravages of time on the engraving of the stone.

On the handle of one of the swords was the portrait of a man, supposed to be Alexander the Great. On the helmet there is sculptured work, that must have been executed by the most exquisite skill, representing *Achilles* dragging the corpse of *Hector* round the walls of Troy; an account of which is familiar to every classic scholar.

This discovery was similar to the Fabula Hieca, the bas-relief stucco, found in the ruins of the Via Appia, at Fratachio, in Spain, belonging to the princess of Colona, which represented all the principal scenes in the Iliad and Odyssey.

From this it is quite clear, says the editor of the Cabinet of Instruction and Literature, from which we have extracted this account, vol. 3, p. 99, that the discovery of this monumental altar is proof that a cotemporary of Aristotle, one of the Greek philosophers, has dug up the soil of Brazil and La Plata in South America.

It is conjectured that this Ptolemaios, mentioned on the stone, was the commander of Alexander's fleet, which is supposed to have been overtaken by a storm at sea, in the great ocean, (the Atlantic) as the ancients called it, and were driven on to the coast of Brazil, or the South American coast, where they doubtless erected the above mentioned monument, to preserve the memory of the voyage to so distant a country;" and that it might not be lost to the world, if any in after ages might chance to find it, as at last it was permitted to be in the progress of events.

The above conjecture, however, that Ptolemaios, a name found engraved on the stone slab which covered the mason work, as before mentioned, was one of Alexander's *admirals*, is not well founded, as there is no mention of such an admiral in the employ of that emperor, found on the page of the history of those times.

But the names of Nearchus and Onesicritus, are mentioned as being admirals of the fleets of Alexander the Great; and the name of Pytheas, who lived at the same time, is mentioned as being a Greek philosopher, geographer and astronomer, as well as a voyager, if not an admiral, as he made several voyages into the great Atlantic ocean; which are mentioned by Eratosthenes, a Greek philosopher, mathematician and historian, who flourished two hundred years befor Christ.

Strabo, a celebrated geographer and voyager, who lived about the time of the commencement of the Christian era, speaks of the voyages of Pytheas, by way of admission, and says that his knowledge of Spain, Gaul, Germany, and Britain, and all the countries of the north of Europe was extremely limited. He had, indeed, voyaged along the coasts of those countries, but had obtained but an indistinct knowledge of their relative situations.

During the adventures of this man at sea, for the very purpose of ascertaining the geography of the earth, by tracing the coasts of countries, there was a great liability of his being driven off in a western direction, not only by the current which sets always towards America, but also by the *trade winds*, which blow in the same direction for several months in the year.

Pytheas, therefore, with his fleet, it is most probable, either by design or storms, is the man who visited the American coast, and caused this subterranean monument of masonry to be erected. The Ptolemaios, or Ptolemy, mentioned on the stone, may refer to *one* of the *four* generals of Alexander, called sometimes Ptolemy Lagus, or Soter. This is the man who had Egypt for his share of the conquests of Alexander; and it is likely the mention of his name on the stone, in connexion with that of Alexander, was caused either by his presence at the time the stone was prepared, or because he patronised the voyages and geographical researches of the philosopher and navigator Pytheas.

Alexander the Great flourished about three hundred years before Christ; he was a Grecian, the origin of whose nation is said to have been Japetus, a descendant of Japheth, one of the sons of Noah, as before shown.

Let it be observed, the kingdom of Macedon, of which Alexander was the last as well as the greatest of its kings, commenced eight hundred and fourteen years before Christ, which was sixty-one years earlier than the commencement of the Romans.

Well, what is to be learned from all this story about the Greeks, respecting any knowledge in possession of the Romans about a continent *west* of Europe? Simply this, which is quite sufficient for our purpose; that an *account* of this voyage, whether it was an accidental one, or a voyage of discovery, *could not but be known* to the Romans, as well as to the Greeks, and entered on the records of the nation on their return. *But where, then, is the record?* We must go to the flames of the Goths and Vandals, who overran the Roman empire, in which accounts of the discoveries of countries and the histories of antiquity were destroyed; casting over those regions which they subdued, the gloom of barbarous ignorance, congenial with the shades of the forests of the north, from whence they originated. On which account, countries, and the knowledge of many arts, anciently known, were to be discovered over again, and among them, it is believed, was America.

When Columbus discovered this country, and had returned to Spain, it was soon known to all Europe. The same we may suppose of the discovery of the same country by the Greeks, though with infinitely less publicity; because the world at the time had not the advantage of printing; yet, in some degree, the discovery must have been known, especially among the great men of both **Greeks and Romans.**

The Grecian or Macedonian kingdom, after the death of Alexander, maintained its existence but a short time, one hundred and forty-four years only: when the Romans defeated Perseus, which ended the Macedonian kingdom, one hundred and sixty-eight years before Christ.

At this time, and thereafter, the Romans held on their course of war and conquest, till four hundred and ten years after Christ,—amounting in all, from their beginning, till Rome was taken and plundered by Alaric, king of the Visigoths, to one thousand one hundred and six-three years.

Is it to be supposed, the Romans, a warlike, enlightened, and enterprising people, who had found their way by sea so far north from Rome as to the island of Britain, and actually sailed round it, would not explore farther north and west, especially as they had some hundred years opportunity, while in possession of the north of Europe?

Morse, the geographer, in his second volume, page 126, says: Ireland, which is situated west of England, was probably discovered by the Phœnicians; the era of whose voyages and maritime exploits commenced more than fourteen hundred years before Christ, and continued several ages. Their country was situated at the east end of the Mediterranean sea; so that a voyage to the Atlantic, through the strait of Gibraltar west, would be a distance of about two thousand and three hundred miles, and from Gibralter to Ireland, a voyage of about one thousand and four hundred miles; which, in the whole amount is near four thousand.

Ireland is farther north, by about five degrees, than Newfoundland, and the latter only about 1800 miles southwest from Ireland; so that while the Phœnicians were coasting and voyaging about in the Atlantic, in so high a northern latitude as Ireland and England, may well be supposed to have discovered Newfoundland, (either by being lost or driven there by storm,) which is very near the coast of America. Phœnician letters are said to be engraven on some rocks on Taunton river, near the sea, in Massachusetts; if so this is proof of the position.

Some hundreds of years after the first historical notice of the Phœnician voyages, and two hundred years before the birth of Christ, the Greeks, it is said, became acquainted with Ireland and was known among them by the name of Juverna. Ptolemy, the

Egyptian geographer, who flourished about one hundred years after Christ, has given a map of that island, which is said to be very correct.—(*Morse.*)

Here, we have satisfactory historical evidence, that Ireland, as well, of course, as all the coast of northern Europe, with the very islands adjacent, were known; first, to the Phœnicians; second, to the Greeks; third, to the Romans; and, fourth, to the Egyptians—in those early ages, from which arises a great probability that America may have been well known to the ancient nations of the old world. On which account, when the Romans had extended their conquests so far north as nearly to old Norway, in latitude 60 degrees, over the greater part of Europe; they were well prepared to explore the North Atlantic, in a western direction, in quest of new countries; having already sufficient data to believe western countries existed.

It is not impossible but the Danes, Norwegians and Welsh, may have at *first* obtained some knowledge of western lands, islands and territories, from the discoveries of the Romans, or from their opinions, and handed down the story, till the Scandinavians or Norwegians discovered Iceland, Greenland and America, many hundred years before the time of Columbus.

But, however this may be, it is *certain* those nations of the north of Europe, *did* visit this country, as we have promised to show in its proper place. Would Columbus have made his attempt if he had not believed, or conjectured, there *was* a western continent; or by some means obtained hints respecting it, or the probability of its existence? It is said, Columbus found, at a certain time, the corpses of two men, of a tawny complexion, floating in the sea, near the coast of Spain, which he knew were not of European origin; but had been driven by the sea from some unknown *western* country; also timber and branches of trees, all of which confirmed him in his opinion of the existence of other countries westward.

If the Romans may have found this country, they may also have attempted its colonization, as the immense *square* forts of the west would seem to suggest.

In 1821, on the bank of the river Desperes, in Missouri, was found, by an Indian, a *Roman coin*, and presented to Gov. Clarke. This is no more singular than the discovery of a *Persian* coin near a spring on the Ohio, some feet under ground; as we have shown in another place of this work; all of which go to encourge the conjecture respecting the presence of the ancient Romans in America. The remains of former dwellings, found along the Ohio, where the stream has, in many places, washed away its banks, *hearths* and *fire places* are brought to light, from two to six feet below the surface.

Near these remains are found immense quantities of muscle shells and bones of animals. From the depths of many of these remnants of *chimnies*, and from the fact that trees as large as any in the surrounding forest, were found growing on the ground above those fire places, at the time the country was first settled by its present inhabitants, the conclusion is drawn that a very long period has elapsed since these subterraneous remnants of the dwellings of man were deserted.

Hearths and fire places.—Are not these evidences that buildings once towered above them? If not such as now accommodate the millions of America, yet they may have been such as the ancient Britons used at the time the Romans first invaded their country.

These were formed of logs set up endwise, drawn in at the top, so that the smoke might pass up at an aperture left open at the summit. They were not square on the ground, as houses are now built, but set in a *circle*, one log against the other, with the hearth and fire place in the centre. At the opening in the top, where the smoke went out, the light came in, as no other window was then used. There are still remaining, in several parts of England, the vestiges of large *stone* buildings made in this way; that is, in a circle.—(*Blair's History of England*, p. 8.)

At Cincinnati there are two museums, one of which contains a great variety of western antiquities, many skulls of Indians, and more than a hundred remains of what has been dug out of the aboriginal mounds. The most strange and curious of all, is a cup, made of clay, with three faces on the sides of the cup, each presenting regular features of a *man*, and beautifully delineated. It is the same represented on the plate.—(*See letter E.*)

A great deal has been said, and not a little written, by antiquarians about this cup. It was found in one of those mysterious mounds, and is known by the name of the *triune cup;* and there are those who think the makers of it had an allusion to the Trinity of the Godhead. Hence its name, triune cup.

In this neighborhood, the Yellow Springs, a day's ride below

Cincinnati, stands one of those singular mounds. Whenever we view those most singular objects of curiosity, and remains of art, a thousand inquiries spring up in the mind. They have excited the wonder of all who have seen or heard of them. Who were those ancients of the west, and *when*, and for *what* purpose these mounds were constructed, are questions of the most interesting nature, and have engaged the researches of the most inquisitive antiquarians. Abundant evidence, however, can be procured, that they are *not* of *Indian* origin.

With this sentiment there is a *general* acquiescence; however, we think it proper, in this place, to quote Dr. Beck's remarks on this point, from his *Gazetteer of the States of Illinois and Missouri.* (*See page* 308.)

"Ancient works exist on this river, the Arkansas, as elsewhere. The remains of mounds and fortifications are almost everywhere to be seen. One of the largest mounds in this country has been thrown up on this stream, (the Wabash,) within the last thirty or forty years, by the Osages, near the great Osage village, in honor of one of their deceased chiefs. This fact proves conclusively the original object of these mounds, and *refutes* the theory that they must necessarily have been erected by a race of men more civilized than the present tribes of Indians. Were it necessary, (says Dr. Beck,) numerous other facts might be adduced to prove, that the mounds are no other than the tombs of their great men."

That this is *one* of their uses there is no doubt, but not their *exclusive* use. The vast height of some of them, which is more than a hundred feet, would seem to point them out as places of lookout, which, if the country in the days when their builders flourished, was cleared and cultivated, would overlook the country to a great distance; and if it were not, still their towering summits would surmount even the interference of the forests.

But although the Osage Indians have so recently thrown up *one* such mound, yet it does not prove them to be of American Indian origin; and as this is an isolated case, would rather argue that the Osage tribe have originally descended from their *more* ancient progenitors, the inhabitants of this country *prior* to the intrusions of the late Indians from Asia.

Before we close this work, we shall attempt to make this appear from their own traditions, which have of late been procured from the most ancient of their tribes, the Wyandots, as handed down for hundreds of years, and from other sources.

The very form and character which Dr. Beck has given the Osage Indians, argues them of a superior stock, or rather a different race of men, as follows: "In person, the Osages are among the largest and best formed Indians, and are said to possess fine *military* capacities; but residing as they do in villages, and having made considerable advances in *agriculture*, they seem less addicted to war than their northern neighbors."

The whole of this character given of the Osage Indians, their *military* taste, their agricultural genius, their noble and commanding forms of person, and being *less* "addicted to war," shows them, it would seem, exclusively of other origin, than that of the common Indians.

It is supposed, the inhabitants who found their way first to this country, after its division, in the days of Peleg, and were here long before the modern Indians, came *not* by the way of Bhering's strait from Kamtschatka, in Asia, but directly from China across the Pacific, to the western coast of America, by means of islands which abounded anciently in that ocean between Chinese Tartary, China, and South America, even more than at present, which are, however, now *very* numerous; and also by the means of boats, of which all mankind have always had a knowledge. In this way, without any difficulty, more than is common, they could have found their way to this, as mankind have to every part of the earth.

We do not recollect that any of those *peculiar* monuments of antiquity appear north of the United States. Mackenzie, in his overland journey to the Pacific, travelling northwest from Montreal, in Canada, does not mention a single vestige of the kind, nor does Carver. If, then, there are none of these peculiar kinds, such as the *mounds*, farther north than about the latitude of the Canadas, it would appear from this, that the *first* authors of these works, especially of the mounds and tumuli, migrated, not from Asia, by way of Bhering's strait, but from Europe, east—China, west—and from Africa, south—continents now separated, then touching each other, with islands innumerable besides, affording the means.

If this supposition, namely, that the continents in the first age, immediately after the flood, were united, is not allowed, how, then, it might be inquired, came every country discovered, of any size, having the natural means of human subsistence, to be found inhabited?

In the very way this can be answered, the question relative to the means by which South America was *first* peopled, can also be answered, namely: the *continents*, as intimated on the first pages of this work, as quoted from Dr. Clarke, were, at first, that is, immediately after the flood, till the division of the earth, in the days of Peleg, *connected* together, so that mankind, with all kinds of animals, might pass to every quarter of the globe, suited to their natures. If such were not the fact, it might be inquired, how then did the several kinds of animals get to every part of the earth from the ARK? They could not, as *man*, make use of the boat, or vessel, nor could they swim such distances.

From Dr. Clarke's Travel's it appears, ancient works exist to this day, in some parts of Asia, similar to those of North America. His description of them, reads as though he were contemplating some of these western mounds. The Russians call these sepulchres *logri;* and vast numbers of them have been discovered in Siberia and the deserts bordering on the empire to the south. Historians mention these *tumuli*, with many particulars. In them were found vessels, ornaments, trinkets, medals, arrows, and other articles; some of copper, and even gold and silver, mingled with the ashes and remains of dead bodies.

When, and by whom, these burying places of Siberia and Tartary, more ancient than the Tartars themselves, were used, is exceedingly interesting. The situation, construction, appearance, and general contents of these Asiatic tumuli, and the American mounds, are however, so nearly alike, that there can be no hesitation in ascribing them to the same races, in Europe, Asia, Africa, and America; and also to the same ages of time, or nearly so, which we suppose, was very soon after the flood; a knowledge of mound building was then among men, as we see in the authors of Babel.

"The *triune cup (see plate, letter E.,)* deposited in one of the museums at Cincinnati, affords some probable evidence, that a part, at least, of the great mass of human population, once inhabiting the valley of the Mississippi, were of Hindoo origin. It is an earthen vessel, perfectly round, and will hold a quart, having three distinct faces, or heads, joined together at the back part of each, by a handle. The faces of these figures strongly resemble the

Hindoo countenance, which is here well executed. Now, it is well known, that in the mythology of India, *three* chief gods constitute the acknowledged belief of that people named BRAHMA, VISHNOO, and SIVA. May not this cup be a symbolical representation of that belief, and may it not have been used for some sacred purpose, here, in the valley of the Mississippi? In this country, as in Asia, the mounds are seen at the junction of many of the rivers, as along the Mississippi, on the most eligible positions for towns, and in the richest lands; and the day may have been, when those great rivers, the Mississippi, the Ohio, the Illinois, and the Muskingum, beheld along their sacred banks, countless devotees assembled for religious rites, such as *now* crowd in superstitious ceremonies, the devoted and consecrated borders of the Indus, the Ganges, and the Burrampooter, rivers of the Indies. Mounds in the west are very numerous, amounting to several thousands, none less than ten feet high, and some over one hundred. One opposite St. Louis measures eight hundred yards in circumference at its base, which is fifty rods. Sometimes they stand in groups, and with their circular shapes, at a distance, look like enormous hay stacks, scattered through a meadow. From their great number, and occasional stupendous size, years and the labors of tens of thousands must have been required to finish them.

Were it not, indeed, for their contents, and design manifested in their erection, they would hardly be looked upon as the work of human hands. In this view, they strike the traveller with the same astonishment as would be felt while beholding those oldest monuments of wordly art and industry, the Egyptian pyramids; and like them the mounds have their origin in the dark night of time, beyond even the history of Egypt itself. Whether or not these mounds were used at some former period, as "high places" for purposes of religion, or fortifications, or for national burying places, each of which theories has found advocates, one inference, however, amidst all the gloom which surrounds them, remains certain: the valley of the Ohio, was once inhabited by an immense agricultural population. We can see their vast funeral vaults, enter into their graves, and look at their dry bones; but no passage of history tells their tale of life; no spirit comes forth from their ancient sepulchres, to answer the inquiries of the living. It is worthy of remark, that Breckenridge, in his interesting travels through these regions, calculates that no less than *five thousand villages* of this forgotten people existed; and that their largest city was situated between the Mississippi and Missouri, not far from the junction of those rivers, near St. Louis. In this region, the mighty waters of the Missouri and Illinois, with their unnumbered tributaries, mingle with the " father of rivers," the Mississippi; (Mississippi, the word in the Indian language means Father of Rivers;) a situation formed by nature, calculated to invite multitudes of men, from the goodness of the soil, and the facilities of water communications.

The present race, who are now fast peopling the unbounded west, are apprised of the advantages of this region. Towns and cities are rising on the very ground where the ancient millions of mankind had their seats of empire. Ohio now contains more than six hundred thousand inhabitants; but at that early day, the same extent of country, most probably, was filled with a far greater population than inhabits it at the present time. Many of the mounds are completely occupied with human skeletons, and millions of them must have been interred in these vast cemeteries, that can be traced from the Rocky mountains, on the west, to the Alleghenies on the east, and into the province of the Texas and New Mexico to the south: revolutions like those known in the old world may have taken place here, and armies, equal to those of Cyrus, of Alexander the Great, or of Tamerlane the powerful, might have flourished their trumpets, and marched to battle, over these extensive plains, filled with the probabale descendants of that same race in Asia, whom these proud conquerors vanquished there.

Course of the Ten Lost Tribes of Israel.

THERE is a strong resemblance between the northern and independent Tartar, and the tribes of the North American Indians, but not of the South American. Besides this reason, there are others for believing our aborigines of North America were descended from the ancient Scythians, and came to this country from the eastern part of Asia.

This view by no means invalidates the opinion, that many tribes of the Indians of North America, are descended of the *Israelites*, because the Scythians, under this particular name, existed long before that branch of descendants of the family of *Shem*, called Israelites; who, after they had been carried away by Salmanasser, the Assyrian king, about 700 years B. C., went *northward*, as stated by Esdras, (see his second book, thirteenth chapter, from verse 40 to verse 45, inclusive,) through a part of Independent Tartary. During this journey, which carried them among the Tartars, *now* so called, but were anciently the Scythians, and probably became amalgamated with them. This was the more easily effected, on account of the agreement of complexion and common origin. If this may be supposed, we perceive at once, how the North American Indians are in possession of both Scythian and Jewish practices. Their Scythian customs are as follows:— "Scalping their prisoners, and *torturing* them to death. Some of the Indian nations also resemble the Tartars in the construction of their canoes, implements of war, and of the chase, with the well known habit of marching in *Indian file*, and their treatment of the aged;" these are *Scythian* customs.

Their Jewish customs are too many to be enumerated in this work; for a particular account of those customs, see Smith's View of the Hebrews. If, then, our Indians have evidently the manners of both the Scythian and the Jew, it proves them to have been, anciently, both Israelites and Scythians; the latter being the more ancient name of the nations now called Tartars,* with whom the ten tribes may have amalgamated. That the Israelites, called the ten tribes, who were carried away from Judea by Salmanasser, to the land of Assyria, went from that country, in a northerly direction, as quoted from Esdras, above, is evident, from the Map of Asia. Look at Esdras again, 43d verse, chap. 13, and we shall percceive, they " entered into the Euphrates by the narrow passes or heads of that river," which runs from the *north* into the Persian gulf.

It is not probable, that the country which Esdras called *Arsareth*, could possibly be America, as many have supposed, because a vast

---

* The appellation of Tartar was not known till the year A. D. 1227, who were at that time, considered a *new* race of barbarians.—*Morse.*

company, such as the ten tribes were at the time they left Syria, (which was about one hundred years after their having been carried away from Judea, nearly 3000 years ago,) could travel fast enough to perform the journey in so short a time as a year and a half.

We learn from the map of Asia, that Syria was situated at the southeasterly end of the Mediterranean sea, and that in entering into the narrow passes of the Euphrates, as Esdras says, would lead them *north* of Mount Ararat, and *southeasterly* of the Black sea, through Georgia, over the Caucassian mountains, and so on to Astracan, which lies north of the Caspian sea. We may, with the utmost show of reason, be permitted to argue, that this vast company of men, women, and their little ones, would naturally be compelled to shape their course so as to avoid the deep rivers which it cannot well be supposed they had the means of crossing, except when frozen. Their course would then be along the heads of the several rivers running north after they had passed the country of Astracan. From thence over the Ural mountains, or that part of that chain running along Independent Tartary. Then, after having passed over this mountain near the northern boundary of Independent Tartary, they would find themselves at the foot of the little Altain mountains, which course would lead them, if they still wished to avoid deep and rapid rivers, running from the little Altain mountains northward, or northwesterly, into the Northern ocean, across the immense and frozen regions of Siberia. The names of those rivers beginning on the easterly side of the Ural mountains, are first, the river Obi, with its many heads, or little rivers, forming at length the river Obi, which empties into the Northern ocean, at the gulf of Obi, in latitude of about 67 degrees north.

The second, is the river Yenisei, with its many heads, having their sources in the same chain of mountains, and runs into the same ocean, further north, towards Bhering's straits, which is the *point* we are approximating, by pursuing this course.

A third river, with its many heads, that rises at the base of another chain of mountains, called the Yablonoy; this is the river Lena.

There are several other rivers arising out of another chain of mountains, farther on northward towards Bhering's straits, which have no name on the map of Asia; this range of mountains is called the St. Anovoya mountains, and comes to a point or end, at the strait which separates Asia from America, which is but a small distance across, about forty miles only, and several islands between.

Allowing the ten tribes, or if they may have become amalgamated with the Tartars as they passed on this tremendous journey toward the Northern ocean, to have pursued this course, the distance will appear from Assyria to the straits, to be some hundreds over six thousand miles. Six thousand two hundred and fifty-five miles, which is the distance, is more, by nearly one-half, than such a vast body, in moving on together, could possibly perform in a year and a half. Six miles a day would be as great a distance, as such a host could perform, where there is no way but that of forests untraced by man, and obstructed by swamps, mountains, fallen trees, and thousands of nameless hindrances. Food must be had, and the only way of procuring it must have been by hunting with the bow and arrow, and by fishing. The sick must not be forsaken, the aged and the infant must be cherished; all these things would delay, so that a rapid progress cannot be admitted

If, then, six miles a day is a reasonable distance to suppose they may have progressed, it follows that nearly *three* years, instead of a year and a half, would not have been more than sufficient to carry them from Syria to Bhering's straits, through a region almost of eternal snow.

This, therefore, cannot have been the course of the *Ten Tribes* to the land of Arsareth, wherever it was: and that it was *north* from Syria, we ascertain by Esdras, who says, they went into the narrow passes of the Euphrates, which means its three heads, or branches, which arise north from Syria. From the head waters of this river, there is no way to pass on, but to go between the Black and Caspian seas, over the Caucassian mountains, as before stated.

From this point they may have gone on to what is now called *Astracan*, as before rehearsed; but *here* we suppose they may have taken a west instead of a *north* direction, which would have been toward that part of Russia, which is now called Russia in Europe, and would have led them on between the rivers Don and Volga; the Don emptying into the Black sea, and the Volga into the Caspian.

This course would have led them exactly to the places where

Moscow and Petersburg now stand, and from thence in a northwesterly direction, along the south end of the White sea, to *Lapland*, *Norway*, and *Sweden*, which lie along on the coast of the North Atlantic ocean.

Now, the distance from *Syria* to Lapland, Norway, and Sweden, on the coast of the Atlantic, is scarcely three thousand miles; a distance which may have easily been travelled in a year and a half, at six miles a day, and the same opportunity have been afforded for their amalgamation with Scythians or Tartars, as in the other course towards Bhering's strait. Norway, Sweden, and Lapland, may have been the land of Arsareth.

But here arises a question; how then did they get into America from Lapland and Norway? The only answer is, America and Europe must have been at that time united by land, or they may have built boats.

The manner by which the original inhabitants and animals reached here, is easily explained, by adopting the supposition, which doubtless is the *most* correct, that the northwestern and western limits of America were, at some former period, united to Asia on the *west*, and to Europe on the east.

This was partly the opinion of Buffon and other great naturalists. *That* connection has, therefore, been destroyed, among other great changes this earth has evidently experienced since the flood.

We have examples of these revolutions before our eyes. Florida has gained leagues of land from the gulf of Mexico; and part of Louisiana, in the Mississippi valley, has been formed by the mud of rivers. Since the Falls of Niagara were first discovered, they have receded very considerably; and it is conjectured, that this sublimest of nature's curiosities was situated originally where Queenstown now stands.

Sicily was united formerly to the continent of Europe, and ancient authors affirm, that the straits of Gibraltar, which divide between Europe and Africa, were formed by a violent irruption of the ocean upon the land. Ceylon, where our missionaries have an establishment, has lost forty leagues by the sea, which is one hundred and twenty miles.

Many such instances occur in history. Pliny tells us, that in his own time, the mountain Cymbotus with the town of Eurites, which stood on its side, were totally swallowed up. He records the like of the city Tantelis in Magnesia, and of the mountain Sopelus, both absorbed by a violent opening of the earth, so that no trace of either remained. Galanis and Garnatus, towns once famous in Phœnicia, are recorded to have met the same fate. The vast promontory, called Phlegium in Ethiopia, after a violent earthquake in the night, was not to be seen in the morning, the earth having swallowed it up and closed over it.

Like instances we have of later date. The mountain Picus, in one of the Moluccas, was so high, that it appeared at a vast distance, and served as a landmark to sailors. But during an earthquake in the isle, the mountain in an instant sunk into the bowels of the earth, and no token of it remained. The like happened in the mountainous parts of China, in 1556 when a whole province, with all its towns, cities, and inhabitants, was absorbed in a moment; an immense lake of water remaining in its place, even to this day.

In the year 1646, during a terrible earthquake in the kingdom of Chili, several whole mountains of the Andes, one after another, were wholly absorbed in the earth. Probably many lakes over the whole earth, have been occasioned in this way. Lake Ontario is supposed to have been formed in this way.

The greatest earthquake we find in antiquity, is that mentioned by Pliny, in which twelve cities in Asia Minor were swallowed up in one night. But one of those most particularly described in history, is that of the year 1693. It extended to a circumference of two thousand six hundred leagues, chiefly affecting the sea coasts and great rivers. Its motions were so rapid, that those who lay at their length were tossed from side to side as upon a rolling billow. The walls were dashed from their foundations, and no less than fifty-four cities, with an incredible number of villages, were either destroyed or greatly damaged. The city of Catanea, in particular, was utterly overthrown. A traveller, who was on his way thither, at the distance of some miles, perceived a black cloud hanging near the place. The sea all of a sudden began to roar: Mount Ætna to send forth great spires of flames; and soon after a shock ensued, with a noise as if all the artillery in the world had been at once discharged. Although the shock did not continue above three minutes, yet near nineteen thousand of the inhabitants of Sicily perished in the ruins.

We have said above, that Norway, Lapland, and Sweden, may have been the very land called the land of Arsareth, by Esdras, in his second book, chapter thirteenth, who may, with the utmost certainty, be supposed to know the very course and place where these Ten Tribes went to, being himself a Jew and a historian, who at the present day is quoted by the first authors of the age.

We have also said, it should be considered impossible for the Ten Tribes, after having left the place of their captivity, at the east end of the Mediterranean sea, which was the Syrian country, for them to have gone in a year and a half to Bhering's strait, through the frozen wilderness of Siberia.

In going away from Syria, they cannot be supposed to have had any place in *view*, only they had conferred among themselves that, as Esdras says, "they would leave the multitude of the heathen, and go forth into a country where never mankind dwelt;" which Esdras called the land of Arsareth.

Now, it is not to be supposed, a *land*, or country, where no man dwelt could have a *name*, especially in that early age of the world, which was about seven hundred years before the Christian era; but on that very account we may suppose the word *Arsareth*, to be descriptive only of a vast wilderness country, where no man dwelt, and is probably a Persian word of that signification, for Syria was embraced within the Persian empire; the Israelites may have, in part, lost their original language, having been there in a state of captivity for more than one hundred years before they left that country.

Esdras says, that Arsareth was a land where no man dwelt; this statement is somewhat corroborated by the fact, that the country which we have supposed was Arsareth, namely, Norway, &c., was anciently unknown to mankind. On this point see Morse's Geography, vol. 2, p. 28:

"NORWAY—A region almost as unknown to the ancients as was America."

But, in this he is mistaken, as will appear by and by, in the course of this work. America was known to the ancients.

Its almost insular situation, having on the west the Atlantic ocean, on the south end the North sea, and on the east the Baltic and the gulf of Bothnia—these waters almost surrounding it—there being a narrow connexion of land with the European continent only on the north, between the gulf of Bothnia and the White sea, which is Lapland, and was a reason quite sufficient why the ancients should have had no knowledge of that region of country which we have supposed to have been the country called by Esdras the land of Arsareth.

Naturalists, as before remarked, have supposed that America was at some remote period before the Christian era, united to the continent of Europe; and that some convulsion in nature, such as earthquakes, volcanos, or the irruptions of the ocean, has shaken and overwhelmed a whole region of earth, lying between Norway and Baffin's bay, of which Greenland and Iceland, with many other islands, are the remains.

But suppose the American and European continents, seven hundred years before the Christian era, were not united; how, then, did such part of the Ten Tribes as may have wandered to that region from Syria, get into America from Norway? The answer is easy. They may have crossed over, from island to island, in vessels or boats, for a knowledge of navigation, and that of the ocean too, was known to the Ten Tribes; for all the Jews and civilized nations of that age were acquainted with this art, derived from the Egyptians.

But it may be said, there are no traces that Jews were ever residents of Norway, Lapland or Scandinavia. From the particular shape of Norway, being surrounded by the waters of the sea, except between the gulf of Bothnia and the White sea, we perceive that the *first* people, whoever they were, *must* have approached it by the narrow pass between those two bodies of water, of only about forty-five miles in width, if they would go there by land.

Consequently, the place now designated by the name of Lapland, which is the northern end of Norway, was first peopled before the more southern parts. An inquiry, therefore, whether the *ancient* people of Lapland had any customs like those of the ancient Jews, would be pertinent to our hypothesis respecting the route of the Ten Tribes, as spoken of by Esdras. Morse, the geographer, says, that of the original population of Lapland very little is known with certainty. Some writers have supposed them to be a colony of *Fins* from Russia; others have thought that they bore a stronger resemblance to the *Semoeids* of Asia. Their language, however, is said by Leems to have less similitude to the Finnish, than the

Danish to the German; and to be *totally unlike any* of the dialects of the Teutonic, or ancestors of the ancient Germans: but according to Leems, as quoted by Morse, in their language are found many Hebrew words, also Greek and Latin.

Hebrew words are found among the American Indians in considerable variety. But how came Greek and Latin words to be in the composition of the Laponic language?

This is easily answered, if we suppose them to be derived from the Ten Tribes; as at the time they left Syria, the Greek and Latin were languages spoken every where in that region, as well as the Syrian and Chaldean. And on this very account, it is likely, the Ten Tribes had in part lost their ancient language as it was spoken at Jerusalem, when Salmanassar carried them away. So that by the time they left Syria, and the region thereabouts, to go to Arsareth, their language had become, from this sort of mixture, an entire *new* language, as they had been enslaved about one hundred years.

So that, allowing the ancient Laplanders to have derived their tongue from a part of these ten wandering tribes, it well might be said by Leems, as quoted by Morse, that the language of Lapland, commonly called the Laponic, *had no words in common* with the Gothic or Teutonic, except a few Norwegian words, *evidently* foreign, and unassociated with any of the languages of Asia or Europe; these being of the Teutonic or *German* origin, which goes back to within five hundred years of the flood, several centuries before the Ten Tribes were carried away by Salmanassar.

This view would seem to favor our hypothesis. We shall now show a few particulars respecting their religious notions, which seem to have, in some respects, a resemblance to those of the Jews. Their deities were of four kinds:

1st. *Super-celestial*, named as follow: Radien, Atzihe, and Kiedde, the Creator. Radien and Atzihe they considered the fountain of all power, and Kiedde or Radien Kiedde, the Son, or Creator. These were their *supreme* gods, and would seem to be borrowed from the Jewish dictrine of the Trinity.

2d. *Celestial*, called *Beiwe*, the Sun, or as other ancient nations had it, Apollo, which is the same, and Ailekies, to whom Saturday was consecrated. May not these two powers be considered as the shadows of the different orders of angels, as held by the Jews?

3d. *Sub-celestial*, or in the air and on the earth. Moderakka, or the Lapland Lucina; Saderakka, or Venus, to whom Friday was holy; and Juks Akka, or the Nurse. These are of heathen origin, derived from the nations among whom they had been slaves and wanderers, the Syrians.

4th. *Sub-terranean*, as Saiwo, and Saiwo-Olmak, gods of the mountains; Saiwo-Guelle, or their Mercury, who conducted the shades, or wicked souls, to the lower regions.

This idea would seem to be equivalent with the doctrine found in both the Jewish and Christian religions, namely, that Satan conducts or receives the souls of the wicked to his hell in the subterranean fire of the earth.

They have another deity, belonging to the fourth order, and him they call *Jabme-Akko*, or he who occupied their Elysium; in which the soul was furnished with a new body, and nobler privileges and powers, and entitled, at some future day, to enjoy the light of *Radien*, the fountain of power, and to dwell with him forever in the mansions of bliss.

This last sentiment is certainly equivalent to the Jewish idea of heaven and eternal happiness in Abraham's bosom. It also, under the idea of a *new* body, shows a relation to the Jewish and Christian doctrine of the resurrection of the body at the last day; and is indeed wonderful.

5th. An *Infernal* deity, called Rota, who occupied and reigned in Rota-Abimo, or the infernal regions; the occupants of which had no hopes of escape. He, together with his subordinates, Fudno, Mubber, and Paha-Engel, were all considered as evil disposed towards mankind.

This is too plain not to be applied to the Bible doctrine of one supreme devil and his angels, who are, sure enough, evil disposed towards mankind.

Added to all this, the Laplanders were found in the practice of sacrificing to *all* their deities, the rein-deer, the sheep, and sometimes the seal, pouring libations of milk, whey, and brandy, with offerings of cheese, &c.

This last item of their religious manners, is too striking not to claim its derivation from the ancient Jewish worship. The Laplanders are a people but few in number, not much exceeding twelve hundred families; which we imagine is a circumstance favoring our idea, that after they had remained a while in Arsareth, or Lapland and Norway, which is much the same thing, that their main body may have passed over into America, either in boats, from island to island; or, if there then was, as is supposed, an isthmus of land, connecting the continents, they passed over on that, leaving, as is natural, in case of such a migration, some individuals or families behind, who might not wish to accompany them, from whom the present race of Laplanders may be derived. Their dress is much the same with that of our Indians; their complexion is swarthy, black hair, large heads, high cheek bones, with wide mouths; all of which is strikingly national. They call themselves *Same*, their speech *Same-giel*, and their country *Same-Edna*. This last word sounds very much like the word *Eden*, and may be, inasmuch as it is the name of their country, borrowed from the name of the region where Adam was created.

When men emigrate from one region of the earth to another, which is very distant, and especially if the country to which they emigrate is a new one, or in a state of nature, it is perfectly natural to give it the *same* name or names which distinguished the country and its parts, from which they emigrated.

Edessa, was the name of an ancient city of Mesopotamia, which was situated in the country or land of Assyria, between the rivers Euphrates and Tigris. In this region the Ten Tribes were held in bondage, who had been carried away by Salmanassar, the Assyrian monarch. We are, therefore, the more confirmed in this conjecture, from the similarity existing between the two names Edna and Edessa, both derived, it is likely, from the more ancient word Eden, which, from common consent, had its situation, before the deluge, not far from this same region where Turkey is now, between the Mediterranean, Black, and Caspian seas, and the Persian gulf, as before argued.

If such may have been the fact, that a part of the Ten Tribes came over to America, in the way we have supposed, leaving the cold regions of Arsareth behind them, in quest of a milder climate, it would be natural to look for tokens of the presence of Jews of some sort, along countries adjacent to the Atlantic. In order to this, we shall here make an extract from an able work, written exclusively on the subject of the Ten Tribes' having come from Asia by the way of Bhering's strait, by the Rev. Ethan Smith, Pultney,

Vt. who relates as follows:—" Joseph Merrick, Esq., a highly respectable character in the church at Pittsfield, gave the following account: That in 1815, he was levelling some ground under and near an old wood-shed, standing on a place of his, situated on *Indian hill*. He ploughed and conveyed away old chips and earth to some depth. After the work was done, walking over the place he discovered, near where the earth had been dug the deepest, a black strap, as it appeared, about six inches in length, and one and a half in breadth, and about the thickness of a leather trace to a harness. He perceived it had at each end a loop of some hard substance, probably for the purpose of carrying it. He conveyed it to his house and threw it into an old tool box. He afterwards found it thrown out at the door, and again conveyed it to the box.

" After some time, he thought he would examine it; but in attempting to cut it, found it as hard as bone; he succeeded, however, in getting it open, and found it was formed of two pieces of thick raw-hide, sewed and made water tight with the sinews of some animal, and gummed over; and in the fold was contained *four* folded pieces of parchment. They were of a dark yellow hue, and contained some kind of writing. The neighbors coming in to see the strange discovery, tore one of the pieces to atoms, in the true Hun and Vandal style. The other three pieces Mr. Merrick saved, and sent them to Cambridge, where they were examined, and discovered to have been written with a pen in *Hebrew*, plain and legible. The writing on the three remaining pieces of parchment, was quotations from the Old Testament. See Deut., chap. vi. from 4th to 9th verse, inclusive; also chap. xi. verse 13 to 21, inclusive; and Exodus, chap. xiii., 11 to 16, inclusive, to which the reader can refer, if he has the curiosity to read this most interesting discovery.

These passages, as quoted above, were found in the strap of raw-hide, which unquestionably had been written on the very pieces of parchment, now in the possession of the Antiquarian Society, before Israel left the land of Syria, more than 2500 years ago; but it is not likely the raw-hide strap in which they were found enclosed, had been made a very great length of time. This would be unnatural, as a desire to look at the sacred characters, would be very great, although they could not read them. This, however, was done at last, as it appears, and buried with some chief, on the place where it was found, called *Indian hill*.

Dr. West, of Stockbridge, relates, that an old Indian informed him, that his fathers in this country had, not long since, been in the possession of a book, which they had, for a long time, carried with them; but having lost the knowledge of reading it, they buried it with an Indian chief.—(*View of the Hebrews*, p. 223.)

It had been handed down, from family to family, or from chief to chief, as a most precious relic, if not as an amulet, charm, or talisman; for it is not to be supposed, that a distinct knowledge of what was contained in the strap could have long continued among them, in their wandering condition, amid woods and forests.

"It is said by Calmet, that the above texts are the very passages of Scripture which the Jews used to write on the leaves of their phylacteries. These phylacteries were little rolls of parchment, whereon were written certain words of the law. These they wore upon their forehead, and upon the wrist of the left arm."—(*Smith's View of the Hebrews*, p. 220.)

This intimation of the presence of the Hebrews in America, is too unequivocal to be passed unnoticed, and the circumstance of its being found so near the Atlantic coast, and at so vast a distance from Bhering's straits, we are still inclined to suppose, that such of the Israelites as found their way to the shores of America, on the coast of the Atlantic, may have come from Lapland or Norway; seeing evident tokens exist of their having once been there, as we have noticed some few pages back.

But there is a third supposition respecting the land of Arsareth; which is, that it is situated exactly east from the region of Syria. This is thought to be the country now known in Asia by the appellation of Little Bucharia. Its distance from Syria is something more than two thousand miles; which, by Esdras, might very well be said to be a journey of a year and a half, through an entire wilderness.

Bucharia, the region of country of which we are about to speak, as being the ancient resort of a part of the lost Ten Tribes, is in distance from England, 3,475 miles; a little southeast from the latitude of London; and from the state of New-York, exactly double that distance, 6,950 miles, on an air line, as measured on an artificial globe, and in nearly the same latitude, due east from this country.

It is not impossible, after all our speculation, and the speculations of others, that instead of America, or of Norway, this same Bucharia is, in truth, the ancient country of Arsareth; although in the country of old Norway, and of America, are abundant evidence of the presence of Jews at some remote period, no doubt derived from this stock, the Ten Tribes.

The country of Bucharia is situated due east from Syria, where the Ten Tribes were placed by Salmanassar, as well as farther east on the river Gozen, or Ganges, of Hindostan. The distance is about 2,500 miles, and at that time was a vast desert, lying beyond the settlements of men, in all probability; and in order to go there they must also pass through the narrow passes of the river Euphrates, or its heads, near the south end of the Caspian sea, and then nearly due east, inclining, however, a little to the north. Two circumstances lead to a supposition that this Bucharia is the Arsareth mentioned by Esdras. The first is, at this place is found a great population of Jews: Second, the word Arsareth is similar to the names of other regions of that country in Asia: as Ararat, Astracan, Samarcand, Yarcund, Aracan, Ala Tau, Alatanian, Aral, Altai, Arnu, Korassan, Balk, Bactriana, Bucharia, Argun, Narrat, Anderab Katlan: (this word is much like the Mexican names of places, as Aztalan, Copallan, and so on,) Anderab, Aktau, Ailak. Names of countries and rivers might be greatly multiplied, which bear a strong affinity in sound and formation to the word Arsareth, which is probably a Persian word, as well as the rest we have quoted, as from these regions, ancient Bucharia, the foundations of the Persian power was derived.

The reader can choose between the three, whether America, Norway, or Bucharia, is the ancient country called Arsareth, as one of the three is, beyond a doubt, the place alluded to by Esdras, to which the Ten Tribes went; and in all three the traits of Jews are found.

In this country, Bucharia, many thousand Jews have been discovered, who were not known by the Christian nations to have existed at all till recently. It would appear from this circumstance, that the Ten Tribes may have divided, a part going *east* to the country now colled Bucharia; and a part *west*, to the country now called Norway; both of which, at that time, were the region of almost endless solitudes, and about equal distances from Syria: and from Bucharia to Bhering's staait, is also about the same distance.

In process of time, both from Bucharia in Asia, and Norway in Europe, the descendants from these Ten Tribes may have found their way into America. Those from Norway, by the way of islands, boats or continent, which may then have existed, between America and north of Europe; and those from Bucharia, by the way of Bhering's strait, which at that time, it is likely, was no strait, but an isthmus, if not a country of great extent, uniting Asia with America. The account of the Bucharian Jews is as follows:

"After having seen, some years past, merchants from Tiflis, Persia, and Armenia, among the visitors at Leipsic, we have had, for the first time, (1826,) *two traders from Bucharia, with shawls, which are there manufactured of the finest wool of the goats of Thibet and Cashmere*, by the Jewish families, *who form a third part of the population*. In Bucharia, (formerly the capitol of Sogdiana,) the Jews have been very numerous ever since the Babylonian captivity, and are there as remarkable for their industry and manufactures, as they are in England for their money transactions. It was not till 1826, that the Russian government succeeded in extending its diplomatic mission far into Bucharia. The above traders exchanged their shawls for coarse and fine woollen cloths, of such colors as are most esteemed in the east."

Much interest has been excited by the information which this paragraph conveys, and which is equally novel and important. In none of the geographical works which we have consulted do we find the the least hint as to the existence in Bucharia of such a body of Jews as are here mentioned, amounting to one-third of the whole population; but as the fact can no longer be doubted, the next point of inquiry which presents itself is, whence have they proceeded, and how have they come to establish themselves in a region so remote from their original country? This question, we think, can only be answered by supposing that these persons are the descendants of the long lost Ten Tribes, concerning the facts of which, theologians, historians, and antiquarians, have been alike puzzled: and however wild this hypothesis may at first appear, there are not wanting circumstances to render it far from being improbable. In the 17th chapter of the second book of Kings, it is said, "in the ninth year of Hoshea the king of Assyria took Samaria, and carried Israel away into Assyria, and placed them in

Helah and in Haber by the river Gozan, and in the cities of the Medes:" and in the subsequent verses, as well as the writings of the prophets, it is said, that the Lord then "put away Israel out of his sight, and carried them away into the land of Assyria unto this day." In the Apocrypha, 2d Esdras, xiii., it is said, that the Ten Tribes were carried beyond the river, (Euphrates,) and so they were brought into another land, when they took counsel together, that they would leave the multitude of the heathen, and go forth into a further country, where never mankind dwelt; that they entered in at the narrow passages of the river Euphrates, when the springs of the flood were stayed, (frozen,) and "went through the country a great journey, even a year and a half;" and it is added, that "there will they remain, until the latter time, when they will come forth again." The country beyond Bucharia was unknown to the ancients, and it is, we believe, generally admitted, that the river Gozan, mentioned in the book of Kings, is the same as the Ganges, which has its rise in those very countries in which the Jews reside, of which the Liepsic account speaks. The distance which these two merchants must have travelled, cannot, therefore, be less than three thousand miles; and there can be but little doubt that the Jews, whom they represent as a third part of the population of the country, are descendants of the Ten Tribes of Israel settled by the river Gozan.

The great plain of Central Asia, forming four principal sides, viz: Little Bucharia, Thibet, Mongolia, and Mantchous, contains a surface of 150,000 square miles, and a population of 20,000,000. This vast country is still very little known. The great *traits* of its gigantic formation compose, for the most part, all that we are certain of. It is an immense plain of an excessive elevation, intersected with barren rocks and vast deserts of black and almost moving sand. It is supported on all sides by mountains of granite, whose elevated summits determine the different climates of the great continent of Asia, and form the division of its waters. From its exterior flow all the great rivers of that part of the world. In the interior are a quantity of rivers, having little declivity, or no issue, which are lost in the sands, or perhaps feed stagnant waters. In the southern chains are countries, populous, rich and civilized; Little Bucharia, Great and Little Thibet. The people of the north are shepherds and wanderers. Their riches consist in their herds.

Their habitations are tents, and towns, and camps, which are transported according to the wants of pasturage. The Bucharians enjoy the right of trading to all parts of Asia, and the Thibetians cultivate the earth to advantage. The ancients had only a confused idea of Central Asia. "The inhabitants of the country," as we learn from a great authority, "are in a high state of civilization; possessing all the useful manufactures, and lofty houses built with stone. The Chinese reckon (but this is evidently an exaggeration) that Thibet alone contains 33,000,000 of persons. The merchants of Cashmere, on their way to Yarkland in Little Bucharia, pass through Little Thibet. This country is scarcely known to European geographers." The immense plain of Central Asia is hemmed in, and almost inaccessible by mountain ranges of the greatest elevation, which surround it on all sides, except China; and when the watchful jealousy of the government of the Celestial Empire is considered, it will scarcely be wondered at, that the vast region in question is so little known.

Such is the country which these newly discovered Jews are said to inhabit in such numbers. The following facts may perhaps serve to throw some additional light on this interesting subject.

In the year 1822, a Mr. Sargon, who had been appointed one of the agents of the London Society, communicated to England some interesting accounts of a number of persons resident at Bombay, Cinnamore, and their vicinity, who are evidently the descenendants of the Jews, calling themselves Beni Israel, and bearing almost uniformly Jewish names, but with Persian terminations. This gentleman, feeling very desirous of obtaining all possible knowledge of their condition, undertook a mission for this purpose to Cinnamore; and the result of his inquiries was, a conviction that they were not Jews of the one tribe and a half, being of a different race to the white and black Jews at Cochin, and consequently, that they were a remnant of the long lost Ten Tribes. This gentleman also concluded, from the information he obtained respecting the Beni Israel, or sons of Israel, that they existed in great numbers in the countries between Cochin and Bombay, the *north of Persia*, among the hordes of Tartary, and in Cashmere; the very countries in which, according to the paragraph in the German paper, they exist in such numbers. So far, then, these accounts confirm each other, and there is every probability that the Beni Israel, resident on the west of the Indian peninsula, had originally proceeded from Bucharia. It will, therefore, be interesting to know something of their moral and religious character. The following particulars are collected from Mr. Sargon's accounts: 1. In dress and manners they resemble the natives so as not to be distinguished from them, except by attentive observation and inquiry. 2. They have Hebrew names of the same kind, and with the same local termination as the Sepoys in the the ninth regiment Bombay native infantry. 3. Some of them read Hebrew, and they have a faint tradition of the cause of their original exodus from Egypt. 4. Their common language is the Hindoo. 5. They keep idols and worship them, and use idolatrous ceremonies intermixed with Hebrew. 6. They circumcise their children. 7. They observe the Kipper, or great expiation day of the Hebrews, but not the Sabbath, or any of the feast or fast days. 8. They call themselves *Gorah Jehudi*, or white Jews; and they term the black Jews *Colla Jehudi*. 9. They speak of the Arabian Jews as their brethren, but do not acknowledge the European Jews as such. They use, on all occasions, and under the most trivial circumstances, the usual Jewish prayer—"Hear, O Israel, the Lord our God is one Lord." 10. They have no cohen, (priest) levite, or kasi, among them, under those terms; but they have a kasi, (reader) who performs prayers, and conducts their religious ceremonies; and they appear to have elders and a chief in each community, who determine in their religious concerns. 11. They expect the Messiah, and that they will one day return to Jerusalem. They think that the time of his appearance will soon arrive, at which they much rejoice, believing that at Jerusalem they will see their God, worship him only, and be despised no more.

These particulars, we should presume, can scarcely fail to prove interesting, both in a moral and religious, as well as in a geographical point of view. The number of the scattered members of the tribes of Judah, and the half tribe of Benjamin, rather exceed than fall short of five millions. Now, if this number be added to the many other millions to be found in the different countries of the east, what an immense power would be brought into action, were the spirit of nationality once roused, or any extraordinary event to occur, which should induce them to unite in claiming possession of that land which was given to them "for an heritage forever," and to which, in every other clime of the earth, their fondest hopes and their dearest aspirations never cease to turn.

But although the opinion that the American Indians are the descendants of the lost Ten Tribes, is now a popular one, and generally believed, yet there are some who totally discard this opinion. And among such, as chief, is Professor Rafinesque, whose opinions on the subject of the flood of Noah not being universal, and of the ark, we have introduced on the first pages of this work.

This gentleman is decidedly, and we may say severely, opposed to this doctrine, and alleges that the Ten Tribes were *never* lost, but are *still* in the countries of the east about the region of ancient Syria, in Asia. He ridicules *all* those authors who have attempted to find in the customs of the Indians, traits of the Jews, and stamps them with being egregiously ignorant of the origin of things pertaining to this subject. This is taking a high stand, indeed, and if he can maintain it, he has a right to the honor thereof. Upon this notion, he says, a new sect of religion has arisen, namely, the Mormonites, who pretend to have discovered a book with golden leaves, in which is the history of the American Jews, and their leader, *Mormon*, who came hither more than 2,000 years ago. This work is ridiculous enough, it is true; as the whole book of Mormon bears the stamp of folly, and is a poor attempt at an imitation of the Old Testament Scriptures, and is without connection, object, or aim; shewing every where language and phrases of too late a construction to accord with the Asiatic manner of composition, which highly characterises the the style of the Bible, and how can it be otherwise as it was written in Ontario county, New York.

As reasons, this philosopher advances as follows, against the American nations being descended from the Ten Tribes of ancient Israel:

"1. These Ten Tribes are *not* lost, as long supposed; their descendants, more or less mixed with the *natives*, are yet found in Media, Iran, Taurin, Cabulistan, Hindostan, and China, where late travellers have traced them calling themselves by various names.

2. The American nations knew not the Sabbath, nor yet the Sabbattical weeks and years of the Jews. This knowledge could never have been lost by the Hebrews. The only weeks known in America, were of three days, five days, and half lunations, (or half a moon) as among the primitive nations, before the week of seven days was used in Asia, which was based upon the seven planets, long before the laws of Moses."

Here is another manifest attempt of this philosopher to invalidate the Scriptures, in attempting to fix the origin of the ancient Jewish and present Christian Sabbath, on the observances of the ancient nations, respecting the motions of the seven primary planets of the heavens; when it is emphatically said, in the Hebrew Scriptures, that the week of seven days was based on the seven days' work of the Creator, in the creation of the world. And as the Creation is older than the astronomical observations of the *most* ancient nations of the earth, it is evident that the Scripture account of the origin of the seven-day week *ought* to have the precedence over all other opinions since sprung up.

3. He says, " The Indians hardly knew the use of iron, although common among the Hebrews, and likely never to be lost; nor did they, the Indians of America, know the use of the plough."

" 4. The same apples to the use of writing; such an art is never lost when once known."

" 5. Circumcision was unknown, and even abhorred by the Americans, except two nations, who used it—the Mayans, of Yucatan, in South America, who worshipped a hundred idols, and the Calchaquis, of Chaco, of the same country, who worshipped the sun and stars, believing that departed souls became *stars*. These beliefs are quite different from Judaism; and besides this, the rite of circumcision was common to Egypt, Ethiopia, Edom, and Chalchis."

But to this we reply, supposing circumcision *was* practised by all those nations, and even more, this does not disprove the rite to be of pure Hebrew or Jewish origin, as we have an account of it in the Scriptures written by Moses, as being in use quite two thousand years before Christ; long enough before Abraham or his posterity knew any thing of the Egyptians; it was therefore, most undoubtedly introduced among the Egyptians by the Jews themselves, or their ancestors, and from them the custom has gone out into many nations of the earth.

Again, Mr. Rafinesque says, *one* tribe there was, namely, the Calchaquis, who worshipped the sun and the stars, supposing them to be the *souls* of the departed.

This notion is not very far removed from, or at least may have had its origin with the Jews; for Daniel, one of their prophets, who lived about 500 years before Christ, expressly says, respecting the *souls* of the departed righteous: " They that be wise shall *shine* as the BRIGHTNESS of the firmament, and they that turn many to righteousness, as the STARS, for ever and ever." A sentiment of such transcendant beauty and consequence is not easily lost. This tribe, therefore, as above named, may *they* not have been of Jewish origin?

" 6. None of the American tribes have the striking, sharp, Jewish features, and physical conformation." [But other authors of equal celebrity, have a contrary opinion.]

" 7. The American Indians eat hogs, hares, fish, and all the forbidden animals of Moses, but each tribe abstain from their *tutelar* animals," (which, as they imagine, presides over their destinies,) " or badges of families of some peculiar sort."

But to this we reply, most certainly the Jews *did* use fish; as in all their history, even in the Bible, frequent reference is had to their use of fishes, and to their fish markets, where they were sold and bought.

" 8. The American customs of scalping, torturing prisoners, cannibalism, painting their bodies, and going naked, even in very cold climates, are totally unlike the Hebrew customs." Scalping, with several other customs of the sort, we have elsewhere in this work shown to be of *Scythian* origin; but does not, on that account, prove, nor in any way invalidate the other opinion, that *some* of the tribes are indeed of Jewish origin.

" 9. A multitude of languages exists in America, which may perhaps be reduced to twenty-five radical languages, and two thousand dialects. But they are often unlike the Hebrew, in roots, words, and grammar; they have, by far, says this author, more analogies with the *Sanscrit*," (the ancient Chinese,) Celtic, Bask, Pelasgian, Berber," (in Europe;) " Lybian, Egyptian," (in Africa;) " Persian, Turan, &c.," (also in Europe;) " or in fact, all the primitive languages of mankind." This we believe.

" 10. The Americans cannot have sprung from a single nation, because, independently of the languages, their features and complexions are as various as in Africa and Asia."

" We find in America, *white*, tawny, brown, yellow, olive, copper, and even black nations, as in Africa. Also, *dwarfs* and *giants*, handsome and ugly features, flat and aquiline noses, thick and thin lips," &c. [Among the Jews is also as great a variety.]

The Rev. Mr. Smith, of Pultney, Vt., a few years since, published a work entitled "A View of the Hebrews," in which he labors to establish that the American Indians worshipped but one God; the great Yohewah, or Jehovah of the Scriptures. This is vehemently opposed by philosopher Rafinesque, as follows, in reply to him.

"You say, *all* the Americans had the *same* God *Yohewa;* this is utterly false. This was the god of the Chactas and Florida Indians only; many other tribes had tripple gods, or trimurtis, as in Hindostan, having names nearly Sanscrit." [But neither does this disprove that *some* of these tribes are of Jewish origin.]

"Polytheism," (a plurality of gods,) "idolatry, and a complex mythology, prevailed among *all* the most civilized nations" of this country.

"All the ancient *religions* were found in America," which have prevailed in the old world, in the earliest ages, as "Theism, Sabaism, Magism, Hindooism, Shamanism, Fetichism, &c., but *no Judaism.*"

He says, the few examples of the affinity between the Indian languages and the Hebrew, given by Mr. Smith, in his work, belong *only* to the Floridan and Caribbean languages. Mr. Rafinesque says, he could show ten times as many in the Aruac, Guarian," (languages of South America,) "but what is that compared with the 100,000 affinities with the primitive languages."

"All the *civilized* Americans had a priesthood, or priestly *caste*, and so had the Hindoos, Egyptians, Persians, Celts, and Ethiopians. Were they all Jews?

"4. *Tribes* are found among *all* the ancient nations, Arabs, Berbers, Celts, Negroes, &c., who are not Jews. The most civilized nations had castes, instead of tribes, in America as well as Egypt and India; the Mexicans, the Mayans, Muhizcas, the Peruvians, &c., had no tribes. The animal badges of tribes, are found among Negroes and Tartars, as well as our Indians."

"5. Arks of covenant and cities of refuge are not peculiar to the Jews; many Asiatic nations had them, also the Egyptians, and nine-tenths of our Indian tribes have none at all, or have only holy bags," (for an ark) somewhat like a talisman, a charm, or as the "Fetiches, of the Africans."

But we reply, there is no evidence that other nations than the

Jews had cities of refuge and imitations of the ark of the covenant, *prior* to the time of Moses, which was full sixteen hundred years before Christ, and from whom it is altogether probable, that all the nations among whom such traits are found, derived them at first from the laws of that Hebrew legislator. Those nations, therefore, among whom, at *this* distance of time, those traits are found most resembling the Jews, may be said, with some degree of propriety, to be their descendants; and among *many* tribes of the western Indians, these traits are found, if we may believe the most credible witnesses.

"6. The religious cry of *aleluya*, is not Jewish, says this author, but *primitive*, and found among the Hindoos, Arabs, Greeks, Saxons, Celts, Lybians, &c., under the modification of *hulili, yululu, tulujah, &c.* Other Americans call it *ululaez, gualulu, aluyah &c.*"

All this being true, which we are willing to allow, does not disprove but that these forms of speech, which are directed in praise and adoration of a supreme or superior being, of some nature, no matter what, may all have originated from the Hebrew Jews, as *this* name of God, namely, Jehovah, was known among that nation, before the existence, as nations, by those names, of either the Hindoos, Arabs, Greeks, Saxons, Celts, or Lybians; for it was known in the family of Noah, and to all the patriarchs before the flood. The original word, translated God, was *Jehova*, and also ELOHIM, which are generally translated *Lord* and *God*.

In the second chapter of Genesis, at the fourth verse, the word *Jehovah* first occurs, says Dr. Clarke, in the original as written by Moses; but was in use long before the days of Abraham, among the ancestors of that patriarch. From this word, *Jehovah*, and *Elohim*, the words aleluia, &c., as above, it is admitted on all hands, were at first derived; and are in all nations, where known and used, directed to the praise and admiration of the *Almighty*, or other objects of adoration.

This most exalted form of praise, it appears, was known to John the Revelator, for he says, in chapter xix., "I heard a great voice of much people in heaven, saying ALLELUIA; and again, they said, *Alleluia.*" This form of praise, says Dr. Clarke, the heathen borrowed from the Jews, as is evident from the *Pæans*, or hymns, sung in honor of Apollo, which began and ended with *eleleuie*, a mere composition of the Hebrew words *alleluia* and *hallelujh.* It is even found among the North American Indians, and adapted by them to the same purpose, viz., the worship of God, or the Great Spirit.

From what we have been able to show on this subject as above, we cannot subscribe to the opinion, that those words are not of Hebrew and Jewish origins; consequently, being of Hebrew origin, it must follow, that where they are found in the most pure and unadulterated use, that the people so using them are most likely to be of Jewish descent; and this is found among the American Indians.

Among *some* of their tribes they have a place denominated the *beloved square.* Here they sometimes dance a whole night; but always in a bowing or worshipping posture, singing continually, hallelujah Ye-ho-wah, Ye-ho-vah; which last word, says Clarke, is probably the true pronunciation of the ancient *Hebrew* word, Jehovah.

It is no marvel, then, that these Jewish customs are found " among nearly all the ancient nations of Asia, Africa, Europe and Polynesia, nay, even among the wild negroes to this day," since they were in use at the very outset of the spread of the nations from Ararat, and are, therefore, of Hebrew *primitive* origin, but not heathen primitive origin, as asserted by Rafinesque. We are not tenacious, however, whether the Ten Tribes were lost or not, nor do we disagree to the opinion that they are found in almost all parts of the old world, having mingled with the various nations of Asia; but if so, we inquire, why may they not, therefore, be found in America? Could they not as easily have found their way hither as the *other* nations of the east? Most assuredly.

It is not the object of this volume to contend on this point; but when we find attempts to overturn the Scriptures, and, if possible, to make it appear, if not by so many words, yet in the manner we understand this writer's remarks, that the Bible itself is nothing else than a collection of heathenism, placed under the plausible idea of *primitive* words, *primitive* usages and *primitive* religion; we think this is placing the (*currus bovem trahit*) cart before the horse, and should not be allowed to pass without reproof.

A further account of the Convulsions of the Globe, with the Removal of Islands.

IF the supposition of naturalists may obtain belief, there has been a whole continent, reaching from the north of Europe to Bhering's strait; uniting, not only Europe with America, on the east, but also Asia on the north, and may have continued on south from Bhering's strait, some way down the Pacific, as Buffon partly believed, uniting America and China on the west.

It was contended by Clavigero, that the equatorial parts of Africa and America were once united. By which means, before the connexion was torn away by the irruption of the sea on both sides, the inhabitants from the African continent came, in the earliest ages, to South America. Whether this be true or not, the two countries approach each other in a remarkable manner, along the coast of Guinea, on the side of Africa, and the coast of Pernambuco, on the side of South America. These are the places which, in reality, seem to stretch towards each other, as though they had been once united.

The innumerable islands scattered all over the Pacific ocean, populous with men, *more* than intimates a period, even since the flood, when all the different continents of the globe were united together, and the sea so disposed of, that they did not break this harmony so well calculated to facilitate the migrations of men and animals.

Several tribes of the present Southern Indians, as they now are called, have traditions that they came from the *east*, or through the Atlantic ocean. Rafinesque says, it is important to distinguish the American nations of eastern origin from those of northern. The latter, he says, were invaders from Tartary, and were as different in their manners as were the Romans and Vandals.

The southern nations, among whom this tradition is found, are the Natchez, Apalachians, Talascas, Mayans, Myhizcas, and Haytians. But those of the Algonquin stock point to a northwest origin, which is the way from the northern regions of Asia.

It is not likely, that immediately after the era of the deluge, there was as much ocean which appeared above ground, as at the present time; but instead of this, lakes were more numerous. Consequently, on the surface of the globe there was much more land than at the present time. But from various convulsions, more than we have spoken of, whose history is now lost, in past ages, many parts, nay, nearly *all* the earthy surface is sunken to the depths below, while the waters have risen above; nearly three-fourths of the globe's surface is known to be water. How appalling is the reflection!

The currents of ocean running through the bowels of the earth, by the disposition of its creator, to promote *motion* in the waters, as motion is essential to all animal life, have, doubtless, by subterranean attrition, affected the foundations of whole islands, which have sunk beneath the waters at different periods. To such convulsions as these, it would seem, Job has alluded, in chapter ix., verse 5, as follows: "Which removeth the mountains, and they know not; which overturneth them in his anger."

Adam Clarke's comment on this verse is as follows: "This seems to refer to earthquakes. By these strong convulsions, mountains, valleys, hills, even *whole* islands, are removed in an instant; and to this latter circumstance the words '*they know not,*' most probably refer. The work is done in the twinkling of an eye; no warning is given; the mountain that seemed to be as firm as the earth on which it rested, was in the *same* moment both *visible* and *invisible*, so suddenly was it swallowed up."—*(See p. 59, 60.)*

It can scarcely be supposed but that Job was either personally, or by information, acquainted with occurrences of the kind, in order to justify the thing as being done by God in his anger

It is not impossible but the fact upon which the following story is founded, may have been known to Job, who was a man supposed in possession of every species of information calculated to interest the nobler faculties of the human mind, if we may judge from the book bearing his own name. The story is an account of a certain island, called by the ancients *Atalantis*; and for aught that can be urged against its having existed, we are inclined to believe it did, as that all learning, uninspired, and general information, was *anciently* in possession of *heathen* philosophers and priests, to whom it was the custom even for princes to resort for learning, before they were considered qualified to sit on the thrones of their fathers. Such were the Egyptian priests to the Egyptians, and the Druids to the Celtic nations; the Brahmins to the Hindoos; the Magi to the Persians; the philosophers to the Greeks and Romans; and the *prophets* of the Indians, to the western tribes.

"This island is mentioned by Plato, in his dialogue of Timaeus. Solon, the Athenian lawgiver, is supposed to have travelled into Egypt," about six hundred years before Christ. Plato's time was three hundred years nearer the time of Christ, who has mentioned the travels of Solon into Egypt. "He arrives at an ancient temple on the Delta, a fertile island formed by the Nile, where he held a conversation with certain learned *priests*, on the *antiquities* of remote ages. When one of them gave Solon a discription of the island Atalantis, and also of its destruction. This island, said the Egyptian priest, was situated in the Western ocean, opposite the straits of Gibraltar;" which would place it exactly between a part of Europe, its southern end, and the northern part of Africa and the continent of America.

"There *was*, said the priest, an easy passage from this to other islands, which lay adjacent to a large continent, exceeding in size *all* Europe and Asia." Neptune settled in this island, from whose son *Atlas*, its name was derived, and divided it between his *ten* sons, who reigned there in regular succession for many ages."

From the time of Solon's travels in Egypt, which was six hundred years before Christ, we find more than seventeen hundred years up to the flood; so that *time* enough had elapsed since the flood to justify the fact of the island having existed, and also of having been inhabited and destroyed even six hundred years before the time of Solon; which would make the time of its destruction twelve hundred years before Christ; and would still leave more than five hundred years from that period back to the flood. So that if King Neptune had not made his settlement on the island Atalantis till two hundred years after the flood, there would have been time for the successive reigns of each of the regal lines of his sons, amounting to three hundred years, before the time of its envelopement in the sea; so that the priest was justified in using the term *antiquities*, when he referred to that catastrophe.

"They made, i. e. the Atalantians, irruptions into Europe and Africa; subduing all Lybia, as far as Egypt, Europe, and Asia Minor. They were resisted, however, by the Athenians, and driven back to their Atlantic territories." If they were resisted and driven back by the Athenians, the era of the existence of this island is easily ascertained; because the Athenians settled at Athens, in Greece, fifteen hundred and fifty-six years before Christ, being a colony from Egypt, under their conductor Cecrops. One hundred years after their establishment at Athens, they had become powerful, so as to be able to take a political stand among the nations of that region, and to defend their country against invasions. Accordingly, at the time the Atlantians were repulsed and compelled to return from whence they came, was in the year fourteen hundred and forty-three, before Christ.

"Shortly after this," says Plato, "there was a tremendous earthquake and an overflowing of the sea, which continued for a day and a night; in the course of which the vast island of Atalantis, and all its splendid cities and warlike nations, were swallowed up, and sunk to the bottom, which spreading its waters over the chasm, added a vast region to the Atlantic ocean. For a long time, however, the sea was not navigable, on account of rocks and shoals of mud and slime, and of the ruins of that drowned country." This occurrence, if the tradition be true, happened about twelve hundred years *before* Christ, three hundred years before the time of Job, and seven hundred and fifty years after the flood. At the period, therefore, of the existence of this island, a land passage to America, from Europe and Africa, was practicable; also by other islands, some of which are still situated in the same direction—the Azores, Madeiras, and Teneriffe islands, about twenty in number.

For this story of the island of Atalantis, we are indebted to Irving's Columbus, a popular work, of recent date; which cannot be denied but is exceedingly curious, and not without some foundation of probability. Was not this island the bridge, so called, reaching from America to Europe, as conjectured by Dr. Robertson, the historian, but was destroyed by the ocean, as he supposes, very far back in the ages of antiquity.

An allusion to this same island, Atalantis, is made by Euclid, who flourished about three hundred years before Christ, in a conversation which he had with Anacharsis, a Scythian philosopher of the same age; who had, in search of knowledge, travelled from the wilds of his own northern regions, to Athens, where he became acquainted with Euclid.

Their subject was the convulsions of the globe. The sea, according to every appearance, said Euclid, has separated *Sicily* from *Italy*, *Eubœa* from *Bœotia* and a number of other islands from the continent of Europe. We are informed, continued the philosopher, that the waters of Pontus Euxinus, (or the Black sea,) having been long enclosed in a basin (or lake,) shut in on all sides, and continually increasing by the rivers of Europe and Asia, rose at length above the highlands which surrounded it, forced open the passage of Bosphorus and Hellespont, and impetuously rushing into the Ægean or Mediterranean sea, extended its limits to the surrounding shores.

If we consult, he says, mythology, we are told that *Hercules*, whose labors have been confounded with those of *nature*, separated Europe from Africa; by which is meant, no doubt, that the Atlantic ocean destroyed the *isthmus*, which once united those two parts of the earth, and opened to itself a communication with the Mediterranean sea.

Beyond the isthmus, of which I have just spoken, said Euclid, existed, according to ancient traditions, an island as large as Africa, which, with all its wretched inhabitants, was swallowed up by an earthquake.

Here, then, is another witness, of great weight, besides Solon, and Plato, who testifies to the past existence of the island ATALANTIS.

Evidences of an Ancient Population in America, different from that of the Indians.

WE shall now attend more particularly, to the evidences of an ancient population in *this* country, anterior to that of the present race of Indians, afforded in the discovery of *forts, mounds, tumuli,* and their contents, as related by western travellers, and the researches of the Antiquarian Society, at Cincinnati. But before we proceed to an account of the traits of this kind of population, more than already given, we will remark, that wherever plats of ground, struck out into *circles, squares* and *ovals*, are found, we are at once referred to an eara when a people and nation existed in this country, more civilized, refined, and given to architectural and agricultural pursuits, than the Indians.

It is well known, the present tribes do not take the trouble of materially altering the face of the ground to accommodate the erection of their places of dwelling; always selecting that which is already fashioned by nature to suit their views; using the earth, where they build their towns, as they find it.

In a deep and almost hidden valley among the mountains of the Alleghany, on the road from Philadelphia to Pittsburgh, is one of those solitary memorials of an exterminated race. It is hid amidst the profoundest gloom of the woods; and is found to consist of a regular circle, a hundred paces in diameter. This is equal to six rods and four paces; and twenty-two rods in circumference. The whole plat is raised above the common level of the earth around, about four feet high; which may have been done to carry off the water, when the snows melted, or when violent rains would otherwise have inundated their dwellings from the surrounding hills.

The neighborhood of Brownville, or Redstone, in Pennsylvania, abounds with monuments of antiquity. A fortified camp, of a very complete and curious kind, on the ramparts of which is timber of five feet in diameter, stands near the town of Brownville. This camp contains about thirteen acres, enclosed in a circle, the elevation of which is seven feet above the adjoining ground; this was a Herculean work. Within the circle a pentagon is accurately described; having its sides four feet high, and its angles uniformly three feet from the outside of the circle, thus leaving an unbroken communication all around. A pentagon is a figure, having five angles or sides. Each side of the pentagon has a postern or small gateway, opening into the passage between it and the circle; but the circle itself has only one grand gateway outward. Exactly in the centre stands a mound about thirty feet high, supposed to have been a place of lookout. At a small distance from this place, was found a stone, eight feet by five, on which was accurately engraved a representation of the whole work, with the mound in the centre; whereon was the likeness of a human head, which signified that the chief who presided there lay buried beneath it. The engraving on this stone, is evidence of the knowledge of stone cutting, as it was executed with a considerable degree of accuracy.

On comparing the description of this circular monument with a description of works of a similar character, found in Denmark, Sweden and Iceland, the conclusion is drawn, that at some era of time the authors of this kind of monumental works, in either of those countries have been the same.

"They are called *Domh-ringr* by the Danes; that is, literally, doom-ring, or, *circle of judgment;* being the solemn place where courts were held." The celebrated *Stonehenge*, in England, is built after the same fashion; that is, in a circle, and is of Belgic origin, the second class of English antiquities, the era of which precedes that of the Romans in England; which would throw the time of their first erection back to a period of some hundred years before Christ.

"*Stonehenge.*—This noble and curious monument of early times, appears to have been formed by *three* principal *circles* of stone, the outer connected together by an uniform pavement, as it were, at the top, to which the chiefs might ascend and speak to the surrounding crowd. A second circle consists of detached upright stones, about five feet in height, while the highest are eighteen. Within this is a grand *oval*, consisting of five huge stones, crossed by another at the top, and enclosing smaller stones, which seem to have been seats, and a large flat stone, commonly called the altar, but which seems to have been the throne or seat of judgment. The whole of the above described monument, with all its apparatus, seems to be enclosed in the midst of a very extensive circle, or embankment of earth, sufficiently large to hold an immense number—a whole tribe or nation."—(*Morse.*)

After the introduction of Christianity into the west of Europe, which was sixty years after Christ, these circles of judgment, which had been polluted with human sacrifices, and other pagan rites, were abandoned, and other customs, with other places of resort, were instituted. This sort of antiquities, says Morse, the geographer, which are found all over Europe, are of this character, that is, of the *tumular* kind, such as are found in the west of our own country, belong entirely to the first era of the settlements of Europe.

The Druidic temples in Europe were numerous, and some of them immense, especially one in the isle of Lewis. In these the gods Odin, Thor, Freyga, and other Gothic deities, were adored;

all such structures were enclosed in circles, some greater and some less, according to their importance, or the numbers of those who supported them. These are of the *first* order of antiquities found in Europe; or, in other words, the *eldest*, and go back very far toward the flood, for their commencement.

The same kind of antiquities are found in Ireland, and are allowed to be of Druidic origin, always enclosed in *circles*, whether a simple stone, or a more spacious temple, be the place where they worshipped. The Scandinavians, who preceded the Norwegians some hundred years, enclosed their rude chapels with circular intrenchments, and were called the *Dane's Raths*, or circular intrenchments.

"In the first ages of the world, the worship of God was exceedingly simple; there were no temples nor covered edifices of any kind. An altar, sometimes a single stone, sometimes it consisted of several, and at other times merely of *turf*, was all that was necessary. On this the fire was lighted, and the sacrifice offered."— (*Adam Clarke.*)

Such were the Druids of Europe, whose *name* is derived from the kind of forest in which they preferred to worship. This was the *oak*, which in the Greek is expressed by the word *druid*, whose worship and principles extended even to Italy, among the Celtic nations, and is celebrated by Virgil, in the sixth book of the *Æneiad*, where he speaks of the *mistletoe*, and calls it the *golden branch*, without which no one could return from the infernal regions.

The mistletoe, an account of which may please the reader, is thus described by Pliny, who flourished about A. D. 23, and was a celebrated writer on natural history, and most learned of the ancient Romans:

"The Druids hold nothing more sacred than the mistletoe, and the tree on which it grows, provided it be the oak. They make choice of groves of oak on this account; nor do they perform any of their sacred rites without the leaves of those trees. And whenever they find it on the oak, they think it is sent from heaven, and is a sign that God himself has chosen that tree; and whenever found, is treated with great ceremony.

"They call it by a name which, in their language, signifies the *curer of ills;* and having duly prepared their feasts and sacrifices under the tree, they bring to it two white bulls. The priest, dressed in a white robe, ascends the tree, and with a golden pruning hook, cuts off the mistletoe, which is received in a *sagum*, or white sheet. Then they sacrifice the victims, praying that God would bless his own gift to those on whom he has bestowed it."—(*Clarke*.)

Discoveries on the Muskingum.

In the neighborhood of Fort Harmer, on the Muskingum, opposite Marietta on the Ohio, were discovered, by Mr. Ash, an English traveller, in the year 1826, several monuments of the ancient nation.

"Having made, (says this traveller,) arrangements for an absence of a few days, I provided myself with an excellent tinder box, some biscuit and salt, and arming my Indian travelling companion with a good axe and rifle, taking myself a fowling piece, often tried, and my faithful dog, I crossed the ferry of the Muskingum, having learned that the left hand side of that river was most accessible and the most abundant in curiosities and other objects of my research." In another part of this work we shall describe works of a similar sort, on the opposite side of the Muskingum, as given by the Antiquarian Society of Ohio.

"On traversing the valley between Fort Harmer and the mountains, I determined to take the high grounds, and after some difficulty, ascended an eminence which commanded a view of the town of Marietta, and of the river up and down, displaying a great distance along the narrow valley of the Ohio, cultivated plains, the gardens and popular walks of that beautiful town.

"After a very short inspection, and cursory examination, it was evident that the very spot or eminence on which I stood, had been occupied by the Indians, either as a place of observation, or a strong hold. The exact summit of the hill I found to be artificial; it expressed an oval, forty-five feet by twenty-three, and was composed apparently of earth and stone, though no stone of a similar character appeared in that place.

"The base of the whole was girded round about by a wall of earth, in a state of too great decay to justify any calculation, and the whole was so covered with heavy timber, that I despaired of gaining any further knowledge, and would have left the place, had I not been detained by my Indian companion, whom I saw occupied in endeavoring to introduce a pole into a small opening between two flat stones, near the root of a tree, which grew on the very summit of this eminence.

"The stones we found were too heavy to be removed by the mere power of hands. Two good oak poles were cut, in lieu of levers and crows. Clapping these into the orifice first discovered, we weighed a large flat stone, tilting it over, when we each assumed a guarded position, in silent expectation of hearing the hissing of serpents, or the rustling of the ground-hog's litter; where the Indian had supposed was a den of one sort or the other.

"All was silent. We resumed our labor, casting out a number of stones, leaves and earth, soon clearing a surface of seven feet by five, which had been covered upwards of fifteen inches deep, with flat stones, principally lying against each other, with their edges to the horizon.

"On the surface we had cleared appeared another difficulty, which was a plain superfices, composed of but three flat stones of such apparent magnitude that the Indian began to think that we should find under them neither snake nor pig; but having once begun, I was not to be diverted from my task.

"Stimulated by obstructions, and animated with other views than those of my companion, I had made a couple of hickory shovels with the axe, and setting to work, soon undermined the surface, and slid the stones off on one side, and laid the space open to view.

"I expected to find a cavern: my imagination was warmed by a certain design I thought I discovered from the very beginning; the manner the stones were placed led me to conceive the existence of a vault filled with the riches of antiquity, and crowded with the treasures of the most ancient world.

"A bed of sand was all that appeared under these flat stones, which I cast off; and as I knew there was no sand nearer than the bed of the Muskingum, a design was therefore the *more* manifest, which encouraged my proceeding; the sand was about a foot deep, which I soon removed.

"The design and labor of man was now unequivocal. The

space out of which these materials were taken, left a hollow in an oblong square, lined with stones on the end and sides, and also, paved on what appeared to be the bottom, with square stones, of about nine inches diameter.

"I picked these up with the nicest care, and again came to a bed of sand, which, when removed, made the vault about three feet deep, presenting another bottom or surface, composed of small square cut stones, fitted with such art, that I had much difficulty in discovering many of the places where they met. These displaced, I came to a substance, which, on the most critical examination, I judged to be a mat, or mats, in a state of entire decomposition and decay. My reverence and care increased with the progress already made; I took up this impalpable powder with my hands, and fanned off the remaining dust with my hat, when there appeared a beautiful tesselated pavement of small, colored stones; the colors and stones arranged in such a manner as to express harmony and shades, and portraying, at full length, the figure of a warrior under whose feet a snake was exhibted in ample folds.

"The body of the figures was composed of dyed woods, bones, and a variety of small bits of terrous and testaceous substances, most of which crumbled into dust on being removed and exposed to the open air.

"My regret and disappointment were very great, as I had flattered myself that the whole was stone, and capable of being taken up and preserved. Little more, however, than the actual pavement could be preserved, which was composed of flat stones, one inch deep, and two inches square. The prevailing colors were white, green, dark blue, and pale spotted red; all of which are peculiar to the lakes, and not to be had nearer than about three hundred miles.

"The whole was affixed in a thin layer of sand, fitted together with great precision, and covered a piece of bark in great decay, whose removal exposed what I was fully prepared to discover, from all previous indications, the remains of a human skeleton, which was of an uncommon magnitude, being seven feet in length. With the skeleton was found, first, an earthen vessel, or urn, in which were several bones, and some white sediment.

"The urn appeared to be made of sand and flint vitrified, and rung, when struck, like glass, and held about two gallons, had a top or cover of the same material, and resisted fire as completely as iron or brass. Second; a stone axe, with a groove round the pole, by which it had been fastened with a withe to the handle. Third; twenty-four arrow points, made of flint and bone, and lying in a position which showed they had belonged to a quiver. Fourth; a quantity of beads, but not of glass, round, oval, and square; colored green, black, white, blue and yellow. Fifth; a very large conch shell, decomposed into a substance like chalk; this shell was fourteen inches long, and twenty-three in circumference. The Hindoo priests, at the present time, use this shell as sacred. It is blown to announce the celebration of religious festivals. Sixth; under a heap of dust and tenuous shreds of feathered cloth and hair, a parcel of *brass* rings, cut out of a solid piece of metal, and in such a manner, that the rings were suspended from each other, without the aid of solder or any other visible agency whatever. Each ring was three inches in diameter, and the bar of the rings an half inch thick, and were square; a variety of characters were deeply engraved on the sides of the rings, resembling the Chinese characters."

Ward's History of the Hindoos, page 41 and 56, informs us, that the god Vishnoo, is represented holding a *sea shell* in his hand, called the " sacred shell;" and, second, he states, that " the utensils employed in the ceremonies of the temple, are several dishes to hold the offerings, a hand bell, a lamp, jugs for holding water; an incense dish, a copper cup, a seat of Kooshu grass for the priests, a large metal plate, used as a bell. Several of the articles found buried in this manner, resemble these utensils of the Brahmin priests, while some are exactly like them. The mat of Kooshu grass resembles the mat of hair and feathers; the earthen dish, the conch shell, are the very same in kind; the brass chain might answer instead of a bell, or iron plate to strike against, which would produce a jingling sound. A quantity of round, oval, and square beads, colored variously, were found; although Mr. Ward does not say, that beads were a part of the utensils of the Hindoo priests, yet we find them on the necks and arms of both their gods and their mendicants.

Pottery of the same kind found in those ancient works, have also the quality of eduring the fire. The art of making vessels of clay, is very ancient; we find it spoken of by Jeremiah the prophet, nearly three thousand years ago.

The art of coloring wood, stones, and shells, with a variety of beautiful tints, was also known, as appears from the pavement above described, and the colored beads.

In many parts of the west, paints of various colors have been found hidden in the earth. On the Chenango river, in the state of New-York, has recently been found, on opening of one of those ancient mounds, though of but small dimensions, three kinds of paint, black, red, and yellow, which are now in the possession of a Dr. Willard, at the village of Greene, in the county of Chenango.

The Indians of both China and America, have, from time immemorial, used paints to adorn themselves and their gods.

But the brass rings and tesselated pavement are altogether the most to be wondered at. A knowledge of the method of manufacturing brass was known to the antediluvians. This we learn from Genesis iv. 22. Tubal Cain was an artificer in brass and iron about eleven hundred years before the flood.

But how this article, the brass chain, of such curious construction, came in the possession of the chief, interred on the summit of the mountain, is a question to be answered, it would seem, in but two ways. They either had a knowledge of the art of making brass, or the article was an item of that king's peculiar treasure, and had been derived either from his ancestors from the earliest ages, or from South America, as an article of trade, a gift from some fellow king, or a trophy of some victorious battle over some southern nation; for, according to Humboldt, brass was found among the native Mexicans, in great abundance.

But how the Mexicans came by this art in mineralogy, is equally a question. Gold, silver, copper, &c., are the natural product of their respective ores; and accident may have made them acquainted with these; as iron was discovered among the Greeks, by fire in the woods having melted the ore. But brass is farther removed from the knowledge of man, being a composition of copper and the calamine stone, or ore of zinc. However, it is said by Morse, that in Chili, in the hills of Huilquilemu, are found mines of native brass, of a fine yellow color, and equally malleable with the best artificial brass; yet this is no common product of mineralogy, and would seem to be an exception, or rather a product extraordinary; and, in a measure, induces a belief, that it is not proper brass, but a metal similar only in complexion, while perhaps its chemical proprieties are entirely different, or it may have been produced by the fusion of copper and the ore of zinc, by the fire of some volcano.

Brass was the metal out of which the ancient nations made all their instruments of war, and defensive armor. The reason of this preference above copper and iron, even by the Greeks and Romans, was probably on account of the excessive bright polish it was capable of receiving; for the Greeks and Romans used it long after their knowledge of iron. Iron was discovered by the Greeks 1406 years before Christ. The ancient Americans must have derived a knowledge of brass from their early acquaintance with nations immediately succeeding the flood, who had it from the antediluvians, by way of Noah; and having found their way to this continent, before it became so isolated as it is at the present time, surrounded on all sides by oceans, made use of the same metal here.

But the tesselated or spotted pavement is equally curious with the brass chain, on account of its resemblance to the Mosaic pavements of the Romans; being small pieces of marble, of various colors, with which they ornamented the fronts of their tents in time of war. This sort of pavement is often dug up in England, and is of Roman origin.

We find the history of the ancient Britons, mentions the currency of *iron rings*, as money, which was in use among them, before the invasion of Julius Cæsar. Is it not possible, that the brass chain, or an assemblage of those rings, as found in this mound, may have been held among those ancients of America in the same estimation? The chain, in their mode of reckoning, being perhaps of an immense amount; its being found deposited with its owner, who was a chief or king, is the evidence of its peculiar value, whether it had been used as an article in trade, or as a sacred implement.

This maculated pavement, arranged in such a manner as to represent in full size, the chief, king, or monarch, who was interred beneath it, shows the knowledge, that people had of painting, sculpture, and descriptive delineation: but most of all, the serpent which lay coiled at his feet is surprising, because we suppose this transaction could not have happened from mere caprice, or the sport of imagination.

It must have been a trait of their theology, and, possibly, an allusion to the serpent, by whose instrumentality Satan deceived the first woman, the mother of us all: and its being beneath his feet, may also have alluded to the promised SEED, who was to *bruise* the *serpent's* head; all of which may easily have been derived from the family of Noah, and carried along with the millions of mankind, as they diverged asunder from Mount Ararat, around the earth. The Mexicans are found to have a clear notion of this thing, and of many other traits of the early history of man, as related in the Hebrew records and the Scriptures, preserved in their traditions and paintings, as we shall show in another place.

The etching on the square sides of those rings of brass, in characters resembling Chinese, shows the manufacturer, and the nation of which he was a member, to have had a knowledge of engraving, even on the metals, equal with artists of the present time, of which the common Indian of the west knows nothing.

The stone hatchet, flint, and bone arrow-points, found in this tomb, are no exclusive evidence that this was all done by the modern Indians; because the same are found in vast profusion in all parts of the old world, particularly in the island of England, and have been in use from remotest antiquity.

We are very far from believing the Indians of the present time to be the most ancient aborigines of America; but, on the contrary, are usurpers; have, by force of bloody warfare, exterminated the original inhabitants, taking possession of their country, property, and, in some few instances, retaining arts learned of those very nations.

The immense sea shell, which was fourteen inches long and twenty-three inches in circumference, found in this tomb, is evidence of this people's having an acquaintance with other parts of the world than merely their own dwellings, because the shell is a marine production, and the nearest place where this element is found from the Muskingum, is nearly a thousand miles in a straight line east to the Atlantic.

If the engravings on this chain be, in fact, Chinese, or if they bear a strong and significant analogy to them, it justifies the opinion that a communication between America and Asia, by means of land or navigation to the west, once existed, but has been destroyed by some convulsion in nature. And also the characters on those rings show the ancient Americans to have had a knowledge of *letters*. A knowledge of letters, hieroglyphics, pictures of ideas, and of facts, was known among men 200 years before the time of Moses, or 1822 years before the Christian era, among the Egyptians. Nations of men, therefore, having, at an early period, found their way to this continent, if indeed it was then a separate continent; consequently, to find the remains of such an art, scattered here and there in the dust and ashes of the nations of America passed away, is not surprising.

The mound which we have described, was apprehended, by Mr. Ash, to be only an advanced guard post, or a place of lookout, in the direction of the Muskingum and the valley of the Ohio. Accordingly, he wandered farther into the woods in a northwesterly direction, leaving on his right the Muskingum, whose course was northeast by southwest. His research in that direction had not long been continued before he discovered strong indications of the truth of his conjecture. He had come to a small valley between two mountains, through which a small creek meandered its way to the Muskingum.

On either side of the stream were evident traits of a very large settlement of antiquity. They consisted, first, of a wall or rampart of earth, of almost *nine* feet perpendicular elevation, and thirty feet across the base. The rampart was of a semi-circular form, its entire circuit being three hundred paces, or something over eighteen rods, bounded by the creek. On the opposite side of the stream was another rampart of the same description, evidently answering to the first; these, viewed together, made one grand circle, of more than forty rods circumference, with the creek running between.

After a minute examination, he perceived, very visibly, the remains of elevated stone abutments, which being exactly opposite each other, suggested the belief that these bridges once connected the two semicircles; one in the centre, and one on either side, or the extreme edges of the ring. The timber growing on the rampart and within the circle, was principally red oak, of great age and magnitude. Some of the trees, being in a state of decay, were not less than seven feet in diameter, and twenty-one in circumference.

Some considerable farther up the brook, at the spot where the beautiful vale commences, where the mountain rises abruptly and discharges from its cleft bosom a delightful creek, are a great number of *mounds* of earth, standing at equal distances from each other, forming three grand circles, one beyond the other, cut in two by the creek, as the one described before, with streets situated between, forming, as do the mounds, complete circles. Here, as at the other, the two half circles were united, as would appear, by two bridges, the abutments of which are distinct, so perfect are their remains.

At a considerable distance, on the sides of the mountain, are two mounds or barrows, which are nearly three feet long, twelve high, and seventeen wide at the base. These barrows are composed, principally, of stone, taken out of the creek, on which are growing, also, very heavy timber. Here were deposited the dead, who had been the inhabitants of the town in the vale. From which it appears that the mounds forming those circles, which were *sixty* in number, are not tumuli, or the places where chiefs and distinguished warriors were entombed, but were the houses, the actual dwellings of the people who built them. However, the distinguished dead were interred in tumuli of the same form frequently, but much more magnificent and lofty, and are fewer in number, situated on the highest grounds adjacent to their towns.

But it may be inquired, how could those mounds of earth have ever been the dwellings of families? There is but one way to explain it. They may have, at the time of their construction, received their *peculiar* form, which is a conical, sugar-loaf form, by the erection of long poles or logs, set up in a circle at the bottom, and brought together at the top, with an opening, so that the smoke might pass out. Against this the earth (being brought from a distance, so as not to disturb the even surface of the spot chosen to build on,) was thrown, till the top and sides were entirely enveloped. This operation would naturally cause the bottom, or base, to be of great thickness, caused by the natural sliding down of the earth, as it was thrown on or against the timbers; and this thickness would be in exact proportion with the height of the poles, at the ratio of an angle of forty-five degrees.

In this way, a dwelling of the most secure description would be the result; such as could not be easily broken through, nor set on fire; and in winter would be warm, and in summer cool. It is true, such rooms would be rather gloomy, compared with the magnificent and well-lighted houses of the present times, yet accorded well with the dark usages of antiquity, when mankind lived in clans and tribes, but few in number compared with the present populousness of the earth, and stood in fear of invasion from their neighbors.

Such houses as these, built in circles of wood at *first*, and *lastly* of stone, as the knowledge of architecture came on, were used by the ancient inhabitants of Britain, Wales, Scotland, and Ireland, and on the continent, as in Norway. No mode of building which can be conceived of, would more effectually shut out the wind. " Houses of this form, made with upright stones, are even now common over all the Danish dominions."—(*See Morse's Geography*, vol. 1, p. 158.)

In the communication of Mr. Moses Fiske, of Hillham, Tennessee, to the American Antiquarian Society, 1815, respecting the remains and discoveries made relative to antiquities in the west, but especially in Tennessee, says, that the description of mounds, whether round, square or oblong in their shapes, which have flat tops, were the most magnificent sort, and seem contrived for the purpose of building temples and castles on their summits; which being thus elevated, were very imposing, and might be seen at a great distance.

" Nor must we," he continues, " mistake the ramparts or fortifications, for farming inclosures; what people, savage or civilized, ever fenced their grrounds so preposterously; bearing no proportion in quantity necessary for tillage;" from which the support of a whole country was expected; and further, there were many neighborhoods which had no such accommodations.

He has also discovered, that within the areas encompassed by these ramparts, are whole ranges of foundations, on which *dwelling houses* once stood, with streets running between, besides mounds and other works.

" The houses generally stood in rows, nearly contiguous to each other," as in all compact towns and cities, though sometimes they stood in an irregular and scattered manner. These foundations " are indicated by rings of the earth, from three to five fathoms in diameter," which is equal to eighteen and thirty feet. The remains of these rings or foundations are from ten to twenty inches high, and a yard or more broad. But they were not always circular; some of which he had noticed were square, and others, also, of the oblong form, as houses are now built by civilized nations.

"The flooring of some is elevated above the common level or surface; that of others is depressed. These tokens are indubitable, and overspread the country; some scattered and solitary, but oftener in groups, like villages, with and without being walled in." From which it is clear, that whoever they were, the pursuits of agriculture were indispensable, and were therefore in use with those nations.

From the forms of the foundations of dwellings discovered and described by Mr. Fiske, we conclude they were the efforts of man at a very early period. We are directed to this conclusion by the writings of Vetruvius, who lived in the time of Julius Cæsar, and is the most ancient writer on the subject of architecture that antiquity can boast of. His account is as follows:

"At first, for the walls, men erected forked stakes, and disposing twigs between them, covered them with loam; others pulled up clods of hay, binding them with wood, and to avoid rain and heat, they made a covering with reeds and boughs; but finding that this roof could not resist the winter rains, they made it sloping, pointed at the top, plastering it over with clay, and by that means discharging the rain water. To this day, (says Vetruvius,) some foreign nations construct their dwellings of the same kind of materials, as in Gaul, Spain, Lusitania, and Aquitain. The Colchins, in the kingdom of Portugal, where they abound in forests, fix trees in the earth, close together in ranks, to the right and left, leaving as much space between them, from corner to corner, as the length of the trees will permit; upon the ends of these, at the corners, others are laid transversely, which circumclude the place of habitation in the middle; then at the top, the four angles are braced together with alternate beams. The crevices, which are large, on account of the coarseness of the materials, are stopped with chips and loam. The roof is also raised by beams laid across from the extreme angles, or corners, gradually rising from the four sides to the middle point at the top, (exactly like a German barrack,) and then covered with boughs and earth. In this manner the barbarians, (says this author,) made their roofs to their towers." By the barbarians he means the inhabitants of Europe, at the time when he wrote these remarks, which was in the reign of Julius Cæsar a short time before Christ.

"The Phrygians, who inhabit a champaign country, being destitute of timber, select natural hills, excavate them, dig an entrance, and widen the space within as much as the nature of the place will permit. Above, they fix stakes in a pyramidal form, bind them together, and cover them with reeds or straw, heaping thereon great piles of earth. This kind of covering renders them very warm in winter and cool in summer. Some also cover the roofs of their huts with weeds of lakes; and thus, in all countries and nations, primeval dwellings are formed upon similar principles."—(*Blake's Atlas*, p. 145.)

The circular, square, and oblong form of foundations, found in the west, would seem to argue the houses built thereon to be made in the same way this author has described the mode of building in his time, among the barbarous nations; and also furnishes reason to believe them to have been made here in America, much in the same ages of the world.

Having this knowledge of the mode of ancient building, we are led to the conclusion, that the town which we have just given an account of, was a *clan* of some of the ancient Celtic nations, who, by some means, had found their way to this part of the earth, and had fixed their abode in this secluded valley.

Celtic or Irish, as Mr. Morse says, who were derived from Gaul or Galatia, which is now France, who descended from Gomer, one of the sons of Japheth, a son of Noah; to whose descendants Europe, with its isles, was given. And whether the people who built this town were of Chinese or Celtic origin, it is much the same; because, if we go far enough back in ages of past time, we shall find they were of the same origin, and had equal opportunities to perpetuate a remembrance of the arts, as known among men immediately after the flood, and might therefore resemble each other in their works.

Here, we may suppose, the gods Odin, Thor, and Friga, were adored under the oaks composing American forests, as taught by the Druids; here their victims, the deer and buffalo, sent up to the skies their smoking odor from the altar of sacrifice, while the priests of the forest invoked the blessing of the beneficent Being upon the votaries of the mystic mistletoe. Here were the means of mutual defence and safety discussed; the sighs of the lover breathed on the winds; parents and children looked with kindness on each other; soothed and bound the wounds of such as returned from the uncertain fate of clanular battles; but have been swept with the besom of extermination from this vale, while no tongue remains to tell the story of their sufferings.

At the distance of about three miles higher up, and not far from the Muskingum, says Mr. Ash, he perceived an eminence very similar to the one just described, in which the brass chain was found, to which he hastened, and immediately perceived their likeness in form.

On a comparison of the two, there could be but one opinion, namely, that both were places of lookout, for the express protection of the settlement in the valley. He says he took the pains of clearing the top of the eminence, but could not discover any stone or mark which might lead to a supposition of its being a place of interment. The country above was hilly, yet not so high as to intercept the view for a presumed distance of twenty miles.

On these eminences the beacon fires of the clan who resided in the valley may have been kindled at the hour of midnight, to show those who watched the portentous flame, the advance or destruction of an enemy. Such fires, on the heights of Scotland, were wont to be kindled in the days of Bruce and Wallace, and ages before their time, originated from the Persians, possibly, who worshipped in this way the great ORAMAZE, as the god who made all things. The idea of a Creator was borrowed from Noah, who received the account of the creation from Seth, who had it from Adam, and Adam from the Almighty himself.

From this excursion, our traveller, after having returned to Marietta, pursued his way to Zanesville, on the Muskingum river, where, learning from the inhabitants that the neighborhood was surrounded with the remains of antiquity, he proceeded to the examination of them, having obtained a number of persons to accompany him with the proper implements of excavation. They penetrated the woods in a westerly direction, to a place known to those who accompanied him, about five miles distance, where the ruins of ancient times were numerous and magnificent in the highest degree; consisting of mounds, barrows and ramparts, but of such variety and form, and covering so immense a track of gronnd, that it would have taken at least ten days to have surveyed them minutely.

These immense works of the ancients, it appears, were, in *this place,* encompassed by outlines of an entirely different *shape* from any other described, being of the *triangular* form, and occupying the whole plain, situated as the one before described, in a place nearly surrounded by mountains.

But we pass over many incidents of this traveller, and come immediately to the object of his research, which was to open such of those mounds as might attract his attention. His first operation was to penetrate the interior of a large barrow, situated at one extremity of the vale, which was its southern. Three feet below the surface was fine mould, underneath which were small flat stones, lying in regular strata or gravel, brought from the mountain in the vicinity. This last covered the remains of a human frame, which fell into impalpable powder when touched and exposed to air.

Towards the base of the barrow, he came to three tiers of substances, placed regularly in rotation. And as these formed two rows four deep, separated by little more than a flag stone between the feet of one and the head of another, it was supposed the barrow contained about 2000 skeletons, in a very great state of decay, which shows their extreme antiquity.

In this search was found a well carved stone pipe, expressing a bear's head, together with some fragments of pottery, of fine texture. Near the centre of the whole works, another opening was effected, in a rise of ground, scarcely higher than a natural undulation, common to the general surface of the earth, even on ground esteemed to be level. But there was one singularity accompanying the spot, which attracted the attention of the company, and this was, there was neither shrub nor tree on the spot, although more than ninety feet in circumference, but was adorned with a multitude of *pink* and *purple* flowers.

They came to an opinion that the rise of ground was artificial, and as it differed in form and character from the common mounds, they resolved to lay it open, which was soon done, to a level with the plain, but without the discovery of any thing whatever. But as Ash had become vexed, having found nothing to answer his expectations in other openings on the spot, he jumped from the bank, in order to take a spade, and encourage the men to dig somewhat deeper. At this instant the ground gave way, and involved the whole company in earth and ruin, as was supposed for the moment, but was soon followed by much mirth and laughter, as no person was hurt by the fall, which was but about three feet.

Ash had great difficulty to prevail on any person to resume the labor, and had to explore the place himself, and sound it with a pole, before any man would venture to aid him further, on account of their fright.

But they soon resumed their courage, and on examination found that a parcel of timbers had given way, which covered the orifice of a square hole seven feet by four, and four feet deep. That it was a sepulchre, was unanimously agreed, till they found it in vain to look for bones, or any substances similar to them, in a state of decomposition. They soon, however, struck an object which would neither yield to the spade, nor emit any sound; but persevering still further, they found the obstruction which was uniform through the pit, to proceed from rows of large spherical bodies, at first taken to be stones.

Several of them were cast up to the suface; they were exactly alike, perfectly round, nine inches in diameter, and of about twenty pounds weight. The superfices of one, when cleaned and scraped with knives, appeared like a ball of base metal, so strongly impregnated with the dust of gold, that the baseness of the metal itself was nearly altogether obscured. On this discovery, the clamour was so great, and joy so exuberant, that no opinion but one was admitted, and no voice could be heard, while the cry of " 'tis gold! 'tis gold!" resounded through the groves.

Having to a man determined on this important point, they formed a council respecting the distribution of the treasure, and each individual, in the joy of his heart, declared publicly the use he intended to make of the part alloted to his share.

The Englishman concluded that he would return to England, being sure, from experience, that there was no country like it. A German of the party said, he would never have quitted the Rhine, had he had money enough to rebuild his *barn*, which was blown down by a high wind; but that he would return to the very spot from whence he came, and prove to his neighbors that he loved his country as well as any man, when he had the means of doing well An Irishman swore a great oath, the day longer he'd stay in America; and the Indian who accompanied Ash, appeared to think, that were he to purchase some beads, rum and blankets, and return to his own nation, he might become *Sachem*, and keep the finest squaws to be found.

Even Ash himself saw in the treasure the sure and ample means of continuing his travels in such parts of the earth as he had not yet visited. The company returned to Zanesville with but one ball of their riches, while they carefully hid the residue, till they should subject it to the ordeal of fire.

They soon procured a private room, where, while it was receiving the trial of fire, they stood around in silence almost dreading to breathe. The dreadful element, which was to confirm or consume their hopes, soon began to exercise its various powers. In a few moments the ball turned black, filled the room with sulphurous smoke, emitted sparks and intermittent flames, and *burst* into ten thousand pieces; so great was the terror and suffocation, that all rushed into the street, and gazed on each other, with a mixed expression of doubt and astonishment.

The smoke subsided, when they were able to discover the elements of the supposed gold, which consisted of some very fine ashes, and a great quantity of cinders, exceedingly porous; the balls were nothing but a sort of metal called spririte or pyrites, composed of sulphur and iron, and abounds in the mountains of that region.

The triangular form of this enclosure, being different from the general form of those ancient works, is perhaps worthy of notice, merely on the account of its form; and might be supposed to be of Chinese origin, as it is well known that the triangular shape is a favorite one of the nations of Hindostan; it is even in the Hindoo theology, significant of the Trinity, of their great Brahma, or god; and on this account, might even characterise the form of national works such as we have just described, under the notion, that the divine protection would the more readily be secured. "One of the missionaries at Pekin," says Adam Clarke, "takes it for granted, that the mystery of the Trinity was known among the ancient Chinese, as that this △ character was its symbol. It is remarkable that Moses and the prophets, the ancient, Chaldee Targumists, the authors of the *Zend Avesta*, a Chinese book, Plato, a celebrated philosopher of antiquity, who died at Athens, 348 B. C., and also the first philosopher of Greece, and Philo the Jew, should all coincide so perfectly in their ideas of a Trinity in the Godhead. This could not be the effect of accident. Moses and the prophets received this from God himself; and all others have borrowed from this first origin."

For what use the balls of which we have given an account were designed, is impossible to conjecture, whether to be thrown by means of engines, as practised by the Romans, as an instrument of warfare, or a sort of medium in trade, or were used as instruments, in athletic games, either to roll or heave, who can tell?

But one thing respecting them is not uncertain, they must have been of great value, or so much labor and care would not have been expended to secure them. Colonel Ludlow, of Cincinnati, a man, it is said, who was well versed in the history of his country, though now deceased, was indefatigable in his researches after the antiquities of America, discovered several hundreds of those balls of pyrites, weighing generally about twenty pounds each, near an old Indian settlement, on the banks of the Little Miami, of the Ohio, and also another heap in an artificial cave, on the banks of the Sciota, consisting of copper pyrites, or quartz.

In that division of South America, called Patagonia, which extends nearly to the extreme southern point of that country, is found a people, denominated Patagonians, who are of a monstrous size and height, measuring from six to seven feet, many af them approaching to eight. Among this people is found an instrument of war, made of heavy stones, wore round by friction; so that in appearance, they are like a cannon ball. These they contrive to fasten in a sling, from which they throw them with great dexterity and force.—*Morse's Geography.*

This kind of ball was used, though of a smaller size, to capture and kill animals with. The manner of using them is as follows: They take *three* of those balls, two of them three inches, and one of them two inches in diameter. The hunter takes the small ball in his right hand, and swings the other two, (which are connected by a thong of a proper length, fastening also to the one in his hand) round his head, till a sufficient velocity is acquired, at the same time taking aim, when it is thrown at the legs of the animal he is pursuing, in such a manner as to entangle its feet by the rotary motion of the balls; so that its capture is easy.

Conjecture might go on to establish it as a fact, that these balls of pyrites, found in many parts of the west, were indeed a warlike instrument, thrown by a sling, out of which, a force almost equivalent to that of powder, might be acquired; and from the top of mounds, or from the sides of their elevated forts, such a mode of defence would be very terrible.

This mode of fighting was known to the Hebrews. David slew Goliath with a stone from a sling. Seven hundred chosen men out of Gibea, could sling a stone at an hair's breadth. Job speaks of this manner of annoying wild beasts, where he is recounting the strength of Leviathan: "Slinged stones are turned with him into stubble."

Dr. Adam Clarke's observation on the *use* and force of the sling, are very interesting, and pertinent to the subject. They are found in his Commentary, 1st. Samuel, chap. xvii. verse 40, "The sling, both among the Greeks and Hebrews, has been a most powerful, offensive weapon. It is composed of two strings and a leather strap;" (or as among the Patagonians, of raw-hide,) "the strap is in the middle, and is the place where the stone or bullet lies. The string on the right end of the strap is firmly fastened to the hand; that on the left, is held between the thumb and middle joint of the fore finger. It is then whirled two or three times round the head; and when discharged, the finger and thumb let go their hold of the string. The velocity and force of the sling is in proportion to the distance of the strap to where the bullet lies, from the shoulder joint. Hence, the ancient Balleares, or inhabitants of Majorca and Minorca, islands in the Mediterranean sea, near the coast of Spain, are said to have had three slings of different lengths; the longest they used when the enemy was at the greatest distance; the middle one on their nearer approach, and the shortest, when they came into the ordinary fighting distance in the field. The shortest is the most certain, though not the most powerful.

"The Balleareans are said to have one of their slings constantly bound about their head; to have used the second as a girdle; and to have carried the third always in their hand.

"In the use of the sling, it requires much practice to hit the mark; but when once this dexterity is acquired, the sling is nearly as fatal as the ball thrown by the explosion of powder.

"David was evidently an expert marksman; and his sling gave him greatly the advantage over Goliah; an advantage of which the giant does not seem to have been aware. He could hit him within any speaking distance; if he missed once, he had as many chances as he had stones; and after all, being unincumbered with armor, young and athletic, he could have saved his life by flight. But David saved himself the trouble of running away, or the giant from throwing his spear or javelin at him, by giving him the first blow.

"Goliah was terribly armed, having a spear, a shield, and a sword; besides, he was every where invulnerable, on account of his helmet of brass, his coat of mail, which was made also of brass, in little pieces, perhaps about the size of a half dollar, and lapped over each other, like the scales of fishes, so that no sword, spear, nor arrow could hurt him."

This coat of mail, when polished and bright, must have been very glorious to look upon, especially when the sun, in his brightness, bent his beams to aid the giant warrior's fulgent habiliments to illumine the field of battle, as the wearer strode, here and there, among the trophies of death.

The only spot left, where he could be hit to advantage, was his broad giant forehead into which the stone of David sunk, from its dreadful impetus received from the simple sling. To some, this has appeared perfectly improbable; but we are assured by ancient writers, that scarcely any thing could resist the force of the sling.

Diodorus Siculus, an historian who flourished in the time of Julius Cæsar, a short time before Christ, and was born in the island of Sicily, in the Mediterranean, says, " the people of the islands of Minorca and Majorca, in time of war, could sling greater stones than any other people, and with such force, that they seemed as if projected from a *capult*," an engine used by the ancients for this purpose.

Therefore, in assaults made on fortified towns, they grievously wound the besieged, and in battle, they break in pieces the shields, helmets, and every species of armor, by which the body is defended. It would seem, from the expertness of the Patagonians, evinced in the use of the sling, that they may have been derived from the ancient inhabitants of those islands, who could as easily have found their way out of the Mediterranean by the strait of

Gibraltar into the Atlantic ocean, and be driven across to South America, by the winds from the east, or by the current of the sea, as the Egyptians, as we have before shown.

The sling was a very ancient warlike instrument; and in the hands of those who were skilled in the use of it, it produced astonishing effects. The people of the above named islands were the most celebrated slingers of antiquity. They did not permit their children to eat till they had struck down their food from the top of a pole, or some distant eminence.

Concerning the velocity of the leaden ball thrown out of the sling, it is said by the ancients, to have melted in its course. Ovid, the Roman poet, has celebrated its speed, in the following beautiful verse:

> "Hermes was fired, as in the clouds he hung;
> So the cold bullet that with fury slung
> From Balearic engines, mounts on high,
> Glows in the whirl, and burns along the sky."

This is no poetic fiction. Seneca, the stoic philospher of Rome, born A. D. 12, says the same thing; "the ball projected from the sling, melts, and is liquified by the friction of the air, as if it were exposed to the action of fire."

Vegetius, who lived in the 14th century, and was also a Roman, tells us, that "slingers could, in general, hit the mark at six hundred feet distance," which is more than thirty rods. From this view we see what havoc the western nations, using the *sling* or *engine*, to throw stones from their vast forts and mounds with, must have made, when engaged in defensive or offensive war.

Discovery of the Remains of Ancient Pottery.

On the subject of pottery we remark, that the remains of this art are generally found, especially of any extent, in the neighborhood of salt springs. It is true, that specimens of earthen ware are frequently taken out of the ancient barrows of the dead, and also are frequently brought to sight on the shores of rivers, where the earth has been suddenly removed by inundations.

A few years since, an instance of this sort occurred at Tawanda, in Pennsylvania. The Susquehannah had risen very high, at the time we are speaking of, and had undermined the bank on the Tawanda shore, to a considerable extent, at the high water mark. On the receding of the waters, the bank was found to be carried away for the distance of about six rods, when there appeared several fire places, made of the stones of the river, with vessels of earthen, of a capacity about equal with a common water pail, in a very good state of preservation.

Between those fire places, which were six in number, were found the skeletons of several human beings, lying in an undisturbed position, as if they, when living, had fallen asleep, and never waked; two of these, in particular, attracted attention, and excited not a little surprise; they were lying side by side, with the arm of one of them under the neck of the other, and the feet were mingled in such a manner as to induce the belief that when death came upon them, they were asleep in each other's embraces. But in what manner they came to their death, so that they appeared not to have moved, from the fatal moment till the bank was carried away, which had covered them for ages, is strange indeed.

It cannot be supposed they died all at once, of some sickness, or that an enemy surprised them while sleeping, and, silently passing from couch to couch, inflicted the deadly blow; because, in any of these ways, their bones, in the convulsions of dissolution, must have been deranged, so that the image and peaceful posture of sleepers could not have characterised their positions, as they were found to have. It was conjectured, at the time of their discovery, that the period of their death had been at the season of the year when that river breaks up its ice; in March or April, the river they supposed, may have been dammed up below them, where, it is true, the stream narrows on the account of the approach of the mountains. Here the ice having jammed in between, caused a sudden rise of the river, and setting back, overflowed them.

But this cannot be possible, as the *noise* of the breaking ice would never allow them to sleep; this operation of nature is accompanied with a tremendous uproar tearing and rending the shores and forests that grow on them, multiplying crash on crash, with the noise of thunder. Neither can it be well supposed, the waters came over them in the way suggested, even if they had slept during the scene we have just described, because on the first touch of the waters to their bodies, they would naturally spring from their sleep in surprise.

Something must have happened that deprived them of life and motion in an instant of time. This is not impossible, because at Herculaneum and Pompeii, are found, where, in digging, they have penetrated through the lava down to those ancient cities, laying bare streets, houses and temples, with their contents, such as have survived the heat which ruined those cities—skeletons, holding between their fingers something they had in their hands at the moment of their death, so that they do not appear even to have struggled.

Something of the same nature, as it respects *suddenness*, must have overtaken these sleepers; so that their natural positions were not disturbed. If the place of their dwellings had been skirted by a steep bank or hill, it might then have been supposed that a land *slip* or mine *spring*, had buried them alive, but this is not the case. They were about four feet under ground, the soil which covered them was the same alluvial with the rest of the flat; it is a mystery, and cannot be solved, unless we suppose an explosion of earth, occasioned by an accumulation of *galvanic* principles, which, bursting the earth near them, suddenly buried them alive.

Dr. Beck, the author of the Gazetteer of Illinois and Missouri, suggests the cause of the earthquakes in the valley of the Mississippi, in 1811 and 1812, which, in many places, threw up in an instant vast heaps of earth, to have been the principle of galvanism bursting from the depths beneath, in a perpendicular direction, overwhelming, in a moment of time, whatever might be asleep or awake, wherever it fell.

Further down the Susquehannah, some thirty or forty miles below Tawanda, at a place called the Black-walnut Bottom, on the farm of a Mr. Kinney, was discovered a most extraordidary specimen of *pottery*.

Respecting this discovery, the owner of the farm relates, as we are informed by a clergyman, who examined the article on the spot, though in a broken state, that soon after the first settlements on that river, and especially on that farm, a great freshet took place which tore a channel in a certain direction across the flat, when the vessel which we are about to describe, was brought to light.

It was *twelve* feet across the top, and of consequence *thirty-six* feet in circumference, and otherwise of proportionable depth and form. Its thickness was three inches, and appeared to be made of some coarse substance, probably mere clay, such as might be found on the spot, as it was not glazed. Whoever its makers were, they must have manufactured it on the spot where it was found, as it must have been impossible to move so huge a vessel. They may have easily effected its construction by building it up by degrees, with layers put on in succession, till high enough to suit the enormous fancy of its projectors, and then by piling wood around, it might have been burnt so as to be fit for use, and then propped up by stones, to keep it from falling apart.

But who can tell for what use this vast vessel was intended? Conjecture here is lost; no ray of light dawns upon this strange remnant of antiquity. One might be led to suppose it was made in imitation of the great *laver* in the court of Solomon's Temple, which was seventeen feet two inches in diameter, and fifty-two feet six inches in circumference, and eight feet nine inches deep.—(*II Chronicles*, iv. 2.)

The discovery of this vast specimen of earthen ware, is, at any rate, a singularity, and refers to some age of the world when the inhabitants used very large implements of husbandry. If there had been in its neighborhood a salt spring, as there are often found farther west, we should not be at a loss to know for what purpose it was constructed.

Remarkable specimens of pottery are often brought up from very great depths at the salt works in Illinois. Entire pots of a very large capacity, holding from eight to ten gallons, have been disinterred at the amazing depth of eighty feet; others have been found at even greater depths, and of greater dimensions.—*Schoolcraft.*

Upon this subject this author makes the following remark: "If these antique vessels are now supposed to lie in those depths where they were anciently employed, the surface of the Ohio, and consequently of the Mississippi, must have been sixty or eighty feet lower than they are at present, to enable the saline water to drain off; and the ocean itself must have stood at a lower level, or extended in an elongated gulf up the present valley of the Mississippi."

Many are of the opinion, that much of this region of country once lay beneath large lakes of water, and that the barriers between them and the ocean, by some means, are broken down, when a rush of water swept the whole country, in its course to the sea, burying all the ancient nations, with their works, at those depths beneath the surface, as low as where those fragments of earthern ware are found. The bottom of those lakes is also supposed to be the true origin of the immense *prairies* of the west; and the reason why they are not, long since grown over with forest trees, is supposed to be because, from the rich and mucky soil found at the bottom of those lakes, a *grass* of immense length, ten and fourteen feet high, peculiar to the prairies, immediately sprung up before trees could take root, and therefore hindred this effort of nature. And as a reason why forest trees have not been able to gain upon the prairies, it is alleged, the Indians annually burn these boundless meadows, which ministers to their perpetuity. Some of those prairies are hundreds of miles in length and breadth, and in burning over, present, in the night, a spectacle too grand, sublime and beautiful for adequate description; belting the horizon with a ruin of fire, the farthest end of which seem dipped in the immeasurable distance, so that even contemplation, in its boldest efforts, is swallowed up and rendered powerless.

A Catacomb of Mummies found in Kentucky.

LEXINGTON, in Kentucky, stands nearly on the site of an ancient town, which was of great extent and magnificence, as is amply evinced by the wide range of its circumvallatory works, and the quantity of ground it once occupied.

There is connected with the antiquities of this place, a catacomb, formed in the bowels of the limestone rock, about fifteen feet below the surface of the earth, adjacent to the town of Lexington. This grand object, so novel and extraordinary in this country, was discovered in 1775, by some of the first settlers, whose curiosity was excited by something remarkable in the character of the stones which covered the entrance to the cavern within. They removed these stones, and came to others of singular appearance for stones in a natural state; the removal of which laid open the mouth of a cave, deep, gloomy, and terrific, as they supposed.

With augmented numbers, and provided with light, they descended and entered, without obstruction, a spacious apartment; the sides and extreme ends were formed into niches and compartments, and occupied by figures representing men. When alarm subsided, and the sentiment of dismay and surprise permitted further research and inquiry, the figures were found to be *mummies*, preserved by the art of embalming, to as great a state of perfection as was known among the ancient Egyptians, eighteen hundred years before the Christian era; which was about the time that the Israelites were in bondage in Egypt, when this art was in its highest state of perfection.

Unfortunately for antiquity, science, and every thing else held sacred by the illumined and learned, this inestimable discovery was made at a period when a bloody and inveterate war was carried on between the Indians and the whites: and the power of the natives was displayed in so savage a manner, that the whites were filled with revenge. Animated by this vindictive spirit, the discoverers of the catacomb delighted to wreak their vengeance even on the mummies, supposing them to be of the same Indian race with whom they were at war.

They dragged them out to the open air, tore the bandages open, kicked the bodies into dust, and made a general bonfire of the most ancient remains antiquity could boast. The descent to this cavern is gradual, the width four feet, the height seven, and the whole length of the catacomb was found to be eighteen rods and a half, by six and a half; and calculating from the niches and shelvings on the sides, it was sufficiently capacious to have contained at least two thousand subjects.

I could never, says Mr Ash, from whose travels we have taken this account, learn the exact quantity it contained; the answers to the inquiries which he made respecting it were, " O, they burnt up and destroyed hundreds!" Nor could he arrive at any knowledge of the fashion, manner, and apparel of the mummies, or receive any other information than that they " *were well lapped up,*" appeared sound, and consumed in the fire with a rapid flame. But not being contented with the uncertain information of persons, who, it seems, had no adequate knowledge of the value of this discovery, he caused the cavern to be gleaned for such fragments as yet remained in the niches, on its shelving sides and from the floor. The quantity of remains thus gathered up, amounted to forty or fifty baskets, the dust of which was so light and pungent as to affect the eyes even to tears, and the nose to sneezing, to a troublesome degree.

He then proceeded on a minute investigation, and separated from the general mass several pieces of human limbs, fragments of bodies, solid, sound, and apparently capable of eternal duration. In a cold state they had no smell whatever, but when submitted to the action of fire, gave out an agreeable effluvia, but was like nothing in its fragrance to which he could compare it.

On this subject Mr. Ash has the following reflections:—" How these bodies were embalmed, how long preserved, by what nations, and from what people descended, no opinion can be formed, nor any calculation made, but what must result from speculative fancy and wild conjecture. For my part, I am lost in the deepest ignorance. My reading affords me no knowledge, my travels no light. I have neither read nor known of any of the North American Indians who formed catacombs for their dead, or who were acquainted with the art of preservation by embalming.

The Egyptians, according to Herodotus, who flourished 450 years before Christ, had three methods of embalming; but Diodorus, who lived before Christ, in the time of Julius Cæsar, observes, that the ancient Egyptians had a *fourth* method of far greater superiority. That method is not described by Diodorus; it had become extinct in his time; and yet I cannot think it presumptuous to conceive that the American mummies were preserved after that very manner, or at least with a mode of *equal* virtue and effect."

The Kentuckians asserted, that the features of the face and the form of the whole body were so well preserved, that they must have been the exact representations of the once living subjects.

This cavern, indeed, is similar to those found in Egypt, where the once polished and powerful inhabitants bestowed their dead, wrapped up in the linens, spices, and aromatics of the east. It is probable that the cave where these were found was partly natural and partly artificial. Having found it suitable to their purpose, they had opened a convenient descent, cleared out the stones and rocks, and fitted it with niches for the reception of those they had embalmed.

This custom, it would seem, is purely Egyptian, and was practised in the earliest age of their national existence, which was about two thousand years before Christ. Catacombs are numerous all over Egypt, vast excavations under ground, with niches in their sides for their embalmed dead, exactly such as the one we have described.

Shall we be esteemed presumptuous, if we hazard the opinion that the people who made this cavern and filled it with the thousands of their embalmed dead were, indeed, from Egypt? If they were not, whither shall we turn for a solution of this mystery? To what country shall we travel? where are the archives of past ages, that shall shed its light here?

If the Egyptians were indeed, reckoned as the *first* of nations; for so are they spoken of, even in the Scriptures: if from them was derived the art of navigation, the knowledge of astronomy, in a great degree, also the unparalleled invention of *letters*, (from whom it is even probable the Phœnecians derived the use of letters,) with many other arts, of use to human society; such as architecture, agriculture, with the science of government, &c.; why not allow the *authors* of the antiquated works about Lexington, together with the immense catacomb, to have been, indeed, an *Egyptian colony;* seeing the art of embalming, which is *peculiarly characteristic* of that people, was found there in a state of *perfection* not exceeded by the mother country itself.

A trait of national practices so strong and palpable, as is this peculiar art, should lead the mind, without hesitation, to a belief, that wherever the thing is practised, we have found in its authors either a colony direct from Egypt, or the descendants of some nation of the countries of Africa acquainted with the art.

But if this be so, the question here arises, how came they in America, seeing the nearest point of even South America approaches no nearer to the nearest point of Africa, than about seventeen hundred miles? Those points are, first, on the American side, Cape St. Roque; and, second, on the African side, Cape de Verd.

But such is the mechanism of the globe, and the operation of the waters, that from the west coast of Africa there is a constant current of the sea setting toward South America; so that if a vessel were lost, or if an eastern storm had driven it far into the ocean or South Atlantic, it would *naturally* arrive at last on the American coast. This is supposed to have been the predicament of the fleet of Alexander the Great, some hundred years before the Christian era, as we have before related. The cause of this current is doubtless, the flow of the waters of the Mediterranean into the Atlantic; the, Mediterranean being fed by a vast number of the rivers of Europe.

The next inquiry to be pursued, is, whether the Egyptians were ever a maritime people, or rather, *anciently* so, sufficient for our purpose? By consulting ancient history, we find it mentioned that the Egyptians, as early as fourteen hundred and eighty-five years before Christ, had shipping, and that one Danus, with his fifty daughters, sailed into Greece, and anchored at Rhodes; which is three thousand, three hundred and eighteen years back from the present year, 1833. Eight hundred and eighty-one years after the landing of this vessel at Rhodes, we find the Egyptians, under the direction of Necho, their king, fitting out some Phœnicians with a vessel, or fleet, with orders to sail from the Red sea, quite around the continent of Africa, and to return by the Mediterranean, which they effected.

It is easy to pursue the very track they sailed, in order to circumnavigate Africa; sailing from some port on the Red sea, they pass down to the strait of Babelmandel, into the Indian ocen; thence south, around the cape of Good Hope, into the South Atlantic;—thence north along the African coast on the west side, which would carry them along opposite, or east of South America.

Pursuing this course, they would pass into the Mediterranean at the strait of Gibraltar, and so on to Egypt, mooring at Alexandria, on the south end of the Mediterranean; a voyage of more than sixteen thousand miles; two-thirds of the distance round the earth. Many ages after their first settlement in Egypt, they were the leading nation in maritime skill and other arts.

It is true, that a knowledge of the compass and magnet, as aids to navigation, in Africa or Europe, was unknown in those early ages; but to counterbalance this defect, they were, from necessity, much more skilful in a knowledge of the heavenly bodies, as guides to their courses, than men are at the present day. But in China, it is *now* believed, that a knowledge of the magnet, and its application to the great purposes of navigatian, was understood before the time of Abraham, more than two thousand years before Christ, of which we shall give a more particular account in another place of this work.

But if we cannot allow the Egyptians to have visited South America, and all the islands between, on voyages of discovery, which by no means can be supposed chimerical, we are ready to admit they may have been *driven* there by an eastern storm; and as favoring such a circumstance, the current which sets from the African coast toward South America, should not be forgotten.

If it be allowed that this mode of reasoning is at all conclusive, the same will apply in favor of their having *first* hit on the coast of the West Indies, as *this* group of islands, as they *now* exist, is much more favorable to a visit from that particular part of Africa, called Egypt, than is South America.

Egypt and the West Indies are exactly in the same latitude, that is, the northern parts of those islands, both being between twenty and thirty degrees north.

Sailing from Egypt, out of the Mediterranean, passing through the straits of Gibraltar would throw a vessel, in case of an eastern storm, aided by the current, as high north as opposite the Bahama islands. A blow of but a few days in that direction, would be quite sufficient to have driven an Egyptian vessel, or boat, or whatever they may have sailed in, entirely on the coast of the West Indies. The trade winds sweep westward across the Atlantic, through a space of 50 or 60 degrees of longitude, carrying every thing within their current directly to the American coast.

If such may have been the case, they were, indeed, in a manner, on the very continent itself, especially, if the opinon of president Jefferson and others be allowed, that the gulf of Mexico, which is situated exactly behind those islands, west, has been scooped out by the current which makes from the equator toward the north.

Kentucky itself, where, we think, we have found the remains of an Egyptian colony, or nation, as in the case of the works and catacomb at Lexington, is in latitude but five degrees north of Egypt. So that whether they may have visited America on a voyage of exploration, or have been driven on the coast against their will; in either case, it would be perfectly natural that they should have established themselves in that region.

Traits of Egyptian manners were found among many of the nations of South America, mingled with those who appeared to be of other origin; of which we shall speak again in the course of this work.

But at Lexington the traits are too notorious to allow them to be other than pure Egyptian, in full possession of the strongest complexion of their national character, that of embalming, which was connected with their *religion*.

The Mississippi, which disembogues itself into the Mexican gulf, is in the same north latitude with Egypt, and may have, by its likeness to the Egyptian Nile, invited those adventurers to pursue its course, till a place suited to their views or necessities may have presented.

Ancient Letters of the Phœnicians and Americans.

The ancient Punic, Phœnician, or Carthaginian language, is all the same; the characters called Punic, or Phœnician, therefore, are also the same. A *fac simile* of those characters, as copied by Dr. Adam Clarke, are herewith presented. See No. 4.

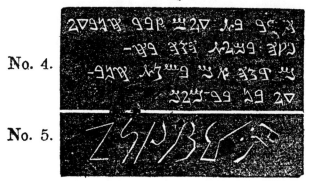

They were discovered in the island of Malta, in the Mediterranean, which was anciently inhabited by the Phœnicians, long before the Romans existed as a nation. These characters were found engraved on a stone, in a cave of that island, in the year 1761, which was a sepulchral cave, so used by the earliest inhabitants. These characters, being found in this ancient repository of the dead, it is believed, marks the place of the burial of that famous Carthaginian general, Hannibal, as they explicitly allude to that character. The reading in the original is as follows:

"*Chadar Beth olam kabar Chanibaal Nukeh becaleth haveh, rachm daeh Am beshuth Chanilaal ben Bar melec.*"

Which, being interpreted, is:—" The inner chamber of the sanctuary of the sepulchre of Hannibal, illustrious in the consummation of calamity. He was beloved. The people lament, when arrayed in order of battle, Hannibal the son of Bar-melec."

This one of the largest remains of the Punic or Phœnician language now in existence. Characters of this description are also found on the rocks of Dighton, Massachusetts, near the sea.

In a chain of mountains between the rivers Oronoco and Amazon, South America, are found engraved in a cavern, on a block of granite, characters supposed also to be Punic letters, a fac similie of which is presented at No. 5. These were furnished by Baron Humboldt, in his volume of Researches in South America; between which and those given us above, by Dr. Clarke, it is easy to perceive a small degree of similarity.

But if the Phœnician letters shown at Nos. 4 and 5 are highly interesting, those which follow at Nos. 1, 2 and 3, are equally so. These are presented to the public by Prof. Rafinesque, in his Atlantic Journal for 1832, with their meaning.

Under figures 1 and 2 are the *African* or *Lybian* characters, the primitive letters of the most ancient nations of Africa. Under figure 3 are the *American* letters, or letters of *Otolum*, an ancient city, the ruins of which are found in South America, being, so far as yet explored, of an extent embracing a circumference of twenty four miles, of which we shall again speak in due time.

The similarity which appears between the African letters and the letters of America, as in use perhaps two thousand years before Christ, is almost, if not exact, showing beyond a doubt, that the same nations, the same languages, and the same arts, which were known in ancient Lybia or Africa, were also known in America; as well also as nations from old China, who came to the western coast in huge vessels, as we shall show in this work.

We here subjoin an account of those characters, numbered 1, 2, 3, by the author Prof. Rafinesque; and also of the American *glyphs*, which, however, are not presented here, but on page 307. They are, it appears, formed by a combination of the letters numbered 1, 2, 3, and resembling very much, in our opinion, the *Chinese* characters, when grouped or combined, with a view to express a sentence or a paragraph in their language. The account is as follows:

		LYBIAN.		AMERICAN.	
		No. 1.	2.	3.	
Ear	AIPS	A			A
Eye	ESH	E			EI
Nose	IFR	I			IZ
Tongue	OMBR	O			OW
Hand	VULD	U			UW
Earth	LAMBD	L			IL
Sea	MAH	M			IM
Air	NISP	N			IN
Fire	RASH	P			IR
Sun	BAP	B p			IB
Moon	CEK	C k			UK
Mars	DOR	D t			ID ET
Mer'cy	GOREG	G			IGH
Venus	UAF	V f			UW
Saturn	SIASH	S sh			ES ISH
Jupiter	THEUE	Thz			UZ

Letter to Mr. Champollion, on the Graphic Systems of America, and the Glyphs of Otolum, or Palenque, in Central America.

ELEMENTS OF THE GLYPHS.

I have the pleasure to present you here a tabular and comparative view of the Atlantic alphabets of the two continents, with a specimen of the groups of letters or glyphs, (see p. 307,) of the monuments of Otolum* or Palenque; which belong to my seventh series of graphic signs, and are in fact words formed by grouped letters or elements as in Chinese characters, or somewhat like the cyphers now yet in use among us, formed by acrostical anagrams or combinations of th first letters of words or names.

When I began my investigation of these American glyphs and became convinced that they must have been groups of letters, I sought for the elementary letters in all the ancient known alphabets, the Chinese Sanscrit and Egyptian above all; but in vain. The Chinese characters offered but few similarities with the glyphs, and not having a literal but syllabic alphabet, could not promise the needful clue. The Sanscrit alphabet, and all its derived branches, including even the Hebrew, Phœnician, Pelagic, Celtic and Cantabrian alphabets were totally unlike in forms and combinations of grouping. But in the great variety of Egyptian form of the same letters, I thought that I could trace some resemblance with our American glyphs. In fact, I could see in them the Egyptian cross, snake, circle, delta, square, trident, eye, feather, fish, hand, &c., but sought in vain for the birds, lions, sphynx, beetle, and a hundred other nameless signs of Egypt.

However, this first examination and approximation of analogy in Egypt and Africa was a great preliminary step in the inquiry. I had always believed that the Atlantes of Africa have partly colonized America, as so many ancient writers have affirmed. This belief led me to search for any preserved fragments of the alphabets of Western Africa and Lybia, the land of the African Atlantes yet existing under the names of Berbers, Tuarics, Shelluhs, &c. This was no easy task. The Atlantic antiquities are still more obscure than the Egyptian. No Champollion had raised their veil; the city of Farawan, the Thebes of the Atlantes, whose splendid ruins exist as yet in the mountains of Atlas, has not even been described properly as yet, nor its inscriptions delineated.

However, I found at last in Gramay, *(Africa Illustrata,)* an old Lybian alphabet, which has been copied by Purchas, in his collection of old alphabets. I was delighted to find it so explicit, so well connected with the Egyptian, being also an acrostic alphabet, and

---

* A late discovered city of South America, nearly equal to the Egyptian Thebes.

above all, to find that all its signs were to be seen in the glyphs of Otolum, the American city. Soon after appeared, in a supplement to Clapperton and Denham's Travels in Africa, another old and obsolete Lybian alphabet, not acrostical, found by Denham in old inscriptions among the Tuarics of Targih and Ghraat, west of Fezan: which, although unlike the first, had many analogies, and also with the American glyphs.

Thinking, then, that I had found the primitive elements of these glyphs, I hastened to communicate this important fact to Mr. Duponceau, (in a printed letter directed to him in 1828,) who was struck with the analogy, and was ready to confess that the glyphs of Palenque might be alphabetical words: although he did not believe before that any American alphabets were extant. But he could not pursue my connection of ideas, analogies of signs, languages and traditions, to the extent which I desired, and now am able to prove.

To render my conclusions perspicuous, I must divide the subject into several parts; directing my inquiries, 1st. On the old Lybian alphabet. 2dly. On the Tuaric alphabet. 3dly. On their element in the American glyphs. 4thly. On the possibility to read them. While the examination of their language, in connection with the other Atlantic languages, will be the theme of my third letter.

I. The old Lybian delineated in the table No. 1, has all the appearance of a very ancient alphabet, based upon the acrostical plan of Egypt; but in a very different language, of which we have 16 words preserved. This language may have been that of a branch of Atlantes, perhaps the Getulians, (Ge-tula, or Tulas of the plains) or of the Ammonians, Old Lybians, and also Atlantes.

Out of these 16 words, only 5 have a slight affinity with the Egyptian, they are:

	Lybian.	Egyptian.		Lybian.	Egyptian.
Nose	Ifr	Nif	Venus	Uaf	Ath
Sea	Mah	Mauh	Ear	Aips	Ap
Saturn	Siash	Sev			

While this Lybian has a greater analogy with the Pelagic dialects, as many as 12 out of 16 being consimilar.

	Lybian.	Pelagic.		Lybian.	Pelagic.
Eye	Esh	Eshas	Earth	Lambd	Landa
Nose	Ifr	Rinif	Sea	Mah	Marah
Hand	Vuld	Hul, chil	Fire	Rash	Purah

	Lybian.	*Pelagic.*		*Lybian.*	*Pelagic.*
Moon	Cek	Selka, kres	Venus	Uaf	Uenas
Mars	Dor	Hares, Thor	Saturn	Siash	Satur, Shiva
Mercury	Goreg	Mergor	Jupiter	Theue	Theos

Therefore, the numerical analogy is only 32 per cent. with the Egyptian, while it is 75 per cent. with the Pelagic. Another proof, among many, that the ancient Atlantes were intimately connected with the Pelagian nations of Greece, Italy, and Spain; but much less so with the Egyptians, from whom they however borrowed perhaps their graphic system.

This system is very remarkable. 1. By its acrostic form. 2. By having only 16 letters like most of the primitive alphabets, but unlike the Egyptian and Sanscrit. 3. By being susceptible of twenty-two sounds by modification of six of the letters, as usual among the Pelagian and Etruscan. 4. Above all, by being based upon the acrostics of three important series of physical objects, the five senses represented by their agents in man, the four elements of nature and the seven planets: which are very philosophical ideas, and must have originated in a civilized nation and learned priesthood. 5. By the graphic signs being also rude delineations of these physical objects or their emblems. The ear, eye, nose, tongue and hand, for the five senses. The triangle for the earth, fish for the sea or water, snake for the air, flame for fire. A circle for the sun, crescent for the moon, a sword for Mars, a purse for Mercury, the V for Venus, double ring for Saturn, and trident for Jupiter. Venus being the fifth planet, has nearly the same sign as U, the fifth letter.

These physical emblems are so natural and obvious, that they are sometimes found among many of the ancient alphabets; the sun and moon even among the Chinese. But in the Egyptian alphabets, the emblems apply very often to different letters, owing to the difference of language and acrostic feature. Thus the hand applies to D in Egyptian instead of U, the eye to R, the circle to O, the snake to L, &c.

II. The second Lybian alphabet, No. 2 in the tables, was the ancient alphabet of Tuarics, a modern branch of the Atlantes, until superseded by the Arabic. Denham found, with some difficulty, its import, and names of letters which are not acrostic but literal, and eighteen in number. It is doubtful whether these names were well applied in all instances, as the explainer was ignorant, and

Denham not aware of the importance of this alphabet. Some appear not well named, and U with V have the same sign W; but these are always interchangeable in old language, and in alphabet No. 1, V is called UAF instead of VAF, and U is VULD instead of UULD!

As we have it, this alphabet is sufficiently and obviously derived from the first, eleven out of the sixteen letters being similar or nearly so, while only five are different, E, M, R, G and Z. This last appears the substitute of TH, of No. 1, and GH represents G. Yet they are by far more alike than the Demotic is from the Hieratic Egyptian, and I therefore deem this No. 2 a Demotic form of the ancient Lybian or Atlantic.

I might have given and compared several other Lybian alphabets found in inscriptions; but as they have been delineated without a key or names, it is at present very difficult to decypher them. I however, recommend them to the attention of the learned, and among others, point out the Lybian inscription of Apollonia, the harbor of Cyrene, given by Lacella, in his travels in the Cyrenaica. The letters of this inscription appear more numerous than sixteen or even twenty-two, and although they have some analogies with the two Lybian alphabets, yet approximate still more to the Demotic of Egypt and the Phœnician. But the inscriptions in Mount Atlas and at Farawan, when collected and decyphered, will be found of much greater historical importance.

III. Meantime in the column No. 3 of the tabular view, are given forty-six elements of the glyphs of Otolum (see page 307, where there is a *fac simile* of these glyphs) or Palenque, a few of these glyphs being given also in column No. 4. These forty-six elements are altogether similar or derived from the Lybian prototypes of No. 1 and 2. In some cases they are absolutely identic, and the conviction of their common origin is almost complete, particularly when taken in connection with the collateral proofs of traditions and languages. These elements are somewhat involved in the grouping, yet they may easily be perceived and separated. Sometimes they are ornamented by double lines or otherwise, as monumental letters often are. Sometimes united to outside numbers represented by long ellipses meaning 10, and round dots meaning unities, which approximates to the Mexican system of graphic numeration. Besides these forty-six elements, some others may be seen in the glyphs, which I left off, because too intricate; although they appear reducible, if a larger table could have been given. There is hardly a single one that may not be traced to these forms, or that baffles the actual theory. Therefore, the conclusion must occur, that such astonishing coincidence cannot be casual, but it is the result of original derivation.

The following remarks are of some importance:

1. The glyphs of Otolum are written from top to bottom, like the Chinese, or from side to side, indifferently, like the Egyptian and the Demotic Lybian of No. 2. We are not told how No. 1 was written, but probably in the same way. Several signs were used for the same letter as in Egypt.

2. Although the most common way of writing the groups is in rows, and each group separated, yet we find some framed, as it were, in oblong squares or tablets like those of Egypt. See plate 12, of the work on Palenque by Delrio and Caberera. In that 12th plate there are also some singular groups resembling our musical notes. Could they be emblems of songs or hymns?

3. The letter represented by a head occurs frequently; but it is remarkable that the features are very different from those of the remarkable race of men or heroes delineated in the sculptures.

4. In reducing these elements to the alphabetical form, I have been guided by the more plausible theory involved by similar forms. We have not here the more certain demonstration of Bilingual inscriptions; but if the languages should uphold this theory, they certainly will be increased of the Atlantic origins of Otolum.

IV. But shall we be able to read these glyphs and inscriptions, without positively knowing in what language they were written? The attempt will be arduous, but it is not impossible. In Egppt, the Coptic has been found such a close dialect of the Egyptian, that it has enabled you to read the oldest hieroglyphs. We find among the ancient dialects of Chiapa, Yucatan and Guatimala, the branches of the ancient speech of Otolum. (See page 241.) Nay, Otolum was perhaps the ancient TOL or TOLA, seat of the Toltecas, (people of Tol,) and their empire; but this subject will belong to my third letter. I will now merely give a few attempts to read some of the groups. For instance:

1. The group or word on the seat of the sitting man of plate 4 of monuments of Palenque, I read UOBAC, being formed by a hand, a tongue, a circle, an ear, and a crescent. It is perhaps his

name. And underneath the seat is an eye with a small circle inside, meaning EB. 2. In plate 5, is an eye with two annexed rings, meaning probably BAB, and perhaps the sun, which is BAP in the Lybian alphabet. 3. In plate 7, the glyph of the corner with a head, a fish, and a crescent, means probably KIM. 4. The first glyph of page 15, is probably BLAKE. 5. I can make out many others reading ICBE, BOCOGO, POPO, EPL, PKE, &c.

If these words and others (although some may be names) can be found in African languages, or in those of central America, we shall obtain perhaps the key of the whole language of old Otolum. And next reach, step by step, to the desirable knowledge of reading those glyphs, which may cover much historical knowledge of high import. Meantime I have opened the path, if my theory and conjectures are correct, as I have strong reasons to believe.

Besides this monumental alphabet, the same nation that built Otolum had a Demotic alphabet belonging to my 8th series; which was found in Guatimala and Yucatan, at the Spanish conquest. A specimen of it has been given by Humboldt in his American researches, plate 45, from the Dresden Library, and has been ascertained to be Guatimalan instead of Mexican, being totally unlike the Mexican pictoral manuscripts. This page of Demotic has letters and numbers, these represented by strokes meaning 5, and dots meaning unities, as the dots never exceed four. This is nearly similar to the monumental numbers.

These words are much less handsome than the monumental glyphs; they are also uncouth glyphs in rows formed by irregular or flexuous heavy strokes, inclosing within small strokes, nearly the same letters as in the monuments. It might not be impossible to decypher some of these manuscripts written on metl paper: since they are written in languages yet spoken, and the writing was understood in central America, as late as 200 years ago. If this is done, it will be the best clue to the monumental inscriptions.

C. S. RAFINESQUE.

This letter as above, strongly corroborates our supposition, that the authors of the embalmed mummies found in the cave of Lexington, were of Egyptian origin. See Morse's Geography, p. 500, and the Western Gazeteer, p. 103, states that several hundred mummies were discovered near Lexington, in a cave, but were wholly destroyed by the first settlers.

A further Account of Western Antiquities with Antediluvian Traits.

CINCINNATI is situated on one of those examples of antiquity, of great extent. They are found on the upper level of that town, but none on the lower one. They are so conspicuous as to catch the first range of the eye.

There is every reason to suppose, that at the remote period of the building of these antiquities, the lowest level formed part of the bed of the Ohio. A gentleman who was living near the town of Cincinnati, in 1826, on the upper level, had occasion to sink a well for his accommodation, who persevered in digging to the depth of eighty feet without finding water, but still persisting in the attempt, his workmen found themselves obstructed by a substance, which resisted their labor, though evidently not stone. They cleared the surface and sides from the earth bedded around it, when there appeared the *stump* of a tree, three feet in diameter, and two feet high, which had been cut down with an axe. The blows of the axe were yet visible. It was nearly of the color and apparent character of coal, but had not the friable and fusible quality of that mineral. Ten feet below, the water sprang up, and the well is now in constant supply and high repute.

Reflections on this discovery are these: 1st. That the tree was undoubtedly antediluvian. 2d. That the river now called the Ohio, did not exist anterior to the deluge, inasmuch as the remains of the tree were found firmly rooted in its original position, several feet *below* the bed of that river. 3d. That America was peopled before the flood, as appears from the action of the axe in cutting down the tree. 4th. That the antediluvian Americans were acquainted with the use and properties of iron, as the rust of the axe was on the top of the stump when discovered.

And why should they not be acquainted with both its properties and utility, seeing it was an antediluvian discovery? Tubal Cain one of the sons of Cain, the son of Adam, we find, according to Genesis iv. 22, was a blacksmith, and worked in iron and brass, more than a thousand years before the flood. It was about 500 years from the creation, when Tubal Cain is noticed in the sacred history to have been a worker in brass and iron; but, says Dr.

Clarke, the commentator, "Although this is the *first smith* on record, who taught how to make warlike instruments and domestic utensils out of brass and iron, yet a knowledge of metal must have existed long before, for Cain was a *tiller* of the *ground*, and so was Adam, which they could not have been without spades, hooks, &c."

The Roman plough was formed of wood, being in shape like the anchor of a vessel; the ploughman held to one fluke, so as to guide it, while the other entered the ground, pointed with iron, and as it was drawn along by the stem, it tore the earth in a streak, mellowing it for the seed. Such, it is likely, was the form of the primitive plough, from which, in the progress of ages, improvements have been made, till the present one, as now formed, and is the glory of the well tilled field.

According to this opinion, it would appear, that in the very first period of time, men were acquainted with the metals; and as they diverged from the common centre, which was near the garden of Eden, they carried with them a knowledge of this all-important discovery. If the stump is, indeed, antediluvian, we learn one important fact, and this is it: America, by whatever name it was called before the deluge, was then a body of earth above the waters, and also was connected with Asia, where, it is allowed on all hands, man was originated. If it were not connected with Asia, it might be inquired, how then came men in America before the flood, the traits of whose industry and agricultural pursuits are discovered in the felling of this tree, as well as a great number of other instances, of which we shall speak by and by?

It is *not* probable, that before the flood there was so small a quantity of dry land on the earth as at the present time; the waters of the globe being generally hid beneath the incumbent soil, so that an easy communication of all countries with each other existed; which must have greatly facilitated the progress of man in peopling and subduing it. We know very well it is said, "the gathering together of the waters, called He seas;" but it does not follow that they were not subterranean; and it is more than intimated that such was the fact, when it is said, " all the fountains of the great *deep* were broken up," on the day the flood commenced.

But by what means were they broken up? This is left to conjecture, as the Scriptures are higher in their aim, than the mere gratification of curious questions of this sort; but in some way this was done. The very terms "broken up," signify the exertion of power and *violence*, of sufficient force to burst at once whole continents from the face of the deep, and also to throw out, at one wide rush, the central waters of the globe.

But can we conceive of any means made use of to effect this, other than the direct pressure of God's power, sinking the earth to the depths beneath, so that the water might rise above, taking the place of the land? We imagine we can.

It is well known, that the velocity of the earth, in its onward motion round the sun, is about twenty miles a second, nearly the speed of lightning. Let Him, therefore, who at first imposed this inconceivable velocity, stop the earth in this motion suddenly; what would the effect be? All the fluids, that is the waters, whether above ground or underneath it, would rush forward with a power equal to their weight, which would be sufficient to burst away mountains, or any impediment whatever; and rushing round the globe, from the extreme western point, rolling one-half of the mighty flood over this side of it, and the other half over the antipode, on the other side, which is relatively beneath us, till the two half worlds of water, should meet at the extreme *east*, where heaping up, by their force, above a common level, would gradually roll back to their original places, as the earth should again go forward. This is our opinion of the way how " all the fountains of the great deep were broken up."

If the earth were to be arrested in its course *now*, the effect would be the same. Suppose we illustrate the position for a moment. Place a vessel of water on a plank, for instance, open on the top, like a common bowl, fastened to the plank, so that it should not be liable to overcast. Cause this plank to move, at first slowly, but increase its steady onward velocity as much as the fluid will bear, without causing a reaction; when, therefore, its utmost speed is obtained, stop it suddenly; the effect would be, the water in the vessel would instantly fly over, leaving the bowl behind. Such, therefore, we imagine, would be the effect, if the earth were now caused to stand suddenly still in its orbit; except this difference, the law of gravitation would prevent the waters of the earth from leaving the surface, but would cause a rapid current in the direction the earth is pursuing.

That the waters of the deluge came from the west, is evident from the manner in which the various strata of the earth are situated over the whole of our country; and that its motion was very violent is also evident from the appearance of native or primitive rock, being found on the top of that which is of secondary formation, and of gravel and sand in hills and smaller eminences, lying on beds of clay and soils of various kinds below it.

The effects of the deluge can be traced in all the earth in this way, and particularly about Albany, Saratoga, and about the lakes, and to the east, showing that the waters flowed in that direction. For a beautiful and able description of this subject, see Thomas's Travels, published at Auburn, under the head, *The Deluge.*

At the same time the waters above the firmament, in the clouds, were permitted to burst downward, which, in its fall, subdivided into drops, as is natural; so that one vast perpetual storm, for forty days and forty nights, rushed with all the violence of a tornado upon the globe, quite around it, by which, in so short a time, the highest hills were buried fifteen cubits deep, and upward; this is what we suppose is meant by the words "and the windows of heaven were opened."

But it may be inquired, from whence did the lands receive water to furnish them with so long a rain as a storm of forty days and nights; and from whence originated vapor enough to becloud the whole circumambient atmosphere of the earth at once. Surely some cause more than existed before the flood, or since, must have transpired at that time, to have produced this great accumulation of clouds and rain.

The answer is, we apprehend, that the central waters bursting suddenly from the great deep, involving the whole globe, presented a greater surface of that fluid to the rays of the sun, so that by its operation on the face of the waters, a dense mist or vapor was at once produced quite round the earth, which, in its ascent, carried up incessantly that quantity of water which furnished the atmosphere for so long and so dreadful a storm, and justify the expression, " and the windows of heaven were opened."

By some it has been imagined that the flood of Noah was produced by the near approach of a comet, the waters of which attracted the waters of the globe from the depths so as to deluge the earth. But this opinion is not admissible, as the same comet which by the laws of gravitation would be compelled to follow the same track or orbit, to endless ages, would long ere this time have deluged the world several times, which has not taken place. Others have supposed that the poles have been entirely shifted. If such may have been the fact, it is true the earth would have been easily flooded, as the frozen oceans, with two continents of ice, would have been placed suddenly beneath the rays of a vertical sun, the effect of which would, even now, were such a catastrophe to take place, bring on a universal deluge, equal to that of Noah's. Also the whirl and shifting of the waters of the ocean would have contributed greatly to this effect. In support of this theory, it is shown that in the high northern latitudes, banks, and even the entire bodies of equatorial animals have been found imbeded in the ice, which have been brought to light by unusual thaws. Even in the the most dreary and desolate northern regions are found in great quantities the tropical plants and trees in a state of preservation.

But these, we believe, are to be accounted for, not on the principle of the shifting of the poles, but rather by the arrest of the globe in its orbit round the sun, occasioning a rapid current of the waters of the earth eastwardly, which, as the strata of the earth generally shows, was the fact, would produce the appearances as above stated by the *lateral* flow of the waters round the earth from the equator toward the poles.

To the arrest of the earth in its orbit, it may be objected, that if such had been the fact, the globe would have fallen during that time a great way toward the sun; to which we assert, that the same power which could arrest the earth in so extraordinary a manner could also hold it suspended in its true place, till the effect should be accomplished for which the arrest was designed.

In this way the surface of the earth was ruined; a disproportionate quantity of water, caused to appear on the surface, while in the same ratio the land is sunk to the depths below.

Sixteen hundred years and rising, was the space of time allowed from the creation till the flood; a time quite sufficient to people the whole earth, even if it were then enjoying a surface of dry land, twice as much as it does at the present time, being but about one-fourth; and America, as appears from this ONE monument, the *stump* of Cincinnati, was a part of the earth which was peopled by the antediluvians.

The celebrated antiquarian, Samuel L. Mitchell, late of New-

York, with other gentlemen, eminent for their knowledge of natural history, are even of the opinion, that America was the country where Adam was created. In a letter to Governor De Witt Clinton, in which this philosopher argued the common origin of the people of America, and those of Asia, he says:—" I avoid the opportunity which this grand conclusion affords me, of stating that America was the *cradle* of the human race; of tracing its colonies *westward* over the Pacific ocean, and beyond the sea of Kamschatka, to *new* settlements; of following the emigrants by land and water, until they reached Europe and Africa. I had no inclination to oppose the current opinions relative to the place of man's creation and dispersion. I thought it was scarcely worth while to inform an European, that in coming to America he had left the new world behind him, for the purpose of visiting the old.—(*American Antiquarian Society*, p. 331.)

But this opinion cannot obtain, if we place the least reliance on the statement of Moses, in the book of Genesis, who gives a circumstantial account of the *place* of man's creation, by stating the names of the very rivers arising out of the regions of country called Paradise; such as Pison, Havilah, Gihon, Hiddekel, and Euphrates; or as they *now* are called, Phasis, Araxes, Tigris, and Euphrates; this last retains its original name.

No such rivers are known in America, nor the countries through which they flow. Here are data to argue from, but the position, or rather the suggestion, of Prof. Mitchell, has absolutely no data whatever. If but a tradition favoring that opinion were found even among the Indians, it would afford some foundation; but as their tradition universally alludes to some part of the earth, far away, from whence they came, it would seem exceedingly extravagant to argue a contrary belief.

This one *stump* of Cincinnati, we consider, surpasses in consequence the magnificence of all the temples of antiquity, whose forsaken turrets, dilapidated walls, tottering and fallen pillars, which speak in language loud and mournful, the story of their ruin; because it is a remnant of matter, in form and fashion, such as it was, before the earth " perished by water," bearing on its top the indubitable marks of the exertion of man, of so remote a time.

It is not impossible but America may have been the country where Noah built his ark, as directed by the Most High. We know very well, when the mind refers to the subject of Noah's ark, our thoughts are immediately associated with Mount Ararat, because it rested there, on the subsiding of the flood. But this circumstance precludes a possibility of its having been built *there*, if we allow the waters of the deluge to have had any current at all. It is said in Genesis that the ark floated, or was borne upon the waters above the earth, and also that the ark "*went upon the face of the waters.*" From which fact we imagine there must have been a current, or it could not have *went* upon the waters. Consequently, it *went from* the place where it was built, being obedient to the current of the flood.

Now, if it had been built any where in the country called Armenia, where the mountain Ararat is situated; and as it is found the waters had a general eastern direction, the ark in going on the face of the waters would have, during the time the waters of the deluge prevailed, which was one hundred and fifty days, or five months, (that is, prevailed after the commencement of the deluge till its greatest depth was effected,) gone in an eastern direction as far perhaps as the regions of the islands of Japan, beyond China, east, a distance of about 6000 miles from Ararat, which would be at the rate of about forty miles a day, or if it had floated faster, would have carried it into the Pacific ocean.

But if we may imagine it was erected in North America, or some where in the latitude of the state of New-York, or even farther west, the current of the deluge would have borne it easterly. And suppose it may have been carried at the rate of forty or fifty miles a day, would, during the time the waters prevailed, in which time, we may suppose, a current existed, have progressed as far as to Ararat, a distance of nearly 6000 miles from America, where it did actually rest.

More than 1600 years had elapsed when the ark was finished, and it may fairly be inferred, that as Noah was born about 1000 years after the creation of the world, that mankind had, from necessity, arising from the pressure of population, gone very far away from the regions round about Eden; and the country where Noah was born may as well be supposed to have been America, as any other part of the earth; seeing there are indubitable signs of antediluvian population in many parts of it. Unite this circumstance with that of the ascertained current of the deluge from America, and with the fact of the ark's having rested in an easterly direction from this country, we come to a conclusion, that here, perhaps, in the very state of New-York, the miraculous vessel was erected, and bore away, treasured in its enormous capacity, the progenitors of the human race renewed. So that if America have not the honor of being the country where Adam was created, as is believed by some, it has, nevertheless the honor, as we suppose, of being the country where the ark was erected.

But as we have argued in the commencement of this volume, that Shem was Melchisedeck, and that from him a knowledge of the exact situation of Eden might have been obtained by the first nations after the flood, it may be inquired, how could he tell them if he was born in America, so far from the location of Eden? To this we reply, that it should not be supposed that the antediluvians were without the means of recording facts, even by the use of letters, or their equivalents, which are pictures, nor that they had no knowledge of the geography of the globe, as it was before the flood, and the means of communication with each other, however distant their colonies may have been.

It is not to be supposed, that more than 1600 years could pass away, without the antediluvians having enjoyed the advantages of art and science, seeing these are the natural results of human society. The ark itself is a demonstration that even ship building was known, or how could Noah have understood what was meant, when it was said to him, "build an ark of gopher wood," &c.

This supposition of the antediluvians having a knowledge of letters or their equivalents, is maintained by discoveries made on opening the vast heaps of bricks which formed the tower of Babel. These bricks, it appears, were much larger and thicker than the same article is *now* made, as they are found to be something over a foot square and three inches thick. On many of these, as stated by M. Beauchamp, a French traveller and astronomer, who visited Babylon in 1781, are *engraven* unknown *characters* and hieroglyphics. On one brick he found a lion presented in *relief*, which shows that the mould in which the brick was formed, had the form of this animal carved or cut into the timber or metal of which the mould was made. On another he found the shape of a half moon formed in the same manner. One of the masons who was employed in digging brick from these ruins, told M. Beauchamp, that there were often found, little cells which contained images of the human shape formed of clay, and that on one brick which had been taken from thence, were represented in *varnish* the figures of a cow, and of the sun and moon, which shows they had also a knowledge of painting, and delineation which belongs to the fine arts.—(See *Evening Recreations*, vol. 1, p. 62, 1830.)

Now it is not reasonable to suppose that the art of *letters, painting,* and *sculpture* were all found out during the short space, from the time the ark rested on Ararat, till the time of the commencement of the building of that tower; and we will add also, the knowledge of brick making, and of architecture. Is it not, therefore, clear that all these were known and practised by the antediluvians?

This knowledge was, therefore, received from the family of Noah, and especially from Shem or Melchesideck, who, it appears, in leaving Ararat came westward from its resting place with some one of the colonies, who settled the land of *Shinar*.

The invention of letters is attributed to the Phœnicians, who were of the race of Ham, and consequently, were black; but the true secret of this is doubtless, that to Melchisedeck, the notions of the continents of Europe, Africa, America, and the knowledge of the use of letters, brought from beyond the flood, even those now in use, as they belong to the same family as *all* letters are found in all ages to have a resemblance to each other in shape.

Shem could therefore tell the latitude of the ancient seat of Paradise, though he may have been born in America, and though the flood had destroyed the beauty and towering grandeur of the pristine situation of the seat of Adam.

In Morse's Universal Geography, first volume, page 142, the discovery of this stump is corroborated : "In digging a well in Cincinnati, the stump of a tree was found in a sound state, ninety feet below the surface; and in digging another well, at the same place, another stump was found, at ninety-four feet below the surface which had evident marks of the axe ; and on its top there appeared as if some iron tool had been consumed by rust."

The axe had, no doubt, been struck into the top of the stump, when the horrors of the deluge first appeared, in the bursting forth of the waters from above, that is from the windows of heaven ;— when sounds terrific, from the breaking forth of the waters of the great deep, and from the shock all sensitve beings must have felt when the earth was caused to stand still in its onward course round the sun, for the space perhaps of a day. Remember Joshua, at whose command and prayer, God stopped the earth for the space of a whole day, but not its onward course around the sun, but its diurnal motion only, which could not have any effect on the fluids of the earth, as the sudden interruption of the other motion would have had.

Who would not flee, when phenomena so terrible, without presage or warning, were changing the face of things, and the feelings of the atmosphere; the earth quivering like an aspen leaf; forests leaning to the east, and snapping asunder in one awful crash over all the wide wilderness; rocks with mountains tumbling from their summits; the stoutest heart would quail at such an hour as this; an *axe*, with all things else, would be left by the owners, and a general flight, if they could stand at all on their feet, would take place, they knew not whither, for safety.

In one of the communications of the admired Dr. Samuel L. Mitchell, professor of Natural History, to the American antiquarian society, he mentions a certain class of antiquities as distinguished entirely from those which are found in and about the mounds of the west, as follows: In the section of country about Fredonia, on the south side of lake Erie, are discovered objects deservedly worthy of particular and inquisitive research. This kind of antiquities, present themselves on digging from thirty to fifty feet below the present surface of the ground. "They occur in the form of fire brands, *split* wood, ashes, coals, and occasionally tools and utensils, buried to those depths." This, it will be perceived, is much below the bed of lake Erie, of consequence must have been antediluvian, and agrees with the discovery of the stumps at Cincinnati. "We are informed, that in Rhode Island, New Jersey, Maryland, North Carolina, and in Ohio, such discoveries have been made." He says, "I wish the members of the society would exert themselves with all possible diligence to ascertain and collect the facts of this description. They will be exceedingly curious, both for the geologist and historian. After such facts shall have been collected and methodised, we may perhaps draw some satisfactory conclusions; light may possibly be shed upon the remote *Pelasgians*, and upon the traditionary *Atlantides*," the inhabitants of the island, we have before spoken of, Atalantis.

But we cannot allow the discoveries made at this vast depth, to belong to any age, or to any of the works of man this side the deluge, as that time enough has not elapsed since that catastrophe, to allow the decomposition of vegetables, nor of convulsions, to have buried these articles so deep beneath the surface extending over so great a tract of country. The draining of lakes, however sudden, could never have had so wide and universal an effect.

It would seem, therefore, that we are compelled to refer them to the works of man beyond the flood, which, by the overflowing of the waters, and the consequent ruin of the original surface, these works, with their makers, have been thus buried in a tomb more dreadful to the imagination than the ordinary receptacles of the dead.

In evidence, that the ocean, at some period in ages past, overwhelmed the American continent, we notice, from the "British Spy," page 112, an account of the discovery of the skeleton of a whale, in Virginia:

"Near Williamsburgh has recently been discovered, by a farmer, while digging a ditch through a plat of ground, about five feet below the surface, a considerable portion of the skeleton of a whale. Several fragments of the ribs, and other parts, were found, with the *whole* of the vertebræ, or backbone, regularly arranged, and very little impaired as to figure. The spot where it was found is about two miles from James river, and about sixty from the sea. In the same region, at depths of from sixty to ninety and an hundred feet, have been found the teeth of sharks." In every region of the earth, as well as America, and on the highest mountains, are found the bones and shells of the ancient inhabitants of the sea. From the universality of those appearances, we conclude they were deposited and cast thither by the billows of the deluge.

From the discoveries of articles of the utensil character, the bones of whales, the teeth of sharks, and the stumps of Cincinnati, at various depths, as stated above; we are led to the conclusion, that the original surface, of what is now called America, was perhaps not much disturbed; but was rather suddenly overwhelmed from the west, by the bursting forth of the subterranean Pacific, which, till then, had been covered with land, mountains and vales, thickly peopled.

The vast depths of strata of loam, sand, clay, gravel, and stone, which lie over each other, evincing, from the unnatural manner of their positions, that they were thrown furiously, by the agent, water, over the whole continent, furnished from the countries of the west.

That such may indeed, have been the fact, is favored from the discovery of the whale's skeleton, found on James river, which could never have been deposited there by other means than the flood; forced onward, till killed by the violence and agitation of the wood, stone, and earth encumbered waters, and sunk finally down, where it was recently discovered.

The pottery of the ancient nations, mentioned by Schoolcraft, found at the vast depth of eighty feet, and even at greater depths, at the great Saline in Illinois, is evidence of an antediluvian population in America.

At Cincinnati there is a barrow or mound of human bones, situated exactly on the edge of the bank, that overlooks the lower town, the principal street leading from the water is cut through it, and exposes its strata and remains to every person passing by. Seven tiers of skeletons lay plainly in sight, where the barrow had caved away, from its being undermined. Among the earth thus fallen down, were found several stone hatchets, pieces of pottery, and a *flute*, made of the great bone of the human leg. This is a very curious instrument, with beautifully carved figures, representing birds, squirrels, and small animals, with perforated holes, in the old *German* manner, which, when breathed into, emitted tones of great melody.

Among the modern Indians, no such instrument has ever been found. At the time when the street was opened through this barrow of the dead, a great variety of interesting and valuable relics were brought to light; among which were human *double teeth*, which, on a moderate calculation, bespoke men as large again as the present race. Also some *brass* rings, which were considered excedingly curious; an instance of which is similar to the one before mentioned in this work. Iron rings, as we have before stated, were anciently used among the Britons before the Christian era, as money; and possibly in this case, the brass rings found in this barrow, may be a specimen of the ancient money of America.

Discovery of an Ivory Image in a Bone Mound at Cincinnati.

In the same barrow of which I have been speaking, was discovered an *ivory* image, which we consider more interesting, and surpasses any discovery yet mentioned. It is said to be now in the cabinet of rare collections, once in the possession of the illustrious Jefferson.

The account of the image is as follows: It is seven inches high; the figure full length; the costume, a *robe*, in numberless folds, well expressed, and the hair displayed in many ringlets; the child naked, near the left breast, and the mother's eye bent on it with a strong expression of affection and endearment.

There are those who think it a representation of the mother of our Lord's humanity, with the child Jesus, in her arms. The Roman Catholics have availed themselves of this image, and made it a testimony of the antiquity of their religion, and of the extensive range of their worship, by attempting to prove thereby, that the idol was nothing less than a Madona and Child—the virgin Mary, and the child Jesus; and that the Roman Catholic religion was the *first* which arose in the earliest Christian age in the east, and the last which set in the west, where it became extinct, by means of a second deluge.

The idea, however, of a second deluge, is inadmissible, as it would have destroyed every vestige of the mounds, pyramids, tumuli, and fortifications, of which this work treats; many of which are supposed older than the Christian era; and the mound in which the image itself was discovered would also have been destroyed.

There is, however, another opinion, which is not impossible may have furnished the imagination with materials for the origin of such a representation. The image may be of Greek origin, and taken from Isaiah the prophet, 7th chap. 14th verse, where it is said,—" Behold a virgin shall conceive and bear a son." This prophecy of Isaiah was known to the Greeks, for the old Testament was translated into their language in the time of Ptolemy Philadelphus, king of Egypt, nearly three hundred years before the Christian era.—(*See Adam Clarke's General Preface to the Old Testament*, p. 27, and is known as the Septugint version.)

The Greek statuaries may, in this way, have easily found the beautiful and captivating idea of a *virgin* mother, by reading Isaiah in the Greek; a work fraught with all the grandeur of images inspired by God himself, and could not fail to challenge the reading of every learned man of the empire, and such were the statuaries, among the Greeks, the fame of whose exquisite skill in this respect, will go down on the historic page to latest time.

From the Greeks such an image, celebrating the idea of a virgin mother and her child, may have easily come into the possession of the Romans, as the Greeks were, soon after the translation of the Hebrew scriptures into the Greek, subdued by the Romans; who, in their conquests, here and there, over the earth, including Europe, England, Scotland, and the northern islands, carrying that kind of image with them as a god, or talisman, and from thence to America.

It is, however, not impossible, but it may be indeed of true Roman Catholic origin; as at the time the Romans evacuated Europe, with its isles, Ireland, England, &c., about the year 450, this church had risen to great importance in the Roman empire which aided her to establish her altars in every country they had conquered. Consequently, long before the Scandinavians colonized Iceland, Greenland, and Labrador, on the American continent, the Christian religion was planted in the north of Europe; first in France, in the year 496, and then soon after in England; and so on farther north among the ancient Scandinavians, Norwegians, &c., and by these to Iceland and Greenland; who may have also brought this trait of that church to America.

The fort at Cincinnati is a circle, embracing about three acres, with a wall seven feet high, and twenty feet broad. At the back part of the upper level, at a distance from the circular fort, are two mounds of about twenty feet high. One of these, by cutting a trench from east to west, four feet wide, and at the depth of ten feet, came to some heavy stones, under which was a body of composition resembling plaster of Paris. This broke with great difficulty, when there were exposed a few fragments of an adult human skeleton, placed on a bed of a similar nature with the covering. It was determined to ascertain whether the monument was erected in memory of one person or more, the lower bed of hard substance was also broken through, and underneath a stratum of stones, gravel and earth, found the fragments of another skeleton, consisting of one *tibia*, or piece of the shin, two pieces of the thigh bone, and the right upper, with the left under jaw.

This was the skeleton of a child, from which was derived the important fact, that this mound was not erected for one individual only, but also for the infant chief or king; and that the nation who erected this mound, in which the child was buried, was governed by a line of *hereditary* chiefs or kings, as is evident from the nature and distinction of the interment of an infant; who certainly could not have been an *elected* chief; the suffrages of a nation could never be supposed to elevate an *infant* as its king; but if it succeeded by right of lineal descent, it might have been their king.

The next relic of antiquity, discovered at Cincinnati, is a spherical stone, found on the fall of a large portion of the bank of the river. It is a green stone, twelve inches in diameter, divided into twelve sides, and each side into twelve equal parts, and each part distinguished by hieroglyphical engravings. This beautiful stone, it is said, is lodged in the cabinet of arts at Philadelphia. It is supposed the stone was formed for astronomical calculations, conveying a knowledge of the movements of the heavenly bodies.

Farther on in this work, is an account of a still more wonderful stone, covered with the engravings of the ancient nations, where a *fac simile* of the stone is presented.

A Cavern of the West, in which are found many interesting Hieroglyphics, supposed to have been done by the Ancient Inhabitants.

On the Ohio, twenty miles below the mouth of the Wabash, is a cavern, in which are found many hieroglyphics, and representations of such delineations as would induce the belief, that their authors were, indeed, comparatively refined and civilized.

It is a cave in a rock, or ledge of the mountain, which presents itself to view, a little above the water of the river when in flood, and is situated close to the bank. In the early settlement of Ohio, this cave became possessed by a party of Kentuckians, called "Wilson's Gang." Wilson, in the first place, brought his family to this cave, and fitted it up, as a spacious dwelling, erected a *signpost* on the water side, on which were these words, " Wilson's Liquor Vault, and House of Entertainment." The novelty of such a tavern, induced almost all the boats descending the river to call for refreshments and amusement. Attracted by these circumstances, several idle characters took up their abode at the cave, after which it continually resounded with the shouts of the licentious, the clamor of the riotous, and the blasphemy of gamblers. Out of such customers, Wilson found no difficulty in forming a band of robbers, with whom he formed the plan of murdering the crews of every boat that stopped at his tavern, and of sending the boats manned by some of his party, to New-Orleans, and there sell their loading for cash, which was to be conveyed to the cave by land, through the states of Tennesse and Kentucky; the party returning with it being instructed to murder and rob, on all good occasions, on the road.

After a lapse of time, the merchants of the upper country began to be alarmed, on finding their property make no returns, and their people never coming back. Several families and respectable men, who had gone down the river were never heard of; and the losses became so frequent, that it raised, at length, a cry of individual distress and general dismay. This naturally led to inquiry, and large rewards were offered for the discovery of the perpetrators of such unparalleled crimes. It soon came out, that Wilson, with an organized party of forty-five men, was the cause of such waste of blood and treasure; that he had a station at Hurricane island, to arrest every boat that passed by the mouth of the cavern, and that he had agents at Natchez and New-Orleans, of presumed respectability, who converted his assignments into cash, though they knew the goods to be stolen, or obtained by the commission of murder.

The publicity of Wilson's transactions soon broke up his party; some dispersed, others were taken prisoners, and he himself was killed by one of his associates, who was tempted by the reward offered for the head of the captain of the gang.

This cavern measures about twelve rods in length, and five in width; its entrance presents a width of eighty feet at its base, and twenty-five feet high. The interior walls are smooth rock. The floor is very remarkable, being level through the whole length of its centre, the sides rising in stony grades, in the manner of seats in the pit of a theatre. On a diligent scrutiny of the walls, it is plainly discerned that the ancient inhabitants at a very remote period, had made use of the cave as a house of deliberation and council. The walls bear many hieroglyphics well executed; and some of them represent animals, which have no resemblance to any now known to natural history.

This cavern is a great natural curiosity, as it is connected with another still more gloomy, which is situated exactly above, united by an aperture of about fourteen feet; which, to ascend, is like passing up a chimney, while the mountain is yet far above. Not long after the dispersion and arrest of the robbers, who had infested it, in the upper vault were found the skeletons of about sixty persons, who had been murdered by the gang of Wilson, as was supposed. But the tokens of antiquity are still more curious and important, than a description of the mere cave, which are found engraved on its sides within, an account of which we proceed to give.

1 The sun, in different stages of rise and declension; the moon, under various phases; a snake, biting its tail, and representing an orb or circle; a viper; a vulture; buzzards tearing out the heart of a prostrate man; a panther held by the ears by a child; a crocodile; several trees and shrubs; a fox; a curious kind of hydra serpent; two doves; several bears; two scorpions; an eagle; an owl; some quails; *eight* representations of animals which are now unknown. Three out of the eight are like the elephant in all respects except the tusk and the tail. Two more resemble the tiger, tne a wild boar, another a sloth; and the last appears a creature of fancy, being a quadrumane instead of a quadruped, the claws being alike before and behind, and in the act of conveying something to the mouth, which lay in the centre of the monster. Besides these were several fine representations of men and women, *not naked*, but clothed; not as the Indians, but much in the costume of Greece and Rome.

We must at once perceive that these objects, with an exception or two, were employed by the ancient Greeks to display the nature of the world, the omnipotence of God, the attributes of man, and the utility of rendering his knowledge systematic and immortal.

All human sciences flourished among the Egyptians long before they were common to any other people; the Grecians in the days of Solon, about 600 B. C.; Pythagoras, about the same time; Herodotus, about 450 B. C.; and Plato, a little later; acquired in Egypt all that knowledge of nature which rendered them so eminent and remarkable. But the Egyptian priests did not divulge their doctrines, but by the aid of signs and figurative emblems. Their manner was, to discover to their auditors the mysteries of God and nature, in hieroglyphics; which were certain visible shapes and forms of creatures, whose inclinations and dispositions led to the knowledge of the truths intended for instruction. All their divinity, philosophy, and their greatest secrets, were comprehended in these ingenious characters for fear they should be profaned by a familiar acquaintance with the commonalty.

It requires but a rapid and cursory view of the hieroglyphics above enumerated, to convince us of design; and also that the cavern wherein they are found eagraved, was originally a place of worship or of council. The sun, the most glorious of all visible beings, represented their chief god, and received their adoration for causing all the vegetation of the earth to bring forth its increase.

2. The moon denoted the next most beautiful object in the creation, and was worshipped for her own peculiar usefulness; and more particularly for supplying the place of the departed sun.

3. The snake, in the form of an orb, or circle, biting its tail, pointed out the continual mutation of creatures, and the change of matter, or the perpetual motion of the world itself. If so, this construction of that hieroglyphic, the snake, agrees with the Greek figure, of the same kind; which implies that the world feeds upon itself, and receives from itself in return, a continual supply for renovation and nourishment; the same symbol designated the year which revolves round, and ends where it first began, like the serpent with its tail in its mouth; it is believed the ancient Greeks gave it this meaning.

4. The viper, the most venomous of all creatures, was the emblem of the devil, or wicked angel; for, as its poison is quick and powerful, so is the destroying spirit in bringing on mankind evils, which can only be opposed by the grace and power of God.

5. The vulture, tearing out the bowels of a prostrate man, seems a moral intending to reprove fierceness and cruelty. Dr. Rush says this hieroglyphic represents *intemperance*, and by them was so understood.

6. The panther, held by the ears by a child, was meant to im-

press a sense of the dominion of innocence and virtue over oppression and vice: or perhaps it bore the Greek meaning of a wretch encompassed with difficulties which he vainly attempts to avoid.

7. The crocodile, from its power and might, was another symbol of the Great Spirit; or its being the only creature without a tongue, might have given it a title to the same honor; all heathen nations concur in representing their gods beholding and doing all things in heaven and earth in profound silence.

8. The several trees and shrubs were undoubtedly emblematical of particular virtues, as represented in this temple, the cave, from a veneration for their aromatic and healing properties. Among the ancients, we know that the palm tree and the laurel were emblems of victory and deserved honor, the myrtle of pleasure, the cedar of eternity, the oak of strength, the olive of fruitfulness, the vine of delight and joy, and the lily of beauty. But what those in the cave imply, it is not possible to determine, as nothing of their character can be deduced from the manner they were sketched on the surface of a rough wall, the design obscured by smoke, or nearly obliterated from the effect of damp, and the gradual decay of time.

9. The fox, from every authority, was put to denote subtlety and craftiness.

10. The hydra serpent probably signified malice and envy, passions which the hieroglyphic taught mankind to avoid.

11. The two doves were hieroglyphics of constancy in love; all nations agree in this, in admiring the attachment of doves.

12. The bears, it is apprehended, signify industry, labor and patience: for the Indians believe the cubs of the bear come into the world with misshapen parts, and that their eyes, ears, and other members are licked into form by the mother, who passes days in that anxious and unceasing employ.

13. The scorpions were calculated to inspire a detestation for malignity and vice; even the present race of Indians hold these animals in great disgust, healing wounds inflicted by them, with a preparation of their own blood.

14. The eagle represents and is held to this day as the emblem of a great, noble and liberal mind; fierce in war, conquering the enemy, and protecting his friends; he among the Indians who can do this, is compared with the eagle.

15. The owl must have been set up to deter men from deceit

and hypocrisy. He cannot endure the light of the sun, nor can hypocrisy bear that of truth and sincerity. He may have been the emblem of death and wretchedness, as among the Egyptians; or of victory and prosperity, when in a flying attitude, as among the Greeks.

16. The quails afford no clue to their hireoglyphic, unless they signify the corn season, and point out the time for the usage of some particular rites and ceremonies of a religious nature. With the Greeks, they were emblematical of impiety, from a belief that they engage and torment themselves when the crescent of the new moon appears.

17. The representations of the larger animals were doubtless indicative of the power and attributes of the Great Spirit. The mammoth showing his greatness, the tiger his strength, the boar his wrath, the sloth his patience, and the nondescript his hidden virtues, which are past finding out.

18. The human figures are more definite, and afford inferences more certain, on account of the dress they are represented in, which rembles the Roman; the figures would be taken for European antiquities, were it not for the character and manner of the heads. The dress of these figures consisted of,—a carbasus, or rich cloak; a sabucala, or waistcoat, or shirt; a supparum, or breeches, open at the knees; solea, or sandals, tied across the toes and heels; the head embraced by a bandeau, crowned with flowers.

19. The dress of the females, carved in this cave, have a Grecian cast, the hair encircled by the crown, and was confined by a bodkin; the remaining part of this costume was Roman. The garments called stolla, or perhaps the toga pura, flounced from the shoulders to the ground; an indusium appeared underneath; the indusium was confined under the breast, by a zone or cestus; and sandals, in the manner of those of the men.

Could all this have been produced by the mere caprice of aboriginal artizans? We think not. They have, in this instance, either recorded their own manners in the one particular of costume, or they have represented that of others, who had come among them as strangers, and wonderfully induces the belief, that such were Greeks, Romans, or some nation of the earth whose mode of dress was similar. Viewed in the most critical manner, this instance of American antiquity cannot fail to excite in the mind surprise, when

We contrast this with the commonly received opinion, that Columbus was the first discoverer of this country.

The hieroglyphic carved in this cave, which represents a child holding or leading a panther, brings forcibly to the mind a similar idea in the Hebrew scriptures, in the book of Isaiah, chapter 14, 6th verse, where it is said, the wolf, the leopard and the young lion shall be led by a child; and relates to the period when both natural and moral evil shall have no existence in the earth, as is believed by some.

In this cave, it appears, there are sketched on the rock the figures of several animals, now extinct; among which are three, much resembling the elephant, the tail and tusks excepted. It would be passing the bounds of credulity to suppose the artists who delineated those figures, would represent no less than eight animals, differing in their configuration, one from the other, which had in reality no being, and such as these had never been seen.

We suppose the animals resembling the elephant, to have been the mammoth, and that those ancients were well acquainted with the creature, or they could never have engraved it on the rock. Job, of the scriptures, who was a native of the land of Uz, in Idumea, which is situated southwest of the lake Asphaltites, or sea of Sodom, was also well acquainted with this animal. (*See Job*, chapter 40.) "Behold now behemoth, which I made with thee; he eateth grass as an ox. Lo, now his strength is in his loins; and his force in the navel of his belly. He moveth his *tail* like a *cedar*; the sinews of his loins are wrapped together. His bones are as strong pieces of brass; his bones are like bars of iron. He is the chief of the ways of God."

Whoever has examined the skeleton of one of those animals, now in the Philadelphia museum, will acknowledge the bones are equal to bars of brass or iron. Its height over the shoulders, eleven feet; from the point of the nose to the end of the tail, following the exterior or curve, is twenty-one feet; a single tooth weighs four pounds ten ounces. The rib bones are six inches in width, and in thickness three; the whole skeleton as it is, with the exception of a few bones, weighs one thousand pounds.

But how tremendous must that animal have been, to which the tooth weighing twenty-five pounds, found in the earth at Cincinnati belonged, more than five times the dimensions of the one described above; arguing, from proportion, that is, if a tooth belonged to a skeleton weighing one thousand pounds, was found to be four pounds ten ounces; a tooth weighing twenty-five pounds would give a skeleton of more than five thousand pounds. And if the calculation be carried forward in this sort of proportion, we shall produce an animal more than forty feet high, and nearly an hundred in length, with a proportionable thickness.

What would be the sensation, were we to meet an animal of this sort in his ancient haunts; it would almost appear a moving mountain; but add to this, the enormous eyes of the animal, set at a frightful distance from each other, with an amplitude of forehead between, clothed like the side of a hill, with a forest of shaggy hair; a mouth, gaping like some drear cavern, set round with teeth sufficient to crush a buffalo at a mouthful; its distended nostrils emitting vapor like the puffs of a steam boat, with a sound, when breathing, that might be heard afar; the legs appearing in size of dimensions sufficient to bear a ship on his shoulders; and his feet or paws spread out like a farmer's corn fan, armed with claws like flukes to an anchor of a vessel of war; the tail, as it is said in Job, waving to and fro, like a cedar bending before the wind. But add to all this, anger; let him but put his fierceness on, his eyes flash fire, his tail elevated aloft, lashing the ground, here and there, at a dreadful distance from his body; his voice like the double rolling of thunder, jarring the wilderness; at which every living thing would tremble, and drop to the earth. Such an animal would indeed be the " chief of the ways of God," it would be perfectly safe in the midst of a tornado in the wilderness; no tree, or a forest of them, could possibly harm the monster by falling against it; it would shake them off, as mere troublesome insects, as smaller animals do the flies in a summer's day.

The one in Peale's museum, of which we have spoken, a page or two back, is one out of nine skeletons of this monster, which were dug out of the earth in the neighborhood of the Shongum mountain, in Ulster county, on the southwestern side of the State of New York, eight of which were sent to Europe.—(See *Spafford's Gazeteer of New York.*)

Near Rochester, in the State of New York, in 1833, two teeth of this animal were discovered, but a small depth beneath the surface. They were found in the town of Perrinton, near Fullam's

Basin, some time ago, by Mr. William Mann, who was engaged in digging up a stump. They were deposited about four feet below the surface of the earth. These were in a tolerably good state of preservation; the roots begin to crumble a little, but the enamel of the teeth is in almost a perfect state. The teeth were the grinders, and from their appearance, were located in the back part of the upper jaw. The largest one weighs three pounds and ten ounces, measuring six inches lengthwise of the jaw, and three inches across the top, the root is about six inches long with several prongs. The other tooth is smaller. If we are to suppose this animal to have the same number of teeth that other animals commonly have, and that the rest of the teeth were of the same proportions, as to size, the circle of the jaw from one end to the other must have been six feet. Again, if we were to estimate the comparative size of this tooth with that of a large ox, and from thence infer the size of the animal to which this tooth belonged, we should probably find that its size was forty times larger than our largest oxen.

A forest of trees would soon be nibbled to their roots by a herd of such animals as these; and the western continent would prove a small enough pasture for a moderate number of them.

Dr. Adam Clarke mentions, in his commentary on the subject of this animal, denominated behemoth in Job, 40th chapter, 15th verse, that he had weighed one of the very smallest grinders of an animal of this supposed extinct race, and found it, in its very dry state, to weigh "four pounds eight ounces;" "the same grinder of an elephant, says Dr. Clarke, I have weighed also, and find it but two pounds; the mammoth, therefore, continues this great author, from this proportion, must have been as large as *two* elephants and a quarter."

If, then, an animal of this kind, having a tooth weighing only four pounds and eight ounces, was more than twice as large as an ordinary elephant, how unwieldily and monsterous must have been the animal to which the tooth just mentioned, weighing *twenty-five* pounds, once belonged, arguing from proportion, as Dr. Clarke has done.

The same author, in his *Biblical Commentary* on the first book of Genesis says, that from a *considerable* part of a skeleton which he had seen and examined, it was computed that the animal, when living, must have been nearly twenty-five feet high and sixty feet in length; the bones of one toe were entire, and were something more than three feet long. The height of the animal, as computed by Dr. Clarke, will agree well with the observations of travellers. In the vicinity of May's lick, or Salt spring, in the state of Kentucky, there are several holes, marked in such a manner as to proclaim at once, that they were formed by animals wallowing in them, after they had bathed and satiated themselves with the waters of the fountain; these were the works of buffaloes, deer, and other small animals.

But the same appearances are evident in some banks in the neighborhood, which were hollowed in a semi-circular manner, from the action of beasts *rubbing* against them, and carrying off quantities of the earth on their hides, forming a thick coat, to defend against the stings of numberless flies, like the rhinoceros of Africa. One of those scooped out hollow banks, appeared as if an hundred thousand loads of soil might have been carried off; the height of the wasted bank, where it was affected by attrition, was at least twenty-five feet. The other animals being smaller, could get down and up again from their wallowing, with ease and quickness; but the mammoths were compelled, from their size, to lean against some hill or mountain, so as to coat their hide with earth.

Near this spot are often found the frames of this animal, sunk in the mire. In the state of Missouri, White river and Strawberry river, are certain ranges of mountains, at whose base, in a certain spot, are found " large quantities of these bones gathered in a small compass, which collection was doubtless occasioned by the appetite these animals had for prey, and had been attracted thither, on account of other animals flocking to the salt licks, at that place; the mammoths, following, became mired when they ventured too far, in pursuit, into the marsh, and of course the struggles of the last one would sink the bones of his predecessor still deeper. Thus, these collections are easily accounted for, although, at first, it seems very strange to see these bones accumulated, like those of some of the extinct Indian tribes of the west."—(*Beck's Gazetteer of Illinois and Missouri, p. 332.*)

Adam Clarke supposes the behemoth to have been a carnivorous animal. See his remarks on this monster, in his *Commentary* on Job, 40th chapter, 15th verse. " The behemoth, on the contrary,

(i. e. in opposition to the habits of the hippopotamus and elephant,) is represented as a *quadruped* of a ferocious nature, and formed for tyranny, if not rapacity; equally lord of the floods and of the mountains; rushing with rapidity of foot, instead of slowness or stateliness; and possessing a rigid and enormous tail, like a cedar tree, instead of a short naked tail of about a foot long, as the hippopotamus, or a weak, slender, hog-shaped tail, as the elephant."

Job says, c. xl. v. 17, that he (this monster) moveth his tail like a cedar, that is, its *motions* were like those of a tall cedar tree moved slowly one way and the other by the wind, which explicitly and emphatically marks the monstrousness of this creature's size. " He moveth his tail like a cedar," slowly one way and the other; exactly as the lion, the tiger, or the leopard, in the motions of this limb, especially when angry, or watching for their prey; on which account, it is probable, Job has seen fit to make mention of this *peculiar* motion of the animal; and also it is an evidence of the overwhelming power or strength of the mammoth. He was, indeed, as it is said in Job, " the chief of the ways of God," in the creation of animals.

At St. Helen's point, north of Guayaquil, in the republic of Colombia, South America, on the coast of the Pacific, on the equator, are found the enormous remains of this animal. The Peruvian tradition of those bones is, that at this very point once landed, from some unknown quarter of the earth, a colony of giants, who mutually destroyed each other. At New Granada in the same province, and on the ridge of the Mexican Cordilleras, vast quantities of the remains of this huge beast are found.—(*Humboldt's Researches in South America.*)

The remains of a monster recently discovered on the bank of the Mississippi, in Louisiana, seventeen feet under ground, may be considered as the greatest wonder of the west. The largest bone, which was thought to be the shoulder blade or jaw bone, is twenty feet long, three broad, and weighed 1200 pounds. The aperture in the vertebræ, or place for the pith of the back bone, is six by nine inches calibre; supposed when alive to have been 125 feet in length. The awful and tremendous size of what this creature must have been, to which this shoulder blade or jaw bone belonged, when alive, is almost frightful to think of. It must have been a water animal.

In President Jefferson's *Notes on Virginia*, we have the following as the tradition of the Indians respecting this animal, which they call the *big* buffalo, and assert that he is carniverous, as Dr. Clarke contends, and still exists in the northern parts of America.

"A delegation of warriors from the Delaware tribe visited the government of Virginia, during the Revolution, on matters of business; after this had been discussed, and settled in council, the governor asked some questions relative to their country, and among others, what they knew or had heard of the animal whose bones were found at the licks on the Ohio.

"Their chief speaker immediately put himself into an attitude of oratory, and with a pomp suited to what he conceived the elevation of his subject, informed him that it was a tradition handed down from their fathers, that in ancient times a herd of these tremendous animals came to the Big-bone lick, and began an universal destruction of the bear, deer, elk, buffaloes and other animals which had been created for the use of the Indians. And that the *Great Man* above, looking down and seeing this, was so enraged, that he seized his lightning, descended on the earth, seated himself on a neighboring mountain, on a certain rock, where the print of his feet are still remaining, from whence he hurled his bolts among them, till the whole were slaughtered, except the big bull; who, presenting his forehead to the shafts shook them off as they fell; but at length one of them missing his head glanced on his side, wounding him sufficiently to make him mad; whereon, springing round, he bounded over the Ohio at a leap, then over the Wabash at another, the Illinois at a third, and a fourth leap over the great lakes, where he is living at this day."

"A Mr. Stanley, taken prisoner by the Indians near the mouth of the Tennessee river, relates that after being transferred through several tribes, was at length carried over the mountains west of the Missouri, to a river which runs westwardly; that these bones abounded there, and that the nations described to him the animal to which these belonged, as still living in the northern parts of their country."

Mr. Jefferson contends, at page 77 of his *Notes on Virginia*, that this animal is *not* extinct. "It may be asked," says this philosopher, "why I insert the mammoth as if it still existed. I ask in return, why I should omit it, as if it did not exist? The northern and western parts still remain in their aboriginal state, unexplored and undisturbed by us, or by others for us. He may as well exist there now as he did formerly, where we find his bones. If he be a carnivorous animal, as some anatomists have conjectured, and the Indians affirm, his early retirement to deeper wilds, may be accounted for, from the great destruction of the wild game, by the Indians, which commenced in the very first instant of their connexion with us, for the purpose of purchasing matchcoats, hatchets, and guns, with their skins."

The description of this monster's habits, as given by the Delaware chief, has a surprising agreement with the account of the behemoth given by Job, especially at this verse:—" Surely the mountains bring him forth food, where all the beasts of the field play." " He frequents those places, (says Dr. Clarke,) where he can have most prey; he makes a mock of all the beasts of the field. They can neither resist his power nor escape his agility. It appears to have been a many-toed animal; the springs which such a creature could make must have been almost incredible; nothing by swiftness could have escaped its pursuit. God seems to have made it as the proof of his power, and had it been prolific, and not become extinct, it would have depopulated the earth of both men and animals.

Tracks of Men and Animals in the Rocks of Tennessee and elsewhere.

AMONG the subjects of antiquity, which are abundant on the American continent, we give the following, from *Morse's Universal Geography*, which in point of mysteriousness is not surpassed, perhaps, on the globe. In the state of Tennessee, on a certain mountain, called the enchanted mountain, situated a few miles south of Braystown, which is at the head waters of the Tennessee river, are found impressed in the surface of the solid rock, a great number of tracks, as turkies, bears, horses, and human beings, as perfect as they could be made on snow or sand. The human tracks are remarkable for having uniformly *six* toes each, like the Anakims of Scripture; one only excepted, which appears to be the print of a negro's foot. One, among those tracks, is distinguished from the rest, by its monstrousness, being of no less dimensions than sixteen inches in length, across the toes thirteen inches, behind the toes, where the foot narrows toward the instep, seven inches, and the heel ball five inches.

One also among the tracks of the animals, is distinguished for its great size: it is the track of a horse, measuring eight by ten inches; perhaps the horse which the great warrior led when passing this mountain with his army. That these are the real tracks of the animals they represent, appears from the circumstance of this horse's foot having slipped several inches, and recovered again; the figures have all the same direction, like the trail of a company on a journey.

Not far from this very spot, are vast heaps of stones, which are the supposed tombs of warriors, slain, perhaps in the very battle this big footed warror was engaged in, at a period when these mountains which give rise to some branches of the Tugulo, Apalachicola, and Hiwassa rivers, were in a state of soft and clayey texture. On this range, according to Mexican tradition, was the holy mountain; temple and *cave* of *Olaimi*, where was also a city and the seat of their empire, more ancient than that of Mexico. To reduce that city, perhaps, was the object of the great warrior, whose track with that of his horse and company, still appear.

We are of the opinion, that these tracks, found sunk in the surface of the rocks of this mountain, is indubitable evidence of their antiquity, going back to the time when men dispersed over the earth, immediately after the flood.

At the period when this troop passed the summit of this mountain, the rock was in a soft and yielding state; time, therefore, sufficient for it to harden to its present rock consistency, is the argument of the great distance of time elapsed since they went over it.

It is probable the whole of these mountains, out of which arise the branches of the rivers above alluded to, were, at the time when the deluge subsided, but a vast body of clay; for even now, the surface, where it is not exposed to the rays of the sun, is of a soft texture, capable of being cut with a knife, and appears to be of the nature of the pipe stone.

In order that those tracks might retain their shape against the operation of rains, the clay must have been of a tough and oily nature; and hardened by slow degrees, after having been brought to feel the influence of the sun's rays, and drying nature of the winds. The changing and revolutionising consequences of the flood, it is likely, unbared these bodies of clay from the depths of the earth, by washing off all the other kinds of strata, not so adhesive as is the nature of this clay; out of which these ranges of mountains have been made, some eighteen hundred years later than the original creation.

In the wild and savage country of Guiana, in South America, are mountains of a prodigious height, on whose smooth and perpendicular sides, which seem once to have been a barrier to mighty waters, are engraved, at a surprising distance from their base, the figures of animals; also the sun, moon, and stars, with other hieroglyphical signs. The tradition respecting them, among the natives, is that their ancestors, in a time of great waters came in canoes, to the tops of these mountains, and that the stones were then so soft, and plastic, that men could easily trace marks on them with their fingers, or with sticks. These rocks, it would appear, were then in a state similar to those in Tennessee, which also had retained the impressions made on them by the feet of the traveller. But these mysterious traces found on the mountain in Tennessee, are not the only impressions of the kind. Mr. Schoolcraft, in his travels in the central parts of the Mississippi regions, informs us, that on the limestone strata of rock, which forms the shores of the Mississippi, and along the neighborhood of St. Louis, were found tracks of the human foot, deeply and perfectly impressed in the solid stone. But two traces of this sort have been, as yet, discovered; these are the same represented on the plate, as given by Schoolcraft.

"The impressions in the stone are, to all appearances, those of a man standing in an erect posture, with the left foot a little advanced, and the heels drawn in. The distance between the heels, by accurate measurement, is six inches and a quarter, and between the extremities of the toes, thirteen and a half. The length of these tracks is ten and a quarter inches, across the toes four inches and a half, as spread out, and but two and a half at the heel. Directly before the prints of these feet, within a few inches, is a well impressed and deep mark, having some resemblance to a *scroll*, or roll of parchment, two feet long, by a foot in width.

To account for these appearances, two theories are advanced;

one is, that they were sculptured there by the ancient nations: the other, that they were impressed there at a time when the rock was in a plastic state; both theories have their difficulties, but we incline to the latter, because the impressions are strikingly natural, says Mr. Schoolcraft, exhibiting even the muscular marks of the foot, with great precision and faithfulness to nature, and on this account, weakens, in his opinion, the doctrine of their being sculptured by the ancient nations.

But why there are no others going to and from these, is unaccountable, unless we may suppose the rest of this rock, at that time, was buried by earth, brush, grass, or some kind of covering. If they were sculptured, why not other specimens appear; this one isolated effort of the kind, would seem unnatural.—(*See the plate which is a true fac simile of those tracks.*)

Cotubamana, the Giant Chief.

On the subject of the stature of the Patagonians, we have the following remarks of Morse, the geographer. "We cannot, without a charge of unreasonable scepticism, deny all credence to the accounts that have been transmitted to us, of a race of men of extraordinary stature, in the country about the strait of Magellan.

Inscrutable as are the ways of Providence, and as limited as is the progress hitherto made in the natural philosophy of the globe we inhabit, no bounds can be assigned to the endless variety of phenomena, which successively appear. The man who can assign a reason why an Irish giant, or a Polish dwarf, should be born amidst nations of ordinary stature, will have solved every problem, as to the existence, either of gigantic Patagonians, or of pigmy Esquimaux.

From an impartial revision of the various authorities, it appears, as an established fact, that the usual stature of one or more tribes of Indians in Patagonia, is from six and a half to seven and a half feet." When the Spaniards conquered and destroyed the nations and tribes of some of the West India islands, among them was a tribe whose chief was a man of great stature. Cotubamana was the name of this cacique, who resided with his nation on the island Higuey, adjacent to Hispaniola.

This chieftian, as related by Las Casas, the historian, was the strongest of his tribe, and more perfectly formed than one man of a thousand, of any nation whatever. He was taller than the tallest of his countrymen, and in width from shoulder to shoulder full three feet, with the rest of his person in admirable proportion. His aspect was not handsome; yet his countenance was grave, strongly marked with the characteristics of a man of courage. His bow was not easily bent by a common man; his arrows were three pronged, pointed with the bones of fishes; all his weapons were large enough for a giant; in a word, he was so nobly proportioned as to be the admiration of even the Spaniards.

Already the murderous Spaniards had been more than conquerors in several battles which drove the poor fugitives to their caves, and the fastnesses of the mountains, whither they had followed their chief. A daily pursuit was continued, but chiefly to capture the as yet invincible Cotubamana. While searching in the woods and hills of the island, at a certain time, and having got on their trail, they came at length to a place where the path which they had followed suddenly divided into many, the whole company of the Spaniards, except one man, chose a path, which they pursued. This one exception, was a man named Juan Lopez, a powerful Spaniard, and skilful in the mode of Indian warfare. He chose to proceed alone, in a blind foot path, leading off to the left of the course the others had taken, winding among little hills, so thickly wooded that it was impossible to see a man at the distance of half a bow shot. But as he was silently darting along this path, he encountered all at once, in a narrow pass, overhung by rocks and trees, twelve Indian warriors, armed with bows and arrows, following each other in Indian file. The poor natives were confounded at the sight of Lopez, imagining there must be a party of soldiers behind him, or they would doubtless have transfixed him with their arrows. Lopez demanded of them where their chief was; they replied, he is behind us, and opening to let him pass, he beheld the dauntless Cotubamana in the rear. At sight of the Spaniard, the gallant cacique bent his gigantic bow, and was on the point of launching one of his three headed arrows into his heart; but Lopez at the instant, rushed upon him, and wounded him with his sword.

The other Indians, struck with terror, had fled. The Spaniard and Cotubamana now grappled with each other; Lopez had seized the chief by the hair of his head with one hand, and was aiming with the other a thrust with his sword at his naked body, but the chief struck down the sword with his arm, and closed in with his antagonist, and threw him with his back upon the rough rocks.

As they were both men of great strength, the struggle was long and violent. The sword lay beneath them, but Cotubamana seized with his great hand the Spaniard's throat, and began to strangle him, when the sound of the contest brought the other Spaniards to the spot. They found their companion writhing and gasping in the agonies of death, in the gripe of the Indian. The whole band now fell, upon him, and finally succeeded in binding his noble limbs, when they carried him to St. Domingo, where the infernal Spaniards hanged him as if he had been a murderer.—(*Irving's Life of Columbus*, vol. 3, p. 159.)

Could this native have been less than twelve feet in height, to be in proportion with the breadth of his back between his shoulders, which was full three feet, as Las Casas relates? In reading the story of the miserable death of this hero, we are reminded of the no less tragical end of Wallace, the Scottish chief, who was, it is said, a man of great size and strength, and was also executed for defending his country.

Goliath of Gath was six cubits and a span high, which, according to the estimate of Bishop Cumberland, was eleven feet and ten inches; Cotubamana and Goliath of the Philistines, were, it appears, much of the same stature, terrible to look upon, and irresistible in strength.

There are those who imagine, that the first inhabitants of the globe, or the antediluvians, were much larger than our race at the present time; and although it is impossible to prove this opinion, yet the subject is not beyond the reach of argument in its support.

The circumstance of their immense longevity favors strongly this opinion; our species, as they are *now* constituted, could not possibly endure the pressure of so many years; the *heart*, with all the blood vessels of the body, would fail. All the organs of the human subject, which appertain to the blood, would ossify, and cease their action, long before five, six and nine hundred years should transpire, unless differently or more abundantly sustained with the proper support, than could *now* be furnished from the little bodies of the present times.

Small streams sooner feel the power of a drought than a river or a lake; great trees are longer sustained beneath the rays of a burning sky, without rain, than a mere weed or shrub; and this is by reason of the greater quantum of the juices of the tree, and of the greater quantum of the water of the river or the lake.

Apply this reasoning to the antediluvians, and we arrive at the conclusion, that their bodies must have been larger than ours, or the necessary *juices* could not have been contained, so as to furnish a heart, and all the blood vessels, with a sufficient ratio of strength and vigor to support life so many ages in succession.

Their whole conformation must have been of a larger, looser, and more generous texture, as the flesh and skin of the elephant, which is the largest as well as the longest lived animal known to the science zoology. The mammoth was undoubtedly a long lived animal. The eagle, the largest of the fowl family, lives to a great age. That the antediluvians were of great stature, is strongly supported by a remark of king Solomon, found in his book of Wisdom, in the Apocrypha, 14th chapter, at the 6th verse, where he calls all the inhabitants of the earth, who were destroyed by the deluge, "*proud giants*," whose history, by tradition, handed down from the family of Noah, through the lineage of Shem, was well known to that king, the wisest of men in his day and age.

And even after the flood, the great stature of men is supported in the Scriptures in several places, who were, for some generations, permitted to live several hundred years, and were all accordingly of great stature. Whole tribes or nations of gigantic inhabitants peopled the country of Canaan, before the Jews drove them out.

Their manners and customs were very horrible, whom Solomon, the king, charges with being guilty, among many other enormities, of glutting themselves with the blood and flesh of human beings; from which we learn they were cannibals.—(*See book of Wisdom*, 12th chap. 5th verse—Apocrypha.)

The very *circumstances* of the human race, before the flood, required that they should be of greater strength of body than now, because it is not likely so many useful and labor saving machines were invented and in use as now. Every thing was to be effected by strength of muscle and bone, which of course would require greater bodies to produce it.

Were we to indulge in fancy on this subject, we should judge them no pigmy race, either in person or in temper; but terrible, broad, and tall in stature, loose and flabby in their flesh and skin; coarse and hideous in their features, slow and strong in their gestures, irascible and ferocious in their spirits, without pity or refinement; given wholly to war, rapine and plunder; formed into bands; clans and small bodies of marauders, constantly prowling round each other's habitations, outraging all the charities of a more refind state of things, measuring all things by mere bodily strength.

From such a state of things we should naturally look for the consequence mentioned in the Bible; which is, that the whole earth was filled with violence before the flood, and extremely wicked every way, so as to justify the Divine procedure in their extermination.

Indications now and then appear, in several parts of the earth, as mentioned by the traveller, of the existence af fowls, of a size compared with the mammoth itself, considering the difference in the elements each inhabit, and approach each other in size as nearly as the largest fowl now known, does the largest animal.

Henderson, in his travels in New Siberia, met with the claws of a bird, measuring three in length; the same was the length of the toes of a mammoth, as measured by Adam Clarke.

The Yakuts, inhabitants of the Siberian country, assured Mr. Henderson, that they had frequently, in their hunting excursions, found the skeleton, and even the feathers of this fowl, the quills of which were large enough to admit a man's arm into the calibre, which would not be out of proportion with the size of the claws mentioned above.

Captain Cook mentions having seen, during his voyages, a monstrous bird's nest in New Holland, on a low sandy island, in Endeavor river, with trees upon it, where were an incredible number of sea fowls. This monstrous nest was built on the ground, with large sticks, and was no less than twenty-six feet in circumference, more than eight feet across, and two feet eight inches high. Geographies speak of a species of eagle, sometimes shot in South America, measuring from tip to tip of the wings, forty feet. This, indeed, must have been of the species celebrated in the tradition of the ancients, called the Phœnix.

In various parts of Ireland, are frequently dug up enormous

horns, supposed to have belonged to a species of deer, now extinct. Some of these horns have been found, of the extent of fourteen feet from tip to tip, furnished with brow antlers, and weighing three hundred pounds. The whole skeleton is frequently found with them. It is supposed the animal must have been about twelve feet high.—(*Morse's Universal Geography.*)

A Further Account of Discoveries in the West, as given by the Antiquarian Society at Cincinnati.

NEAR Newark, in the county of Licking, Ohio, is situated one of those immense works or fortifications. Its builders chose, with good taste and judgment, this site for their town, being exactly on the point of land at the junction of Racoon creek and South fork, where Licking river commences. It is in form resembling somewhat a horse shoe, accommodated, however, to the sweep of those two streams; embracing in the whole, a circumference of about six hundred rods, or nearly two miles.

A wall of earth, of about four hundred rods, is raised on the sides of this fort next to the small creek, which comes down along its sides from the west and east. The situation is beautiful, as these works stand on a large plain, which is elevated forty or fifty feet above the stream just noticed, and is almost perfectly flat, and as rich a soil as can be found in that country. It would seem the people who made this settlement, undertook to encompass with a wall, as much land as would support its inhabitants, and also sufficient to build their dwellings on, with several fortifications, arranged in a proper manner for its defence.

There are, within its ranges *four* of those forts, of different dimensions; one contains forty acres, with a wall of about ten feet high; another, containing twenty-two acres, also walled; but in this fort is an elevated observatory, of sufficient height to overlook the whole country. From this, there is the appearance of a secret or subterranean passage to the water, as one of the creeks runs near this fort. A third fort, containing about twenty-six acres, having a wall around it, thrown out of a deep ditch on the inner side of the wall. This wall is now from twenty-five to thirty feet in height. A fourth fortification, enclosing twenty acres, with a wall of about ten feet high. Two of these forts are perfect circles; one a perfect square; another an octagon or eight sided. These forts are severally connected by roads running between parallel walls; and also in the same way communicate with the creeks; so that these important points, in case of invasion, should not be deprived of water. There are, besides the forts, four other small works of defence, of a circular form, situated in such a manner as to protect, in a measure, the roads running from fort to fort.

The fort which is of the eight sided form, containing the greatest space within, has eight gateways, with a mound in front of each of them, and were doubtless placed there to aid in a defence against invaders. The other forts have no gateways connected with the roads that lead to them, except one, and this is a round fort united to the octangular fort, containing twenty-two acres; the gateway to this looks toward the wilderness; at this gate is also a mound, supposed to be for its defence.

On the southern side of this great town, is a road running off to the country, which is also walled in the same way; it has been surveyed a few miles, and is supposed to connect other similar works on the Hokhoking, thirty miles distance, at some point a few miles north of Lancaster, as walls of the description connected with this work, of ten or twelve miles in extent, have been discovered. It is supposed, also, that the walls on each side of the road were made for the double purpose of answering as a fence to their fields, with gateways to accommodate their farms, and for security in time of danger, so that communion between friendly settlements might not be interrupted. About the walls of this place have been discovered very beautiful rock crystal and horn stone, suitable for arrow and spear heads, a little lead, sulphur, and iron.

This kind of stone, suitable for spears, was, undoubtedly, valuable on other accounts, as axes, knives, mallets, &c., were made of it. It is likely that, as very little iron has been discovered, even in its oxydized state, their vast works of excavation were carried on by means of wooden shovels and scrapers, which would answer very well in the easy and stoneless soil of that country.

A second fort, situated southwesterly from the great works on the Licking, and four or five miles, in a northwestern direction

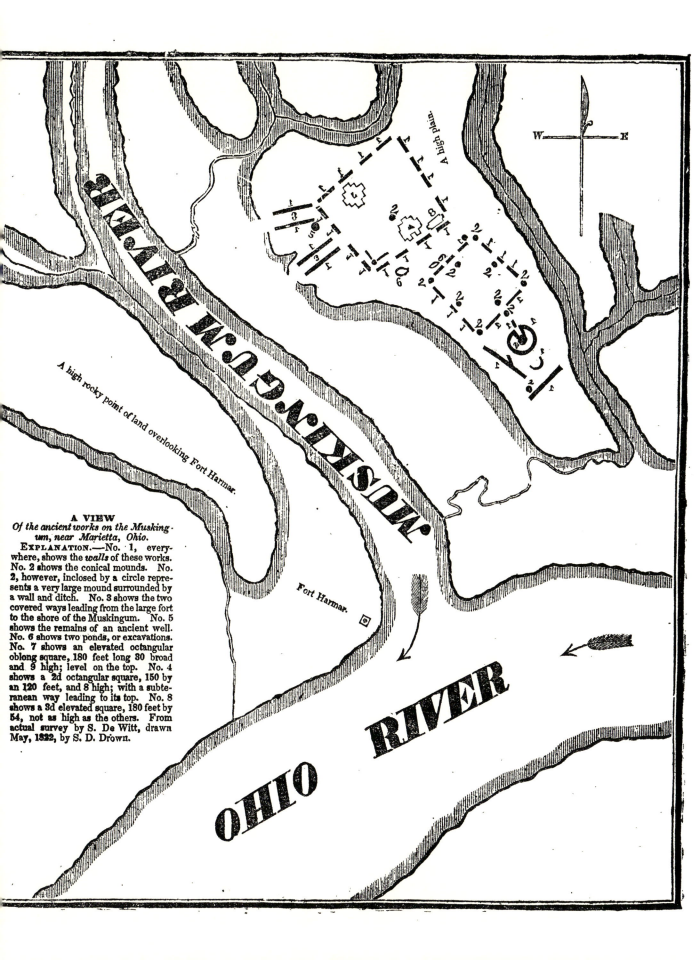

from Somerset, the seat of justice for Perry county is found. This work encloses about forty acres; its wall is entirely of stone, not regularly laid up in a wall, agreeably to the rules of masonry, but a huge mass of stones and rocks of all shapes and sizes, as nature formed them, without the mark of an iron tool upon them. These are in sufficient quantity to form a wall, if laid in good order, of about fourteen feet in height, and three in thickness.

Near the centre of the area of this enclosure, is a stone mound, of a circular form, fifteen feet high, and was erected, as is conjectured, for an altar, on which were performed their religious rites, and also for a monument to perpetuate the memory of some great event in the history of its builders. It is also believed, that the whole of this vast preparation was devoted solely to the purposes of worship of some kind; as it is situated on very high grounds, where the soil is good for nothing, and may have been, what is called, an *high place* in Scripture, according to the customs of the ancient pagans of the old world.

It could not have been a military work, as no water is found there, nor a place of dwelling, for the same reason, and from the poverty of the soil; but must have been a place of resort on great occasions, such as a solemn assembly to propitiate the gods; and also a place to anoint and crown their kings, elect legislators, transact national affairs, judge among the people, and inflict condign punishment.

Who will believe for a moment, that the common Indians of the west, who were derived in part from the wandering hordes of the northern Tartar race of Asia, were the authors of these works; bearing the marks of so much labor and scientific calculation in their construction? It cannot be.

Vast Works of the Ancient Nations on the east side of the Muskingum.

This fort, town, or fortification, or whatever it may have been, is between three and four hundred rods, or rising of a mile in circumference, and so situated as to be nearly surrounded by two small brooks, running into the Muskingum. Their site is on an elevated plain, above the present bank of that river, about a half mile from its junction with the Ohio.

We give the account in the words of Mr. Atwater, president of the Antiquarian Society. "They consist of walls and mounds of earth, in direct lines, and in square and circular forms. The largest *square* fort, by some called the *town*, contains forty acres, encompassed by a wall of earth, from six to ten feet high, and from twenty to thirty in breadth at the base.

"On each side are three openings at equal distances, resembling twelve gateways. The entrances at the middle are the largest, particularly on the side next to the Muskingum. From this outlet is a covert way formed of two parallel walls of earth, two hundred and thirty-one feet distant from each other, measured from centre to centre. The walls at the most elevated part, on the inside, are twenty-one feet in height, and forty-two in breadth, at the base, but on the outside average only about five feet in height. This forms a passage of about twenty rods in length, leading by a gradual descent to the low grounds, where, at the time of its construction, it probably reached the river. Its walls commence at sixty feet from the ramparts of the fort, and increase in elevation as the way descends to the river; and the bottom is rounded in the centre, in the manner of a well founded turnpike road.

Within the walls of the fort, at its northwest corner, is an oblong *elevated* square, one hundred and eighty feet long, one hundred and thirty-two broad, and nine feet high, level on the summit, and even now, nearly perpendicular at the sides. Near the south wall is an elevated square, one hundred and fifty by one hundred and twenty, and eight feet high, similar to the other, excepting, that instead of an ascent to go up on the side next the wall, there is a hollow way, ten feet wide, leading twenty feet towards the centre, and then rising with a gradual slope to the top. This was, it is likely, a secret passage. At the southeast corner is a third elevated square, of one hundred and eighty by fifty-four feet, with ascents at the ends, ten feet wide, but not so high nor perfect as two others.

Besides this forty acre fort, which is situated within the great range of the surrounding wall, there is another, containing twenty acres, with a gateway in the centre of each side, and at each corner these gateways are defended by circular mounds.

On the outside of the smaller fort is a mound, in form of a sugar loaf; its base is a regular circle, one hundred and fifteen feet in diameter, or twenty-one rods in circumference; its altitude is thirty feet. It is surrounded by a ditch four feet deep, fifteen feet wide, and defended by a parapet four feet high, through which is a gateway towards the foot, twenty feet in width. Near one of the corners of the great fort, was found a reservoir or well, twenty-five feet in diameter, and seventy-five in circumference, with its sides raised above the common level of the adjoining surface, by an embankment of earth, three and four feet high."

It was, undoubtedly, at first, very deep, as, since its discovery by the first settlers, they have frequently thrust poles into it to the depth of thirty feet. It appears to run to a point, like an inverted cone or funnel and was undoubtedly that *kind* of well used by the inhabitants of the old world, which were so large at their top as to afford an easy descent down to the fountain, and up again with its water in a vessel borne on the shoulder, according to the ancient custom. (*See Genesis* xiii, 24.) "And she, (that is Rebecca, the daughter of Bethuel,) went *down* to the well, filled her pitcher and came up." Bethuel was an Assyrian, who, it seems, had made a well in the same form with that described above. Its sides were lined with a stratum of fine ash colored clay, eight and ten inches thick, beyond which is the common soil of the place. It is conjectured, that at the bottom of this well might be found many curious articles which belonged to the ancient inhabitants. Several pieces of copper have been found in and near these ancient works, at various places; and one was in the form of a cup, with low sides, the bottom very thick and strong, showing their enlarged acquaintance with that metal, more than the Indians ever had.

Ruins of Ancient Works at Circleville.

At Circleville, in Ohio, are the remains of very great works of this description, evidently of a military character, two of which are united; one is exactly square, the other an exact circle. The square fort is fifty rods on each side; the round one is nearly three hundred feet, or eighteen rods in circumference; the circle and square touching each other, and communicate at the very spot where they united.

The circular fort is surrounded by *two* walls, with a deep ditch between them; the square fort is also encompassed by a wall, without a ditch. The walls of the circular fort were at least twenty feet in height, measuring from the bottom of the ditch, before the town of Circleville was built. The inner wall is formed of clay, brought from a distance, but the outside one was formed with the earth of the ditch, as it was thrown out.

There were eight gateways, or openings, leading into the square fort, and only one into the circular. Before each of these openings was a mound of earth, about four feet high, forty feet in diameter at the base, and twenty feet and upwards at the top, situated about two rods in front of the gates; for the defence, no doubt, of these openings. The walls of this work vary a few degrees from north and south, and east and west, but no more than the needle varies; and not a few surveyors have, from this circumstance, been impressed with the belief, that the authors of these works were acquainted with *astronomy*, and the four cardinal points.

Within the great square fort are eight small mounds, placed opposite the gateways, for their defence, or to give opportunity to privileged spectators to review the thousands passing out to war, or coming in with the trophies of victory. Such was the custom of ancient times. David, the most potent king of the Jews, stood at the gateway of the city, as his armies went to quell the insurrection of his son Absalom. (*See 2d Samuel*, xviii, 4.) "And the king stood by the gate side, and all the people came out by hundreds and by thousands." It cannot be supposed the king stood on the ground, on a common level with his armies. Such a situation would be extremely inconvenient, and defeat, in a great measure, the opportunity of review. How impressive, when soldiers, fired with all the ardor of expected victory, to behold their general, chief, king, or emperor, bending over them, as they pass on, from some commanding position near at hand, giving counsel to their captains; drawing, in this way, large draughts on the individual confidence and love of the soldiery. Such may have been the spectacle at the gateways of the forts of the west, at the eras of their grandeur.

In musing on the structure of these vast works found along the western rivers, enclosing such immense spaces of land, the mind is irresistibly directed to a contemplation of ancient Babylon, the first city of magnitude built immediately after the flood. That city was of a square form, being fifteen miles distance on each of its sides, and sixty in circumference, surrounded with a wall eighty-seven feet in thickness, and three hundred and fifty in height. On each side it had twenty-five gateways, amounting in all, to a hundred; the whole, besides the wall, surrounded with a deep and wide ditch. At each corner of this immense square, was a strong tower, ten feet higher than the walls. There were fifty broad streets, each fifteen miles long, starting from each of its gates, and an hundred and fifty feet broad, crossing each other at right angles; besides four half streets, surrounding the whole, two hundred feet broad. The whole city was divided into six hundred and seventy-six squares, four and a half furlongs on each side. In the centre of the city stood the temple of Belus, and in the centre of this temple stood an immense tower, six hundred feet square at its base, and six hundred feet high, narrowing in the form of a pyramid as it ascended. The ascent to the summit was accomplished by spiral stairs, winding eight times round the whole. This tower consisted of eight distinct parts, each on the top of the other, seventy-five feet high, till the whole, in aggregate, finished the tower.

In the different stories were temples, or chapels, for the worship of the sun; and on its top, some authors say, was an image of gold, forty feet in height, equal in value to three millions five hundred thousand dollars.—(*Blake's Atlas.*)

The model of this city, with its towers at the corners, and pyramid in its centre, having been made at so early a period of time, being not far from one hundred years after the flood, was doubtless of sufficient influence to impress its image on the memory of tradition, so that the nations spreading out from that region over all the earth, may have copied this Chaldean model in their various works.

This thought is strengthened when we compare its counterpart, the vast works of the west, with this Babylonian prototype of architectural effort, and imagine we see in the latter, the features and general outlines of this giant, among cities, in the towers, walls, and pyramids of the western states.

Near the round fort at Circleville, is another fort, ninety feet high, and was doubtless erected to overlook the whole works of that enormous military establishment. That it was a military establishment is the decided opinion of the president of the Western Antiquarian Society, Mr. Atwater. He says, the round fort was *picketed* in, if we are to judge from the appearance of the ground, on and about the walls. Half way up the outside of the inner wall, is a place distinctly to be seen, where a row of pickets once stood, and where it was placed when this work of defence was originally erected. Finally, this work about its walls and ditch, a few years since, presented as much of defensive aspect, as forts which were occupied in our war with the French, such as Oswego, Fort Stanwix, and others.

Respecting this place, it is said, that the Indian, even to this day, will on no account enter within its outlines, which circumstance proves beyond a doubt, that it was also, a holy, or sacred place, where the mysteries of ancient paganism were celebrated, with all the pomp and circumstance, necessary to the belief of that which is mere fiction.

Ancient Works on Paint Creek.

On Paint creek, in Ohio, about fifteen miles from Chilicothe, are works of art, still more wonderful than any yet described. There are six in number, and are in the neighborhood of each other. In one of those grand enclosures are contained three forts, one embraces seventeen, another twenty-seven, a third seventy-seven, amounting in all, to one hundred and fifteen acres of land.

One of those forts is round, another square, and a third is of an irregular form, approaching however, nearer to the circular than any other; and the wall which embraces the whole, is so contrived in its courses, as to favor those several forms; the whole being, evidently, one work, separated into three compartments.

There are fourteen gateways, going out of the whole work, besides three which unite the several forts one with the other, inwardly; all these, especially those leading outwardly, are very wide, being, as they now appear, from one to six rods. At three of those gateways, on the outside of the wall, are as many ancient wells; and one on the inside, where doubtless, the inhabitants procured water. Their width at the top is from four to six rods, but their depth unknown, as they are now nearly filled up. Within the greatest enclosure, containing the seventy-seven acres, is an eliptical elevation of twenty-five feet in height, and so large, that its area is nearly one hundred and fifty rods in circumference, composed almost entirely of stone in their rough and natural state, brought from a hill adjacent to the place.

This elevated work is full of human bones, and some have not hesitated to express a belief, that on this work, human beings were once sacrificed. The surface is smooth and level, favoring the idea of the horrid parade, such occasions would produce; yet they may have been erected for the purpose of mere military manœvreing, which would produce a spectacle very imposing, composed of thousands, harnessed in their war attire, with nodding plumes. About a mile from this fort, there is a work in the form of a half moon, set round the edges with stones, exactly resembling the stone circles of the Druids, in which they performed their mystic rites in Europe two thousand years ago. Near this semicirle is a very singular mound of only five feet in height, but ninety feet in circumference, composed entirely of red ochre; which answers well as a paint. An abundance of this ochre is found on a hill, not a great distance from this place; from which circumstance, the stream which runs along here, is called Paint creek.

So vast a heap of this paint being deposited, is pretty clear evidence, that it was an article of commerce among these nations. Here may have been a store house, or a range of them, attended by salesmen, or merchants; who took in exchange for it, copper, feathers, bow and arrow timber, stone for hatchets, spears, and knives, wooden ploughs and shovels; with skins and furs, for clothing; stones for building their rude altars and works; with food to sustain the populace, as the manner of cities of the present time. Red paint in particular, is used now among the Hindoos, which they mark themselves with, as well as their gods. This vast collection of red paint, by the ancient nations, on Paint creek, favors the opinion, that it was put to the same use, by the same people.

Near this work is another, on the same creek, enclosing eighty-four acres, part of which is a square fort, with seven gateways; and the other a fort, of an irregular oval, with seven gateways, surrounded with a wall like the others. But the most interesting work of the three contiguous forts, is yet to be described. It is situated on a high hill, of more than three hundred feet elevation, and in many places almost perpendicular. The wall running round this work, is built exactly on the brow of the precipice, and in its courses, is accommodated to the variations of this natural battlement, enclosing, in the whole, one hundred and thirty acres. On its south end the ground is level, where the entrance to the fort is easy. At the north end, which approaches pretty near to Paint creek, appears to have been a gateway descending to the water, the ground favoring it at this point, as well as at one other, leading to a little stream, which runs along its base, on the east side of this eminence, where is also another gateway; these three places are the only points which are at all accessible. The wall round the whole one hundred and thirty acres, is entirely of stone, and is in sufficient quantity, if laid up in good order, to make it ten feet high, and four thick. At the north gateway, stones enough now lie, to have built two considerable round towers, taken from the hill itself, and are of the red sand stone kind.

Near the south end of this enclosure, at the place where it is easiest of access, " appear to have been a row of furnaces, (says Mr. Atwater) or smith's shops, where the cinders now lie, many feet deep; but was not able to say with certainty, what manufactures were carried on here, whether brick or iron, or both." It was a clay, that had been exposed to the action of fire; the remains of which are four and five feet in depth; which shows in a good degree, the amount of business done was great. "Iron ore, in this country, is sometimes found in such clay; brick and potter's ware are now manufactured out of it. This fort is, from its natural site, one of the strongest positions of the kind in the state of Ohio, so high is its elevation, and so nearly perpendicular are the sides of the hill on which it was built." At the several angles of the wall, and at the gateways, the abundance of stone lying there, leads to the belief, that those points, towers and battlements once overlooked the country to an immense distance; from whence stones and arrows might have been launched away, from engines adapted to that purpose, among the approaching enemy, with dreadful effect. " No military man could have selected a better position for a place of protection to his countrymen, their temples and their gods," than this.

Ancient Wells found in the Bottom of Paint Creek.

In the bed of Paint creek, which washes the foot of the hill, on which the walled town stood, have been discovered four wells. They were dug through a pyritous slate rock, which is very rich in iron ore. When first discovered, by a person passing over them in a canoe, they were covered, each by stones of about the size and shape of the common mill stone. These covers had holes through their centre, through which a large pry, or handspike might be put for the purpose of removing them off and on the wells. The hole through the centre of each stone, was about four inches in diameter. The wells at their tops were more than nine feet in circumference; the stones were well wrought with tools, so as to make good joints, as a stone mason would say, which were laid around them severally, as a pavement. At the time they were dug, it is not likely Paint creek run over these wells. For what they were sunk, is a mystery; as that for the purposes of water, so many so near each other, would scarcely appear necessary; perhaps for some kind of ore or favorite stone, was the original object, perhaps for salt water.

There is, at Portsmouth, Ohio, one of those works, which is very extensive and wonderful, on account of walled roads, a " high place," with many intricate operations in its construction.

On the east bank of the Little Miami, about thirty miles east from Cincinnati, are vast works of this character; having the form almost exactly of the continent of North and South America, as presented on the map, on which account some have supposed they were made in imitation of it.

A Recent Discovery of one of those Ancient Works among the Alleghanies.

New discoveries are constantly making of these ancient works, the farther we go west, and the more minutely the research is prosecuted, even in parts already settled.

During the last year, 1832, a Mr. Ferguson communicated to the editor of the Christian Advocate and Journal, a discovery of the kind, which he examined, and describes as follows:

"On a mountain called the Lookout mountain, belonging to the vast Alleghanian chain, running between the Tennessee and Coos rivers, rising about one thousand feet above the level of the surrounding valley. The top of the mountain is mostly level, but presents to the eye an almost barren waste. On this range, notwithstanding its height, a river has its source, after traversing it for about seventy miles, plunges over a precipice. The rock from which the water falls, is circular, and juts over considerably. Immediately below the fall, on each side of the river, are bluffs, which rise about two hundred feet. Around one of these bluffs, the river makes a bend, which gives it the form of a peninsula. On the top of this are the remains of what is esteemed fortifications; which consist of a stone wall, built on the very brow of this tremendous ledge. The whole length of the wall, following the varying courses of the brink of this precipice, is thirty-seven rods and eight feet, including about two acres of ground."

The only descent from this place is between two rocks, for about thirty feet, when a bench of the ledge presents itself, from two to five feet in width, and ninety feet long. This bench is the only road or path up from the water's edge to the summit. But just at the foot of the two rocks, where they reach this path, and within thirty feet of the top of the rock, are five rooms, which have been formed by dint of labor. The entrance to these rooms is very small, but when within, they are found to communicate with each other, by doors or apertures. Mr. Ferguson thinks them to have been constructed during some dreadful war, and those who constructed them, to have acted on the defensive; and believe that *twenty* men could have withstood the whole army of Xerxes, as it was impossible for more than one to pass at a time; and might by the slightest push, be hurled at least a hundred and fifty feet down the rocks. The reader can indulge his own conjectures, whether, in the construction of this inaccessible fortress, he does not perceive the remnant of a tribe or nation, acquainted with the arts of excavation and defence; making a last struggle against the invasion of an overwhelming foe; where, it is likely, they were reduced by famine, and perished amid the yells of their enemies.

A Description of Western Tumuli or Mounds.

ANCIENT Tumuli are considered a kind of antiquities, differing in character from that of the other works; both on account of what is frequently discovered in them, and the manner of their construction. They are conical mounds, either of earth or stones, which were intended for sacred and important purposes. In many parts of the world, similar mounds were used as monuments, sepulchres, altars, and temples. The accounts of these works, found in the Scriptures, show, that their origin must be sought for among the antediluvians.

That they are very ancient, and were used as places of sepulture, public resort, and public worship, is proved by all the writers of ancient times, both sacred and profane. HOMER frequently mentions them, particularly describing the tumulus of Tydeus, and the spot where it was. In memory of the illustrious dead, a sepulchral mound of earth was raised over their remains; which, from that time forward, became an altar, whereon to offer sacrifices, and around which to exhibit games of athletic exercise. These offerings and games were intended to propitiate their manes, to honor and perpetuate their memories. Prudentius, a Roman bard, has told us, that that there were in ancient Rome, just as many temples of gods, as there were sepulchres of heroes; implying that they were the same. Need I mention the tomb of Anchies, which Virgil has described, with the offerings there presented, and the games there exhibited? The sanctity of Acropolis, where Cecrops was inhumed? The tomb of the father of Adonis, at Paphos, whereon a temple dedicated to Venus, was erected? The grave of Cleomachus, whereon stood a temple dedicated to the worship of Apollo? Finally, I would ask the classical reader, if the words translated *tomb*, and *temple*, are not used as synonymous, by the poets of Greece and Rome? Virgil, who wrote in the days of Augustus Cæsar, speaks of these tumuli, as being as ancient as they were sacred, even in his time.

The conical mounds in Ohio, are either of stones or of earth. The former, in other countries, and in former ages, were intended as monuments, for the purpose of perpetuating the memory of some important event, or as altars whereon to offer sacrifices. The latter were used as cemeteries and as altars, whereon, in later times, temples were erected, as among the people of Greece and Rome.

The tumuli "are of various altitudes and dimensions, some being only four or five feet, and but ten or twelve in diameter, at their base; while others, as we travel to the south, rise to the height of eighty, ninety, and some more than a hundred feet, and cover many acres of ground. They are, generally, when completed, in the form of a cone. Those in the north part of Ohio, are of inferior size, and fewer in number, than those along the river. These mounds are believed to exist, from the Rocky mountains in the west, to the Alleghanies in the east; from the southern shore of lake Erie to the Mexican gulf; and though few and small in the north, are numerous and lofty in the south, yet exhibit proof of a common origin.

On Jonathan creek, in Morgan county, are found some mounds, whose bases are formed of well burnt bricks, between four and five inches square. There are found lying on the bricks, charcoal cinders, and pieces of calcined *human bones*. Above them the mounds were composed of earth, showing, that the dead had been buried in the manner of several of the eastern nations, and the mounds raised afterwards to mark the place of their burial.

One of them is about twenty-four feet in circumference, and the stones yet look black, as if stained with fire and smoke. This circle of stones seems to have been the nucleus on which the mound was formed, as immediately over them is heaped the common earth of the adjacent plain. This mound was originally about ten feet high, and ninety feet in circumference at its base; and has every appearance of being as old as any in the neighborhood, and was, at the first settlement of Marietta, covered with large trees.

A particular account of many curious articles, which go to show the person buried there was a member of civilized society, is given farther on in this work, under the head of "a description of implements found in the tumuli."

The person buried here was about six feet in height, nothing differing from other men in the form of his bones, except the skull, which was uncommonly thick. "The timber growing on this mound, when it was cleared off, was ascertained to be nearly five hundred years old, from counting the concentric circles or grains of the wood on the stumps. On the ground beside them were other trees in a state of decay, that had fallen from old age."

If we were to conjecture, from this sort of data, how great a lapse of years has ensued since the abandonment of this mound, we should pursue the following method. From the time when the country became desolate of its inhabitants, till trees and forests would begin to grow, cannot well be reckoned less than five years. If then they are permitted to grow five hundred years, till as large and as old as some of the trees were on the mound when it was cleared by the people of Marietta, from that time till their natural decay and fall to the earth, and reduction to decayed wood, as was found on the mound, could not be less than three hundred years, in decaying so as to fall, and then fifty years to rot in; this would give eight hundred and fifty-five years for the first growth of timber. From this time we reckon a second crop, which we will suppose, was the one growing when the mound was cleared of its timber; which was, according to Mr. Atwater's statement, " between four and five hundred years;" add this to the age of the first crop, say four hundred and fifty, and we have, in the whole, one thousand three hundred and five years since it was deserted of its builders. Dr. Cutler supposes at least a thousand years. Then it will follow, taking out the time since Marietta was settled, and the mound cleared of its timber, that the country was deserted about five hundred years after the commencement of the Christian era.

About the same time, say from the year 410 to 500 of the Christian era, the greater part of Europe was devastated by the Goths, the Huns, the Heruli, the Vandals, the Swevri, the Alians, and other savage tribes, all from the northern wilds of ancient Russia. By these the western empire of the Romans, comprehending Italy, Germany, France, Spain, and England, was subverted; all literature was obliterated, and the works of the learned, which contained the discoveries and improvements of ages, were annihilated.

And from all we can make out by observing the growth of timber, with that which is decayed, as found on the deserted works of the west, we are inclined to believe, that about the same period of time when Europe was overrun by the northern hordes, that the region now called the United States, where the ancient inhabitants had fixed their abode, was also overrun by northern hordes from toward Bhering's strait, who had, in ages before, got across from Asia, the Tartars, or Scythians, and had multiplied; and as they multiplied, progressed farther and farther southerly till they discovered an inhabited country, populous, and rich, upon whom they fell with all the fury of Attila and his Huns; till after many a long and dreadful war, they were reduced in numbers, and driven from their country far to the south; when the rich fields, vast cities, innumerable towns, with all their works, were reduced to the ancient dominion of nature, as it was when first overgrown immediately after the flood, except their vast pyramids, fortifications, and tumuli, these being of the same nature and durability of the hills and mountains, have stood the shock of war and time—the monuments of powerful nations disappeared.

"In clearing out a spring near some ancient ruins of the west on the bank of the Little Miami, not far from its entrance into the Ohio, was found a copper coin, four feet below the surface of the earth; from the *fac simile* of which it appears, that the characters on the coin are *old Persian* characters.—(*Morse's Universal Geography*, vol. 1, p. 442.)

The era of the Persians, as noticed on the page of history, was from 559, after the flood, till 334, before Christ, and were a people of great strength, of enterprising character, and enlightened in the arts and sciences; and for aught that can be objected, traversed the globe, planted colonies, perhaps even in America, as the coin, which lay so deep beneath the surface of the earth, would seem to justify; which was truly a Persian coin of copper.

At Cincinnati, a mound, only eight feet high, but one hundred and twenty long, by sixty in breadth, has been opened, and is now almost obliterated, by the construction of Main-street, which has furnished many curious discoveries relative to the ancient inhabitants who built it. Of the articles taken from thence, many have been lost; but the most worthy of notice are embraced in the following catalogue:

1st. Pieces of jasper, rock crystal, granite and some other stones, cylindrical at the extremes, and swelled in the middle, with an annular groove near the end. 2d. A circular piece of stone coal, with a large opening in the centre, as if for an axis or axeltree, and a deep groove; the circumference suitable for a hand; it has a number of small perforations, disposed in four equidistant lines, which run from the circumference towards the centre. 3d. A small article of the same shape, with eight lines of perforations, but composed of argilaceous earth, well polished; 4th. A bone ornamented with several lines, supposed to be hieroglyphical. 5th. A sculptured representation of the head and beak of a rapacious bird, resembling the eagle. 6th. A mass of lead ore, lumps of which have been found in other tumuli. 7th. A quantity of isinglass, (mica membranacea,) several plates of which have been found in and about other mounds. 8th. A small oval piece of sheet copper, with two perforations; a large oblong piece of the same metal, with longitudinal grooves and ridges.

These articles are described in the fourth and fifth volumes of the American Philosophical Transactions, by Governeur Sargeant and Judge Turner, and were supposed, by philosopher Barton, to have been designed, in part, for ornament, and, in part, for superstitious ceremonies. In addition to which, the author of the foregoing, (Mr. Atwater,) says, he has since discovered, in the same mound, a number of beads, or sections, of small hollow cylinders, apparently of bone or shell.

Several large marine shells, cut in such a manner as to serve for domestic utensils, and nearly converted into a state of chalk; several copper articles, each consisting of two sets of circular concavo convex plates, the interior of each set connected with the other by a hollow axis, around which had been wound some lint, and the whole encompassed by the *bones* of a man's hand. About the precincts of this town, Cincinnati, human bones have been found " of different sizes; sometimes enclosed in rude stone coffins, but oftener lying blended with the earth; generally surrounded by a portion of ashes and charcoal," as if they had been burnt either alive or dead, as the Hindoos burn both the dead husband and the living wife, on the same funeral pile. (See Ward's *History of the Hindoos*, p. 57;) where he states, " that not less than five thousand of these unfortunate women, it is supposed, are burnt annually." On the shores of the Pacific, to the west, about the mouth of the Columbia river dwell a tribe of Indians, known by the name of Tolkotins, who compel the widows of their tribe to sleep by the dead bodies of their deceased husbands, nine nights in succession immediately after their death, however offensive it may be. When this period is accomplished, the body is laid on a pile of dry wood and burnt to ashes, at which time, the unfortunate wife is forced, by the friends of the deceased, into the fire, while her own relations stand by, and as often as she is pushed on to the fire, these pull her off. This kind of persecution, they continue till the poor wretch is severely blistered, when they desist. The body of her lord is now consumed, when she gathers up the bones from among the ashes of the wood, and carefully envelopes them in the bark of the birch tree, and is doomed to carry them about on her back, a year or two. When the prescribed time is accomplished, the relations on both sides assemble, and having feasted, discharge her from farther penance, when, if she chooses, she can marry again. So far as is known, it appears that this practice, which is purely of Hindoo origin, is peculiar to this tribe.—(*Ross Cox's late travels on the Columbia*, p. 329.)

This practice, as above, is ample evidence, that the Hindoos once filled with their idolatry, and cruel ceremonies, the regions of the west, who came hither in vessels, in the early ages, as we shall show in another part of this volume.

The ancient Jews practised the same thing; (*See Amos*, vi. 10.) "And a man's uncle shall take him up, and he that *burneth* him, to bring out the bones out of the house." The ancient Edomites burnt the dead bodies of their captured enemies. (*See Amos*, ii. 1:) " He," that is Edom, "burned the *bones* of the king of Edom into lime." The same may have been practised in America.

Besides these relics found at Marietta, others equally interesting, have been procured from a mound on the Little Muskingum, about four miles from Marietta. There are some pieces of copper which appear to have been the front part of a *helmet*. It was originally about *eight* inches long and *four* broad, and has marks of having been attached to *leather;* it is much decayed, and is now quite a thin plate. The helmet was worn by the ancients as a defence against the blows of the sword, aimed at the head. The Greeks, the Romans, with many other nations of antiquity, made use of this majestic, beautiful, warlike covering of the head. But how came this part of the ancient armor in America? This is the mystery, and cannot be solved, only on the principle, that we believe the wearers lived in those ages coeval with the martial exploits of the Medes, Persians, Carthaginians, Egyptians, Greeks, Romans and of the Celtic nations of Europe. In the same mound on the Muskingum, was found a copper ornament; this was on the forehead of a human skeleton, no part of which retained its form, except that part of the forehead where the copper ornament lay, and had been preserved no doubt by the salts of that mineral. In Virginia, near Blacksburgh, eighty miles from Marietta, there was found the half of a *steel bow*, which, when entire would measure five or six feet; the other part was corroded or broken. The father of the lad who found the bow, was a blacksmith, and worked up this curious article with as little remorse as he would an old gun barrel. In the 18th Psalm, 34th verse, mention is made by David, king of Israel, of the steel bow, which must have been a powerful instrument of death, of the kind, and probably well known to the Jews, as superior to the wooden bow. This kind of warlike *artillery*, the bow and arrow, has been used by all nations, and in all ages of time. The time of king David was about one thousand one hundred years before Christ; when he says, a bow of *steel* was broken by his own arm. This must have been done in some of his fights with the enemies of Saul, as it is not very probable that he fought personally after he came to the kingdom; and from his earnestness in the fight, drew the string of his bow too far, so that the instrument could not bear it, consequently it snapped asunder; which circumstance he has celebrated in the praises of the God of Israel, as an evidence of the aid and strength derived from Heaven in the heat of battle. But Dr. Clarke supposes, steel is out of the question, as he thinks the art of making steel was unknown at that time, and believes the bow alluded to, which was broken by David, was a *brass* one, but it is unknown to the writer of this work, whether brass will *spring* at all so as to throw an arrow with an effect. But why may not steel have been known, and the art of producing it from iron, in the time of David, as well as the art of making brass, which is equally hidden, and more so than that of steel? Tubal Cain was a worker in *brass* and *iron*, before the flood; and we should suppose the way to procure *steel* from iron, would as soon have been discovered by the antediluvian blacksmiths, as a knowledge how to make brass from a union of copper and zinc.

The discovery of this steel bow, in the west, is exceedingly curious, and would seem to justify the belief, that it came from the old world, as an instrument of warfare in the hands of some of the Asiatic, African, or *European* nations, possibly Danes, as the present Indian nations were found destitute of every kind of bow and arrow, except that of wood.

"In Ross county, near Chilicothe, a few years since, was found, in the hand of a skeleton, which lay buried in a small mound, an ornament of pure gold; this curiosity, it is said, is now in the Museum at Philadelphia."—(*Atwater.*) The tumuli, in what is called the Sciota country, are both numerous and interesting. But south of Lake Erie, until we arrive at Worthington, nine miles north of Columbus, they are few in number, and of comparatively small magnitude. Near Columbus, the seat of government of Ohio, were several mounds, one of which stood on an eminence in the principal street, which has been entirely removed, and converted into bricks. It contained human bones, some few articles, among which was an *owl* carved in stone, a rude but very exact representation. The *owl*, among the Romans, was the emblem of wisdom, and it is not impossible but the ancients of the west, may have carved it in the stone for the same reason; who may have been, in part, Romans, or nations derived from them, or nations acquainted with their manners, their gods, and their sculpture, as we suppose the Danes were. "In another part of the town of Columbus, was a tumulus of clay, which was also manufactured into bricks. In this were many human bones; but they lay in piles, and in confusion," which would seem to elicit the belief, that these were the bones of an enemy, or they would have been laid in their accustomed order. Or they may have been the bones of the conquered, thrown together in a confused manner, and buried beneath this mound.

As we still descend the Sciota, through a most fertile region of country, mounds and other ancient works, frequently appear, until we arrive at Circleville. Near the centre of the circular fort at Circleville, was a tumulus of earth, about ten feet high, and several rods in diameter at its base. On its eastern side, and extending six rods from it, was a semicircular pavement, composed of pebbles such as are now found in the bed of Sciota river, from whence they appear to have been taken. The summit of this tumulus was nearly ninety feet in circumference, with a raised way to it, leading from the east, like a modern turnpike. The summit was level. The outline of the semicircular pavement, and the wall, are still discernible. Mr. Atwater was present when this mound was removed, and carefully examined the contents it developed. They were as follows:—1. Two skeletons, lying on what had been the original surface of the earth. 2. A great quantity of arrow heads, some of which were so large as to induce a belief that they were used for spear heads. 3. The handle, either of a small sword, or a large knife, made of an elk's horn; around the end where the blade had been inserted, was a ferule of silver, which, though black, was not much injured by time; though the handle showed the hole where the blade had been inserted, yet no iron was found, but an oxyde or rust remained, of similar shape and size. The swords of the ancient nations of the old world, it is known, were very short. 4. Charcoal, and wood ashes, on which these articles lay, were surrounded by several bricks, very well burnt. The skeleton appeared to have been burnt in a large and very hot fire, which had almost consumed the bones of the deceased. This skeleton was deposited a little to the south of the centre of the tumulus; and about twenty feet to the north of it was another, with which was found a large mirror, about three feet in length, one foot and a half in width, and one inch and a half in thickness; this was of isinglass, (mica membranacea.)

On this mirror was a plate of iron, which had become an oxyde; but before it was disturbed by the spade, resembled a plate of *cast iron*. The mirror answered the purpose very well for which it was intended. This skeleton had also been burned like the former, and lay on charcoal and a considerable quantity of wood ashes; a part of the mirror is in the possession of Mr. Atwater, as also a piece of brick, taken from the spot at the time. The knife, or sword handle, was sent to Peale's museum, Philadelphia. To the southwest of this tumulus, about forty rods from it, is another, more than ninety feet in height. It stands on a large hill, which appears to be artificial. This must have been the common cemetry, as it contains an immense number of human skeletons, of all sizes and ages. These skeletons are laid horizontally, with their heads generally towards the centre, and the feet towards the outside of the tumulus. In it have been found, besides these skeletons, stone axes and stone knives, and several ornaments, with holes through them, by means of which, with a cord passing through these perforations, they could be worn by their owners, round the neck.

Sir Robert Ker Porter says, that in Persia thousands of such stones are found belonging to the early ages of that people, and that they were considered by the Persians to be endowed with supernatural qualities, and were, therefore, made by the people to defend them from evil spirits; they are found in great abundance among the Hindoos even now. On the south side of this tumulus, and not far from it, was a semicircular fosse, or ditch, six feet deep; which, when examined at the bottom, was found to contain a great quantity of human bones, which, it is believed, were the remains of those who had been slain in some great and destructive battle; because they belonged to persons invariably who had attained their full size; while those found in the mound adjoining, were of all sizes, great and small, but laid in good order, while those in the ditch were in the utmost confusion; and were, no doubt, the conquered invaders, buried thus ingloriously, where they had intrenched themselves, and fell in the struggle. The mirror was a monstrous piece of isinglass, a lucid mineral, larger than we recollect to have ever heard of before, and used among the rich of the ancients, for lights and mirrors. A mirror of any kind, in which men may he enabled to contemplate their own form, is evidence of a considerable degree of advancement in the arts, if not even of luxury itself.

The Rev. Robert G. Wilson, D. D., of Chilicothe, furnished the Antiquarian Society, with information concerning the mound, which once stood near the centre of that town. He took pains to write down its contents at the time of its demolition. Its perpendicular height was about fifteen feet, and the circumference of its base about one hundred and eighty feet, composed of sand. It was not till this pile of earth had been removed, that the original design of its builders could be discovered. On a common level with the surrounding earth, at the very bottom of this mound, they had devoted about twenty feet square; this was found to have been covered at first with bark, on which lay, in the centre, a human skeleton, overspread with a mat, manufactured from weeds or bark, but greatly decayed. On the breast of this person lay what had been a piece of copper in the form of a *cross*, which had become verdigris; on the breast also lay a stone ornament, three inches in length, and two and a half in width, with two perforations, one near each end, through which passed a string, by means of which it was suspended from the wearer's neck. On this string, which appeared to have been made of the sinews of some animal, which had been cured or tanned, but were very much injured by time, was strung a great many *beads*, made of *ivory*, or bone, he could not tell which. With these facts before us, we are left to conjecture at what time this individual lived, what were his heroic deeds in the field of battle; his wisdom, his virtues, his eloquence in the councils of his nation; for his cotemporaries have testified in a manner not to be mistaken, that among them he was held in honorable and grateful remembrance, by the mound which was raised over him at his decease. The cross on the breast of this skeleton, excites the most surprise, as that the cross is the emblem of the Christian religion. It is true, a knowledge of this badge of Christianity, may have been disseminated from Jerusalem, even as far east as China; as we know it was at a very early period, made known in many countries of Europe, Africa, and Asia; especially, at the era when the Roman emperor Constantine, in the year 331, ordered all the heathen temples to be destroyed, for the sake of Christianity, throughout his vast dominion. The Gnostic heresy of the *first* centuries of the Christian era, which spread itself into more than fifty sects, wandered into all the countries of the known world; in Africa, Asia, and Europe, are still found gems, coins and various precious stones, having engravings upon them, the emblems of their deities, their genii and their mystical characters, mingled with allusions, also, to the Christian religion. This cross, therefore, may it not have been left on the bosom of this skeleton by some officiating priest of the Gnostics, even here in America? (For an account of the Gnostics, see the *Amulet*, 1832, by Marmion Savage, A. B., p. 282.)

The reader may recollect, we have elicited an argument, from the age of the timber, or forest trees, growing on the mound, at Marietta, proposing to show the probable era when the country became depopulated; and come to the conclusion, that at least, about thirteen hundred years have passed away since that catastrophe.

This would give about five hundred years from Christ till the depopulation of the ancient western country; so that, during the lapse of those five centuries, a knowledge of what had been propagated at Jerusalem about Christ, may have been, easily enough by missionaries, travelling philosophers of the Romans, Greeks, or of other nations, carried as well to China, as to other distant countries, as we know was the fact. The string of beads, and the stone on his breast, which we take the liberty of calling the *Shalgramu* stone, or the stone in which the Hindoos suppose the god Vishnoo resides; together with the copper cross on his breast, and beads on his neck, are circumstances, which strongly argue that a mixture of *Gnosticism, Brahminism,* and *Christianity* were embraced by this individual. To prove that the wearing of beads around the neck, or on the arm, for the purposes of devotion, is a Hindoo custom, we refer to Ward's late history of those nations, who was a Baptist missionary, among that people, and died in that country. This author says, page 40, that *Brumha,* the grandfather of the gods, holds in his hand, a string of beads, as an evidence of his devotion or goodness. *Ungee,* the regent of fire, is represented with a bead roll in his hand, to show that he is merciful or propitious to those who call upon him.—*Page* 45.

The Hindoo mendicants, or *saints,* as they suppose themselves, have invariably, a string of beads, made of bone, teeth of animals, ivory, stones, or the seeds of plants, or of something, hanging about their necks, or on their arms, which they recount, calling over and over, without end, the name of the god, as evidence of devotion to him.—*Page* 422.

The devotions of the ascetic disciples among the Hindoos, consists in repeating incessantly the name of their god, using, at the same time, the bead roll, or rosary, as the catholics do.—*Page* 427.

"Strings of beads were used for this purpose, from remotest antiquity, in all eastern Asia."—(*Humboldt,* p. 204.)

This author further says, "*the rosarie,*" which is a string of beads, " have been in use in Thibet and China, from time immemorial; and that the custom passed from the east, viz: China, to the Christians in the west, viz: Europe;" and are found among the catholics; no other sect of Christians, that we know of, have borrowed any trappings from the pagans, to aid their devotions, but this. The stone found on his breast, as before remarked, we assume to call the Shalgramu stone. See also, Ward's account of this stone, page 41 and 44, as follows:—A stone called the Shalgramu is a form of the god Vishnoo, and is in another case, the representative of the god Saoryu, or the sun.—*Page* 52.

The Shalgramu, or Lingu, is a black stone, found in a part of the Gundeekee river. They are mostly perforated, in one or more places, by worms, while at the bottom of the river; but the Hindoos believe the god Vishnoo, in the shape of a reptile, resides in this stone, and caused the holes. With this belief, how very natural it would be to wear on the breast, either in view or concealed, this stone, as an amulet, or charm, as found on the breast of this skeleton, in the union with the cross. We are inclined to believe, that the Roman catholic religion, borrowed, at a very early period, after their peculiar formation and corruption, subsequent to the time of Constantine, the notion of the rosary, or bead roll, which they recount while saying prayers, from the Hindoos; and that from Christian missionaries, the Hindoo Brahmins borrowed the idea of the cross, which they might also wear, together with Lingu stone, as an amulet or charm. For we see on the breast of this person, both the emblem of Christianity, and of the Hindoos' superstition, on which account, we are of the opinion, that the ministers of the Brahmin religion, lie buried beneath many of the western mounds.

Mr. Ward informs us, page 272, that near the town of Dravina, in Hondostan-hu, are shown to this day, or at the time he lived in India, four small elevations, or mounds, from the top of which, the great ascetic philosopher, Shunkuracharyu, used to teach and harangue the people and his disciples. From this circumstance, we catch a glimpse of the *oratorial* use of the mounds in the east; and why not the same use be derived from them to the ancient people of the west; and more especially so, if they may be believed to have, in any measure, derived themselves from any nations of the Chinese world.

Great Works of the Ancient Nations on the North Fork of Paint Creek.

On the north branch of this creek, five miles from Chilicothe, are works so immense, that although we have given the reader several accounts of this kind, yet we cannot well pass over these. They are situated on an elevated piece of land, called the second bottom. The first bottom, or flat, extends from Paint creek, till it is met by a bank of twenty-five feet in height, which runs in a straight line, and parallel with the stream. One hundred rods from the top of this first bank, is another bank, of thirty feet in height; the wall of the works runs up this bank, and twenty rods beyond it. The whole land enclosed, is six hundred and twenty rods in circumference, and contains one hundred and twenty-six acres of land. This second bank runs also parallel with the creek, and with the first. On this beautiful elevation, is situated this immense work, containing within it, *seventeen mounds* of different sizes. Three hundred and eight rods of this fort are encompassed with a wall twelve feet high, a dicth twenty feet wide, and the wall the same at its base. Two hundred and forty rods, running along on the top of the first bank, is the rest of the wall; but is without a ditch; this is next to the river or creek, between which and the water, is the first bottom or flat. Within this great enclosure, is a circular work of one hundred rods in circumference, with a wall and ditch surrounding it, of the same height of the other wall. Within this great circle, are six mounds, of the circular form; these are full of human bones; the rest of the mounds, eleven in number, are for some other purpose. There are seven gateways, of about five rods in width each. "The immense labor, and numerous cemeteries filled with human bones, denote a vast population, near this spot, in ancient times."—(*Atwater.*)

"Tumuli are very common on the river Ohio, from its utmost sources to its mouth, although on the Monongahela, they are few, and comparatively small, but increase in number and size, as we descend towards the mouth of that stream at Pittsburgh, where the Ohio begins; after this they are still more numerous and of greater dimensions, till we arrive at Grave creek, below Wheeling. At this place, situated between two creeks, which run into the Ohio, a little way from the river, is one of the most extraordinary and august monuments of antiquity, of the mound description. Its circumference at its base, is fifty-six rods, its perpendicular height ninety feet, its top seven rods and eight feet in circumference. The centre at the summit, appears to have sunk several feet, so as to form a kind of amphitheatre. The rim enclosing this concavity is seven or eight feet in thickness; on the south side, in the edge of this rim, stands a large beech tree, the bark of which is marked with the initials of a great number of visitants."

This lofty and venerable tumulus has been so far opened as to ascertain that it contains many thousands of human skeletons, but no farther; the proprietor will not suffer its demolition, in the least degree, for which he is highly praiseworthy.

Following the river Ohio downwards, the mounds appear on both sides, erected uniformly on the highest alluvials along that stream, increasing in numbers all the way to the Mississippi, on which river they assume the largest size. Not having surveyed them, (says Mr. Atwater,) we shall use the description of Mr. Breckenridge, who travelled much in the west, and among the Indians, and devoted much attention to the subject of these astonishing western antiquities.

These tumuli, (says Mr. Breckenridge,) as well as the fortifications, are to be found at the junction of all the rivers along the Mississippi, in the most eligible positions for towns, and in the most extensive bodies of fertile land. Their number exceeds, perhaps, three thousand; the *smallest*, not less than twenty feet in height, and three hundred in circumference at the base. Their great number, and their amazing size, may be regarded as furnishing, with other circumstances, evidences of their great antiquity.

I have been sometimes induced to think, that at the period when these were constructed, there was a population as numerous as that which once animated the borders of the Nile, or of the Euphrates. The most numerous, as well as the most considerable of these remains, are found precisely in those parts of the country where the traces of a numerous population might be looked for, namely, from the mouth of the Ohio, on the east side of the river, to the Illinois, and on the west side, from the St. Francis to the Missouri. I am perfectly satisfied that *cities*, similar to those of ancient Mexico, of several hundred thousand souls, have existed in this western country.

From this view we are *compelled* to look upon those nations as agriculturists, or they could not have subsisted; neither wild game nor fish could possibly support so great a population. If agriculturists, then it must follow, of necessity, that many modes of building, as with stone, timber, earth or clay, were practised and known, as well as methods of clearing the earth of heavy timber. And if they had not a knowledge of metals, we cannot well conceive how they could have removed the forests for the purposes of husbandry, and space for building. But if we suppose they did not build houses with wood, stone and brick, but lived in tents or some fragile hut, yet the use of metals cannot be dispensed with, on account of the forests to be removed for agricultural purposes. Baron Humboldt informs us, in his *Researches in South America*, that when he crossed the Cordillera mountains, by the way of Panama and Assuay, and viewed the enormous masses of stone cut from the porphyry quarries of Pullal, which was employed in constructing the ancient highroads of the Incas, that he began to doubt whether the Peruvians were not acquainted with *other* tools than hatchets made of flint and stone; and that grinding one stone on another to make them smooth and level, was not the *only* method they had employed in this operation. On which account he adopted a new opinion, contrary to those generally received. He conjectured that they must have had tools made of copper, hardened with *tin*, such as it is known the early nations of Asia made use of. This conjecture was fully sustained by the discovery of an ancient Peruvian mining chisel, in a silver mine at Vilcabamba, which had been worked in the time of the Incas. This instrument of copper was four inches long, and three-fourths of an inch wide; which he carried with him to Europe, where he had it analyzed, and found it to contain ninety-four parts of copper and six of tin. He says, that this keen copper of the Peruvians is almost identically the same with that of the ancient *Gallic axe*, which cut wood nearly as well as if made of iron and steel.

Every where on the old continent, at the beginning of the civilization of nations, the use of copper, mixed with tin, prevailed over that of iron, even in places where the latter had been for a long time known. Antonio de Herera, in the tenth book of his *History of the West Indies*, says expressly that the inhabitants of the maritime coast of Zocatallan, in America, prepared two sorts of copper, of which one was *hard* and cutting, and the other malleable. The hard copper was to make hatchets, weapons and instruments of agriculture with, and that it was tempered with tin.—(*Humboldt*, vol. 1, pp. 260—268.

Among a great variety of the gods of the people of the Tonga islands, in the South Pacific ocean, is found one god named *To-gi Ocunmeu*, which is, literally, the iron axe. From which circumstance we imagine the people of those islands, sometimes called the *Friendly Islands*, were, at some period before their having been discovered by Captain Cook, acquainted with the use of *iron*, and consequently in a more civilized condition. Because men, in those early times, were apt to deify almost every thing, but especially those things the most useful?

Were the people of Christendom to lose their knowledge of the true God, and to fall back into nature's ignorance, is there an article within the compass of the arts which would from its usefulness have a higher claim to deification than the metal called *iron*.

That group of islands belongs to the immense range shooting out from New-Holland, in south latitude about 20 deg. and once perhaps were united to China, forming a part of the continent. But, however this may be, the *first* inhabitants of those islands were derived from China, and carried with them a knowledge of the arts; among which was that of the use of iron, in the form of the axe, which, it appears, had become deified from its usefulness. The reason of the loss of this knowledge, must have been the separation of their country from the continent by convulsions, from age to age; which not only altered the shape and condition of the land, but threw the inhabitants into confusion, separating them far from each other, the sea running between, so that they became reduced to savagism, as they were found by the first Christian nations.

Traits of ancient Cities on the Mississippi.

NEARLY opposite St. Louis, there are the traces of two ancient cities, in the distance of a few miles, situated on the Cohokia creek, which empties into the Mississippi but a short distance below that place. Here is situated one of those pyramids, which is one hundred and fifty rods in circumference at its base, (nearly half a mile,) and one hundred feet high. At St. Louis is one with two stages or landing places, as the architectural phrase is. There is another with three stages, at the mouth of the Missouri, a few miles above St. Louis. With respect to the stages, or landing places of these pyramids, we are reminded of the tower once standing in old Babylon, which had eight stages from its base to the summit, making it six hundred feet high. At the mouth of the Cahokia creek, a short distance below St. Louis, are two groups of those mounds, of smaller size, but we are not informed of their exact number. At Bayeau Manchac and Baton Rouge, are several mounds, one of which is composed chiefly of shells, which the inhabitants burn into lime. There is a mound on Black river, which has two stages or stories; this is surrounded with a group of lesser ones, as well as those at Bayeau Manchac, and Baton Rouge. There is one of those pyramids near Washington, in the State of Mississippi, which is one hundred and forty-six feet high; which is little short of nine rods perpendicular elevation, and fifty-six rods in circumference. Mr. Breckenridge is of the opinion that the largest city belonging to this people, the authors of the mounds and other works, was situated on the plains between St. Francis and the Arkansas. There is no doubt but in the neighborhood of St. Louis must have been cities or large towns of these ancient people; as the number and size of the mounds above recounted would most certainly justify.

Fifteen miles in a southwesterly direction from the town of St. Louis, on the Merrimack river, was discovered, by a Mr. Long, on lands which he had purchased there, several mounds of the ordinary size, as found in the valley of the Mississippi, all of which go to establish that this country, lying between the Missouri and the Mississippi rivers, below St. Louis, and between the junction of the Illinois and the Mississippi above, with the whole region about the union of those rivers with each other,—which are all not far from St. Louis—was once the seat of empire, equal, if not surpassing, the population and the arts as once they flourished on the plains of Shinar, the seat of Chaldean power, and on the banks of the Euphrates.

It was on the lands of this gentleman, Mr. Long, that the discovery of a burying-ground, containing a vast number of small tumuli, or graves, took place. On opening the graves, there were found deposited in stone coffins, composed of stone slabs, six in number, forming the bottom, sides and top, with end pieces, the skeletons of a race of human beings, apparently of but from three to four feet in height. This discovery excited much surprise, and called forth, from several pens, the conjectures of able men, who published a variety of opinions respecting them. Some imagined them to be the relics of a race of pigmy inhabitants who had become extinct. Others on account of the size of the teeth, which denoted full grown and adult persons, conjectured them to be the skeletons of a race of baboons or monkeys, from the shortness of their stature. From this opinion arose another conjecture, that they had been the objects of worship to the ancient nations, as they had been sometimes among the earlier Egyptians.

The bones of these subjects were entirely destroyed, and reduced to ashes of a white chalky consistency, except the teeth, which were perfect, being made imperishable from their enamel. Many of these graves were opened, and the inmates found not to exceed three and four feet. At length one was opened, and the skeleton it contained appeared to be of the full size of a large man, except its length; however, this, on close inspection, was found to have had its legs disjointed at the knees, and placed along side the thigh bones, which at once, in the eyes of some, accounted for the statures of the whole.

Such a custom is, indeed, singular; and among all the discoveries of those ancient traits, nothing to compare with this has come to light. Respecting this instance of short skeletons, it has been also urged, that as certain tribes of the common Indians, now inhabiting the upper shores of the Missouri, place their dead on scaffolds and in baskets, fastened to the limbs of trees, till their flesh becomes separated from the bones, that the authors of these short graves did the same. And that when by this process, they had become fair and white, they deposited them in small coffins, as discovered on the farm of Mr. Long. But although this is doubtless true respecting the Missouri Indians, yet we have no account of short graves having been found among others. But as we are unable to cast light on this discovery, we shall leave it as we found it—a great curiosity.

Tradition of the Mexican Natives respecting their Migration from the North.

In corroboration of Mr. Atwater's opinion, with respect to the gradual remove of the ancient people of the west toward Mexico, we subjoin what we have gathered from the Researches of Baron Humboldt, on that point. See Helen Maria William's translation of Humboldt's Researches in South America, vol. 2, p. 67. From which it appears the people inhabiting the vale of Mexico, at the time the Spaniards overrun that country, were called Aztecks, or Aztekas; and were, as the Spanish history informs us, usurpers, having come from the north, from a country which they called *Aztalan.*

This country of Aztalan, Baron Humboldt says, " we must look for at least north of the 42d degree of latitude." He comes to this conclusion from an examination of the Mexican or Azteca manuscripts, which were made of a certain kind of leaves, and of skins prepared; on which, an account in painted hieroglyphics or pictures, was given of their migration from Aztalan to Mexico, and how long they halted at certain places, which, in the aggregate, amounts to " four hundred and sixteen years."

The following names of places appear on their account of their journeyings, at which places they made less or more delay, and built towns, forts, tumuli, &c.

1st. A place of *Humiliation*, and a place of *Grottoes*. It would seem at this place they were much afflicted and humbled; but in what manner is not related; and also at this place, from the term *grottoes*, that it was a place of caverns and dens, probably where they at first hid, and dwelt till they built a town and cleared the ground. Here they built the places which they called Tocalco and Oztatan.

2d Journey; they stopped at a place of *fruit trees;* probably meaning, as it was farther south, a place where nature was abundant in nuts, grapes, and wild fruit trees. Here they built a mound or tumuli, and, in their language, it is called a Teocali.

3d Journey; when they stopped at a place of *herbs*, with *broad leaves;* probably meaning a place where many succulent plants grew, denoting a good soil; which invited them to pitch their tents here.

4th Journey; when they came to a place of *human bones;* where they, either during their stay had battles with each other, or with some enemy, or they may have found them already there, the relics of other nations before them; for, according to Humboldt, this migration of the Aztecas, took place A. D. 778; so that other nations certainly had preceded them, also from the north.

5th Journey; they came to a place of *Eagles.*

6th Journey; to a place of *precious stones,* and *minerals.*

7th Journey; to a place of *spinning,* where they manufactured clothing of cotton, barks, or of something proper for clothing of some sort, and mats of rushes and feathers.

8th Journey; they came to another place of eagles, called the Eagle mountain, or in their own language, *Quauktli Tepec: Tepec,* says Humboldt, in the Turkish language, is the word for mountain; which two words are so near alike, *tepec* and *tepe,* that it would seem almost an Arab word, or a word used by the Turks.

9th Journey; when they came to a place of walls, and the seven grottoes; which shows the place had been inhabited before, and these seven grottoes were either caves in the earth, or were made in the side of some mountain, by those who had preceded them.

10th Journey; when they came to a place of thistles, sand and vultures.

11th Journey; when they came to a place of *Obsidian Mirrors,* which is much the same with that of isinglass, scientifically called mica membranacea. This mineral substance is frequently found in the tumuli of the west, and is called, by the Mexicans, the *shining* god. The obsidian stone, however, needs polishing, before it will answer as a mirror.

12th Journey; came to a place of water, probably some lake, or beautiful fountains, which invited their residence there; on the account not only of the water, but for fishing and game.

13th Journey; they came to the place of the *Divine Monkey,* called in their own language, *Teozomoco.* Here, it would seem, they set up the worship of the monkey, or baboon, as the ancient Egyptians are known to have done. This animal is found in Mexico or New Spain, according to Humboldt.

14th Journey; when they came to a high mountain, probably with table lands on it; which they called *Chopaltepec,* or mountain of locusts. A place, says Baron Humboldt, celebrated for the magnificent view from the top of this hill; which, it appears, is in the Mexican country, and probably not far from the vale of Mexico; where they finally and permanently rested.

15th Journney; when they came to the vale of Mexico; having here met with the prodigy, or fulfilment of the prophecy, or oracle, which at their outset from the country of Aztalan, Huehuetlapallan, and Amaquemecan; which was (see Humboldt, vol 2, p. 185,) that the migrations of the Aztecks should not terminate till the chiefs of the nation should meet with an *eagle* perched on a *cactus tree* or *prickly pear;* at such a place they might found a city. This was, as their bull-hide books inform us, in the vale of Mexico.

We have related this account of the Azteca migration from the country of Aztalan, Huehuetlapallan, and Amaquemecan, from the regions of north latitude 42 degrees, merely to show that the country, provinces, or districts, so named in their books, must have been the country of Ohio, Mississppi and Illinois, with the whole region thereabout; for these are not far from the very latitude named by Humboldt as the region of Aztalan, &c.

The western country is *now* distinguished, by the general name of the " lake country," and why, because it is a countty of lakes; and for the same reason, it was called by the Mexican, Azteca, Indians, *Aztalan*, because in their language, ATL is water, from which Aztalan is doubtless a derivitive as well also as their own name as a nation, or title, which was *Astecas*, or people of the Lakes.

This account, derived from the Mexicans since their reduction by the Spaniards, gathered from the researches of learned travellers, who have, for the very purpose of learning the origin of the people of this country, penetrated not only into the forest retreats in the woods of Mexico, but into the mysteries of their hard language, their theology, philosphy and astronomy. This account of their migration, as related above, is corroborated by the tradition of the Wyandot Indians.

We come to a knowledge of this tradition, by the means of a Mr. William Walker, some time Indian agent for our government; who, it seems, from a pamphlet published, 1823, by Frederick Falley, of Sandusky, giving Mr. Walker's account, that a great many hundred years ago the ancient inhabitants of America, who were the authors of the great works of the west, were driven away from their country and possessions, by barbarous and savage hordes of warriors, who came from the north and northeast; before whose power and skill in war, they were compelled to flee, and went to the south.

After having been there many hundred years, a runner came

back into the same country, from whence the ancient people had been driven, which we suppose is the very country of Aztalan, or the region of the western states; bringing the intelligence, that a dreadful *beast* had landed on their coast along the sea, which was spreading among them havoc and death, by means of fire and thunder; and that it would no doubt, travel all over the country, for the same purpose of destruction. This beast whose voice was like thunder, and whose power to kill was like fire, we have no doubt, represents the cannon and small arms of the Spaniards, when they first commenced the murder of the people of South America.

Supposed uses of the Ancient Roads connected with the Mounds.

Ancient roads, or highways, which in many parts of the west, are found walled in on both sides for many miles, where the forest trees are growing as abundant, and as large, and aged, as in any part of the surrounding woods. We have already mentioned several roads which have always been found connected with some great works; as at Piketon, Portsmouth, Newark, Licking county, and at the works on the Little Miami river. These roads, where they have been traced, are found to communicate with some mound, or mountain, which had been shaped by art to suit the purposes of those who originated these stupendous works. The circumstance of their being walled in by banks of earth, leaving from one to four and six rods space between, has excited much inquiry, as to the reason and purposes of their construction. But may not this grand characteristic of the people of the west, in road building, be illustrated by comparing a practice of the Mexicans with this fact. We will show the practice, and then draw the conclusion.

" The Mexicans believed, according to a very ancient tradition, that the end of the world would take place at the termination of every cycle of fifty-two years; that the sun would no more appear on the horizon, and that mankind would be devoured by evil genii of hideous appearance, known under the name of Tzitzimimes,

On the last day of this great cycle of time, of fifty-two years, the sacred fires were extinguished in all their temples, and dwellings, and every where, all the people devoting themselves to prayer, no person daring to light a fire at the approach of the night; the vessels of clay were broken, garments torn, and whatever was most precious was destroyed, because every thing appeared useless at the tremendous moment of the last day. Amidst this frantic superstition, pregnant women became the objects of peculiar horror to the men; they caused their faces to be hidden with masks made with paper of the agave; they were even imprisoned in the store houses of maize or corn, from a persuasion, that if the catastrophe took place, the women transformed into tigers, would make common cause with the evil genii, and avenge themselves of the injustice of the men. As soon as it was dark, the grand procession, called the festival of the new fire, commenced. The priests took the dresses of the gods, and followed by an immense crowd of people, went in solemn train to the mountain of Huzachthcatl, which was two leagues or six miles from Mexico. This lugubrious march was called the march of the gods; which was supposed to be their final departure from their city, and possibly never to return; in which event, the end of the world was come. When the procession had reached the summit of the mountain, it waited till the moment when the Pleiades, or the seven stars, ascended the middle of the sky, to begin the horrible sacrifice of a human victim, stretched on the stone of sacrifice, having a wooden disk on the breast, which the priest inflames by friction. The corpse, after having received a wound in the breast, which extinguished life, while he was held on the fatal stone, was laid on the ground; and the instrument made use of to produce fire by friction, was placed on the wound, which had been made with a knife of obsidian stone. When the bits of wood, by the rapid motion of the cylinder, or machine made use of for that purpose, had taken fire, an enormous pile, previously prepared to receive the body of the unfortunate victim, was kindled, the flames of which, ascending high into the air, were seen at a great distance; when the vast populace of the city of Mexico, and surrounding country, filled the air with joyful shouts and acclamations. All such as were not able to join in the procession, were stationed on the terraces of houses, and on the tops of teocallis, or mounds, and tumulis, with their eyes fixed on the spot where the flame was to appear: which, as soon as it was perceived, was a token of the benevolence of the gods, and of the preservation of mankind during another cycle of fifty-two years. Messengers posted at proper distances from each other, holding branches of wood, of a very resinous pine, carried the new fire from village to village to the distance of many leagues; and deposited it anew in every temple, from whence it was distributed to all private dwellings. When the sun appeared on the horizon, the shouting was redoubled, the procession went back from the mountain to the city, and they thought they could see their gods also returning to their sanctuaries. The women were then released from their prisons, every one put on a new dress, the temples were whitewashed, their household furniture renewed, their plate, and whatever was necessary for domestic use. "This secular festival, this apprehension of the sun being extinguished at the epoch of the winter solstice, seems to present a new instance of analogy between the Mexicans and the inhabitants of Egypt. When the Egyptians saw the sun descend from the *Crab* towards *Capricorn*, and the days gradually grow shorter, they were accustomed to sorrow, from the apprehension that the sun was going to abandon the earth, but when the orb began to return, and the duration of the days grew longer, they robed themselves in white garments, and crowned themselves with flowers." (*Humboldt*, p. 380, 384.)

This Mexican usage may have been practised by the people of the west, as the roads would seem to justify, leading as they do, either to some mountain prepared by art, or at some mound: and as these processions took place in the night, so that the Pleiades, or seven stars, might be seen, it was necessary that the roads should be walled as a defence against an enemy, who might take advantage under cover of the night. After having examined these accounts of the ancient works of the west, it is natural to ask, who their authors were: this can be answered only by comparison and conjecture, more or less upheld, as circumstances, features, manners, and customs of the nations, many resemble each other. "If we look into the Bible, we shall there learn, that mankind, soon after the deluge, undertook to raise a tower, high as heaven, designed to keep them together. But in this attempt they were disappointed, and themselves dispersed throughout the world. Did they forget to raise afterwards similar monuments and places of worship? They *did not*, and to use the words of an inspired writer, "high places," of various altitudes and dimensions, were raised on every high hill throughout the land of Palestine, and all the east, among the pagan nations. Some of these "high places" belonged to single families; some to mighty chieftains, a petty tribe, a city, or a whole nation. At those "high places," belonging to great nations, great national affairs were transacted. Here they crowned and deposed their kings; here they concluded peace, and declared war, and worshipped their gods. The Jews, on many great occasions, assembled at Gilgal; which word signifies " an *heap*." Shiloh, where the Jews frequently assembled to transact great national affairs, and perform acts of devotion, was on the top of a high hill. When this was forsaken, the loftier hill of Zion was selected in its stead; upon Sinai's awful summit the law of God was promulgated. Solomon's temple was situated upon a high hill, by Divine appointment. Samaria, a place celebrated, for the worship of idols, was built upon a high hill of Shemer, by Omri, one of the kings of Israel, who was buried there. How many hundreds of mounds in this country are situated on the highest hills, surrounded by the most fertile soils? Traverse the counties of Licking, Franklin, Pickaway, and Ross; examine the loftiest mounds, and compare them with those described in Palestine, and a conviction will remain, that as in the earliest ages, men preferred the summit of the highest mountains, as a love of the same, as a memorial of ancestry, would influence posterity to the like custom." (*Atwater.*)

But the most extraordinary mound we have heard of, is mentioned by Schoolcraft, *Travels in the West*. It is called *Mount Joliet*, and is situated on the river Des Plains, one of the head water rivers of the Illinois. Its situation is such as to give to its size its fullest effect, being on a level country with no hill in sight to form a contrast. Its height is sixty feet, nearly four rods perpendicular, its length eighty-four rods, its width fourteen, and is one hundred and ninety-six rods in circumference on its top, but considerably larger, measuring round the base. It has been remarked by Dr. Beck, that this is probably the largest mound within the limits of the United States. This mound is built on the horizontal lime stone stratum of the secondary formation, and is fronted by the beautiful lake Joliet, which is but fifteen miles long, furnishing the most "noble and picturesque spot in all America."—(*Schoolcraft.*) This mound consists of eighteen million two hundred and fifty thousand solid feet of earth. How long it took to build it, is more than can be made out, as the number of men employed, and the facilities to carry on the work, are unknown.

In England, Scotland, and in Wales, they are thus situated. At Inch Tuthel, on the river Tay, there is a mound which resembles this on the Licking, near Newark. The camp at Comerie is on a water of Ruchel, situated on a high alluvion, like that in the west. The antiquities of Ardoch are on a water *Kneck*, their walls ditches, gateways, mounds of defence before them, and every thing about them, resemble our works of this character in America.

What Pennant, in his *Antiquarian Researches* in the north of Europe, calls a *prætorium*, is exactly like the circular works round our mounds, when placed within walls of earth. Catter-thun, two miles from Angus, is ascribed to the ancient Caledonians, or Scotch. Such works are very common in Ohio. One on the river Loden, or Lowthe, and another near the river Emet, are exactly like those in the west. The strong resemblance between the works in Scotland and those of the west, I think, says Mr. Atwater, n man will deny. In various parts of the British isles, as well as England, Scotland, Ireland, and Wales, are abundance of those works, which were places of worship, burial, and defence, built by the ancient Picts, so called by the Romans, because they *painted* themselves, like the aborigines of this country. At a very early period of the globe, a small mound of earth served as a sepulchre and an altar, wheron the officiating priest could be seen by the surrounding worshippers. Such sacred works may be traced from Wales to Russia, quite across that empire north, to our continent; and then across this continent, from the Columbia on the Pacific ocean, to the Black river, on the east end of lake Ontario; thence turning in a southwestern direction, we find them extending quite to the southern parts of Mexico and Peru.

"If there exists," says Dr. Clarke, "any thing of former times which may afford evidence of antediluvian manners, it is this mode of burial; which seems to mark the progress of population in the first ages after the dispersion, occasioned by the confusion of languages, at Babel. Whether under the form of a mound in Scandinavia and Russia, a barrow in England, or cairn in Ireland, Scotland and Wales, or heaps of earth, which the modern Greeks and Turks call *tepe*, and the Mexicans *tepec;* and lastly, in the more artificial shape of a pyramid, in Egypt: they had universally the same origin."

Here we have the unequivocal opinion of a man who has scarcely his fellow, respecting a knowledge of the ancient manners of mankind; who says, that the tumuli, found in all parts of the earth, belong solely to the age immediately succeeding Noah's flood; which greatly favors our opinion, that this country was settled as early as the other parts of the earth, which are at as great a distance from Mount Ararat and Babylon.

But what is the distance from Mount Ararat by way of Bhering's strait, to the middle of the United States, which is the region of the Missouri? It is something over ten thousand miles; nearly half the circuit of the globe. Here, in the region of the western states, we have, by the aid of Baron Humboldt, supposed the country of Aztalan was situated; where the great specimens of labor and ancient manners are most abundant. If this was the way the first people came into America, it is very clear they could not, in the ordinary way of making a settlement here and there, have arrived soon enough to show signs of as great antiquity, in their works in America, as those of the same sort found in the north of Europe. Some other way, therefore, we are confident, the first inhabitants must have pursued, so that their works in America might compare, in character and antiquity, with those of other nations. From Ararat, in a westerly course, passing through Europe, by way of the countries now situated in Russia in Europe, to the Atlantic, the distance is scarcely 5000 miles; not half the distance the route of Bhering's strait would have been. And if the Egyptian tradition be true respecting the island Atalantis, and the conjectures of naturalists about a union of Europe and America on the north, there was nothing to hinder their settling here, immediately after their dispersion.

It is supposed the *first* generations immediately succeeding the flood, were much more enlightened than many nations since that period; the reason is, they had not yet forgotten that which they had learned of the manners of their antediluvian ancestors, from Noah: but as they spread and diverged asunder, what they had learned from him concerning the creation, architecture, and the culture of the earth before the flood, they lost, and so retrograded to savagism.

It is true, the family of Shem, of whom were Abraham, Isaac, and Jacob, by the particular Providence of God, retained, unadulterated, the traditional history of the creation, and of man, till the time Moses embodied it in a book, 857 years after the flood. But the rest of the nations were left, in this respect, to mere recollections; which, as soon as they divided and subdivided, became contradictory and monstrous in their accounts.

But the authors of the great works found in the west, seem to have retained the *first* ideas received from their fathers at the era of the building of Babel, equally, if not superior, to many nations of Europe, as they were in the year 800 after Christ. This is consented to on all hands, and even contended for by the historian Humboldt. In order to show the reader the propriety of believing that a colony, very soon after the confusion of the language of mankind, found their way to what is now called America, we give the tradition of the Azteca nation, who once inhabited Aztalan, the country of the western states, but were, at the era of the conquest of South America, found inhabiting the vale of Mexico, because they had, as we have shown, been driven away by the irruptions of the Tartarian Indians, as follows:

Traits of the Mosaic History found among the Azteca Nations.

The tradition commences with an account of the deluge, as they had preserved it in books made of the buffalo and deer skin, on which account there is more certainty than if it had been preserved by mere oral tradition, handed down from father to son.

They begin by painting, or as we would say, by telling us that Noah, whom they call Tezpi, saved himself, with his wife, whom they call Xochiquetzal, on a raft or canoe. Is not this the ark? The raft or canoe rested on or at the foot of a mountain, which they call Colhuacan. Is not this Ararat? The men born after this deluge were born dumb. Is not this the confusion of language at Babel? A *dove* from the top of a tree distributes languages to them in the form of an olive leaf. Is not this the dove of Noah, which returned with that leaf in her mouth, as related in Genesis? They say, that on this raft, beside Tezpi and his wife, were several *children*, and animals, with grain, the preservation of which was of importance to mankind. Is not this in almost exact accordance with what was saved in the ark with Noah, as stated in Genesis?

When the Great Spirit, Tezcatlipoca, ordered the waters to withdraw, Tezpi sent out from his raft a *vulture*, which never returned, on account of the great quantities of dead carcasses which it found to feed upon. Is not this the raven of Noah, which did not return when it was sent out the second time, for the very reason here assigned by the Mexicans? Tezpi sent other birds, one of which was the humming bird; this bird alone returned, holding in its beak a branch covered with leaves. Is not this the dove? Tezpi, seeing that fresh verdure now clothed the earth, quitted his raft near the mountain of Colhuacan. Is not this an allusion to Ararat of Asia? They say the tongues which the dove gave to mankind, were infinitely varied; which, when received, they immediately dispersed. But among them there were fifteen *heads* or *chiefs* of families, which were permitted to speak the same language, and these were the Taltecs, the Aculhucans, and Azteca nations, who embodied themselves together, which was very natural, and travelled, they knew not where, but at length arrived in the country of Aztalan, or the lake country in America.

The plate or engraving presented here, is a suprising representation of the deluge of Noah, and of the confusion of the ancient language, at the building of the tower of Babel, as related in the book of Genesis, (see chap. vii. and xi.)

We have derived the subject of this plate from Baron Humboldt's volume of *Researches in Mexico*, who found it painted on a manuscript book, made of the leaves of some kind of tree, suitable for the purpose, after the manner of the ancient nations of the sultry parts of Asia, around the Mediterranean.

Among the vast multitude of painted representations found by this author, on the books of the natives, made also frequently of prepared skins of animals, were delineated all the leading circumstances and history of the deluge, of the fall of man, and of the

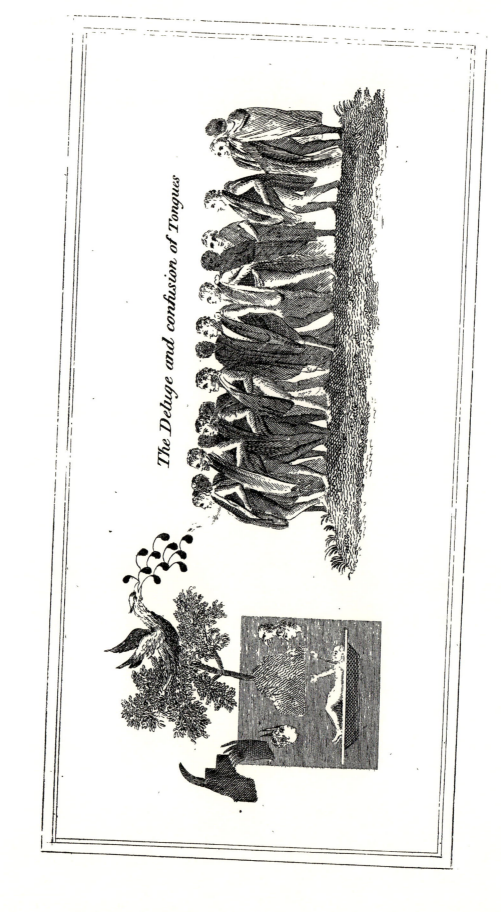
The Deluge and confusion of Tongues

seduction of the woman by the means of the serpent, the first murder as perpetrated by Cain, on the person of his brother Abel.

The plate, however, here presented, shows no more than a picture of the flood, with Noah afloat on a raft, or as the traditions of some of the nations say, on a tree, a canoe, and some say even in a vessel of huge dimensions. It also shows, by the group of men approaching the bird, a somewhat obscure history of the confusion of the ancient language, at the building of Babel, by representing them as being born dumb, who receive the gift of speech from a dove, which flutters in the branches of the tree, while she presents the languages to the mute throng, by bestowing upon each individual a leaf of the tree, which is shown in the form of small commas suspended from its beak.

Among the different nations, according to Humboldt, who inhabited Mexico, were found paintings which represented the deluge, or the flood of Tezpi. The *same* person among the Chinese is called *Fohi* and *Yu-ti*, which is strikingly similar in sound to the Mexican *Tezpi*, in which they show how he saved himself and his wife, in a bark, or some say, in a canoe, others, on a raft, which they call, in their language, a huahuate.

The painting, of which the plate is the representation, shows Tezpi, or Noah, in the midst of the waters, lying on his back. The *mountain*, the summit of which is crowned by a tree, and rises above the waters, is the peak of Colhucan, the Ararat of the Mexicans. At the foot of the mountain, on each side, appear the heads of Noah and his wife. The woman is known by the two points extending up from her forehead, which is the universal designation of the female sex among the Mexicans. The horn at the left hand of the tree, with a human hand pointing to it, is the character representing a mountain, and the head of a bird placed above the head of Tezpi or Noah, shows the vulture which the Mexicans say Tezpi sent out of his acalli or boat to see if the waters had subsided.

In the figure of the bird, with the leaves of a tree in its beak, is shown the circumstance of the dove's return to the Ark, when it had been sent out the second time, bringing a branch of the olive in its mouth; but in their tradition it had become misplaced, and is made the author of the languages. That birds have a language, was believed by the nations of the old world. Some of those nations retain a surprising traditional account of the deluge; who say, that Noah embarked in a spacious *acalli* or boat, with his wife, his children, several animals, and grain, the preservation of which was of great importance to mankind. When the Great Spirit, Tezcatlipoca, ordered the waters to withdraw, Tezpi, or Noah, sent out from his boat a vulture. But as the bird's natural food was that of dead carcasses, it did not return, on account of the great number of dead carcasses with which the earth, now dried in some places, abounded.

Tezpi sent out other birds, one of which was the humming bird; this bird alone returned again to the boat, holding in its beak a branch, covered with leaves. Tezpi now knowing that the earth was dry, being clothed with fresh verdure, quitted his bark near the mountain Colhucan, or Ararat.

The purity of this tradition is evidence of two things: first., that the book of Genesis, as written by Moses, is not as some have imagined, a cunningly devised fable, as these Indians cannot be accused of Christian priestcraft, nor yet of Jewish priestcraft, their religion being solely of another cast, wholly idolatrous. And second, that the continents of America, Europe, Africa, and Asia, were anciently united, so the earlier nations came directly over after the confusion of the ancient language and dispersion—on which account its purity has been preserved more than among the more wandering tribes of the old continents.

As favoring this idea of their coming immediately from the region of the tower of Babel, their tradition goes on to inform us, that the tongues distributed by this bird were infinitely various, and dispersed over the earth; but that it so happened that fifteen heads of families were permitted to speak the same language, these are the same shown on the plate. These travelled till they came to a country which they called Aztalan, supposed to be in the regions of the now United States, according to Humboldt. As favoring this idea, we notice, the word *Aztalan* signifies in their language, *water*, or a country of much water. Now, no country on the earth better suits this appellation than the western country, on account of the vast number of lakes found there, and is even, by us, called the lake country.

There is another particular in this group of naked, dumb human beings, worthy of notice, which is, that neither their countenances nor form of their persons agree at all with the countenances or formation of the common Indians; they suit far better to the face of the ancient Britons, Greeks, Romans, Carthaginians and Persians the progenitors of the German tribes.

If so, it is evident, that the Indians are not the first people who found their way to this country. Among these ancient nations are found many more traditions corresponding to the accounts given by Moses, respecting the creation, the fall of man by the means of a serpent—the murder of Abel by his brother, &c.; all of which are denoted in their paintings, as found by the earlier travellers among them, since the discovery of America by Columbus, and carefully copied from their books of prepared hides, which may be called parchment, after the manner of the ancients of the earliest ages.

We are pleased when we find such evidence, as it goes to the establishment of the truth of the historical parts of the old Testament, evidence so far removed from the sceptic's charge of priestcraft here among the unsophiscated nations of the earlier people of America.

Clavigero, in his history of Mexico, says that among the Chiapanese Indians, was found an ancient manuscript in the language of that country, made by the Indians themselves, in which it was said, according to their ancient tradition, that a certain person, named *Votan*, was present at that great building, which was made by order of his uncle, in order to mount up to heaven; that then every people was given its language, and that Votan himself was charged by God to make the division of the lands of Anahuac—so Noah divided the earth among his sons. Votan may have been Noah, or a grandson of his.

Of the ancient Indians of Cuba, several historians of America relate, that when they were interrogated by the Spaniards concerning their origin, they answered, they had heard from their ancestors, that God created the heavens and the earth, and all things: that an old man having foreseen the deluge with which God designed to chastise the sins of men, built a large canoe and embarked in it with his family, and many animals; that when the inundation ceased, he sent out a raven, which, because it found food suited to its nature to feed on, never returned to the canoe; that he then sent out a pigeon, which soon returned, bearing a branch of the *Hoba* tree, a certain fruit tree of America, in its mouth; that when the old man saw the earth dry, he disembarked, and having made himself wine of the wood grape, he became intoxicated and fell asleep; that then one of his sons made ridicule of his nakedness, and that another son piously covered him; that, upon waking, he blessed the latter and cursed the former. Lastly, these islanders held that they had their origin from the accursed son, and therefore went almost naked; that the Spaniards, as they were clothed, descended perhaps from the other.

Many of the nations of America, says Clavigero, have the same tradition, agreeing nearly to what we have already related. It was the opinion of this author, that the nations who peopled the Mexican empire, belonged to the posterity of Naphtuhim—(the same, we imagine, with Japheth;) and that their ancestors having left Egypt not long after the confusion of the ancient language, travelled towards America, crossing over on the isthmus, which it is supposed once united America with the African continent, but since has been beaten down by the operation of the waters of the Atlantic on the north, and the Southern ocean on the south, or by the operation of earthquakes.

Now we consider the comparative perfection of the preservation of this *Bible* account, as an evidence that the people among whom it was found must have settled in this country at a very early period of time, after the flood, and that they did not wander any more, but peopled the continent, cultivating it, building towns and cities, after their manner; the vestiges of which are so abundant to this day; and on this account, viz., their fixedness, their traditionary history was not as liable to become lost, as it would have undoubtedly been, had they wandered, as many other nations of the old world have, among whom scarcely a vestige of their origin is found, of credible tradition, compared with this.

Even the Hindoo nations, who, in their origin wandered also from Ararat, have not, with all their boasted refinement and antiquity of origin, as clear an account of the first age of the earth, as these Mexicans. But there is another additional reason for it: those countries of the east have been frequently overrun by savage hordes from the wilds of northern Tartary; while the ancient people of *this* continent have rested in peace, till similar hordes found their way across Bhering's strait in later years; and, as is believed, an account of the tradition, both of some of the western tribes, and of the Azteca nations in Mexico, were driven from their ancient possessions.

If, then, we believe that the *first* people who visited this country did not come here by the way of Bhering's strait, from Tartary, how then is it that we find such evident marks in the mounds and tumuli of the west, of the presence of a Hindoo population, as well as of other nations.

Let the traditions of the nations of Taltec and Azteca extraction in Mexico answer it. These say, that a wonderful personage, whom they name *Quetzalcoatl*, appeared among them, who was a white and bearded man. This person assumed the dignity of acting as a priest and legislator, and became the chief of a religious sect, which like the Songasis, and the Boudhists of Hindostan, inflicted on themselves the most cruel penances. He introduced the custom of piercing the lips and ears, and lacerating the rest of the body, with the prickles of the agave and leaves, the thorns of the cactus, and of putting reeds into the wounds, in order that the blood might be seen to trickle more copiously. In all this, says Humboldt, we seem to behold one of those Rishi, hermits of the Ganges, whose pious austerity is celebrated in the books of the Hindoos.

Jewitt, a native of Boston, who lately died at Hartford, Conn.; was, some few years since, captured with the crew of the vessel in which he had sailed, by the Nootka Indians, at Nootka sound, on the Pacific. In his narrative of his captivity and sufferings, he states that those Indians had a religious custom, very similar to those of the Hindoos, now in use about the temple of Juggernaut, in India; which was, piercing their sides with long rods, and leaping about while the rods were in the wound.

Respecting this white and bearded man, much is said in their tradition, recorded in their books of skin, and among other things, that after a long stay with them he suddenly left them, promising to return again, in a short time, to govern them and renew their happiness. This person resembles, very strongly, in his promise to return again, the behavior of Lycurgus, the Spartan lawgiver, who, on his departure from Lacedæmon, bound all the citizens under an oath, both for themselves and posterity, that they would neither violate nor abolish his laws till his return; and soon after, in the Isle of Crete, he put himself to death, so that his return became impossible.

It was the posterity of this man whom the unhappy Montezuma

thought he recognized in the soldiers of Cortez, the Spanish conqueror of Mexico. "We know," said the unhappy monarch, in his first interview with the Spanish general, "by our books, that myself and those who inhabit this country, are not natives but strangers, who came from a great distance. We know, also, that the chief who led our ancestors hither, returned for a certain time, to his primitive country, and thence came back to seek those who were here established, who after a while, returned again, alone. We always believed that his descendants would one day come to take possession of this country. Since you arrive from that region where the *sun rises*, I cannot doubt but that the king who sends you is our natural master."

Humboldt says, that the Azteca tribes left their country, Aztalan, in the year of our Lord 544; and wandered to the south or southwest, coming at last to the vale of Mexico. It would appear, from this view, that as the nations of Aztalan, with their fellow nations, left vast works, and a vast extent of country, apparently in a state of cultivation, with cities and villages, more in number than three thousand, as Breckenridge supposed, that they must, therefore, have settled here long before the Christian era.

The peculiar doctrines of the Hindoos, we are informed, were commenced to be taught in the east, among what is *now* called the Hindoo nations, by Zoroaster, about the time of Abraham, 1449 years before the time of Confucius, who was born 551 B. C. So that there was time for those doctrines of Confucius and Zoroaster to take root in China, and to become popular, and also to reach America, by Hindoo missionaries, and overspread these regions even as early as the commencement of the Christian era.

Of Zoroaster, it is said, that he predicted the coming of the Messiah in plain words; and that the "wise men" of the east, who saw his star, were of his disciples, or sect. This doctrine he must have learned of Shem, who, we have attempted to show, was Melchisedek, or of Abraham, as it had been handed down from Adam, the first of men. But the peculiar doctrine of Confucius, which was the worship of fire as well as that of the sun, by Zoroaster, it is likely, was derived from the account he found among the archives of the Jews, respecting the *burning bush* of Moses, which had taken place more than a thousand years before the time of Confucius. From this originated, in all probability, as taught by Confucius, the burning of heroes, when dead, among many nations; and from this, that of immolating widows, as among the Hindoos, on the funeral pile, taught by the Brahmin missionaries, who, undoubtedly, visited America, and planted their belief among these nations; the tokens of which appear so abundantly in the mounds and tumuli of the west.

And this Quetzalcotl, a celebrated minister of those opinions, appears to have been the *first* who announced the religion of the east among the people of the west. There was also one other minister, or Brahmin, who appeared among the Mozca tribes in South America, whom they name *Bochica*. This personage taught the worship of the sun; and if we were to judge, should pronounce him a missionary of the Confucian system, a worshipper of fire, which was the religion of the ancient Persians, of whose country Confucius was a native. This also is evidence that the first inhabitants of America came here at a period near the flood, long before that worship was known, or they would have had a knowledge of this Persian worship, which was introduced by *Bochica*, among the American nations; which, it seems, they had not until taught by this man.

Bochica, it appears, became a legislator among those nations, and changed the form of their government to a form, the construction of which, says Baron Humboldt, bears a strong analogy to the governments of Japan and Thibet, on account of the *pontiffs'* holding in their hands both the secular and the spiritual reins. In Japan, an island on the east of Asia, or rather many islands, which compose the Japanese empire, is found a religious sect, stiled *Sinto*, who do not believe in the sanguinary rites of shedding either human blood, or that of animals, to propitiate their gods. They even abstain from animal food, and detest bloodshed, and will not touch any dead body.—(*Morse's Geography*, p. 523.)

There is, in South America, a whole nation who eat nothing but vegetables, and who hold in abhorrence those who feed on flesh.— (*Humboldt*, p. 200.)

Such a coincidence in the religion of nations, can scarcely be supposed to exist, unless they are of one origin. Therefore, from what we have related above, and a few pages back, it is clear, both from the tradition of the Aztecas, who lived in the western regions before they went to the south, and from the fact that nations on the Asiatic side of Bhering's strait, having come *annually* over the strait to fight the nations of the northwest, that we, in this way, have given conclusive and satisfactory reasons why, in the western mounds and tumuli, are found evident tokens of the presence of a Hindoo population, or at least of nations influenced by the superstitions of that people, through the means of missionaries of that cast; and that they did not bring those opinions and ceremonies with them when they *first* left Asia, after the confusion of the antediluvian language, as led on by their fifteen chiefs; till by some means, and at some period, they finally found this country; not by the way of Bhering's strait, but some nearer course, as we have conjectured in other places in this work.

Perhaps a few words on the supposed native country of Quetzalcotl may be allowed; who, as we have stated, is reported to have been a *white* and *bearded* man, by the Mexican Aztecas. There is a vast range of islands on the northeast of Asia, in the Pacific, situated not very far from Bhering's strait, in latitude between 40 and 50 degrees north. The inhabitants of these islands, when first discovered, were found to be far in advance in the arts and civilization, and a knowledge of government, of their continental neighbors, the Chinese and Tartars. The island of Jesso, in particular, is of itself an empire, comparatively, being very populous; and are also highly polished in their manners. The inhabitants may be denominated white; their women, especially, whom Morse in his geography of the Japan, Jesso, and others in that range, says expressly, are white, fair and ruddy. Humboldt says they are a bearded race of men, like Europeans.

It appears the ancient government of these islands, especially that of Japan, which is neighbor to that of Jesso, was in the hands of spiritual monarchs and pontiffs, till the seventeenth century. As this was the form of government introduced by Quetzalcotl, when he first appeared among the Azteca tribes, which we suppose was in the country of Aztalan, or western states, may it not be conjectured that he was a native of some of those islands, who in his wanderings had found his way to the place now called Bhering's strait; for, indeed, anciently there may have been only an isthmus at that place, and thence to this country, on errands of benevolence; as it is said in the tradition respecting him, that he preached peace among men, and would not allow any other offering to the divinity than the first fruits of the harvest; which doctrine was in character with the mild and amiable manners of the inhabitants of those islands. And that peculiar and striking record, found painted on the Mexican skin-books, which describes him to have been a white and bearded man, is our other reason for supposing him to have been a native of some of these islands, and most probably Jesso, rather than any other country.

The inhabitants of these islands originated from China, and with them undoubtedly carried the Persian doctrines of the worship of the sun and fire; consequently we find it taught to the people of Aztalan and Mexico, by such as visited them from China, or the islands above named; as it is clear the sun was not the original object of adoration in Mexico, but rather the power which made the sun. So Noah worshipped.

Their traditions recognize also another important chief, who led the Azteca tribes *first* to the country of Aztalan, long before the appearance of Quetzalcotl, or Bochica, among them. This great leader they name Tecpaltzin, and doubtless allude to the time when they first found their way to America, and settled in the western region.

A Description of the Ceremonies of Fire-Worship, as practised by certain Tribes on the Arkansas.

Mr. Ash witnessed an exhibition of fire-worship, or the worship of the sun, as performed by a whole tribe, at the village of Ozark, near the mouth of the Ozark, or Arkansas river, which empties into the Mississippi from the west.

He says, he arrived at the village at a very fortunate period; at a time when it was filled with Indians, and surrounded with their camp. They amounted to about 900, and were composed of the remnants of various nations, and were worshippers of the sun. The second day after his arrival happened to be the grand festival among them. He had the most favorable opportunity of witnessing their adorations at three remarkable stages, the sun's rising, meridian and setting.

The morning was propitious, the air serene, the horizon clear, the weather calm. The nations divided into classes; warriors, young men and women, and married men with their children. Each class stood in the form of a quadrant, that each individual might behold the rising luminary, and each class held up a particular offering to the sun the instant he rose in his glory. The warriors presented their arms, the young men and women offered ears of corn and branches of trees, and married women held up to his light their infant children. These acts were performed in silence, till the object of their adoration visibly rose; when, with one impulse, the nations burst into praise, and sung a hymn in loud chorus. The lines, which were sung with repetitions, and marked by pauses, were full of sublimity and judgment. Their meaning, when interpreted, is as follows:

Great Spirit! master of our lives. Great Spirit! master of things visible and invisible, and who daily makes them visible and invisible. Great Spirit! master of every other spirit, good or bad; command the good to be favorable to us, and deter the bad from the commission of evil. O Grand Spirit! preserve the strength and courage of our warriors, and augment their number, that they may resist the oppression of the Spanish enemies, and recover the country, and the rights of our fathers. O Grand Spirit! preserve the lives of such of our old men as are inclined to give counsel and example to the young. Preserve our children, multiply their number, and let them be the comfort and support of declining age. Preserve our corn and our animals, and let no famine desolate the land. Protect our villages, guard our lives. O Great Spirit! when you hide your light behind the western hills, protect us from the Spaniards, who violate the night, and do evil which they dare not commit in the presence of your beams. Good Spirit! make known to us your pleasure by sending to us the Spirit of Dreams. Let the Spirit of Dreams proclaim your will in the night, and we will perform it through the day; and if it say the time of some be closed, send them, Master of Life! to the great country of souls, where they may meet their fathers, mothers, children and wives, and where you are pleased to shine upon them with a bright, warm and perpetual blaze! O Grand! O Great Spirit! harken to the voice of *nations*, harken to all thy children, and remember us always, for we are descended from thee.

Immediately after this address, the four quadrants formed one immense circle, of several deep, and danced and sung hymns descriptive of the power of the sun, till near ten o'clock. They then amused and refreshed themselves in the village and camp, but assembled precisely at the hour of twelve, and formed a number of circles, commenced the adoration of the meridian sun. The following is the *literal* translation of the mid-day address.

Courage, nations! courage! the Great Spirit looks down upon us from his highest seat, and by his lustre appears content with the children of his own power and greatness. Grand Spirit! how great are his works, and how beautiful are they! How good is the Great Spirit! He rides high to behold us. 'T is he who causes all things to augment and to act. He even now stands for a moment to hearken to us. Courage, nations! courage! The Great Spirit, now above our heads, will make us vanquish our enemies; he will cover our fields with corn, and increase the animals of our woods. He will see that the old be made happy, and that the young augment. He will make the nations prosper, make them rejoice, and make them put up their voice to him, while he rises and sets in their land, and while his heat and light can thus gloriously shine out.

This was followed by dancing and hymns, which continued from two to three hours, at the conclusion of which, dinners were served and eaten with great demonstrations of mirth and hilarity. Mr. Ash says he dined in a circle of chiefs, on a barbecued hog, and venison very well stewed, and was perfectly pleased with the repast. The dinner and repose after it continued till the sun was on the point of setting. On this being announced by several who had been on the watch, the nations assembled in haste, and formed themselves into segments of circles, in the face of the sun, presenting their offerings during the time of his descent, and crying aloud,

The nations must prosper; they have been beheld by the Great Spirit. What more can they want? Is not that happiness enough? See, he retires, great and content, after having visited his children with light and universal good. O Grand Spirit! sleep not long in the gloomy west, but return and call your people once again to light and life, to light and life, to light and life.

This was succeeded by dances and songs of praise, till eleven o'clock at night; at which hour they repaired to rest, some retiring to the huts that formed their camp, and others to the vicinity of fires made in the woods, and along the river bank. Mr. Ash took up his abode with a French settler in the village. He understood that these Indians have four similar festivals in the year—one for every season. When the sun does not shine or appear on the adoration day, an immense fire is erected, around which the ceremonies are performed with equal devotion and care."

Origin of Fire-Worship.

For many ages the false religions of the east had remained stationary; but in this period *magianism* received considerable strength from the writings of Zoroaster. He was a native of Media. He pretended to a visit in heaven, where God spake to him out of a fire. This fire he pretended to bring with him, on his return. It was considered holy; the dwelling of God. The priests were forever to keep it, and the people were to worship before it. He caused fire temples every where to be erected, that storms and tempests might not extinguish it. As he considered God as dwelling in the fire, he made the sun to be his chief residence, and therefore the *primary* object of worship. He abandoned the old system of two gods, one good and the other evil, and taught the existence of one Supreme, who had under him a good and evil angel; the immediate authors of good and evil. To gain reputation, he retired into a cave, and there lived a long time a recluse, and composed a book called the *Zend-Avesta*, which contains the liturgy to be used in the fire temples, and the chief doctrines of his religion. His success in propagating his system was astonishingly great. Almost all the eastern world, for a season, bowed before him. He is said to have been slain, with eighty of his priests, by a Scythian prince, whom he attempted to convert to his religion.

It is manifest that he derived his whole system of God's dwelling in the fire, from the burning bush, out of which God spake to Moses. He was well acquainted with the Jewish Scriptures. He gave the same history of the creation and deluge that Moses had given, and inserted a great part of the Psalms of David into his writings. The Mehestani, his followers, believed, in the immortality of the soul, in future rewards and punishments, and in the purification of the body by fire, after which they would be united to the good.—(*Marsh's Ecclesiastical History*, p. 78.)

From the same origin, that of the burning bush, it is altogether probable, the worship of fire, for many ages, obtained over the whole habitable earth; and is still to be traced in the funeral piles of the Hindoos, the beacon fires of the Scotch and Irish, the periodical midnight fires of the Mexicans, and the council fires of the North American Indians, around which they dance.

A custom among the natives of New Mexico, as related by Baron Humboldt, is exactly imitated by a practice found still in some parts of Ireland, among the descendants of the ancient Irish.

At the commencement of the month of November, the great fire of *Samhuin* is lit up, all the culinary fires in the kingdom being first extinguished, as it was deemed sacrilege to awaken the winter's social flame, except by a spark snatched from this sacred fire; on which account, the month November is called, in the Irish language, Samhuin.

To this day, the inferior Irish look upon bonfires as sacred; they say their prayers, walking round them, the young dream upon their ashes, and the old take this fire to light up their domestic hearths, imagining some secret undefinable excellence connected with it.

A Further Account of Western Antiquities.

"I have a brick," says Mr. Atwater, "now before me, over which lay, when found, wood, ashes, charcoal, and human bones, burnt in a large and hot fire. And from what was found at Circleville, in the mound already described, it would seem that females were sometimes burnt with the males. I need not say, that this custom was derived from Asia, as it is well known, that is the only country to look to for the origin of such a custom. The Greeks and Romans practised burning their illustrous dead; it was practised by the several other nations, but they all derived it from Asia.

In Dr. Clarke's volume of Travels from St. Petersburgh to the Crimea, in the year 1800; and in his Travels in Russia, Tartary, and Turkey, it is said conical mounds of earth, or tumuli, occur very frequently. The most remarkable may be seen between Yezolbisky and Voldai, on both sides of the road, and they continue over the whole country, from the latter place to Jedrova, and finally, over the whole Russian empire. The author of the travels above alluded to, says, "There are few finer prospects than that of Woronetz, viewed a few miles from the town on the road to Pautoosky. Throughout the whole of this country, are seen, dispersed over immense plains, mounds, of earth, covered with fine turf, the sepulchres of the ancient world, common to almost every habitable country."

This country, (Russia in Europe) from Petersburgh to the Crimea, a seaport on the Black sea, the region over which Adam Clarke travelled, is in the very neighborhood of Mount Ararat; and from the circumstance of the likeness existing between the mounds and tumuli there, which Clarke says are the "tombs of the ancient world," and those of the same character, North and South America, we draw the conclusion, that they belong, nearly to one and the same era of time; viz: that immediately succeeding the confusion of language, at the building of Babel.

We are told in the same volume of travels, that "the Cossacks at Ekaterindara, dug into some of these mounds, for the purpose of making cellars, and found in them several ancient vases," earthen vessels, corresponding exactly with vases found in the western mounds. Several have been found in our mounds, which resemble one found in Scotland, described by Pennant. A vessel apparently made of clay and shells, resembling in its form, a small keg, with a spout on one side of it, formed like the spout of a tea-kettle, with a chain fastened to each end, made probably of copper, of which Mr. Atwater has not informed us. This chain answered as a bail or handle; exactly on its top, or side, under the range of the chain handle, is an opening of an exact circle, which is the mouth of this ancient tea-kettle.—(*See plate, letter A.*)

In the Russian tumuli are found the bones of various animals, as well as those of men. In the western tumuli are found also, the bones of men, as well as the teeth of bears, otters, and beavers.

Thus we learn, from the most authentic sources, that these ancient works existing in Europe, Asia, Africa and America, are similar in their construction, in the materials with which they were raised, and in the articles found in them.

Let those who are constantly seeking for some argument to overthrow the history of man by Moses, consider this fact. Such persons have affected to believe, that there were different stocks or races of men derived from different original fathers; and in this way they account for the appearance of human beings found on islands. But this similarity of works, language, and of tradition, relating to the most ancient history of man, indicates, nay *more*, establishes the fact, that all men sprung from but one origin, one first man and woman, as Moses has written it in the book of Genesis.

When Dr. Clarke was travelling in Tartary, he found a place called *Iverness*, situated in the *turn* of a river; he inquired the meaning of the word, and found that Iverness, in their language, signifies *in a turn*. Whoever looks into Pennant's Tour, will see a plate, representing a town in the turn of a river, in Scotland, called by the same name, *Iverness*. The names of not a few of the rivers in England, Scotland, and Wales, are the names also of rivers in Tartary.

Some have supposed that all the great works of the west, of which we have been treating, belong to our present race of Indians; but from continued wars with each other, have driven themselves from agricultural pursuits, and thinned away their numbers, to that degree, that the wild animals and fishes of the rivers, and wild fruit of the forests, were found sufficient to give them abundant support; on which account, they were reduced to savagism.

But this is answered by the Antiquarian Society, as follows: "Have our present race of Indians ever buried their dead in mounds by thousands? Were they acquainted with the use of silver, or copper? These metals curiously wrought have been found. Did the ancients of our Indians burn the bodies of distinguished chiefs, on funeral piles, and then raise a lofty tumulus, over the urn containing their ashes? Did the Indians erect any thing like the "walled towns," on Paint creek? Did they ever dig such wells as are found at Marietta, Portsmouth, and above all, such as those in Paint creek? Did they manufacture vessels from calcareous breccia, equal to any now made in Italy? Did they ever make and worship an idol representing the three principal gods of India, called the triune cup?—(*See plate, letter E.*)

To this we respond, they never have: no, not even their traditions afford a glimpse of the existence of such things as forts, tumuli, roads, wells, mounds, walls enclosing between one and two hundred, and even five hundred acres of land; some of them of stone, and others of earth twenty feet in thickness, and exceedingly high, are works requiring too much labor for Indians ever to have performed.

The skeletons found in our mounds never belonged to a people like our Indians. The latter are a tall and rather slender, straight limbed people; but those found in the barrows and tumuli, were rarely over five feet high, though a few were six. Their foreheads were low, cheek bones rather high, their faces were very short and wide, their eyes large, and their chins very broad.

But Morse the geographer says, p. 629, that the Tartars have small eyes, and not of the oblique form, like the Monguls and Chinese, neither of which seem to correspond with the large eyed race who built the mounds and tumuli of the west; on which account we the more freely look to a higher and more ancient origin for these people. The Indians of North America, in features, complexion, and form, and warlike habits, suit far better the Tartaric character, than the skeletons found in the mounds of the west. The limbs of our fossils are short and thick, resembling the *Germans* more than any other Europeans with whom we are acquainted.

Germany is situated east of England, and parts of it lie along the coast of the Atlantic, or the North sea, in north latitude 53 degrees. From whence voyagers may have passed out between the north end of Scotland and the south extremity of old Norway, by the Shetland and Faroe islands, directly in the course of Iceland, Greenland and the Labrador coast of America. This is as possible for the Germans to have performed, as for the Norwegians, Danes and Welch, in the year of our Lord 1000, as shown in another part of this work. White Indians, as found far to the west, must have had a white origin.

An idol found in a tumulus near Nashville, Tennessee, (*see plate, letter B,*) and now in the Museum of Mr. Clifford, of Lexington, is made of clay, peculiar for its fineness. With this clay was mixed a small portion of gypsum, or plaster of Paris. This idol was made to represent a man, in a state of nudity or nakedness, whose arms had been cut off close to the body, and whose nose and chin have been mutilated, with a fillet and cake upon its head. In all these respects, as well as in the peculiar manner of plating the hair, it is exactly such an idol as professor Pallas found in his travels in the southern part of the Russian empire.

A custom among the ancient Greeks, may have given rise to the formation of such an idol; which was copied by the Asiatic ancestors of the people who brought it with them from Asia to the woods of America. This custom was—when a victim was destined to be sacrificed, the sacred fillet was bound upon the head of the idol, the victim and priest. The *salted* cake was placed upon the head of the victim only; it was called " Mola," hence *immolare*, or immolation, in later times was used to signify any kind of sacrifice.

On this idol, (*see the plate, letter B.,*) found near Nashville, the sacred fillet and salted cake are represented on its head: it is supposed the copy of this god was borrowed by the Greeks from the Persians from whence it might also have been copied, in later times, by the Chinese nations, and from thence have been brought to America.

" If the ancestors of our North American Indians, were from the northern parts of Tartary, those who worshipped this idol came from a country lying farther to the south, where the population was more dense, and where the arts had made grater progress; while the Tartar of the north was hunter and a savage, the Hindoo and southern Tartar were well acquainted with most of the useful arts," who, at a later period than that of the first people who settled this country, came, bringing along with them the *arts*, the *idols*, and the religious *rites* of Hindostan, China, and the Crimea."

The ancestors of our northern Indians were mere hunters; while the authors of our tumuli were shepherds and husbandmen. The temples, altars and sacred places of the Hindoos were always situated on the banks of some stream of water. The same observation applies to the temples, altars and sacred places of those who erected our tumuli. " To the consecrated streams of Hindostan devotees assembled from all parts of the empire, to worship their gods, and purify themselves by bathing in the sacred waters. In this country, their sacred places were uniformly on the banks of some river; and who knows but the Muskingum, the Sciota, the

Miami, the Ohio, the Cumberland, and the Mississippi, were once deemed as sacred, and their banks as thickly settled, and as well cultivated, as are now those of the Ganges, the Indus, and the Burempooter."—(*American Antq. Researches.*)

" Some years since a clay vessel was discovered, about twenty feet below the surface, in alluvial earth, in digging a well near Nashville, Tennessee, and was found standing on a rock, from whence a spring of water issued. This vessel was taken to Peale's museum, at Philadelphia. It contains about one gallon; was circular in its shape, with a flat bottom, from which it rises in a somewhat globose form, terminating at the summit with the figure of a female head; the place where the water was introduced, or poured out, was on the one side of it, nearly at the top of the globose part. The features of the face are Asiatic; the crown of the head is covered by a cap of pyramidal figure, with a flattened circular summit, ending at the apex, with a round button. The ears are large, extending as low as the chin. The features resemble many of those engraved for Raffle's history; and the cap resembles Asiatic head dresses."—(*Am. Ant. Researches.*)

Another idol was, a few years since, dug up in Natchez, on the Mississippi, on a piece of ground where, according to tradition, long before Europeans visited this country, stood an Indian temple. This idol is of stone, and is nineteen inches in height, nine inches in width, and seven inches thick at the extremities. On its breast, as represented on the plate of the idol, were five marks, which were evidently characters of some kind, resembling, as supposed, the Persian; probably expressing, in the language of its authors, the name and supposed attributes of the senseless god of stone. (*See the plate, letter G.*)

It has been supposed the present race of Indians found their way from Asia, by the way of Bhering's strait, and had passed from thence along down the chian of northern lakes, till they finally came to the Atlantic, south of Hudson's bay, in latitude about 50 degrees north; *long* before the people who made the great works of the west. That this was the fact, is argued by those who contend for its belief, from their having greater knowledge of the arts diffused among them than the Indians.

It is, say they, among a dense population, that these improvements are effected; it is here that necessity, the mother of invention, prompts man to subject such animals to his dominion, as he discovers most docile, and best calculated to assist him in his labors, and to supply him with food and raiment. All this we believe; and for this very reason we hold the authors of our western works were thus enlightened, before they came here, on the plains of Shinar, amid the density of the population of the region immediately round about the tower of Babel. For it is evident, they never would have undertaken to build a work so immense as that tower, unless their numbers were considered equal to it; and much less, unless this *was* the fact, could they have in reality effected it.

While the thousands and tens of thousands, who are employed in that work, were thus engaged, there must also, for their support, have been a large country, densely peopled, under contribution. In order to this, agriculture must have been resorted to; instruments of metal were indispensible, both in clearing the earth and in erecting the tower. All this was learned from Noah, who had brought, with himself and family, the knowledge of the antediluvians; of whom it is said expressly, in the book of Genesis, that they both understood the use of iron and brass, as well as agriculture. Abel was a tiller of the ground; Tubal Cain was a worker in iron and brass.

It cannot, therefore, be possible that Noah's immediate descendants, to the third or tenth generations, could have forgotten these things. And such as wandered least after the dispersion, after such as may have spoken the same language, had found a place to settle in, would most certainly retain this antediluvian information more than such as wandered, as the Tartars always have done.

One of the arts known to the builders of Babel, was that of brick making; this art was also known to the people who built the works in the west. The knowledge of copper was known to the people of the plains of Shinar, for Noah must have communicated it, as he lived one hundred and fifty years among them after the flood; also copper, was known to the antediluvians. Copper was also known to the authors of the western monuments. Iron was known to the antediluvians; it was also known to the ancients of the west; however, it is evident that very little iron was among them, as very few instances of its discovery in their works have occurred; and for this very reason we draw a conclusion that they came to this country very soon after the dispersion, and brought with them such few articles of iron as have been found in their works in an oxydized state.

Copper ore is very abundant, in many places of the west; and therefore, as they had a knowledge of it when they first came here they knew how to work it, and form it into tools and ornaments. This is the reason why so many articles of this metal are found in their works; and even if they had a knowledge of iron ore, and knew how to work it, all articles made of it must have become oxydized as appears from what few specimens have been found, while those of copper are more imperishable. Gold ornaments are said to have been found in several tumuli. Silver, very well plated on copper, has been found in several mounds, besides those at Circleville and Marietta. An ornament of copper was found in a stone mound near Chilicothe; it was a bracelet for the ancle or wrist.

The ancients of Asia, immediately after the dispersion, were acquainted with ornaments made of the various metals; for in the family of *Terah*, who was the father of *Abraham* and *Nahor*, we find these ornaments in use for the beautifying of females. See the servant of Abraham, at the well of Bethuel in the country of " Ur of the Chaldeans," or Mesopotamia, which is not very far from the place where Babel stood—putting a jewel of gold upon the face or forhead of Rebecca, weighing half a shekel, and two bracelets for her wrists, or arms. Bracelets for the same use have been found in the west; all of which circumstances go to establish the acquaintance of those who made those ornaments of silver and copper found in the mounds of the west, equal with those of Ur in Chaldea. The families of Peleg, Reu, Serug, and Nahor, who were the immediate progenitors of Abraham, lived at an era but little after the flood; and yet we find them in the possession of ornaments of this kind; from which we conclude a knowledge both of the metals, and how to make ornaments, as above described, was brought by Noah and his family from beyond the flood.

A knowledge, therefore, of these things must have gone with the different people who spread themselves over the whole earth, and were retained by those who wandered least, as we suppose was the fact in relation to the first settlers of this continent, in the regions of the west. It is believed by some that the common Indian nations came first to this country to the northwest, and following the northern lakes, found their way to the Atlantic; while at a later period, they suppose, the more enlightened nations of China came the same way, and followed along down the shore of the Pacific, till they found a mild climate, along in latitudes 50, 40 and 30 degrees.

But this is not possible: *First,* Because the Indians were found by us as numerous on the shores of the Pacific as on the shores of the Atlantic, and in all the vast country between; dwelling where a people still more ancient than they, once lived, but had forsaken their fields, their houses, their temples, mounds, forts and tumuli, and either were nearly exterminated in wars with them, or wandered to the south; the small residue, the descendants of whom are found in several of the nations inhabiting South America, as we have shown heretofore.

Second, It would seem impossible for the people, or nations, who built the vast works of the west, and are evidently of the shepherd or agricultural cast, to have crossed the strait, and fought their way through hostile, opposing and warlike nations, till they had established themselves in their very midst. It is, therefore, much more agreeable to reason, and also to the traditions, both of the Azteca nations in Mexico and the Wyandot tribes in the west, to believe that our Indians came on the continent at a much later period than those who are the authors of the works we have described, and that they had many wars with them, till, at length, they slowly moved to the south, abandoning forever their country, to wander, they knew not whither, as we have also shown. This conclusion is not mere fancy, for it is a matter of historic notice, that the " Tchautskis annually crossed Bhering's strait to make war on the inhabitants of the northwest coast of America."—(*Humboldt*, vol. 1, p. 919.)

The reader will recollect our description of the walled towns of the west, surrounded with deep ditches, as found on Paint creek, Little Miami, Circleville, Marietta, Cincinnati, Portsmouth, and in Perry county, Ohio. There is a town, (*See Morse's Geography,* vol 2, p. 631,) situated in the regions of Mount Ararat, in the ancient country called Independent Tartary, by the name of Khiva, which stands on a rising ground, like the town in Perry county. It is surrounded with a high wall of earth, very thick, and much higher than the houses within. It has three gateways; there are turrets at small distances and a broad, deep ditch; the town is large, and occupies a considerable space, and commands a beautiful prospect of the distant plains, which the industry of the inhabitants has rendered very fertile; but the houses of this town are very low, and mostly built of clay, and the roofs flat, and covered with earth. This town, which so exactly corresponds with the ruins of the west, is in that part of Asia east of Ararat, where the primitive inhabitants, immediately after the deluge, made the first settlements. And from this coincidence, we are led to a belief, drawn from this and abundant other evidence, that the antiquity of the one is equal with that of the other; that its construction is indeed of the primitive form; which strengthens our opinion, that the first inhabitants of America came here with the very ideas relative to the construction and security of towns and fortifications, that dictated the building of Khiva. It is allowed on all hands, that the people of Asia are wholly of the primitive stamp; their antiquities, therefore, are of the same character with those of America.

"Proofs of primitive times, (says Mr. Atwater,) are seen in their manners and customs, in their modes of burial and worship, and in their wells, which resemble those of the patriarchal ages. Here the reader has only to recollect the one at Marietta, those at Portsmouth, on Paint creek, at Cincinnati, and compare them with those described in Genesis. Jacob rolled the stone from the well's mouth, (that is, from the fountain at the bottom,) Rachel descended with her pitcher, and brought up water for her future husband, and for the flocks of her father."

Before men were acquainted with letters, they raised monuments of unwrought fragments of rocks, for the purpose of perpetuating the memory of events. Such we find raised in America. In the patriarchal ages men were in the habit of burying their dead on high mountains and hills, with mounds or tumuli raised over them; such we find in America. Mr. Atwater asks the question, "Did they not come here as early as the days of Lot and Abraham?" The latter of whom lived something more than 2000 B. C., which would be only about 340 years after the flood, and about 150 years after the confusion of language at Babel.

If so, they were acquainted more or less with a knowledge of the true God, the creation of the world, with the circumstances of the building of the ark, the fact of the deluge, the number of persons saved in the ark, or, as they say, on a raft; and also, with circumstances which transpired after the flood, as mentioned in Scripture; all of which are plainly alluded to in Mexican tradition. But other nations than the progenitors of the Mexicans have also found this country, at other eras, one after another, as accident or design may have determined.

Fortification.—On the shores of the Mississippi, some miles below lake Pepin, on a fine plain, exists an artificial elevation of about four feet high, extending a full mile, in somewhat of a circular form. It is sufficiently capacious to have covered 5000 men. Every angle of the breast work is yet traceable, though much defaced by time. Here, it is likely, conflicting realms as great as those of the ancient Greeks and Persians, decided the fate of ambitious monarchs, of the Chinese Mongol descent.

Weapons of brass have been found in many parts of America, as in the Canadas, Florida, &c. with curiously sculptured stones, all of which go to prove that this country was once peopled with civilized, industrious nations, now traversed the greater part by savage hunters.

Discovery of America by the Norwegians and Welch, before the Time of Columbus.

This is contended by Lord Monboddo, a native of Scotland, and a philosophical and metaphysical writer of the 17th century. He wrote a dissertation on the origin and progress of language, in which he is sure he has found among the nations of America, who are of the aboriginal class, the ancient Celtic or Gælic dialect. He goes further, and supposes that all the nations of America, from the Labrador Esquimaux, to the natives of Florida, are derived of Celtic origin: but to this we cannot subscribe, as that many nations of the common Indians are evidently of Tartaric or Scythian origin; the descendants of the race of Shem, and not of Japheth, who was a white man.

Monboddo, however, argues in support of his opinion, from a

number of curious circumstances. He says, that when in France, he was acquainted with a French Jesuit, a man of great and celebrated erudition, who related to him that a companion of his, who was engaged in the missionary service, with himself, among the northern Indians in America, having lost his way in the woods, travelled on, he knew not whither, till he found himself among the Esquimaux Indians.

Here he stayed long enough to learn their language; after which he returned to Quebec in Canada; and happening one day to be walking along the docks of that city, observed among the crew of a ship that was moored there, a sailor who was a native of the country at the foot of the Pyrennean mountains, on the side of France. On hearing this man speak, who was a Basque, from his knowledge of the Esquimaux, obtained as above related, he understood what he said, so that they conversed together a while.

Now, the language which the Basques speak, Lord Monboddo informs us, is absolutely a dialect of the ancient Celtic, and differs but little from the language of the ancient Highlanders of Scotland. This opinion is corroborated by a fact noticed in a Scotch publication, respecting an Esquimaux Indian, who accompanied one of the English expeditions towards the north pole, with a view to reach it, if possible, or to find a passage from the North Atlantic through to the North Pacific, by the way of Bhering's strait; but did not succeed on account of the ice.

On board of this vessel was a Scotch Highlander, a native of the island of Mull, one of the Hebrides; who, in a few days time, was enabled to converse fluently with the Esquimaux; which would seem to be a proof absolute, of the common origin, both of the Esquimaux language, and that of the Basque, which is the ancient Scotch or Celtic.

Also the same author states, that the Celtic language was spoken by many of the tribes of Florida, which is situated at the north end of the gulf of Mexico; and that he was well acquainted with a gentleman from the Highlands of Scotland, who was several years in Florida, in a public character, and who stated that many of the tribes with whom he had become acquainted, had the greatest affinity with the Celtic in their language; which appeared particularly, both in the form of speech and manner of reciprocating the common salutation of *how do you do?*

But what is still more remarkable, in their war song he discovered, not only the sentiments, but several lines, the very same words as used in Ossian's celebrated majestic poem of the wars of his ancestors, who flourished about thirteen hundred years ago. The Indian names of several of the streams, brooks, mountains and rocks of Florida, are also the same which are given to similar objects, in the highlands of Scotland.

This celebrated metaphysician was a firm believer in the anciently reported account of America's having been visited by a colony from Wales, long previous to the discovery of Columbus; and says the fact is recorded by several Welch historians, which cannot be contested. It is reported by travellers in the west, that on the Red river, which has its origin north of Spanish Texas, but empties into the Mississippi, running through Louisiana; that on this river, very far to the southwest, a tribe of Indians has been found, whose manners, in several respects, resemble the Welch, especially in their marriage and funeral ceremonies. They call themselves the McCedus tribe, which having the Mc or Mack attached to their name, points evidently to a European origin, of the Celtic description. It is further reported by travellers, that northwest from the head waters of the Red river, which would be in the region called the great American desert, Indians have come down to the white settlements, some thirty or forty years since, who spoke the Welch language quite intelligibly. These Indians, bearing such strong evidence of Welch extraction, may possibly be descended from the lost colony from Wales, an account of which is given in Powel's History of Wales, in the 12th century; which relates, that Prince Madoc, weary of contending with a brother for their father's crown, left his country, and sailed from Wales a due west course, which, if they came to land at all must have been Newfoundland, which lies opposite the mouth of the river St. Lawrence, exactly in latitude 50 degrees north, and which is contiguous to this continent. But the account relates that he discovered an unknown country; that he returned to Wales, and gave such a favorable history of his discoveries and of the goodness of the land, that many were induced to embark with him on his second voyage, which he accomplished. He returned again to Wales, but after a while sailed a third time to the newly discovered country, but has never since been heard of.

The same account as above, is here again related, but with other circumstances attending. "In the year 1170," 663 years ago, which was as before stated, in the 12th century, "Madoc, son of Owen Groynwedk, Prince of Wales, dissatisfied with the situation of affairs at home, left his country, as related by the Welch historian, in quest of some new place to settle. And leaving Ireland to the north, proceeded west, till he discovered a fertile country; where leaving a colony, he returned, and persuading many of his countrymen to join him, put to sea with *ten ships*, and was never more heard of."

We are not in the belief that all the tribes of the west, who have the name of Indian, are indeed such. There are many tribes which have been discovered in the western regions, as on the Red river, in the great American desert, west of the head waters of that river, and in wilds west of the Rocky mountains; who are evidently not of the Tartar stock, whose complexion, language, and heavy bearded faces, show them to be of other descent.

The Indians who were living on the river Taunton, in Massachusetts, when the whites first settled there, had a tradition that certain strangers once sailed up Asoonset, or Taunton river, in wooden houses, and conquered the red men. This tradition does not go to lessen the probability of the expedition of the Welch fleet, as above related, but greatly to strengthen it.

This account of the Welch expedition, has several times drawn the attention of the world; but as no vestige of them has been found, it was concluded, perhaps too rashly, to be a fable; or at least, that no remains of the colony exist. Of late years, however, western settlers have received frequent accounts of a nation inhabiting at a great distance up the Missouri, in manners and appearance resembling the other Indians, by speaking Welch, and retaining some ceremonies of the Christian worship; and, at length, says Imlay, in his work, entitled *Imlay's America*, this is universally believed to be a fact.

Near the falls of Ohio, six brass ornaments, such as soldiers usually wear in front of their belts, was dug up, attached to six skeletons. They were cast metal, and on one of them which was brought to Cincinnati, was represented a *mermaid*, playing upon a harp, which was the ancient coat of arms for the principality of Wales. The tradition from the oldest Indians, is that it was at the falls of the Ohio, that the first white people were cut off by the natives.

It is well authenticated that upwards of thirty years ago, Indians came to Kaskaskia, in the territory, now the state of Illinois, who spoke the Welch dialect, and were perfectly understood by two Welchmen then there, who conversed with them. From information to be relied on, tomb stones, and other monuments of the existence of such a people, have been found, with the year engraved, corresponding very near to that given above, being in the twelfth century.

But long before this lost colony left Wales, Lord Monboddo says, America was visited by some Norwegians, from Greenland, who, it was well known, were the discoverers of Greenland, in A. D. 964, and on that very account, it might be safely supposed they would push their discoveries still farther west.

Accordingly, his lordship says, the Norwegians having made a settlement in Greenland, in the end of the tenth century, some adventurers from thence about that time, which would be more than eight hundred years ago, discovered, or rather visited, North America; for this writer supposes the continent to have been known to the people of the old world, as early as the time of the seige of Troy; which was about eleven hundred years before Christ; about the time of Solomon, or rather, one hundred years before the time of that king, nearly 3000 since.

This is a point at which the publication of this book aims, viz: to establish that this part of the earth was settled as soon after the flood as any other country as far from Ararat, and perhaps sooner.

Lord Monboddo says, these Greenland Norwegian adventurers made a settlement about the mouth of the River St. Lawrence; where having found wild grapes, a German among them named the country Vinland, as is related in the history of this discovery. Mr. Irving, in his late life of Columbus, says, that as the Norwegians have never seen the grape vine, did not know what it was, but there being a German with them, who was acquainted with the grape of his own native country, told them its name, from which they named it as above.

This account is recorded in the annals of Iceland; which was peopled from Norway, which is in the north of Europe; and from Iceland the colony came that settled in Greenland, from thence to the mouth of the river St. Lawrence, about the year 1000 A. D. If such was the fact, there is nothing more natural, than that they may have pursued up the river, even to the lakes, and have settled around them, and on the islands in the St. Lawrence. There is an island in that river, called *Chimney Island*, so named, on account of the discovery of ancient *cellars* and *fire places*, evidently more ancient than the first acquaintance of the French with that country, which we suppose to have been made by these Norwegians.

This Scottish author, in his admired work on the origin and progress of language, as well as in other works of his, relates a vast number of curious and interesting circumstances, which relate to our subject; one of the most remarkable, is an account of an Indian mummy, discovered in Florida, wrapped up in a cloth manufactured from the bark of trees, and adorned with hieroglyphical characters, precisely the same, with characters engraved on a metal plate, found in an ancient burying ground, in one of the Hebride islands, north of Scotland.

This country, (Scotland) boasts of the most ancient line of kings that have reigned in Europe, having settled in Scotland, more than three hundred years before the Christian era, in the time of Alexander the Great. They are of Cimbrick Chersonese origin, who are derived probably, from some wandering tribe, descended from Japheth, the white son of Noah, whose independence, the Greeks nor Romans were never able, in their wide-spread conquests, to wrest from them; this was reserved for the English to accomplish, which was done in 1603.

These islands, therefore, north and west of Scotland, became peopled by their descendants at an early day. Their hardiness of constitution, perseverance of character, and adventuring disposition, favors, in the strongest sense, the accounts as recorded in their national documents. And a reason why those documents have not come to light sooner, is, because they were penned some hundred years before the invention of printing; and laid up in the cabinet of some Norwegian chief, at a time when but few could read at all, and the means of information did not exist, to be compared with the facilities of the present time: therefore, it has been reserved to this late era, to unravel, in *any* degree, the mysteries of antiquity.

In the work entitled "Irving's Life of Columbus," is an account of the discovery of this continent, by those northern islanders, given in a more circumstantial and detailed manner. See his Appendix to vol. 3, p. 292, as follows:

"The most plausible or credible account respecting those discoveries is given by Snoro Sturleson, or Sturloins, in his *Saga*, or *Chronicle of King Olaus*. According to this writer, one Biorn, of Iceland, voyaging to Greenland in search of his father, from whom he had been separated by a storm, was driven by tempestuous weather far to the southwest, until he came in sight of a low country, covered with woods, with an island in its vicinity. The weather becoming favorable, he turned to the northeast, without landing, and arrived safe at Greenland. His account of the country he had seen, it is said, excited the enterprise of Lief, son of Eric Rauda, (or red head,) the first settler of Greenland. A vessel was fitted out, and Lief and Biorn departed together in quest of this unknown land. They found a rocky and sterile island, to which they gave the name of Helleland; also a low sandy country, covered with wood, to which they gave the name of Markland; and two days afterwards they observed a continuance of the coast, with an island to the north of it. This last they described as fertile, well wooded, producing agreeable fruits, and particularly grapes; a fruit with which they were not acquainted; but on being informed by one of their companions, a German, of its qualities and name, they called the country from it, Vinland.

They ascended a river well stored with fish, particularly salmon, and came to a lake from which the river took its origin, where they passed the winter. It is very probable that this river was the St. Lawrence, as it abounded with salmon, and was the outlet of a lake, which, it is likely, was Ontario. There is no other river capable of being navigated, very far from its mouth, with a sea vessel, and which comes from a lake, and empties into the sea, on that side of the coast, but the St. Lawrence.

The climate appeared to them mild and pleasant, in comparison, being accustomed to the more rigorous seasons of the north. On the shortest day in the winter the sun was but eight hours above the horizon; hence it has been concluded, that the country was about the 49th degree of north latitude, and was either Newfoundland, or some part of the coast of North America, about the gulf of St. Lawrence. It is said in those Chronicles of Sturloins, that the relatives of Lief made several voyages to Vinland; that they traded with the natives for peltry and furs; and that in 1121, 173 years ago, a bishop named Eric, went from Greenland to Vinland, to convert the inhabitants to Christianity.

A knowledge of Christianity among the savage Britons, Caledonians and the Welch, was introduced, as is supposed, by St. Paul, or some of his disciples as early as A. D. 63, more than 1700 years since.

"From this time, about 1121, we know nothing of Vinland," says Forester, in his book of northern voyages, vol. 3, p. 36, as quoted by Irving. "There is every appearance that the tribe which still exists in the interior of Newfoundland, and who are so different from the other savages of North America, both in their appearance and mode of living, and always in a state of warfare with the Indains of the northern coast, are descendants of the ancient Normans, Scandinavians or Danes."

In the chronicles of these northern nations, there is also an account of the voyages of four boat crews in the year 1354, which corroborates the foregoing relations. This little squadron of fishing boats being overtaken by a mighty tempest, were driven about the sea for many days, until a boat containing seven persons, was cast upon an island called Estotiland, about 1000 miles from Friesland. They were taken by the inhabitants and carried to a fair and populous city, where the king sent for many interpreters to converse with them, but none that they could understand, until a man was found who likewise had been cast upon that coast some time before. They remained several days upon the island, which was rich and fruitful. The inhabitants were intelligent and acquainted with the mechanical arts of Europe. They cultivated grain, made beer, and lived in houses built of stone. There were Latin books in the king's library, though the inhabitants had no knowledge of that language, and in manuscript, as the art of printing was not yet discovered. They had many towns and castles, and carried on a trade with Greenland for pitch, sulphur and peltry. Though much given to navigation, they were ignorant of the use of the compass, and finding the Frieslanders acquainted with it, held them in great esteem, and the king sent them, with twelve barks, to visit a country to the south called Drogeo.

Drogeo is, most likely, a Norman name; as we find *Drogo* was a leader of the Normans against the ancient baronies of Italy, about A. D. 787. Drogeo is supposed to have been the continent of America. This voyage of the fishing squadron, it appears, was in 1354, more than fifty years after the discovery of the magnetic needle, which was in 1300.

They had nearly perished in this storm, but were cast away upon the coast of Drogeo. They found the people cannibals and were on the point of being killed and devoured, (these were our Indians,) but were spared on account of their great skill in fishing. Drogeo they found to be a country of vast extent, or rather a *new world;* that the inhabitants were naked and barbarous; but that far to the southwest there was a more civilized region and temperate climate, where the inhabitants had a knowledge of gold and silver, lived in cities, erected splendid temples to idols, and sacrificed human victims to them. The same it is likely, the ruins of which have been recently discovered and are now being explored, an account of which we shall partially give at page 241, and onward.

After the fisherman who relates this account had resided many years on the continent of Drogeo, during which time he had passed from the service of one chieftain to another, and traversed various parts of it, certain boats of Estotiland, (now supposed to be Newfoundland,) arrived on the coast of Drogeo. The fisherman got on board of them, and acted as interpreter, and followed the trade between the mainland of Drogeo and the island Estotiland, for some time, until he became very rich; he then fitted out a bark of his own, and with the assistance of some of the people of the island, made his way back across the intervening distance between Drogeo and his native country, Friesland, in Germany.

The account he gave of this country, determined Zichmni, the prince of Friesland, to send an expedition thither: and Antonio Zeno, a Venetian, was to command it. Just before starting, the fisherman, who was to have acted as pilot, died; but certain mariners who accompanied him from Estotiland, were taken in his place. The expedition sailed under command of Zichmni; the Venetian Zeno merely accompanied it. It was unsuccessful. After having discovered an island, called *Icaria,* where they met with a rough reception from the inhabitants, and were obliged to withdraw, the ships were driven by storm to Greenland. No record remains of any farther prosecution of the enterprise. The countries mentioned in the account written by this Zeno, were laid down on a map originally on wood.

The island Estotiland has been supposed by M. Malte-Brun, to be Newfoundland; its partially civilized inhabitants, the descendants of the Scandinavian colonists of Viñland, and the Latin books in manuscript, found in the king's library, to have belonged to the remains of the library of the Greenland bishop, who emigrated thither in 1121, 922 years ago.

Drogeo, according to the same conjecture, was Nova Scotia and New-England; the civilized people to the southwest, who sacrificed human beings in rich temples, he supposes to have been the Mexicans, or some ancient nations of Florida or Louisiana.

A distinguished writer of Copenhagen, it is said, was not long since engaged in the composition of a work on the early voyages of discovery to this continent, as undertaken by the inhabitants of the north of Europe more than eight hundred and thirty years ago. He has in his hands genuine ancient documents, the examination of which leads to curious and surprising results. They furnish various and unquestionable evidence, not only that the coast of North America was discovered soon after the discovery of Greenland by northern explorers, a part of whom remained there; and that it was again visited in the 11th, 12th and 13th centuries, but also that Christianity was introduced among the Indians of America. The documents of this writer furnish even a map, cut in wood, of the northern coast of America, and also an account of the sea coast south, as far down as to the Carolinas, and that a principal station of these adventurers was at the mouth of the river St. Lawrence.

He says that it was in the year 985 that America was *first* discovered by Baiske Her Juefser, but that he did not land; and that in the year 1000 the coast was visited by a man named Lief, a son of Eric the *Red*, who colonized Greenland.—(*Cabinet of Literature*, vol 3.)

From the discoveries of Baron Humboldt in South America, it would appear that the continent of America has indeed been not only visited by the northern nations of Europe, at a very early day, but also to have settled on it, and to have become the head of tribes, nations, and kingdoms, as follows:

In the kingdom of Guatemala, North America, the descendants of the original inhabitants preserve traditions which go back to the epoch of a great deluge, after which their ancestors, led by a chief called Votan, had come from a country lying toward the north. As late as in the 16th century, in a village in Guatemala, there were of the natives who boasted their descent from the family of Votan, or Vodan. They who have studied the history of Scandinavian (old Norway) nations, says Humboldt, in the heroic times, must be struck at finding in Mexico a name which recalls that of Vodan or Odin, who reigned among the Scythians, and whose race according to the very remarkable assertion of Bede, (an ecclesiastical historian of the 17th century,) gave kings to a great number of nations. This wonderfully corroborates the opinion of America's having been settled in several parts by Europeans, at a period more *ancient* than even the history of Europe can boast of.

The Shawanese tribe of Indians, who now live in Ohio, once lived on the Suaney river, in West Florida, near the shores of the southwest end of the gulf of Mexico; among these Indians, says Mr. Atwater, there is a tradition that Florida had once been inhabited by *white* people, who had the use of iron tools. Their oldest Indians say, when children, they had often heard it spoken of by the old people of the tribe, that anciently stumps of trees, covered with earth, were frequently found, which had been cut down by edged tools.—(*Am. Antq. Researches*, p. 273.)

Whoever they were, or from whatever country they may have originated, the account, as given by Morse, the geographer, of the subterranean wall found in North Carolina, goes very far to show, they had a knowledge of *iron ore;* and consequently knew how to work it, or they could not have had iron tools, as the Shawanese Indians relate. Morse's account is as follows:

"In Rowan county, North Carolina, about ten miles southwest from Salisbury, two hundred from the sea, and seventy from the mountains, which run across the western end of the State, is found a remarkable subterraneous wall. It stands on uneven ground, near a small brook. The stones of the wall are all of one kind, and contain iron ore. They are of various sizes, but generally weighing about four pounds. All are of a long figure, commonly seven inches in length, sometimes twelve. The *ends* of the stones form the sides of the wall; some of these ends are square, others nearly of the form of a parallelogram, triangle, rhombus or rhomboids; but most of them are irregular. Some preserve their dimensions through the whole length, others terminate like a wedge. The alternate position of great and little ends, aids in keeping the work square. The surface of some is plain, of some concave, of others convex. The concave stone is furnished with one convex, so as to suit each other. Where the stones are not firm, or shelly, they are curiously wedged in with others. The most irregular are thrown into the middle of the wall. Every stone is covered with cement, which, next to the stone, has the appearance of iron rust. Where it is thin, the rust has penetrated through. Sometimes the cement is an inch thick, and where wet, has the fine, soft, oily feeling of putty. The thickness of the wall is uniformly twenty-two inches, the length discovered is rising of eighteen rods, and the height twelve or fourteen feet. Both sides of this are plastered with the substance in which the stones are laid. The top of the wall appears to run nearly parallel with the top of the ground, being generally about a foot below the surface. In one place it is several feet. There is a bend or curve of six feet or more, after which it proceeds in its former direction. The whole appears to be formed in the most skilful manner. Six or eight miles from this wall, another has been since discovered, forty feet long, four and five feet high, seven inches thick only. The stones of this wall are all of one length.—(*Universal Geog.* p. 515.)

In the State of Tennessee, which is situated exactly on the western end of North Carolina, are also found the vestiges and remains of ancient dwellings, towns and fortifications, with mounds, barrows, utensils and images, wherever the soil is of prime quality, and convenient to water.

The bodies of two of these people were discovered in the autumn of 1810, in Warren county, in the State of Tennessee; one of a man, the other of a child, to appearance about four years old. They were four feet below the surface, in a situation perfectly dry, there being a mixture of copperas, alum, sulphur and nitre, in the soil that covered them. Their skin was preserved, though its original complexion could not be ascertained; but the hair of their heads was of an auburn shade. The child was deposited in a basket, well wrought of smooth splits of reeds, (*arundo gigantucu,*) and several singular species of cloth, as well as deer skins, dressed and undressed, were wrapped round and deposited with them, and two feather fans, and a curious belt.—(*Morse.*)

From the discovery of these two bodies we think we ascertain the inhabitants to have been white, like the Europeans, from the color of their hair; as it is well known the Australasians, Polynesians and Malays, as well as the common Indians, have universally *black*, long and shining hair. The body which is mentioned by Prof. Mitchill, late of New-York, discovered in a nitrous cave, in the western country, had *red* or *sandy* hair; such was the color of the hair of the Scandinavians of the north of Europe, and are supposed, upon authority indubitable, to have settled at Onondaga, and round about that region. (See toward the close of this work.)

The wall drscovered in North Carolina, as related above, is doubtless a part of a wall built for the defence of a town or city; the rest may have been thrown down by an enemy, or it may have been never finished. The regular manner in which it was built and laid in mortar, shows a considerable knowledge of masonry. This is by no means very extraordinary, as in Europe a considerable knowledge of the arts was in possession of the people of that country, derived from the Romans, who had subdued all the island of England, and abandoned the country, some hundred years before the time of the Welch expedition to the west of Europe, as we shall relate by and by.

What traits of iron instruments are found scattered over this country, except such as have been buried or lost in conflicts and battles with the Indians, since the discovery of the country by Columbus, as to be attributed to these Scandinavian and Welch settlers from the old country; the latter about the ninth or tenth century, and the former long before.

If the Welch, as we shall show, a few pages hence, found this country about the year 950, there was time enough for them to have established themselves in many parts, and to have built themselves towns and cultivated the earth to a great extent; as from about 950, till its discovery by Columbus, in 1492, would be not far from 542 years. A longer time than this has elapsed, since its last discovery, and also time enough for their deserted works to become covered with forests of the age of four and five hundred years.

According to Morse, the ancestors of the Welch were the Cimbri, or northern Celts: but he says, the Goths from Asia having seized on Germany, and a great part of Gaul, or France, gradually repelled the Celts, and placed colonies on the island of Britain, three or four centuries before the Christian era; that the Romans found many tribes of the Belgæ, or ancient Germans, when they first invaded that island; consequently, not only the Welch, but the English also, had, in part, the Goths, or ancient Germans, for their ancestors, and were the people who, as well as the Scandinavians, discovered America and settled here.

It may be, that from such causes as these, are found, far to the west, several tribes of white Indians, originated from Welch, German and Scandinavian ancestors; who well might be supposed to have had, not only a knowledge of masonry, sufficient to build walls, but of iron also; the traits of which are found in many parts sufficiently marked by oxydization to throw the time of their formation beyond the last discovery of America.

On the river Gasconade, which empties into the Missouri, on the southern side, are found the traces of ancient works, similar to those in North Carolina. In the saltpetre caves of that region, and Gasconade county in particular, was discovered, when they were first visited, axes and hammers made of iron; which led to the belief that they had formerly worked those caves for the sake of the nitre.

Dr. Beck, from whose Gazetteer of Missouri and Illinois, p. 234, we have this account, remarks, however, that " it is difficult to decide whether these tools were left there by the present race of Indians, or a more civilized race of people." He says it is unusual for the savages of our day to take up their residence in caves; considering them places to which the devil resorts; and that they are not acquainted with the uses of saltpetre, and would rather avoid them than collect it. This author considers the circumstance of finding those tools in the nitre caves, as furnishing a degree of evidence that the country of Gasconade river was formerly settled by a race of men who were acquainted with the use of iron, and exceeded the Indians in civilization and a knowledge of the arts.

But there are other facts, he says, connected with these, about which there can be no mistake. Not far from this cave is found the ruins of an ancient town. It appears to have been regularly aid out, and the dimensions of the squares, streets, and some of the houses, can yet be discovered.

Stone walls are found in different parts of the area, which are frequently covered with huge heaps of earth. Missouri joins Tennessee on the west, the same as the latter does North Carolina; and from a similarity of the works discovered, it would appear, that a population, similar in manners and pursuits, inhabited a vast region of country, from the Atlantic side of North Carolina, to the Missouri Territory.

These discoveries rank with the architectural works of Europe, in the 9th and 10th centuries; as that long before that period, the use of stone work had been introduced, even in the island of Britain, by the all-conquering bands of the Romans.

If, therefore, the Germans, Danes, Welch, Normans, Icelanders, Greenlanders, or Scandinavians, settled in this country, who are all of much the same origin, there need be no great mystery respecting these discoveries, as they are to be referred to those nations from Europe, beyond all doubt. The ancient monuments of a country, says Dr. Morse, are intimately connected with the epochs of its history; consequently, as the state of masonry, or the knowledge of stone work, discovered, as above described, in North Carolina, Tennessee, and Missouri, is of the same character with those of Europe, about the time of the 9th, 10th, 11th, and 12th centuries, we conclude them to be wholly of European origin.

About ten miles from the spot where the relics of this town are discovered, on the west side of the Gasconade river, is also found another stone work, still more extraordinary, as it is evident that its builders had indeed, a competent knowledge of constructing buildings of that material. It is about thirty feet square, and although in a dilapidated condition appears to have been erected with a great degree of regularity. It is situated on a high bold cliff, which commands a fine and extensive view of the country on all sides. From this stone work was found a foot path, running a devious course down the cliff, to the entrance of a cave. These antiquities evidently *form* a distinct class, says Dr. Beck, of which, as yet, he had seen no description.

Of the same class has been discovered on Noyer creek, in Missouri, the foundation of a large stone building, fifty-six feet in length, and twenty-two in breadth, divided into four apartments. The largest room occupies about one half of the whole building, and is nearly square; a second in size is twelve feet by sixteen, partly oval, third, four by sixteen, fourth, three by sixteen feet. The outer wall is eighteen inches thick, consisting of rough, unhewn stone; the partitions between the rooms is of the same material, of equal thickness with the outer wall. As an entrance into the largest room, are two door ways, the second size, one, and the same of the two others.—(*See at the bottom of the Frontispiece.*)

About eighty rods from this structure, is also found the remains of the foundation of a stone building, nineteen feet by fifteen, in size, of the same character of architecture. One large oval room, twelve feet by twelve on an average, occupies the centre, with a door way, and at each end of the room, three feet by twelve, without any door way. It is probable the largest of these buildings was the palace of the chief, or king, of the tribe, clan, or nation; where was held the legislatve councils, and the affairs of government were transacted.

The second building, placed at the respectful distance of eighty rods, was probably the prison house, and place of execution, which the small narrow cells, without any outside door way, would seem to suggest. The prison in which St. Paul was confined at Rome, is exactly of this form and size; which we consider a remarkable coincidence, unless it is allowed, this American prison house, as we have supposed it was, had been fashioned after the same manner.

We have an account of this prison, in which St. Paul was confined, which was built several hundred years before the Christian era, as given by a gentleman now making the tour of Europe. It is as follows:

"All parts of Italy are interesting to the scholar, and many parts to the Christian. Thus, near Naples, at Puteoli, I saw where Paul landed, and I travelled between Naples and Rome on the very same road over which he was led prisoner to Rome; and if he was incarcerated in this city, (which I see no reason to doubt) he doubtless lived the greater part of the time he was here, in his own hired house. I have been in the same dungeon, and seen the very pillar to which he must have been chained.

The prison is the *Mamertine*, the name and history of which, is familiar to every one acquainted with Roman history, as it was, for a long time, the only prison of the Romans. It consits of but two apartments, circular, and about twelve feet diameter, and six feet in height, the one over the other, both under ground. The only entrance to them originally, was through a small hole in the top of each, through which the prisoner must have been let down with ropes, passing through the upper to reach the lower prison. These dungeons were large enough for the Romans, as the trial soon followed the imprisonment of an offender, who, if found innocent, was at once liberated, but if guilty, immediately executed."—(*Journal and Telegraph, vol. IV., No.* 191,—1832.)

From the Romans the German or Belgic tribes may have derived their first ideas of stone work, as from the Germans the Danes derived the same. The style and manner of this building, as it now appears, in its ruined state, agrees well with the buildings of the ancient Danes of the north of Europe, in the 10th and 11th centuries; which also consisted of unhewn stone, laid up in their natural state, the squarest, and best formed, selected, of course. In these buildings, says Morse, were displayed the first elements of the Gothic style, in which the ancient Belgæ or Germans used to erect their castles, in the old world, eight or nine hundred years ago. These works of these distinct kind of antiquities, are numerous in the western countries; the regularity, form and structure of which, says Dr. Beck, favors the conclusion that they were the work of a more civilized race than those who erected the former, or more ancient works of America; and that they were acquainted with the rules of architecture, &c., [of Danish and Belgic origin,] and perhaps with a perfect system of warfare.

At present, the walls of this trait of ancient times, are from two to five feet high, the rooms of which are entirely filled with forest trees; one of which is an oak, and was, ten years ago, nine feet in circumference.—(*Beck's Gazetter*, p. 306.)

Ruins of the city of Otolum, discovered in North America.

In a letter of C. S. Rafinesque, whom we have before quoted, to a correspondent in Europe; we find the following: " Some years ago, the Society of Geography in Paris offered a large premium for a voyage to Guatimala, and for a new survey of the antiquities of Yucatan and Chiapa, chiefly those fifteen miles from Palanque, which are wrongly called by that name."

"I have," says this author, "restored to them the true name of OTOLUM, which is *yet* the name of the stream running through the ruins. They were surveyed by Captain Del Rio, in 1787, an account of which was published in English, in 1822.

"This account describes partly the ruins of a *stone* city, of no less dimensions than seventy-five miles in circuit; length thirty-two, and breadth twelve miles, full of palaces, monuments, statues and *inscriptions;* one of the earliest seats of American civilization, about equal to Thebes of ancient Egypt.

It is stated in the Family Magazine, No. 34, p. 266, for 1833, as follows:—"Public attention has been recently excited respecting the ruins of an *ancient* city found in Guatemala. It would seem that these ruins are now being explored, and much curious and valuable matter in a literary, and historical point of view is anticipated. We deem the present, a most auspicious moment, now, that the public attention is turned to the subject, to spread its contents before our readers, as an introduction to future discoveries during the researches now in progress."

The following are some particulars, as related by Captian Del Rio, who partially examined them as above related, 1787:—"From Palenque, the last town northward in the province of *Ciudad Real de Chiapa*, taking a southwesterly direction, and ascending a ridge of high land that divides the kingdom of Guatemala from Yucatan at the distance of six miles, is the little river *Micol* whose waters flowing in a westerly direction and unites with the great river *Tulija* which bends its course towards the province of *Tabasco.* Having passed Micol the ascent begins, and at half a league or a mile and a half, the traveller crosses a little stream called OTOLUM; from this point heaps of stone ruins are discovered, which render the road very difficult for another half league, when you gain the height whereon the stone houses are situated, being still fourteen in number, in one place, some more dilapidated than others, yet still having many of their apartments perfectly discernable.

A rectangular area, three hundred yards in breadth by four hundred and fifty in length," which is a fraction over fifty-six rods wide and eighty-four rods long, being in the whole circuit two hundred and eighty rods, which is three-fourths of a mile and a trifle over. This area "presents a plain at the base of the highest mountain forming the ridge. In the centre of this plain is situated the largest of the structures which has been as yet discovered among these ruins. It stands on a mound or pyramid twenty yards high, which is sixty feet, or nearly four rods, in perpendicular altitude, which gives it a lofty and beautiful majesty, as if it were a temple suspended in the sky. This is surrounded by other edifices, namely, five to the northward, four to the southward, one to the southwest and three to the eastward, fourteen in all. In all directions, the fragments of other fallen buildings are seen extending along the mountain that stretches east and west, either way from these buildings, as if they were the great temple of worship, or their government house, around which they built their city and where dwelt their kings and officers of state. At this place was found a subterranean stone aqueduct of great solidity and durability, which in its course passes beneath the largest building.

Let it be understood, this city of Otolum, the ruins of which are so immense, is in North, not South America, in the same latitude with the island Jamaica, which is about 18 degrees north of the equator, being on the highest ground between the northern end of the Caribbean sea and the Pacific ocean, where the continent narrows toward the isthmus of Darien, and is about 700 miles south of New-Orleans, merely across the gulf of Mexico.

The discovery of these ruins, and also of many others, equally wonderful in the same country, are just commencing to arouse the attention of the schools of Europe, who hitherto have denied that America could boast of her antiquities. But these immense ruins are now being explored under the direction of scientific persons, a history of which, in detail, will be forthcoming, doubtless, in due time; two volumes of which, in manuscript, we are informed, have already been written, and cannot but be received with enthusiasm by Americans.

By those deeply versed in the antiquities of past ages, it is contended that the first people who settled in America came directly from Chaldea, immediately after the confusion of language at Babel.—(*See description of the ruins of the American city, published in London,* 1832, *p.* 33, *by Dr. Paul Felix Cabrera.*) Whoever the authors of the city may have been, we seem to find in their sculptured deities, the idolatry of even the Phœnicians, a people whose history goes back nearly to the flood, or to within a hundred and fifty years of that period.

It appears from some of the historical works of the Mexicans, written in pictures, which fell into the hands of the Spaniards, that there was found one which was written by *Votan*, and sets himself forth to be the third gentile, (reckoning from the flood or family of Noah,) and lord of the *Tapanahuasec*, or the sacred drum. In the book above alluded to, Votan says that he saw the great house which was built by his grandfather, meaning the tower of Babel, which went up from the earth to the sky. In one of those picture books, the account is given by the Indian historian, whoever he was, or at whatever time he lived, that Votan had written it himself. He gives the account that he made no less than four voyages to this continent, conducting with him at one time seven families. He says that others of his family had gone away before himself, and that he was determined to travel till he should come to the *root* of heaven, (in the west,) in order to discover his relation, the *Culebras*, or Snake people, and calls himself *Culebra*, (a snake,) and that he found them, and became their captain. He mentions the name of the town which his relation had built at first, which was *Tezequil*.

Agreeing with this account, it is found by exploring the ruins of this city, and its sculptures, that among a multitude of strange representations are found two which represent this *Votan*, on both continents. The continents are shown by being painted in two parallel squares, and standing on each is this Votan, showing his acquaintance with each of them. The pictures engraven on the stones which form the sides of the houses or temples of this ruined city, are a series of hieroglyphics which show, beyond all doubt, that the era of its construction, and of the people who built it, excels in antiquity those of the ancient Greeks, the Romans, and the most celebrated nations of the old world, and is worthy of being compared even with the first progenitors of the Hebrews themselves, after the flood.—(See *History of American city, as before quoted*, p. 39.)

It is found that the gods of the ancient Egyptians, even *Osiris*, *Apis* and *Isis*, are sculptured on the stones of this city, the worship of which passed from Egypt to many nations, and is found under many forms, but all traceable to the same original.

But as it respects the *true founders* of this city, the discovery and contents of which are now causing so great and general interest in both this country and Europe, it is ascertained in the most direct and satisfactory way, in the work to which we have just alluded, published in London, 1832, on the subject of this city, that they were the ancient *Hivites,* one of the nations which inhabited Palestine, or Canaan, a remnant of which, it is ascertained, fled into the kingdom of Tyre, and there settled, and into Africa, to avoid annihilation by the wars of Joshua, the captain of the Jews; and that among them was one who acted as a leader, and was called *Votan,* and that he sailed from a port in ancient Tyre, which before it was known by that name, was called *Chivim,* and that this Votan was the third in the gentile descent from Noah, and that he made several voyages to and from America. But the kingdom which was founded by Votan, was finally destroyed by other nations, and their works, their cities and towns turned into a wilderness, as they are now found to be.

The *Hivites,* it appears, were the ancestors of the Moors, who spread themselves all along the western coast of Africa, at an early period, and in later times they overran the country of Spain, till the Romans supplanted them; who in their turn were supplanted by the northern nations of Germany, the Goths, &c.

The Moors were not the proper Africans, as the hair of their heads was long, straight and shining. They were a different race, and of different manners and attainments. The contour of the faces of the authors of the American city, found sculptured on the stones of its ruins, are in exact correspondence with the *forehead* and *nose* of the ancient Moors, the latter of which was remarkable for its aquiline shape, and was a national trait, characteristic of the Moors as well as the Romans.

When the Spaniards overran Peru, which lies on the western side of South America on the coast of the Pacific were found statues, obelisks, mausolea, edifices, fortresses, all of stone, equal, fully so, with the architecture of Egypt, Greece, and Rome, six hundred years before the Christian era. Roads were cut through the Cordillera mountains; gold, silver, copper, and led mines, were opened and worked to a great extent; all of which is evidence of their knowledge of architecture, mineralogy and agriculture. In many places of that country, are found the ruins of noble aqueducts, some of which, says Dr. Morse, the geographer, would have been thought works of difficulty in civilized nations. Several pillars of stone are now standing, which were erected to point out the equinoxes and solstices. In their sepulchres were found their paintings, vessels of gold and silver, implements of warfare, husbandry, &c.

To illustrate the architecural knowledge of the Peruvians as well as of some other provinces of South America, we quote the following from Baron Humboldt's Researches, 1st vol. Eng. trans. Amer. edt., p 255. "This plate," referring to one which is found in one of the volumes of his Researches, in the French language; "represents the plan and inside of the small building which occupies the centre of the esplanade, in the citadel of Cannar, supposed to be a guard house. I sketched, he says, this drawing with the greater exactness, because the remains of Peruvian architecture, scattered along the ridge of the Cordilleras, from Cuzco to Cajambe, or from the 13th degree of north latitude to the equator, a distance of nearly a thousand miles. What an empire, and what works are these, which all bear the same character, in the cut of the stones, the shape of the doors to their stone buildings, the symmetrical disposal of the niches, and the total absence of the exterior ornaments. This uniformity of construction is so great that all the stations along the high road, called in that country palaces of the Incas, or kings of the Peruvians, appear to have been copied from each other; simplicity, symmetry, and solidity, were the three characters, by which the Peruvian edifices were distinguished. The citadel of Cannar, and the square buildings surrounding it, are not constructed with the same quartz sandstone, which covers the primitive slate, and the prophyries of Assuay; and which appears at the surface, in the garden of the Inca, as we descend toward the valley of Gulan, but of trappean prophyry, of great hardness, enclosing nitrous feldspar, and hornblende. This prophyry was perhaps dug in the *great* quarries which are found at 4000 metres in height, (which is 13000 feet and a fraction, making two and a third miles in perpendicular height,) near the lake of Culebrilla, nearly ten miles from Cannar. To cut the stones for the buildings of Cannar, at so great a height, and to bring them down and transport them ten miles, is equal with any of the works of the ancients, who built the cities of Pompeii, Herculaneum, and Stabia, long before the Christian era, in Naples of Italy.

"We do not find, however," says Humboldt, "in the ruins of

Cannar, those stones of enormous size, which we see in the Peruvian edifices of Cuzco and the neighboring countries, Acosto, he says, measured some at Traquanaco, which were twelve metres (38 feet) long, and five metres eight tenths, (18 feet) broad, and one metre nine tenths (6 feet) thick." The stones made use of in building the temple of Solomon, were but a trifle larger than these, some of which were twenty-five cubits, (43 feet 9 inches) long, twelve cubits (29 feet) wide, and eight cubits, (14 feet) thick, reckoning twenty-one inches to the cubit.

"One of the temples of ancient Egypt is now, in its state of ruin, a mile and a half in circumference. It has twelve principal entrances. The body of the temple consists of a prodigious hall or portico; the roof is supported by 134 columns. Four beautiful obelisks mark the entrance to the shrine, a place of sacrifice, which contains three apartments, built entirely of granite. The temple of *Luxor*, probably surpasses in beauty and splendor all the other ruins of Egypt. In front are two of the *finest obelisks* in the world; they are of rose colored marble, one hundred feet high.

But the objects which most attract attention, are the *sculptures* which cover the whole of the northern front. They contain, on a great scale, a representation of a victory gained by one of the ancient kings of Egypt over an enemy. The number of human figures, cut in the solid stone, amounts to 1,500; of these, 500 are on foot, and 1,000 in chariots. Such are the remains of a city, which perished long before the records of ancient history had a being."—(*Malte-Brun.*)

We are compelled to ascribe some of the vast operations of the ancient nations of this country, to those ages which correspond with the times and manners of the people of Egypt, which are also beyond the reach of authentic history.

It should be recollected that the fleets of king Hiram navigated the seas in a surprising manner, seeing they had not, as is supposed, (but not proven,) a knowledge of the magnetic needle; and in some voyage out of the Mediterranean, into the Atlantic, they may have been driven to South America; where having found a country, rich in all the resources of nature, more so than even their native country, founded a kingdom, built cities, cultivated fields, marshalled armies, made roads, built aqueducts, became rich, magnificent and powerful, as the vastness and extent of the ruins of Peru, and other provinces of South America, plainly show.

Humboldt says, that he saw at Pullal, three houses made of stone, which were built by the Incas, each of which was more than fifty metres, or a hundred and fifty feet long, laid in a cement, or true mortar. This fact, he says, deserves attention, because travellers who had preceded him, had unanimously overlooked this circumstance, asserting, that the Peruvians were unacquainted with the use of mortar, but is erroneous. The Peruvians not only employed a mortar, in the great edifices of Pacaritambo, but made use of a cement of *asphaltum*; a mode of construction, which on the banks of the Euphrates and the Tigris, may be traced back to the remotest antiquity. The tools made use of to cut their stone was copper, hardened with tin, the same made use of among the Greeks and Romans, and other nations, of which we have spoken, in another place of this work.

To show the genius and enterprise of the natives of Mexico, before America was last discovered, we give the following as but a single instance: Montezuma, the last king but one of Mexico, A. D. 1446, forty-six years before the discovery of America by Columbus, erected a dyke to prevent the overflowing of the waters of certain small lakes in the vicinity of their city, which had several times deluged it. This dyke consisted of a bank of stones and clay, supported on each side by a range of palisadoes; extending in its whole length about seventy miles, and sixty-five feet broad, its whole length sufficintly high to intercept the overflowings of the lakes, in times of high water, occasioned by the spring floods. In Holland, the Dutch have resorted to the same means to prevent incursions of the sea; and the longest of the many is but forty miles in extent, nearly one half short of the Mexican dyke. " Amidst the extensive plains of Upper Canada, in Florida, near the gulf of Mexico, and in the deserts bordered by the Orinoco, in Colombia, South America, dykes of a considerable length, weapons of brass, and sculptured stones, are found, which are the indications that those countries were formerly inhabited by industrious nations, which are now traversed only by tribes of savage hunters." (*Humboldt*.) Samuel R. Brown, author of the Western Gazetteer, 1817, says, he examined one of those remains of the ancient nations, situated upon the mouth of big Scioto river on a high bank of the Ohio, a half mile from the water. He has no doubt it was a military position of great strength, and describes it as follows:

"The walls are yet standing, and enclosing as nearly as I could ascertain by pacing, fourteen acres of ground. It is of a *square form*" (like the ancient Roman military works.) "The officious hand of civilized man has not yet marred the wood which shade these venerable *ruins;* nor has any curious antiquarian mutilated the *walls* by digging in search of hidden treasure. The walls in many places are yet sixteen feet high, and no where less than eight. At their base they are about thirty feet wide, and wide enough at their top to admit a horse team and waggon. There are seven gateways, three on the west, two on the east, and two on the north, all being about 20 feet wide. On the northwest side are the ruins of a covered way, extending to a creek, at the distance of 280 rods. The covering is fallen in, and large trees are growing in the ditch. On the west side are *two* covered ways leading also to the same creek, these are apart from each other about 30 feet, and extending about 40 rods till they reach the stream. These walls are as wide and as high as the walls of the fort. On the east side, are also two covered ways at convenient distances from each other, leading to another small creek.

Thus the garrison of this ancient fortification had *five* avenues through which they could safely procure water." This could never have been the work of the common Indians.

Great Stone Calendar of the Mexicans.

THIS stone was found near the site of the present city of Mexico, buried some feet beneath the soil, of the same character on which was engraven an almost infinite number of hieroglyphics, signifying the divisions of time, the motions of the heavenly bodies, the twelve signs of the Zodiac, with reference to the feasts and sacrifices of the Mexicans, and is called by Humboldt the *Mexican Calendar*, in relief, on basalt.

This deservedly celebrated historiographer and antiquarian, has devoted a hundred pages, and more, of his octavo work, entitled *Researches in America*, in describing the similarity which exists between its representations of astrolgy, astronomy, and the divisions of time, and those of a great multitude of the nations of Asia; Chinese, Japanese, Calmucks, Moghols, Mantchaus, and other Tartar nations; the Egyptians, Babylonians, Persians, Phœnicians, Greeks, Romans, Hebrews, and ancient Celtic nations of Europe. See the American edition by Helen Maria Williams, vol 1. The size of this stone was very great, being a fraction over twelve feet square, three feet in thickness, weighing twenty-four tons. It is of the kind of stone denominated trappean porphyry, of the blackish grey color. We here present a fac similie of this stone.

The place where it was found was more than thirty miles from any quarry of the kind; from which we discover the ability of the ancient inhabitants, not only to transport stones of great size, as well as the ancient Egyptians, in building their cities and temples of marble, but also to cut and engrave on stone, equal with the present age.

It was discovered in the vale of Mexico, in A. D. 1791, in the spot where Cortez ordered it to be buried, when, with his ferocious Spaniards, that country was devastated. That Spaniard universally broke to pieces all idols of stone which came in his way, except such as were too large and strong to be quickly and easily thus affected. Such he buried, among which this sculptured stone was one. This was done to hide them from the sight of the natives, whose strong attachment, whenever they saw them, counteracted their conversion to the Roman Catholic religion.

The sculptured work on this stone, is in circles; the outer one of all, is a trifle over twenty-seven feet in circumference; from which the reader can have a tolerable notion of its size and appearance. The whole stone is intensely crowded with an infinity of representations and hieroglyphics; arranged however, in order and harmony, every way equal with any astronomical calendar of the present day. It is further described by Baron Humboldt, who saw and examined it on the spot.

"The concentric circles, the numerous divisions and subdivisions, engraven in this stone, are traced with mathematical precision; the more minutely the detail of this sculpture is examined, the greater the taste we find in the repetition of the same forms. In the centre of the stone is sculptured the celebrated sign *nahui-olin-Tonatiuh*, the SUN; which is surrounded by eight triangular radii. The god *Tonatiuh* or the SUN, is figured on this stone, opening his large mouth, armed with teeth, with the tongue protruded to a great length. This yawning mouth, and protruded tongue, is like the image of *Kala*, or in another word, *Time*, a divinity of Hindostan. Its dreadful mouth, armed with teeth, is meant to show, that the god, Tonatiuh, or time, swallows the world, opening a firey mouth devouring the years, months, and days, as fast as they come into being. The same image we find under the name of *Moloch*, among the Phœnicians," the ancient inhabitants of a part of Africa, on the eastern side of the Mediterranean; from which *very country*, there can be but little doubt, America received a portion of its earliest inhabitants; hence, a knowledge of the arts to great perfection, as found among the Mexicans, was thus derived. Humboldt says, the Mexicans have evidently followed the Persians, in the division of time, as represented on this stone. The Persians flourished 1500 years before Christ.

"The structure of the Mexican aqueducts, leads the imagination at once, to the shores of the Mediterranean."—(*Thomas' Travels*, p. 293.) The size, grandeur, and riches, of the tumuli on the

European and Asiatic sides of the Cimmerian strait," (which unites the black sea with the Archipelago, a part of the Mediterranean, the region of ancient Greece, where the capital of Turkey in Europe now stands, called Constantinople,) "excite astonishing ideas of the wealth and power of the people by whom they were constructed; and in view of labor so prodigious, as well as expenditure so enormous, for the mere purpose of inhuming a single body, customs and superstitions which illustrate the origin of the pyramids of Egypt, the cavern of Elephanta, and the first temples of the ancient world."—(*Thomas' Travels.*)

But whatever power, wealth, genius, magnitude of tumuli-mounds, and pyramids, are found about the Mediterranean; where the Egyptian, the Phœnician, Persian, and the Greek, have displayed the monuments of this most ancient sort of antiquities: all, all is realised in North and South America; and doubtless under the influence of the same superstition, and eras of time; having crossed over, as before argued; and among the various aboriginal nations of South and North America, but especially the former, are undoubtedly found the descendants of the fierce Medes and Persians, and other warlike nations of the old world.

The discoveries of travellers in that country, show, even at the present time, that the ancient customs, in relation to securing their habitations with a wall, still prevails. Towns in the interior of Africa, on the river Niger, of great extent, are found to be surrounded by walls of earth, in the same manner as those of the west in North America.

See the account as given by Richard Lander: "On the 4th of May we entered a town of prodigious extent, fortified with three walls, of little less than twenty miles in circuit, with ditches, or moats between. This town, called *Boo-hoo*, and is in latitude of about 8 degrees 43 minutes north, and longitude 5 degrees 10 minutes, east. On the 17th we came to *Roossa*, which is a cluster of huts walled with earth."

This traveller states, that there is a kingdom there called *Yaorie*, which is large, powerful, and flourishing; a city which is of prodigious extent; the wall surrounding it is of clay or earth, and very high, its circuit between twenty and thirty miles. He mentions several other places, enclosed by earth walls in the same manner.

It is easy to perceive the resemblance between these walled towns in central Africa, and the remains of similar works in this country, America.

A further Account of European Settlements.

THERE are the remains of one of those efforts of Scandinavian defence, situated on a hill of singular form, on the great sand plain between the Susquehannah and Chemung rivers, near their junction. The hill is entirely isolated, about three-fourths of a mile in circumference, and more than one hundred feet high. It has been supposed to be artificial, and to belong to the ancient nations to which all works of this sort generally belong. However, the inhabitants living round it, do not believe it to be artificial, on account of large stones situated on its sides, too heavy to have been placed there by art of man.

In the surrounding plain are many deep holes, of twenty or thirty rods circumference, and twenty feet deep; favoring a belief that from these, the earth was scooped out to form the hill with. It is four acres large on its top, and perfectly level, beautifully situated to overlook the country, to a great distance, up and down both rivers. But whether the hill be artificial nor not, there are on its top the remains of a wall, formed of earth, stone and wood, which runs round the whole, exactly on the brow. The wood is decayed and turned to mould, yet it is traceable and easily distinguished from the natural earth. Within is a deep ditch or entrenchment, running round the whole summit. From this it is evident, that a war was once waged here; and were we to conjecture between whom, we should say, between the Indians and Scandinavians; and that this fortification, so advantageously chosen, is of the same class of defensive works with those about Onondaga, Auburn, and the lakes Ontario, Cayuga, Seneca, Oneida, and Erie. As it is known, or not pretended, that the Scandinavians did not make settlements on the continent earlier than 985; there cannot be a doubt but they had to fight their way among the Indians, more or less, the same as we did when first we colonized the coast of the Atlantic, along the seaboard of the New-England states.

But as these Scandinavians, Norwegian, Scotch, and Welch, were fewer in number than the Indians, and without the means of recruiting from the mother country, as was *our case;* they at length fell a prey to this enemy, or became amalgamated with them, and so were lost; the traces of whom appear, now and then, among the tribes, as we have shown.

We are strongly inclined to believe the following articles, found in the town of Pompey, Onondaga county, New-York, are of Scandinavian origin. In Pompey, on lot No. 14, is the site of an ancient burying ground, upon which, when the country was first settled, was found timber growing apparently of the second growth, judging from the old timber reduced to mould, lying round, which was one hundred years old, ascertained by counting the concentric grains. In one of these graves was found a glass bottle about the size of a common junk bottle, having a stopple in its muzzle, and in the bottle was a liquid of some sort, but was tasteless. This fact was related to us by a Mr. Higgins, some time sheriff of Onondaga county, who both saw the bottle and tasted the liquid at the time it was discovered, but could not tell of what kind, as it was tasteless.

But is it possible that the Scandinavians could have had glass in their possession at so early a period as the year 950, and thereabout, so as to have brought it with them from Europe when their first settlements were made in this country? We see no good reason why not, as glass had been in use nearly 300 years in Europe, before the northern Europeans are reputed to have found this country; the art of making glass having been discovered in A. D. 644. In the same grave with the bottle was found an iron hatchet, edged with steel. The eye, or place for the helve, was round, and extended or projected out, like the ancient Swiss, or German axe.

On lot No. 9, in the same town, was another aboriginal burying ground, covered with forest trees, as the other. In the same town, on lot No. 17, were found the remains of a blacksmith's forge. At this spot have been ploughed up crucibles, such as mineralogists use in refining metals.

These axes are similar, and correspond in character with those found in the nitrous caves on the Gasconade river, which empties into the Missouri, as mentioned in Prof. Beck's Gazetteer of that country. In the same town are the remains of two ancient forts or fortifications, with redoubts, of a very extensive and formidable character. Within the range of these works have been found pieces of cast iron, broken from some vessel of considerable thickness. These articles cannot well be ascribed to the era of the French war, as time enough since then till the region round about Onondaga was commenced to be cultivated, had not elapsed to give the growth of timber found on the spot, of the age above noticed; and added to this, it is said that the Indians occupying that tract of country, had no tradition of their authors.

The reader will recollect, a few pages back, we have noticed the discovery of a place called Estotiland, supposed to be Nova-Scotia, in 1354, the inhabitants of which were Europeans, who cultivated grain, lived in stone houses, and manufactured *beer*, as in Europe at that day. Now, from the year 1354, till the time of the first settlements made in Onondaga county, by the present inhabitants, is about 400 years. Is it not possible, therefore, that this glass bottle, with some kind of liquor in it, may have been derived from this Estotiland, having been orginally brought from Europe; as glass had been in use there, more or less, from the year 644, till the Scandinavians colonized Iceland, Greenland, and Estotiland, or Newfoundland. The hatchets or iron axes found here, were likely of the same origin with the pieces of cast iron.

In ploughing the earth, digging wells, canals, or excavating for salt waters, about the lakes, new discoveries are frequently made, which as clearly show the operations of ancient civilization here, as the works of the present race would do, were they left to the operations of time for five or six hundred years; especially were this country to be totally overrun by the whole consolidated savage tribes of the west, exterminating both the worker and his works, as appears to have been done in ages past.

In Scipio, on Salmon creek, a Mr. Halsted has, from time to time, during ten years past, ploughed up, on a certain extent of land on his farm, seven or eight hundred pounds of brass, which appeared to have once been formed into various implements, both of husbandry and war; helmets and working utensils mingle together.

The finder of this brass, we are informed, from time to time, as he discovered it by ploughing, carried it to Auburn, and sold it by the pound, where it was worked up, with as little curiosity attending it as though it had been but an ordinary article of the country's produce: when, if it had been announced in some public manner, the finder would have doubtless been highly rewarded by some scientific individual or society, and preserved it in the cabinets of the antiquarian, as a relic of by-gone ages of the highest interest.

On this field, where it was found, the forest timber was growing as abundantly, and had attained to as great age and size, as elsewhere in the heavy timbered country of the lakes.

In the same field was also found much wrought iron, which furnished Mr. Halsted with a sufficiency to shoe his horses for several years. Hatchets of iron were also found there, formed in the manner the ancient Swiss or German hatchet, or small axe is formed.

From the above account, we cannot resist the conclusion that on this farm in Scipio, was situated an European village of Danes, or Welch, who were cut off and exterminated by the fortunes of war, some hundred years before the discovery of America by Columbus, when it is likely their town was destroyed by the fire of the enemy, their articles of brass broken in pieces, and in the course of ages became buried by the earth, by the increase of vegetable mould, and the growth of the wilderness.

If, then, we have discovered the traits of a clan or village of Europeans, who had a knowledge of the use of brass and iron, as the Danes certainly had, long before they colonized Iceland, Greenland and Labrador, why not be allowed to conjecture, nay more, to believe, that many others in different parts overspread the lake country to a great extent.

On the Black river, running from the northern part of the state of New-York, into lake Ontario, a man was digging a well, when at the depth of several feet he came to a quantity of *China* and *Delph* ware. This is equally surprising with the field of brass.

A Mr. Thomas Lee discovered, not long since, on his farm, in Tompkins county, in the State of New-York, the entire iron works of a wagon, reduced to rust. From this discovery much might be conjectured respecting the state of cultivation, as a wagon denotes not only a knowledge of the mechanic arts, equal, perhaps, in that respect, with the present times; but also that roads existed, or a wagon could not have traversed the country.

That the wagon was brought there by the Spaniards, who it is said, very soon after the discovery of America, explored these northern and further regions, in quest of minerals, because roads at that time did not exist; and for the same reason none of the first settlers of the New-England coast had penetrated so far in the wilds with a wagon as to give time for it to rust *entirely away* before the last settlement of the western country.

If *one* wagon existed, there were doubtless many; which plainly shows a civilized state of things, with all the conveniences of an agricultural life, which would also require towns and places of resort—as market places for produce—or a wagon could not have been of any use to the owner. Anvils of iron have been found in Pompey, in the same quarter of the country with the other discoveries, as above related; which we should naturally expect to find, or it might be inquired how could axes, and the iron works of wagons, be manufactured?

On the flats of the Genesee river, on the land of Mr. Liberty Judd, was found by this gentleman a bit of silver, about the length of a man's finger, hammered to a point at one end, while the other was square and smooth, on which were cut or engraved, in Arabic figures, in the year of our Lord 600.

The discovery of the remains of a wagon, as above stated, goes also to prove that some kind of animal must have been domesticated to draw it with. The horse, it is said, was not known in America till the Spaniards introduced it from Europe, after the time of its discovery by Columbus, which has multiplied prodigiously on the innumerable wilds and prairies of both South and North America; yet the track of a horse is found on a mountain of Tennessee, in the rock of the enchanted mountain, as before related, and shows that horses were known in America in the earliest ages after the flood.

It is likely, however, that the Danes, who are believed once to have occupied the whole lake country, had domesticated the buffalo and moose, as other nations have done, by which they were aided in agricultural pursuits, as we are now by the ox.

A further Account of Western Antiquities.

But as to the state of the arts among the more ancient nations of America, some idea may be gathered from what has been already said. That they manufactured brick of a good quality, is known from the discoveries made on opening their tumuli. A vast many instances of articles made of copper and sometimes plated with silver, have been met with on opening their works. Circular pieces of copper, intended either as medals or breast plates, have been found, several inches in diameter, very much injured by time. In several tumuli, the remains of knives, and even of swords, in the form of rust, have been discovered.

Glass has not been discovered in any of their works in the Ohio except one; from which we learn at once that these works were made at least more than eleven hundred and sixty years ago; as the manufacture of glass was not discovered till A. D. 664. But there is no doubt of their having inhabited this country from the *remotest* antiquity, drawn from data heretofore noticed in this work. "Mirrors made of *isinglass*, have been found in as many as fifty places, within my own knowledge, says Mr. Atwater, besides the large and very elegant one at Circleville. From the great thickness of those mica membranacea mirrors, they answered the purpose for which they were made very well.

Their houses, in some instances, might have been built of stone and brick, as in the walled towns on Paint creek, and some few other places, yet their habitations were of wood, or they dwelt in tents; otherwise their ruins would be met in every part of this great country.

Along the Ohio, where the river is, in many places, wearing and washing away its banks, hearths and fire places are brought to light, two, four, and even six feet below the surface, these are also found on the banks of the Muskingum, at its mouth, and at Point Harman, opposite Marietta. Two stone covers of stone vessels, were found in a *stone* mound, in Ross county, in Ohio, ingeniously wrought and highly polished. These covers resembled almost exactly, and were quite equal to vessels of that material manufactured in Italy at the present time.

An urn was found in a mound, a few miles from Chilicothe,

which, a few years since, was in the hands of a Mr. J. W. Collet, who lived in that place, about a foot high, and well proportioned; it very much resembles one found in a similar work in Scotland, mentioned in Pennant's Tour, vol. 1, p. 154. It contained arrow heads, ashes and calcined or burnt human bones. In digging a trench on the Sandusky river, in alluvial earth, at a depth of six feet, was found a pipe, which displays great taste in its execution. The rim of the bowl is in high relief, and the front represents a beautiful female face. The stone of which it is made is the real *talc graphique*, exactly resembling the stone of which the Chinese make their idols. No talc of this species is known to exist on the west side of the Alleghanies; it must therefore have been brought, at some remote period, from some part of the old world.

Fragments of fishing nets and moccasins, or shoes made of a species of weed, have been found in the nitrous caves of Kentucky. The mummies which have been found in these places, were wrapped in a coarse species of *linen cloth*, of about the consistency and texture of cotton bagging. It was evidently woven by the same kind of process which is practised in the interior of Africa. The warp being extended by some slight kind of machinery, the woof was passed across it, then twisted, every two threads of warp together, before the second passage of the filling. This seems to have been the first rude method of weaving in Asia, Africa and America.

A second envelope of these mummies, is a kind of net work, of coarse threads, formed of very small loose meshes, in which were fixed the feathers of various kinds of birds, so as to make a perfectly smooth surface, lying all in one direction. The art of this manufacture was well understood in Mexico, and still exists in the northwest coast of America, and in the Pacific islands. The third and outer envelope of these mummies, is either like the one first described, or consists of leather, sewed together.—*(Am. Antq. Soc.)*

The manufacture of leather from the hides of animals is a very ancient invention, known to almost all the nations of the earth; but to find it in America, wrapped around mummies, as in several instances found in nitrous caves, and the Kentucky caverns, shows a knowledge of a branch of the arts, in the possession of the people of America, at an era coeval with the Egyptians—as the art of embalming is found in connection with that of tanning the skins of animals.

Among the vast variety of discoveries made in the mouuds, tumuli and fortifications of these people, have been found, not only hatchets made of stone; but axes as large, and much of the same shape with those made of iron at the present day; also pickaxes and pestles, (see plate Nos. 11 and 12,) with various other instruments, made of stone. But besides, there have been found very well manufactured swords and knives of iron, and possibly *steel*, says Mr. Atwater: from which we are to conclude, that the primitive people of America, either discovered the use of iron themselves, as the Greeks did, or that they learned its use from this circumstance; or that they carried a knowledge of this ore with them at the time of their dispersion; as received from Noah's family, who brought it from beyond the flood, discovered in or before the days of Tubal Cain, which was only about five hundred years after the creation.

Dr. Clarke says, that from the manufacture of certain articles in the wilderness by the Israelites, iron, and even steel *must have been known*, which was an age preceding its knowledge by the Greeks, nearly a hundred years. If this was so, it follows that they must have learned it, or rather they must have taken these very instruments of iron and steel when they left Egypt; as they had no means of making such instruments from the ore, in the wilderness.

Great Stone Castle of Iceland.

In Iceland, which is not far from Greenland, and Greenland is not far from the coast of America, has been found the remains of ancient architecture, of no less dimensions than 200 rods in circumference, built of stone, the wall of which, in some places, as related by Van Troil, was 120 feet high. This was a Norwegian castle, of wonderful strength and magnitude, and of the same character with ruins found in this country, and in South America.

Iceland is but 120 miles east of Greenland, and Greenland is supposed to be connected with America far to the north. This island is considerably larger than the state of New-York, being 400 miles in length, and 270 in breadth. It was discovered by a Norwegian pirate, named Nardoddr, in the year 861, as he was driven out to sea by an eastern storm, on his way from Norway, which is the northern part of Europe, to the Feroe islands.

Soon after this, in the year 870, it was colonized from Norway, under the direction of a man named Ingalf, and sixty years after, which would bring it to 930, the whole island was inhabited. But they were without any regular government, being distracted with the wars of several chiefs, for a long series of years, during which Iceland was a scene of rapine and butchery. It is natural to suppose, during such conflicts, many families, from time to time, would leave the island, in quest of some other dwelling. This was in their power to do, as they had a knowledge of navigation, in a good degree, derived from the Romans, at the time they ruled the most of Europe, 900 years before.

That Greenland, or countries lying west of Iceland, existed, could not but be known to the Icelanders from the flights of birds of passage, and from driftwood, which, to this day, is driven in large quantities from America, by the gulf steam, and deposited on the western coast of that Island.—(*Morse.*)

In this way, it is highly probable, the first Europeans found their way to America, and became the authors of those vast ruins built of stone, found in various parts of America. The language of the Icelanders is, even now, after so long a lapse of ages, much the same with that spoken in Sweden, Denmark and Norway; so that they understand the most ancient traditional history of their ancestors. The characters they made use of were Runic, and were but sixteen in number. But about the year 1000, the Latin or Roman letters superceded the use of the ancient Runic.

Dr. Morse says, the arts and sciences were extensively cultivated in Norway, at the time when Iceland was first settled by them; and while the traces of literature were diminished, and at length destroyed, in Norway, by the troubles which shook the whole north of Europe for several ages; they were, on the contrary, carefully preserved in Iceland.

From this we may safely infer, that America, having received its *first European* colonies from Iceland; who had not only a knowledge of architecture, in a degree, but of navigation also, with that of science; that in the very regions where villas, cities, cultivated fields, roads, canals, rail-ways, with all the glory of the present age, exist along the Atlantic coast,—also flourished the works of a former population—the Danes, Swedes and Norwegians, civilized nations, centuries before Columbus was born, but who have passed away by the means of wars, with the more ancient nations of America, or with the common enemy of both, the Tartar hordes from Asia, now called the American Indians, leaving forever the labor of ages, which, here and there, are discovered, the relics of their architectural knowledge.

One hundred and twenty-one years after the discovery of Iceland, Greenland was discovered also, by the Norwegians, who planted a colony there, and in a little time after the country was provided with two Christian churches and bishops; between which and Norway, the mother country, a considerable amount of commerce was carried on, till 1406; a lapse of years amounting to about 483, before the discovery of America by Columbus; when all intercourse between the two countries ceased, occasioned probably by the convulsions and wars of Europe at that period.

The whole of that population, it is supposed, was lost, as no traces of them are found; the climate of that region, as is evident, has since undergone a great change, from an accumulation of ice and snow from the northern sea, so as to render the coast, where those settlements *were,* wholly inaccessible.—(*Morse.*)

Is it not possible, that as they found the severity of the weather increasing rapidly upon them, they may have removed to the coast of Labrador, and from thence down the coast, till they came to the region of the Canadas, where are discovered the traces of ancient nations, in vast lines of fortifications, as attested to by the most approved authority, Humboldt, and others.

A Description of Instruments found in the Tumuli.

In removing the earth which composed an ancient mound, situated where now one of the streets of Marietta runs, several curious articles were discovered in 1819. They appear to have been buried with the body of the person to whose memory this mound was erected.

Lying immediately on the forehead of this skeleton, were found *three* large circular ornaments, which had adorned a sword belt, or buckler, and were composed of copper, overlaid with a plate of silver. The *fronts,* or show sides were slightly convex, with a deep depression, like a cup, in the centre, and measured *two* inches and a quarter across the face of each. On the back side, opposite the depressed portion, is a copper rivet, around which are two separate plates by which they were fastened to the leather belt. The two pieces of leather resembled the skin of a mummy, and seemed to have been preserved by the salts of the copper; the plates were nearly reduced to an oxyde or rust. The *silver* looked quite black, but was not much corroded, as on rubbing it became bright and clear.

Around one of the rivets was a small quantity, of what appeared to be, flax or hemp, in a tolerable state of preservation. Near the side of the body was found a *plate of silver,* which appeared to have been the upper part of a *sword scabbard;* it was six inches long, and two broad, with two longitudinal ridges, which probably corresponded with the edges or ridges of the sword once sheathed by it, and appeared to have been fastened to the scabbard by several rivets, the holes of which remain in the plate.

Two or three pieces of a copper tube, were also found with this body, filled with iron rust. The pieces, from their appearances, composed the lower end of the scabbard, near the point of the sword, but no sign of the sword itself, except a streak of rust its whole length.

We learn from this that the person who was buried there, was a warrior, as the sword declares; and also that the people, of whom he was an individul, were acquainted with the arts of civilized life, which appears from the sheath, the flax, the copper, and the silver, but more especially as the silver was *plated* on the copper. Near the feet was found a piece of copper, weighing three ounces, which from its shape, appeared to have been used as a plumb, as near one of the ends is a crease or groove, for tying a thread; it is round and two inches and a half in length, one inch in diameter at the centre, and an half inch at the small or upper end. It was composed of small pieces of native copper, pounded together, and in the cracks between the pieces were stuck several bits of silver, one nearly the size of a sixpence. This copper plumb was covered with a coat of green rust, and was considerably corroded. A piece of red ochre, or paint, and a piece of iron ore, which had the appearance of having been partially vitrified, or melted, was also found in this tumulus; the bit of ore was nearly pure iron.

The body of the person here buried, was laid *on the surface* of the earth, with his face upwards, and his feet pointing to the northeast, and his head to the southwest.

From the appearance of several pieces of charcoal, and bits of partially burnt wood, and the black color of the earth, it would appear that the funeral obsequies had been celebrated by fire; and that while the ashes were yet hot and smoking, a circle of flat stones had been laid around and over the body, from which the tumulus had been carried up.

For a view of each article, the reader can refer to the Frontispiece engraving, by observing the numbering of each specimen. Nos. 1, 2, 3, 4, 5, and 6, are articles found in the mound at Marietta, in 1819.

No. 1. Back view of the silver ornament for a sword scabbard.

No. 2. Front view of the same.

No. 3. Front view of an ornament for a belt, with a silver face.

No. 4. Back view of the same ornament, of copper.

No. 5. A plumb, or pendant, formed of pieces of copper pounded together, leaving fissures or openings, which were filled with bits of silver; an implement, as to its shape, resembling the instruments used by carpenters and masons, now-a-days, to ascertain perpendiculars with, and was doubtless used by these ancients for the same purpose.

No. 6. A stone with seven holes, like a screw plate, fourteen inches long, finely polished, and very hard; this, however, was not found in the mound, but in a field near this tumulus.

Letter A represents a small keg in its construction, and a tea-kettle in the use of which it seems to have been put, which is indicated by its spout; and appears to have been made of a composition of clay and shells.

Letter B represents the *idol*, before spoken of, on pages 217 and 218, in three views, a front, side and back view.

Letter C represents the *idol*, or image of stone, on page 219.

Letter D is the stone, or *Shalgramu*, described on pages 180, 181, and 182.

Letter E represents the *triune cup*, found on the Cany fork of Cumberland river, in an ancient work, about four feet below the surface. The drawing is an exact likeness, taken originally by Miss Sara Clifford, of Lexington, Kentucky; it is by some called the triune idol.

"The object itself may be thus described. It consists of three heads joined together at the back part, near the top, by a stem or handle, which rises above the head about three inches. This stem is hollow, six inches in circumference at the top, increasing in size as it descends.

The heads are all of the same dimensions, being about four inches from the top to the chin. The face, at the eyes, is three inches broad, decreasing in breadth, all the way to the chin. All the strong marks of the Tartar countenance are distinctly preserved and expressed with so much skill, that even a modern artist might be proud of the performance. The countenances are all different from each other, and denote one old person, and two younger ones.

The face of the oldest is painted around the eyes with yellow, shaded with a streak of the same color, begining from the top of the ear, running in a semicircular form, to the ear on the other side of the head. Another painted line begins at the lower part of the eye, and runs down before each ear, about one inch.—(*See the right hand figure on the cup, or image on frontispiece.*)

The face engraved alone, is the back view, and represents a person of a grave countenance, but much younger than the preceding one, painted very differently, and of a different color. A streak of reddish brown surrounds each eye. Another line of the same color, begining at the top of one ear, passes under the chin, and ends at the top of the other ear. The ears also, are slightly tinged with the same color.

The third figure, in its characteristical features resembles the others, representing one of the Tartar family. The whole of the face is slightly tinged with vermilion, or some paint resembling it. Each cheek has a spot on it, of the size of a quarter of a dollar, brightly tinged with the same paint. On the chin is a similar spot. One circumstance worthy of remark, is, that though these colors must have been exposed to the damp earth for many centuries, they have, notwithstanding, preserved every shade in all its brilliancy.

This triune vessel stands upon three necks, which are about an inch and a half in length. The whole is composed of a fine clay, of a light umber color, which has been rendered hard by the action of fire. The heads are hollow, and the vessel is of capacity to hold about one quart.

Does not this cup represent the three gods of India—Brahma, Vishnoo, and Siva? Let the reader look at the plate representing this vessel, and consult the *Asiatic Researches*, by Sir William Jones; let him also read Buchanan's *Star in the East*, and accounts there found, of the idolatry of the Hindoos, and he cannot fail to see in this idol, one proof at least, that the people who raised our ancient works were idolaters; and, that some of them worshipped gods resembling the three principal deities of India. What tends to strengthen this inference, is, that nine *murex shells*, the same as described by Sir William Jones, in his Asiatic Researches, and by Symmes, in his Embassy to Ava, have been found within twenty miles of Lexington, Kentucky, in an ancient work.

The *murex shell*, is a sea shell fish, out of which the ancients procured the famous *Tyrian purple dye*, which was the color of the royal robes of kings, so celebrated in ancient times. Their component parts remained unchanged, and they were every way in an excellent state of preservation. These shells, so rare in India, are highly esteemed, and consecrated to their god, Mahadeva, whose character is the same with the Neptune, of Greece and Rome. This shell, among the Hindoos, is the musical instrument of their *Tritons;* (sea gods, or trumpeters of Neptune.) Those, of the kind discovered as above, are deposited in the museum, at Lexington. The foot of the Siamese god, Gudma, or Boodh, is represented by a sculpture statue, in Ava, of six feet in length, and the *toes* of this god, are carved, each to represent a shell of the murex.

These shells have been found in many mounds which have been opened in every part of this country; and this is a proof that a considerable value was set upon them by their owners. From these discoveries it is evident, that the people who built the ancient works of the west, were idolaters; it is also inferred from the age of the world in which they lived; history, sacred and profane, affords the fact, that all nations, except the Jews, were idolaters at the same time and age.

Medals, representing the sun with its rays of light, have been found in the mounds, made of a very fine clay, and colored in the composition, before it was hardened by heat, from which it is inferred they worshipped the sun. It is also supposed, that they worshipped the moon, both from their semicircular works, which represent the *new* moon; and also from the discovery of copper medals, round like the moon in its full, being smooth, without any rays of light, like those which represent the sun. The worship of the sun, moon, and stars, was the worship of many nations, in the earliest ages, not only soon after the flood, but all along, cotemporary with the existence of the Jews as a nation, and also succeeding the Christian era, and till the present time, as among the pagan Mexicans.

Nos. 8, 9, 10, 11, and 12, represent the shapes of the stone axes, pestle, and other articles spoken of a few pages back.—(*See the plate.*)

As it respects the scientific acquirements of the builders of the works in the west, now in ruins, Mr. Atwater says, " when thoroughly examined, have furnished matter of admiration to all intelligent persons, who have attended to the subject. Nearly all the lines of ancient works found in the whole country, where the form of the ground admits of it, are right ones, pointing to the four cardinal points. Where there are mounds enclosed, the gateways are most frequently on the east side of the works, towards the rising sun. Where the situation admits of it, in their military works, the openings are generally towards one or more of the *cardinal points*. From which it is supposed they must have had some knowledge of astronomy, or their structures would not, it is imagined, have been thus arranged. From these circumstances also, we draw the conclusion, that the first inhabitants of America, emigrated from Asia, at a period coeval with that of Babylon, for here it was that astronomical calculations were first made, 2234 years before Christ.

" These things could never have so happened, with such invariable exactness, in almost all cases, without design. " On the whole," says Atwater, " I am convinced from an attention to many hundreds of these works, in every part of the west which I have visited, that their authors had a knowledge of astronomy." He strengthens his opinions as follows: " The pastoral life, which men followed in the early ages, was certainly very favorable to the attainment of such a knowledge. Dwelling in tents, or in the open air, with the heavenly bodies in full view, and much more liable to suffer from changes in the weather, than persons dwelling in comfortable habitations, they would, of course, direct their attention to the prognostics of approaching heat or cold, stormy or pleasant weather. Our own sailors are an example in point. Let a person, even wholly unaccustomed to the seas, be wafted for a few weeks by the winds and waves, he will become all ear to every breeze, all eye to every part of the heavens. Thus, in the *earliest ages* of mankind, astronomy was attended to, partly from necessity; hence, a knowledge of this science was early diffused among men, the proofs of which are seen in their works, not only here, but in every part of the globe. It was reserved, however, for the geniuses of modern times, to make the most astonishing discoveries in this science, aided by a knowledge of figures, and an acquaintance with the telescope."

Our ancient works continued into Mexico, increasing in size and grandeur, preserving the same forms, and appear to have been put to the same uses. The form of our works is round, square, triangular, semicircular and octangular, agreeing, in all these respects, with those in Mexico. The first works built by the Mexicans, were mostly of earth, and not much superior to the common ones on the Mississippi." The same may be said of the works of this sort over the whole earth, which is the evidence that all alike belong to the first efforts of men, in the very first ages after the flood.

"But afterwards temples were erected on the elevated squares, circles, &c., but were still like ours, surrounded by walls of earth. These sacred places, in Mexico, were called "*teocalli*," which in the vernacular tongue of the *most ancient* tribe of Mexicans, signifies "*mansions of the gods.*" They included within their sacred walls, gardens, fountains, habitations of priests, temples, altars, and magazines of arms. This circumstances may account for many things which have excited some surprise among those who have hastily visited the works on Paint creek, at Portsmouth, Marietta, Circleville, Newark, &c.

It is doubted by many to what use these works were put; whether they were used as forts, camps, cemeteries, altars, and temples; whereas they contained all these either within their walls, or were immediately connected with them. Many persons cannot imagnie why the works, at the places above mentioned, were so extensively complicated, differing so much in form, size, and elevation, among themselves." But the solution is, undoubtedly, "they contained within them, altars, temples cemeteries, habitations of priests, gardens, wells, fountains, places devoted to sacred purposes, of various kinds, and the whole of their warlike munitions, laid up in arsenals. These works were calculated for defence, and were resorted to in cases of the last necessity, where they fought with desperation. We are warranted in this conclusion, by knowing that these works are exactly similar to the most ancient now to be seen in Mexico, connected with the fact, that the Mexican works did contain within them *all* that we have stated.

Great size of some of the Mexican Mounds.

THE word *Teocalli*, Humboldt says, is derived from the name of one of the gods to which they were dedicated, *Tezcatlipoca*, the Brahma of the Mexicans. The pyramid of Cholula, was seated on a tumulus with four stages, and was dedicated to Quetzalcotl, one of the mysterious characters that appeared among the ancient Mexicans, said to have been a *white* and *bearded* man, before spoken of in this work.

The *teocalli*, or pyramid of Cholula, is sixty rods in circumference, and ten rods high. In the vale of Mexico, twenty-four miles northeast from the capital, in a plain that bears the name of Micoatl, or the path of the dead, is a group of pyramids, of several hundred in number, generally about thirty feet high.

In the midst of these are *two* large pyramids, one dedicated to the *sun*, the other to the *moon*. The sun pyramid is ten rods thirteen feet high, and its length nearly thirty-five rods, and of a proportionable thickness, but is not a circle; that of the moon is eight rods and eleven feet in perpendicular height, but its base is not specified by Humboldt; from whose Researches we have derived this information.

The small pyramids, which surrounded the two dedicated to the sun and moon, are divided by spacious streets, running exactly north and south, east and west, intersecting each other at right angles, forming one grand palace of worship, and of the dead. It is the tradition of the Mexicans, that in the small tumuli, or pyramids, were buried the chiefs of their tribes. We also here ascertain that the builders of these two vast houses of the sun and moon, had indeed a knowledge of the cardinal points of the compass; for this arrangement could never have taken place from mere chance, it must have been the result of calculation, with the *north star*, or pole, in view. On the top of those teocallis, were two colossal statues of the sun and moon, made of stone, and covered with plates of gold, of which they were stripped by the soldiers of Cortez. Such were some of the pyramids of Egypt, with colossal statues.

This tremendous work is much similar to one found in Egypt, called the " Cheops and the Mycerinus ;" round about which were eight small pyramids; only the Egyptian work is much less than the Mexican one, yet their fashion is the same.

Predilection of the Ancients to Pyramids.

In those early ages of mankind, it is evident there existed an unaccountable ambition among the nations, seemingly to outdo each other in the height of their pyramids; for Humboldt mentions the pyramids of Porsenna, as related by Varro, styled the most learned of the Romans, who flourished about the time of Christ; and says there were, at this place, four pyramids, eighty meters in height, which is a fraction more than *fifteen* rods perpendicular altitude; the meter is a French measure, consisting of 3 feet 3 inches.

Not many years since was discovered, by some Spanish hunters, on descending the Cordilleras, towards the gulf of Mexico, in the thick forest, the pyramid of Papantla. The form of this teocalli, or pyramid which had seven stories, is more tapering than any other monument of this kind, yet discovered, but its height is not remarkable; being but fifty-seven feet, its base but twenty-five feet on each side. However, it is remarkable on one account; it is built entirely of hewn stones, of an extraordinary size, and very beautifully shaped. Three stair-cases lead to its top; the steps of which were decorated with hieroglyphical sculpture and small niches, arranged with great symmetry. The number of these niches seems to allude to the 318 simple and compound signs of the days of their civil calendar. If so, this monument was erected for astronomical purposes; besides, here is evidence of the use of metalic tools, in the preparation and building of this temple.

In those mounds were sometimes hidden the treasures of kings and chiefs, placed there in times of war and danger. Such was found to be the fact on opening the tomb of a Peruvian prince, when was discovered a mass of pure gold, amounting to 4,687,500 dollars.—(*Humboldt's Researches*, vol. 1, p. 92.)

The pyramids of the Ohio are, in several instances, built in the same manner, with several stages, on the tops of which were, unquestionably, temples of wood, in the day of their glory, when their builders swarmed in populous ten thousands, over all the unbounded west; but time has destroyed all fabrics of this sort, while the mounds on which they stood, in giddy grandeur, remain, but stripped of the habiliments of architecture, and the embellishments of art.

There is, in Central America, to the southeast of the city of Cuernuvaca, on the west declivity of the Cordillera of Anahuac, an isolated hill, which, together with the pyramid, raised on its top by the ancients of that country, amounts to thirty-five rods ten feet high, which is but thirty feet higher than the hill we are describing [perpendicular height. The ancient tower of Babel, around which the city Babylon was afterwards built, was six hundred ing; but the base of Babel is a mere nothing, compared with the gigantic work of Anahuac, being but 600 feet square, which is 150 rods, or nearly so; while the hill in America, partly natural and partly artificial, is at its base 12,066 feet; this thrown into rods gives 754, and into miles is $2\frac{3}{8}$, wanting eight rods, which is five times greater than that of Babel.

The hill of Xochicalco is a mass of rocks, to which the hand of man has given a regular conic form, and which is divided into five stories or terraces, each of which is covered with masonry. These terraces are nearly sixty feet in perpendicular height, one above the other, besides the artificial mound added at the top, making its height near that of Babel: besides, the whole is surrounded with a deep broad ditch, more than five times the circumference of that Babylonian tower.

Humboldt says, we ought not to be surprised at the magnitude and dimensions of this work, as on the ridge of the Cordilleras of Peru, and on the other heights, almost equal to that of Teneriffe, he had seen monuments still more considerable. Also in Canada, he had seen lines of defence, and entrenchments of extraordinary length, the work of some people belonging to the early ages of time. Those in Canada, however, we imagine to be of the Danish origin, and to have been erected in the 9th, 10th and 11th centuries of the Christian era, for reasons hereafter shown.

If then, as Humboldt states, there were found on the plains of Canada, lines of defence of extraordinary length, it affords an argument that the Norwegians, and other northern nations, may not only have made settlements there, but became a kingdom, a body politic and military, and waged long and dreadful wars with opposing powers, who were unquestionably the Indians, who had already driven away the more ancient inhabitants of America, the authors of the western mounds and tumuli. But respecting this stone monument of art, found by the hunters, which we have described above, it is said that travellers, who have attentively examined it, were struck with the polish and cut of the stones, the care with which they have been arranged, without cement between the joints, and the execution of the sculpture with which the stones are decorated; each figure occupying several stones, and from the outlines of the animals which they represent, not being broken by the joints of the stones, it is conjectured the engravings were made after the edifice was finished. But the animals and men sculptured on the stone of this pyramid, afford a strong evidence of the country from which the ancestors of those who built it came. There are crocodiles spouting water, and men sitting even cross legged, according to the custom of several Asiatic nations; finally, the whole of the American works, of the most ancient class, from Canada to the extreme parts of South America, resemble those which are daily discovered in the eastern parts of Asia.

From the deep ditch, with which the greater monument we have been describing, is surrounded, the covering of the terraces, the great number of subterranean apartments, cut into the solid rock, on its northern side, the wall that defends the approach to its base, it is believed to have been a military work of great strength. The natives, even to this day, designate the ruins of this pyramid by the name that signifies a citadel or castle. The pyramid of Mexitli, found in another part of Mexico, called the great temple of Tenochtitlan, contained an arsenal, and during the war of the Spaniards with the devoted Mexicans, was alternately resorted to as a fort of defence, and a place of security.

Nothing of the warlike character, could exceed the grandeur of a fight maintained from the base to the summit of one of these tremendous *teocallis*, or pyramids. We may suppose the foe already gathered from their more scattered work of ruin, and circling, with yells of fury, the immediate precincts of the mound, while the rushing multitude fly from thier burning habitations towards this last resort. The goal is gained; the first who reach it ascend to its top; rank after rank succeed, till in frightful circles of ferocious warriors, the whole pyramid is but one living mass of fury. Now the enemy come pouring round as a deluge, and begirt this final refuge of the wailing populace; while warrior facing warrior, each moment fells its thousands by the noiseless death-stab of the dirk of copper; while from the ranks above, the silent but vengeful arrow does its work of death. Here, from the strong arm and well practised, sling stones with furious whizzing through the air, cover in showers the distant squadron with dismay. Circle after circle, at the base, both of invader and invaded, fall together in glorious ruin. Now the top where waved such signals of defiance as rude nations could invent, becomes thinned of its defenders; who, pressing downward, as the lower ranges are cut in pieces, renew the fight. Now the farthest circle of the enemy nears the fatal centre. Now the destinies of conflicting nations draw nigh; those of the pyramid have thrown their last stone; the quiver is emptied of its arrows; the last spear of flint and battle-axe have fled, with well-directed aim, amid the throng. Surrender, captivity, slavery and death, wind up the account; a tribe becomes extinct, whose bones, when heaped together, make a new pyramid. Such doubtless, is the origin of many of the frightful heaps of human bones found scattered over all the west.

We learn from Scripture that in the earliest times the temples of Asia, such as that of Baal-Berith, at Shechim, in Canaan, were not only buildings consecrated to worship, but also intrenchments, in which the inhabitants of a city defended themselves in times of war. The same may be said of the Grecian temples; for the wall which formed the parabolis, alone afforded an asylum to the besieged.—(*Humboldt.*)

The ancient Carthaginians, the sworn and eternal enemies of the Romans, practised raising mounds of earth over their glorious dead. Hannibal, their famous general, who for a while so successfully combated the Roman armies, almost in sight of the imperial city, was thus honored. At the place where he fell by his own hand, having poisoned himself to escape the scorn of his victors, was raised a lofty mound of earth over his remains, exactly like the one which marks the place where sleeps the ashes of Achilles on the plains of Troy.

The mound of Hannibal was erected 182 years before Christ. If, therefore, the Carthaginians, the Greeks, the Romans, the more ancient Phœnicians, the Egyptians, the Jews, and all the first nations immediately succeeding the flood, were found in this practice, is it not fairly inferred, that branches or colonies of these same nations and races of men, were also the authors of many of the mounds of America found scattered over its mighty regions.

Clavigero, who was well acquainted with the history of the Mexicans and Peruvians, professes to point out the places from whence they emigrated, several places they stopped at, and the times which they continued to sojourn there. This, we understand, is the same as related before in this work, written by Humboldt, and describes the emigration of the Azteca tribes, from Aztalan, or the western states, to Mexico, which commenced to take place not long after the conquest of Judea by Titus. Clavigero supposes these nations of Aztalan came from Asia, across the Pacific, from the region along the coast of the Chinese sea and islands, reaching America not far from Bhering's strait, and from thence followed along the coast of the Pacific, till they came, in process of time, to a milder climate.

To this Mr. Atwater adds, and supposes them to have from thence worked across the continent, as well as in other directions, as far as the regions of the western states and territories, where they may have lived thousands of years, as their works denote.

Others may have found their way into South America, by crossing the Pacific and Atlantic at different times and places. Greenlanders have been driven upon the coast of Iceland, which is a distance of at least a thousand miles. Thus transported by winds, waves and stress of weather, man has found all the islands of all the seas. In the same way may have arrived persons from Africa, and Europe, Australasians, Chinese, Hindoos, Japanese, Birmans, Kamschadales and Tartars, on the coasts of America in the first ages after the flood.

A Specimen of Antediluvian Letters.

Although we have bestowed a few thoughts on the subject of antediluvian letters on pages 132 and 133, yet we are inclined to state, farther, that our opinion is still more confirmed that letters, whether as pictures of articles, or of ideas and words, were in use before the flood, from the late discoveries made on pulling down the foundations of the tower of Babel.

The reason we introduce this subject again is, that at the time the above quoted pages went to press we had not obtained the beautiful fac-similie specimen of some of the letters of that tower built by Nimrod, son of Ham, and grandson of Noah, and are here set forth.

These letters are presented to the public by Sir Robert Ker Porter, who examined them on the spot, that is at the tower in 1820, on the Euphrates: an account of which can be seen at large, in his Travels in Persia, Armenia, the country round about the mountains of Ararat, Georgia, Babylon, and the vast plains and regions of the ancient Tartars, or more properly Scythians, vol. 2, p. 395.

The invention of letters is, by all who have given their attention to this exceedingly interesting subject, ascribed to the Phœnicians, who were black, as the very climax of antiquity, going back to the time coeval with Abraham, 2000 B. C.

But from the abundance of *letters*, not *pictures* of things, found on the bricks of Babel, it certainly is ascertained that Nimrod has here availed himself of the art learned from his grandfather Noah, to record his own history, that of the deluge, the family of man saved in the ark, the institutions of men before the flood, the creation of the first man and woman, as also the erection of the tower, and his own laws and religion. We do not certainly know that such *is* the history written on these bricks, yet it is highly probable, as those subjects would be the most likely to engross his attention, and that of all other men, at the time, and are therefore supposed to compose a history, as above expressed.

The reader will perceive that the writing is in perpendicular columns, a mode known to the *most* ancient in China, although horizontal writing is practised in that country yet, more frequently according to Good, and by the Chinese is said to be the most ancient. The *varieties* of these letters are found to be immense, yet they all partake of a similar formation, which is arrow-headed, and in our opinion, stand at the head of all the letters of the human race, and are the same which were in use before the flood. But whether they were invented by man at first, or were received from God by Adam, Seth or Enoch, is a question among the most learned. Some are of the opinion that the *letters* are the result of improvement from picture writing, and others that they were received by inspiration. We incline, however, to believe them the invention of man, yet we do not forget that "Man hath his understanding by the inspiration of God."—(*Job.*)

It is said by the same traveller, that on his leaving the bank of the river Ingouletz he entered on the dreary steppe or desert plains, where he observed innumerable tumuli, or mounds; and some of a breadth and height hardly credible. He says the mounds in this immense region of the dead, vary greatly in size, and that where one of unusual magnitude is found, it is generally surrounded by several smaller ones. So also in America.

It is the opinion of this most intelligent traveller that there should be no doubt but the larger sort of these tumuli were raised over the bodies of princes and heroes, and that the smaller ones cover the remains of the followers of their armies, or of their state. But that so vast an expanse should be occupied by monuments of the dead, extending regularly to the very farthest extent of sight, seemed almost beyond belief: yet, there they were; and the contemplation was as awful, as the view was amazing.

His first impression, he says, on beholding the immensity of these tumuli, was, that he was in some famous field of battle, vast enough for the world to have been lost in. Herodotus thus describes the burial place of princes among the ancient Scythians. He says a large quadrangular excavation was made in the earth in dimensions more like a hall of banquet than a grave, and within it was placed a sort of bier bearing the body of the deceased prince. Daggers were laid at various distances around him, and a number of golden goblets; the whole then covered with pieces of wood, and branches of the willow tree. This done, the hollow was soon filled up, and surmounted with earth by the multitudes following in the train.

Herodotus also describes the great tumulus erected over the remains of Alyates, the father of Crœsus, which in part still exists near the ancient city of Sardis. He describes it as of a prodigious height, having a base of stones, and that three classes of people were employed to raise up its enormous bulk. This tumulus was, in the time of Strabo, though partly destroyed, still two hundred feet high, and its circumference three-fourths of a mile. This mound or tumulus was erected about 600 years before Christ; as this Alyates, the father of Crœsus, was contemporary with Nebuchadnezzar, the king of Babylon, the same of whom the Scriptures give an account. All about that region, the tower of Babel, mounds are still immense in numbers, copied from the first, that of Babel, and Babel, it is likely, from the same practice once in use before the flood, to mark the places where slept the remains of the mighty dead, whose deeds attracted the eye of heaven itself, and provoked its thunders to exterminate the race.

Voyages and Shipping of the Mongol Tartars, and Settlements on the Western Coast of America.

The whole western coast of the American continent, from opposite the Japan islands, in latitude from 40 to 50 degrees north, down to Patagonia, in latitude 40 south—a distance of more than six thousand miles—it would appear, was once populous with such nations as peopled the Japan islands, and the eastern shores of Asia, Chinese Tartary, China, and Farther India; who also peopled the islands between, with their various nations.

A cross made of fine marble, beautifully polished, about three feet high, and three fingers in width and thickness, was found in an Indian temple. This, it appears, was kept as *sacred*, in a palace of one of the Incas, and held in great veneration by the natives of South America. When the Spaniards conquered that country they enriched this cross with gold jewels, and placed it in the cathedral of Cuzco.

But how came this emblem of Christianity in America? There were in the service of the Mongols, in the 13th century, many Nestorians, a sect of Christians. The conqueror of the king of Eastern Bengal, was a Christian, which was in 1272, A. D.

Under this king a part of an expedition was sent to conquer the islands of Japan, in large Chinese vessels, and supposed to have been commanded by these Christian Nestorians, as officers; being more trust-worthy and more expert in warlike manouvres than the Mongol natives. This expedition by some means found their way from the Japan islands, (which are west from North America, in north latitude 35 degrees,) to the coast of America in the same latitude, and landed at a place called in the Mexican language Culcaan, opposite New-California, in north latitude about 35 degrees.

In 1273 A. D., Kublai, a Mongol emperor, it appears, became master of all China. At that time they were in the possession of the knowledge of ship building, so that vessels of enormous size were constructed by them; so great as to carry more than a thousand men; being four masted, not rigged as vessels now are, yet well adapted to take advantage of the winds; in this way this emblem may have found its way here.

They were so solidly and conveniently made, as to carry elephants on their decks. The Peruvians had a tradition that many ages before their conquest by the Spaniards, there landed on their coast at St. Helen's point, vessels manned with giants, having no beard and were taller from their knees downward than a man's head; that they had long hair, which hung loose upon their shoulders, and that their eyes were wide apart, and very big in other parts of their bodies.

This description is supposed descriptive of the elephants only, with their riders blended both in one animal; as they did in after years, when the Spaniards rode on horses, they took them at first to be all one animal.

There remains not a doubt, that the Mongol Tartars found their way from China to the west of America in shipping. The voyage is not so great as to render it impossible, as that a French vessel in the year 1721 sailed from China, and arrived at a place called Valle de Nandras, on the coast, in fifty days.

The Phœnician letters were known among the Mongol nations. If, therefore, they found their way to South America, we at once account for the Phœnician characters found in caverns, and cut in rocks of that country.

A description of what is supposed a Chinese Mongol town, to the west, in latitude 39, in longitude 87, called by themselves, when first visited by the Spaniards *Talomeco*, is exceedingly curious, and situated on the bank of a river running into the Pacific from the territory now called Oregon, only four degrees south of Lake Erie, and in longitude 87, or exactly west of Ohio, in latitude 39.

It was well built, and contains five hundred houses; some of which are large and show well at a distance. It was situated on the banks of a river. Hernando Soto dined with a cacique named Guachaia, and was entertained with as much civility as exists among polished nations. The suit of servants stood in a row with their backs against the wall. This is an eastern fashion. While the cacique was at dinner, he happened to sneeze, on which the attendants respectfully bowed. This too was an ancient eastern usage. After the repast was finished, the servants all dined in another hall. The meat was well cooked, the fish properly roasted or broiled.

They had the knowledge of dressing furs with neatness, and deer skins were prepared with softness and delicacy, with which they clothed themselves.

The principal pride and grandeur of his people, however, consisted in their temple, which stood in the town of Talomeco, which was also the sepulchre of their caciques or chiefs.

The temple was a hundred paces long, which is eighteen rods, and forty wide, which is seven rods and eight feet. Its doors were wide in proportion to its length. The roof was thatched neatly with split twigs, and built sloping to throw off the rain. It was thickly decorated with different sized shells, connected together in festoons, which shine beautifully in the sun.

On entering the temple, there are twelve wooden statues of gigantic size, with menacing and savage faces, the tallest of which was eight feet high. They held in their hands, in a striking posture, clubs, adorned with copper. Some had copper hatchets, edged with flint; others had bows and arrows, and some held long pikes, pointed with copper.

The Spaniards thought these statues worthy of the ancient Romans. On each of the four sides of the temple, there was two rows of statues, the size of life; the upper row of men with arms in their hands; the lower row of women. The cornice in the temple was ornamented with large shells mingled with pearls, and festoons.

The corpses of these caciques were so well embalmed that there was no bad smell; they were deposited in large wooden coffers, well constructed, and placed upon benches two feet from the ground.

In smaller coffers and in baskets, the Spaniards found the clothes of the deceased men and women; and so many pearls, that they distributed them among the officers and soldiers by handfulls. The prodigious quantity of pearls; the heaps of colored chamois or goat skins; clothes of marten and other well dressed furs; the thick, well made targets of twigs, ornamented with pearls; and other things found in this temple and its magazines, which consisted of eight halls of equal magnitude, made even the Spaniards who had been in Peru, admire this as the wonder of the new world.

The remains of cities and towns of an ancient population, exists every where on the coast of the Pacific, which agree in fashion with the works and ruins found along the Chinese coasts, exactly west from the western limits of North America, showing beyond all dispute, that in ancient times the countries were known to each other, and voyages were reciprocally made.

The style of their shipping was such as to be equal to voyages of that distance, and also sufficient to withstand stress of weather, even beyond vessels of the present times, on account of their great depth of keel and size.

"The Chinese ships have a single deck, below the space of which is divided into a great number of cabins, sometimes not less than sixty, affording accommodations for as many merchants with their servants.

They have a good helm, some of the larger ships have *besides* the cabin, *thirteen* bulk-heads, or divisions, in the hold, formed of thick planks mortised together. The object of this is to guard against springing a leak, if they strike on a rock, or should be struck by a whale, which not unfrequently occurs.

By this plan, if an accident *did* happen, only *one* of the divisions could be effected; the whole vessel was double planked, laid over the first planking; and so large were some of these vessels as to require a crew of three hundred sailors to manage them when at sea.—(*See Marco Polo, Book* 3*d., chap. 1, and note* 1128—*Rankin.*)

In A. D. 1275, the Tartars, under their general, called *Moko*, undertook the invasion of the Japan empire, which lies along adjacent to China, between the western coast of North America and China, with a fleet of 4000 sail, having on board two hundred and forty thousand men. But the expedition proved unsuccessful, as it was destroyed by a storm, driven and scattered about the Pacific ocean.—(*Kempfer's History of Japan—Rankin.*)

From this we discover the perfect ability of the western nations, that is, west of America, to explore the ocean, as suited their inclinations, in the earliest ages; for we are not to suppose the Tartars had just then, in 1275, come to a knowledge of navigation, but rather, the greatness of this fleet is evidence, that the art had arrived to its highest state of perfection.

But had they a knowledge of the compass? This is an important enquiry. On this subject we have the following from the pen of the most learned antiquarian of the age, C. S. Rafinesque, whose writings we have several times alluded to in the course of this work.

This author says, that in the year of the world 1200, or 2800 B. C., or 450 years before the flood, the magnetic needle was known and in use, and that under the Emperor Hoangti, which was about 130 years nearer the time of the flood, reckoning from the creation, ships began to be invented. He even gives the names of two ship builders, *Kong-ku*, and *Ho-ahu*, who by order of the above named emperor, built boats, at first with hollow trees, and furnished them with oars, and were sent to explore places where no man had ever been.

In the year 2037 B. C., or 307 years after the flood, under the *Hia* dynasty, embassies were sent to China from foreign countries beyond sea, who came in ships to pay homage to the *Hias* or emperor.

If a knowledge of the magnet, and its adaptation to navigation, was known before the flood, as appears from this writer's remarks, who derives this discovery from a perusal of the Chinese histories; it was, of necessity, divulged by Noah, to his immediate posterity, who, it is said, went soon after the confusion of the language at Babel, and planted a colony in China, or in that eastern country; as all others of mankind had perished in the flood, consequently there were none else to promulge it to but this family.

Dr. Clarke has given his opinion, in his comment on the book of Job, that the needle was known to the ancients of the east. He derives this from certain expressions of Job, chap. xxviii. verse 18, respecting precious stones, which are:—"*No mention shall be made of coral pearls: for the price of wisdom is above rubies.*" That is, it is understood that the wisdom which aided man to make this discovery, and to apply it to the purposes of navigation, on the account of its polarity, is that wisdom which is above the price of *rubies*.

"The attractive properties of loadstone *must* have been observed from its first discovery; and there is every reason to believe that the magnet and its virtues were known in the east long before they were discovered in Europe."—(*Clarke.*)

But it may be inquired, if the knowledge of the magnet and its application to the great purpose of navigation, and surveying, were understood in any degree, how came *one* branch of the descendants of the family of Noah, those who went east from Ararat, to have it; and the others, who went in other directions, to be ignorant of it, and had to discover it over again in the course of ages. We can answer this, *only* by noticing that many arts of the ancients of Europe and of Africa are lost; but how, we cannot tell; but in the same way this art was lost. Wars, convulsions, revolutions, sweeping diseases, often change the entire face and state of society; so that if it were even known to all the *first* generation, immediately succeeding the flood, a second generation may have lost it, not dwelling in the vicinity of great waters; having no use for such an art, would of necessity loose it, which remained lost till about A. D. 1300.

In the year 1197, before Christ, about the time of Job; a large colony from China, under the *Yu* dynasty was sent to Japan, and other western islands, who drove out the *Oni*, or black inhabitants, the first settlers of those islands, a branch, it appears, of the family of *Ham*, who had found their way across the whole continent of Asia, from Ararat, or else had, by sea, coasted along from the countries of the equator, their natural home, to those beautiful islands.

From this trait of early settlement, we see the African, as he is now designated, as enterprising in the colonizing of new countries, as they were in the study of astronomy, and of building, and the invention of letters, at the time the Egyptians first merge to notice on the page of history. And if the Japan islands, a part of the earth as far from Ararat, the great starting point of man after the flood, as is America, and much farther, was found settled by the black race of Ham, why not therefore parts of America.

The pure negro has been found on some of the islands between China and America; which would seem to indicate that this race of people have preceded even the whites, or at least equalled them, in first peopleing the globe after the deluge.

Rafinesque, the great antiquarian, says, the exact time when the Chinese first discovered or reached America, is not given in their books, but it was known to them, he says, and to the Japanese at a very early period, and called by them *Fu Sham*, and frequented for trade. But who were here for them to trade with? Our answer is; those first inhabitants, the white, the red and the black, the sons of the sons of Noah, Shem, Ham and Japheth, who got on to the continent before it was severed from Asia and Africa, in the days of Peleg, one or two hundred years after the flood of Noah.

But there is another way of accounting for the appearance of the cross, the emblem of Christianity, besides the supposition of its having been introduced by the Nestorians, as stated on page 273. There was a tradition among the Mexican Indians, when that country was first overrun by the Spaniards, that the gospel of Christianity had once been introduced into that country by a person whom they worshipped under the name of *Quetzalcotl*; and according to the *tradition* of the Catholic church, and the opinions of several Spanish writers, this was none other than the apostle St. Thomas.

But whether this is so or not, one thing is certain; the Saviour himself stated that before the *end* of the Jewish nation should come, and the destruction of their city, that the gospel of the kingdom of the Messiah *should* be preached in *all the world*. Are we therefore to suppose, that one whole continent, a fourth part of the earth, was *not* visited according to that statement? We may therefore rest assured, that in *some way* the gospel was preached in America, before forty years had passed away from the time of the crucifixion of Christ, although its traces had nearly become obliterated here when first discovered, as it had in many other countries, till its recent revival under the influence of the great Protestant reformation.

A further Account of Western Discoveries.

Six miles from Lebanon, on the Little Miami, above the mouth of Todd's fork, are curious remains of ancient works. The form of one of the forts is trapezoidal; the walls are of earth, and generally eight or ten feet high; but in one place, where it crosses the brow of the hill where it stands, it is eighteen feet high. The Little Miami passes by on the west, on the north are deep ravines, and on the south and southeast the same ravines continue, making it a position of great strength. The area of the whole enclosure is nearly a hundred acres; the wall has numerous angles, retreating, salient and acute, from which are eighty outlets or gateways. From which circumstance we learn that its citizens were very great in number, or so many gateways would not have been needed. Two mounds are in its neighborhood, from which walls run in different directions to the adjoining ravines. Round about this work are the traces of several roads, two of them are sixteen feet wide, elevated about three feet in their centre, and like our turnpikes.

The Sioux country, on the Wabispinekan, St. Peters, and Yellow rivers, abound with ancient entrenchments, mounds and fortications. Six miles from St. Louis is a place called the *valley of bones*, where the ground is promiscuously strewed with human and animal bones; some of the former are of an enormous size.

On the river Huron, thirty miles from Detroit, and about eight miles from lake St. Clair, are a number of small mounds situated on a dry plain or bluff of the river. Sixteen baskets full of human bones, of a remarkable size, were discovered in the earth, while sinking a cellar on this plain for the missionary. Near the mouth of this river, (Huron,) on the east bank, are ancient works, representing a fortress, with walls of earth, thrown up similar to those of Indiana and Ohio.

At Belle Fontaine, or Spring Wells, three miles below Detroit, are three mounds or tumuli, standing in a direct line, about ten rods apart. One of these having been opened, bones, stone axes, and arrow-heads, were found in abundance. Within the distance of a quarter of a mile of these, are still to be seen the remains of ancient fortifications, a breast-work, in some places three and four feet high, enclosing several acres of firm ground, in the centre of an extensive swamp.

"In the state of Indiana, Franklin county, near Harrisonville, on the Whitewater river, eight miles from its mouth, on the north side, the traces of an ancient population literally strew the earth in every direction. On the bottoms or flats are a great number of mounds, very unequal in size. The small ones are from two to four feet above the surface, and the growth of timber upon them small, not being over one hundred years old, while the others are from ten to thirty feet high, with trees growing on them of the largest and most aged description."—(*Brown's Western Gazetteer.*)

Mr. Brown, the author of the *Western Gazetteer*, from whose work we extract the following, says he obtained the assistance of the inhabitants for the purpose of making a thorough examination of the internal structure of these mounds. He examined from fifteen to twenty of them, and found them all except one to contain human bones; some filled with hundreds of all ages, thrown promiscuously together, into great heaps. He found several sculls, leg and thigh bones, which plainly shows that their possessors were persons of gigantic stature.

The teeth of all the subjects he examined were remarkably even and sound, handsomely and firmly planted. The fore teeth were very deep, and not so wide as those of the generality of white people. He discovered in one mound an article of glass, in form resembling the bottom of a tumbler, weighing five ounces; it was concave on both of its sides.

It is true, that although glass is said not to have been found out till 644 of the Christian era, yet it was known to the ancient Romans, but was considered an article of too great value to be in common use. That the Romans were actually in possession of this knowledge, we learn from the discoveries made in the disinterred cities of the ancient Romans, Pompeii and Herculaneum, buried by the volcanic eruption of Mount Vesuvius. Among the vast discoveries of temples, dwellings, streets, gardens, paintings, sculptures, skeletons, with treasures of gold, has been found one bow window, lighted with a glass of a green tinge or color. The discovery of this article of glass in the tumuli, is a proof of its being of European manufacture, and probably of the Roman, brought by its owner as a valuable jewel in those early times.

In this mound were found several stone axes, such as are shown on the plate, with grooves near the heads to receive a withe, which unquestionably served to fasten the helve on, and several pieces of earthen ware. Some appeared to be parts of vessels, once holding six or eight gallons; others were obviously fragments of jugs, jars and cups. Some were plain, where others were curiously ornamented with figures of birds and beasts, drawn while the clay, or material of which they were made, was soft before the process of glazing was performed. The glazer's art appears to have been well understood by the potters who manufactured this aboriginal crockery. One of the skulls taken out of a mound at this place was found pierced with a flint arrow, which was still sticking in the bone; it was about six inches long.

At the bottom of all the mounds he examined, there was found a stratum of ashes, from six inches to two feet thick, which rests on the original soil. These ashes contain coals, fragments of brands, and pieces of calcined or burnt human bones. It is somewhat singular to find that these people both buried and burnt their dead; yet it may be that such as were burnt were prisoners of war, who being bound and laid in heaps, were thus reduced to ashes, by heaping over them brush and dry wood.

Near this place, (Harrisonville,) on the neighboring hills northeast of the town, are a number of the remains of stone houses. They were covered with soil, brush, and full grown trees. Mr. Brown cleared away the earth, roots and rubbish from one of them, and found it to have been anciently occupied as a dwelling. It was about twelve feet square. The walls had fallen nearly to the foundation, having been built with the rough stone of nature, like a stone wall. At one end of the building was a regular hearth, on which was yet the ashes and coals of the last fire its owners had enjoyed; before which were found the decayed skeletons of eight persons, of different ages, from a small child to the heads of the family. Their feet were found pointing towards the hearth : and they were probably murdered while asleep.

From the circumstance of the kind of house these people lived in, (which is the evidence of their not belonging to the mound inhabitants,) we should pronounce them to be a settlement of Welch, Scandinavians or Scotch, who had thus wandered to the west, from the first settlements made along the Atlantic, and were exterminated by the common Indians, who had also destroyed or driven away the authors of the mounds, many hundred years before these Europeans came to this country.

Various Opinions of Antiquarians respecting the Original Inhabitants of America.

But we hasten to a conclusion of this work, by furnishing the reader with the opinions of several antiquarians, who stand high in the estimation of the lovers of research; and among these is the late celebrated Dr. Samuel L. Mitchill, professor of natural History. And as we have not room to give at length all that these gentleman have published on this subject, we shall only avail ourselves of extracts, such as will show their final judgment as to what nations or races of men they were who built the works of which we have given an account.

In the following we have, in extract, the remarks and opinions of Dr. Mitchill in his communication to the American Antiquarian society, of which he was a member, 1815 : " I offer you some observations on a curious piece of American antiquity, now in New-York. It is a human body found in one of the limestone caverns of Kentucky. It is a perfect exsiccation ; all the fluids are dried up. The skin, bones, and other firm parts are in a state of entire preservation.

" In exploring a calcareous chamber, in the neighborhood of Glasgow, in the west, for saltpetre, several human bodies were found enwrapped carefully in skins and cloths. The outer envelope of the body is a deer skin, dried in the usual way, and perhaps softened before its application by rubbing. The next covering is a deer skin, the hair of which had been cut away by a sharp instrument, resembling a hatter's knife. The remnant of the hair, and the gashes in the skin, nearly resemble a sheared pelt of beaver. The next wrapper is of cloth, made of twine, doubled and twisted ; but the threads do not appear to have been formed by the wheel, nor the web by the loom. The warp and filling seem to have been crossed and knotted by an operation like that of the fabrics of the northwest coast, and of the Sandwich islands. The innermost tegument is a mantle of cloth like the preceding, but is furnished with large brown feathers, arranged and fashioned with great art, so as to be capable of guarding the living wearer from wet and cold. The plumage is distinct and entire, and the whole bears a near similitude to the feathery cloaks now worn by the nations of the northwest coast of America.

" The body is in a squatting posture, with the right arm reclining forward, and its hand encircling the right leg. The left arm hangs down by its side. The individual was a male, supposed to be not more than fourteen at its death. There is a deep and extensive fracture of the scull near the occiput, which probably killed him. The skin has sustained but little injury, and is of a dusky color, but the natural hue cannot be decided with exactness from its present appearance. The scalp, with small exceptions, is covered with reddish hair. The teeth are white and sound. The hands and feet, in their shrivelled state, are slender and delicate. "It may now," adds Dr. Mitchill, "be expected that I should offer some opinion as to the antiquity and race of this singular exsiccation. First, then, I am satisfied that it does not belong to the class of white men, of which we are members. Nor do I believe that it ought to be referred to the bands of Spanish adventurers, who, between the fifteenth and sixteenth centuries rambled up the Mississippi, and along the tributary streams. I am equally obliged to reject the opinion that it belonged to any of the tribes of aborigines now or lately inhabiting Kentucky. The mantle of feathered work and the mantle of twisted threads, so nearly resemble the fabrics of the natives of Wakash, and the Pacific islands, that I refer this individual to that era of time, and that generation of men which preceded the Indians of Green river, and of the place where these relics were found."

In another letter to the Society, of a later date, he requests the preservation of certain papers, "as worthy of being recorded in its archives, showing the progress of his mind in coming to the great conclusion that the three races, Malays, Tartars and Scandinavians, contributed to make up the great American population," who were the authors of the various works and antiquities found on the continent.—(*Am. Antiquarian*, p. 315.)

The fabrics accompanying the Kentucky bodies, resemble, very nearly, those which encircled the mummies of Tennessee. On comparing the two sets of samples, they were ascertained to be as much alike as two pieces of goods of the same kind, made at different factories of this country.

Other antiquities of the same class have come to light; specimens of cloths, and some of the raw materials, all dug out of that unparalleled natural excavation, the Kentucky cavern, which is found to extend many miles, in different directions, very deep in the earth; has many vast rooms, one in particular, of 1800 feet in circumference, and 150 in height. For a very grand description of this cave, see *Blake's Atlas*, 1826, published at New-York, for subscribers.

The articles found in this cave were sent to Dr. Mitchill, of the city of New-York, which were accompanied with the following note: "There will be found in this bundle two moccasins, in the same state they were when dug out of the Mammoth cave, about two hundred yards within its mouth. Upon examination it will be perceived that they are fabricated out of different materials; one is supposed to be made of a species of flag or lily, which grows in the southern parts of Kentucky; the other of the bark of some tree, probably the pappaw. There is a part of what is supposed to be a *kinniconecke*, or pouch, two meshes of a fishing net, and a piece of what is supposed to be the raw material, and of which the fishing net, pouch and moccasins were made. Also a bowl, or cup, containing about a pint, cut out of wood, found also in the cave: and, lately, there has been dug out of it the skeleton of a human body, enveloped in a matting similar to that of the pouch. This matting is substantially like those of the plain fabric, taken from the copperas cave of Tennessee, and the saltpetrous cavern near Glasgow, in Kentucky."

And what is highly remarkable, and worthy the attention of antiquarians is, that they all have a perfect resemblance to the fabrics of the Sandwich, Caroline and the Fejee islands, in the Pacific. We know the similitude of the manufactured articles, from the following circumstance:—After the termination of the war in the island of Toconroba, wherein certain citizens of the United States were engaged, as principals or allies, many articles of Fejee manufacture were brought to New-York by the victors. Some of them agree almost exactly with the fabrics discovered in Kentucky and Tennessee. They bear a strict comparison, the marks of a similar state of the arts, and point strongly to a sameness of origin in the respective people who prepared them. Notwithstanding the distance of their several residences at the present time, it is impossible not to look back to the common ancestry of the Malays, who formerly possessed the country between the Allegany mountains and the Mississippi river, and those who now inhabit the islands of the Pacific ocean.

All these considerations lead to the belief, that colonies of Australasians or Malays, landed in North America, and penetrated across the continent in process of time, to the region lying between the great lakes and the gulf of Mexico. There they resided, and constructed the fortifications, mounds, and other ancient structures which are the wonder of all who have seen them.

What has become of them? They have probably been overcome by the more warlike and ferocious hordes that entered our hemisphere from the northeast of Asia. These Tartars of the higher latitudes have issued from the great hive of nations, and desolated, in the course of their migrations, the southern tribes of America, as they have done those of Asia and Europe. The greater part of the present American natives are of the Tartar stock, the descendants of the hardy warriors who destroyed the weaker Malays that preceded them. An individual of their exterminated race now and then rises from the tomb, by which their identity of origin is ascertained.

In a communication of Samuel L. Mitchill to De Witt Clinton, 1826, he remarks, that " the parallel between the people of America and Asia affords this important conclusion; that on both continents the hordes dwelling in higher latitudes have overpowered the more civilized though feebler inhabitants of the countries situated towards the equator."

As the Tartars have overrun China, so the Aztecas subdued Mexico; as the Huns and Alans desolated Italy, so the Chippewas and Iroquois prostrated the populous settlements on both banks of the Ohio. The surviving race, in these terrible conflicts between the different nations of the ancient native residents of North America, is evidently that of the Tartars. The opinion is founded upon four considerations.

1st. *The similarity of physiognomy and features.* His excellency M. Genet, sometime minister plenipotentiary from France to the United States, is well acquainted with the faces, hues and figures of our Indians, and of the Asiatic Tartars, and is perfectly satisfied of their national resemblance.

Mons. Cazeaux, consul of France to New-York, has drawn the same conclusion, from a careful examination of the man of North America and Northern Asia.

M. Smibert, who had been employed in executing paintings of Tartar visages for the Grand Duke of Tuscany, was so struck with the similarity of their features to those of the Narragansett Indians, that he pronounced them members of the same great family of mankind. This opinion of the Grand Duke's portrait painter, is preserved, with all its circumstances, in the fourteenth volume of the *Medical Repository*.

I have examined with the utmost care seven or eight Chinese sailors, who had assisted in navigating a ship from Macao to New-

York. The thinness of their beards, the bay complexion, the black lank hair, the aspect of the eyes, the contour of the face, and in short the general external character, induced every person who observed them to remark how nearly they resemble the Mohegans and Oneidas of New-York.

Sidi Mellimelli, the Tunisian envoy to the United States in 1804, entertained the same opinion on beholding the Cherokees, Osages and Miamis, assembled at the city of Washington, during his residence there. Their Tartar physiognomy struck him in a moment.

2d. *The affinity of their languages.* The late learned and enterprising professor Barton took the lead in this inquiry. He collected as many words as he could from the languages spoken in Asia and America, and concluded, from the numerous coincidences of sound and signification, that there must have been a common origin.

3d. *The existence of corresponding customs.* I mean to state, at present, that of shaving away the hair of the scalp from the fore part and sides of the head, so that nothing is left but a tuft on the crown.

The custom of smoking the pipe on solemn occasions, to the four cardinal points of the compass, to the heavens and to the earth, is reported, upon the most credible authority, to distinguish equally the hordes of the Asiatic Tartars, and the bands of the American Sioux, the most dreadful warriors of the west.

"In addition to the considerations, already stated in favor of this opinion, may be urged the more recent discoveries concerning the quadrupeds which inhabit the respective countries. There is conculsive evidence, for example, that the wild *sheep* of Louisiana and California is the Tartarian animal of the same name. Yes, the *taye-taye* of Northwestern America is an animal of the same species with the *argali* of Northern Asia. Our mountain ram, or big horn, is their *ovis ammon.*"—(Am. Antq. Soc. p. 333.)

But we remark, this opinion of the learned antiquarian, professor Mitchill, by no means lessens the probability, as is contended by many learned men, and also is the popular belief, that notwithstanding this Tartar physiognomy of our Indians, that they are, in part, but in a mixed relation, descended of the Jews; or in other words, a part of the ten lost tribes of Israel; and do in reality, in many things, imitate the worship of the ancient Israelites. Having taught the same to the Tartars, after they left Syria, in mass, as is related by 2d Esdras, chap. xiii, 7—47. But we resume the remarks of professor Mitchill to Governor Clinton, in reference to the authors of the works in the west.

"The exterminated race, in the savage intercourse between the nations of North America, in ancient days, appears clearly to have been that of the Malays. The bodies and shrouds and clothing of those individuals have, within a few years, been discovered in the caverns of saltpetre and copperas, within the States of Kentucky and Tennessee. Their entire dried or exsiccated condition, has led intelligent gentlemen, who have seen them, to call them mummies.

They are some of the most memorable of the antiquities that North America contains. The race, or nation, to which they belonged is extinct; but in preceding ages, occupied the region situated between lakes Ontario and Erie, on the north, and of Mexico on the south, and bounded eastwardly by the Alleghany mountains, and westwardly by the Mississippi river.

That they were similar in their origin and character, to the present inhabitants of the Pacific islands, and of Australasia, is argued from various circumstances. 1st. The sameness of texture in the plain cloth or matting that enwraps the mummies, and that which our navigators bring from Wakash, the Sandwich islands, and the Fejees. 2d. The close resemblance there is between the feathery mantles brought, now-a-days, from the islands of the South Sea, and those wrappers which surround the mummies lately disinterred in the western states. The plumes of birds are twisted or tied to threads, with peculiar skill, and turn water like the back of a duck. 3d. Meshes of net regularly knotted and tied, and formed of a strong and even twine. 4th. Moccasins, or coverings of the feet, manufactured with remarkable ability, from the bark or rind of plates, worked into a sort of stout matting. 5th. Pieces of antique sculpture, especially of human heads, and of some other forms, found where the exterminated tribes had dwelt, resembling the carving at Otaheite, New-Zealand, and other places. 6th. Works of defence or fortifications, overspreading the fertile tract of country, formerly possessed by these people, who may be supposed capable of building works of much greater magnitude than the *morais*, or burial places, and the *hippas*, or fighting stages, of the Society islands. 7th. As far as observation has gone, a belief, that the shape of the skull, and the angle of the face, in the mummies, (found in the west,) correspond with those of the living Malays.

I reject, therefore, the doctrine taught by the European naturalists, that the man of *western* America differs, in any material point from the man of *eastern* Asia. Had the Robertsons, the Buffons, the Raynals, the De Pauwys, and the other speculators upon the American character, and the villifiers of the American name, procured the requisite information concerning the hemisphere situated west of us, they would have discovered that the inhabitants of vast regions of Asia, to the number of many millions, were of the *same blood* and lineage with the millions of America, whom they affect to undervalue and despise.

But notwithstanding the celebrity, founded on the great erudition and critical research of professor Mitchill, we cannot subscribe to this opinion respecting the red-headed mummy now in the New-York museum, found in a saltpetre cave in Kentucky. It is a well known fact, that invariably all the nations of the earth, who are of the swarthy or black complexion, have black hair, either straight or curled.

But those nations belonging to the white class, have a great variety of color of the hair; black, white, auburn, and red. We are sure this is a characteristic of the two classes of mankind, the dark and the white. If so, then the Kentucky body, found in the cave, is not of Malay origin, but of Scandinavian; of whom, as a nation, it is said that the predominant color of the hair was red.

And further, we object, that the traits of ancient population found in Canada, between lakes Ontario and Erie, to be of Malay origin, but rather of Scandinavian also. Our reason is as follows: It is unreasonable to suppose the Malays, Australasian, and Polynesian nations of the islands of the Pacific, who were originally from the eastern coasts of China, situated in mild climates, should penetrate so far north as the countries in Canada, to fix their habitations. But it is perfectly natural that the Scandinavian, the Welch, or the Scottish clans, all of whom inhabit cold, very cold countries, should be delighted with such a climate, as any part of either Upper or Lower Canada.

And farther, as a reason that the Malay nations never inhabited any part of the Canadas, we notice, that in those regions there are found no traces of their peculiar skill and labor ascribed to them by professor Mitchill, which are the great *mounds* of the west. In Canada we know not that any have been discovered. But other works, of warlike character, abound there in the form of long lines of defensive preparations, corresponding with similar works in the north of Europe, and in many places in the state of New-York, and in other Atlantic states, as before noticed. On which account, we do not hesitate to ascribe the ancient traits of a former civilized population, found between lakes Ontario and Erie, to be of European, rather than of Malay origin.

Voyages of the Ancients from Italy and Africa to the Continent of America and its adjacent Islands.

CALMET, a celebrated writer, and well known as an ecclesiastic of the Catholic communion, who was highly versed in the antiquities of past ages, brings forward the most classic authors of ancient times respecting the discovery of America, and the origin of its inhabitants.

He produces the writings of Hornius, son of Theodosius the Great, and Emperor of the West, who lived in the third century, as supported by the writings of Strabo, a native of Cappadocia, and was a historian and geographer at or about the time of the commencement of the Christian era, affirms as *certain*, that voyages from Africa and Spain into the Atlantic ocean, were both frequent and celebrated. He says that Eudoxius, sailing from the Arabian gulf to Ethiopia and India, found a *prow* of a *ship* that had been wrecked, which, from its having the head of a horse carved on it, he knew belonged to a Phœnician bark; and some Gaditani merchants declared it to have been a fishing vessel. Laretius relates nearly the same circumstance. Hornius says, (continues Calmet,) that in very remote ages *three* voyages were made to America. The first by the *Atlantes*, or descendants of Atlas, who gave his name to the Atlantic ocean, and the island Atlantides; this name, (Atlantides,) Plato, who lived nearly 400 B. C., appears to have learned from the Egyptian priests, the general depositories of knowledge.

The second voyage mentioned by Hornius, is given on the authority of Diodorus Siculus, who lived in the time of Julius Cæsar, who says, that the Phœnicians having passed the columns of Hercules, (out of the Mediterranean sea at the strait of Gibraltar,) and being impelled by the violence of the wind, abandoned themselves to its fury, and after experiencing many tempests, were thrown upon an island in the Atlantic ocean, distant *many* days navigation to the westward of the coast of Lybia or Africa; which island possessed a fertile soil, had navigable rivers, and there were large buildings upon it. On their return, by the means of other adventurers, the report of this discovery soon spread among the Carthaginians and Romans, the former being harrassed by the wars of the latter, and the people of Mauritania sent a colony to that island with great secresy, that in the event of being overcome by their enemies, they might possess a place of safe retreat.

Such were the descriptions which the Phœnicians gave of the beauty and fertility of this island, as well as of its opulent inhabitants, that the Romans became desirous of making themselves masters of it, and of settling a colony there. This perplexed the Carthaginians, who began to fear that their countrymen would be enamored of a fertility so much praised, and abandon their native country to settle there. And on the other hand they viewed it as a safe refuge in event of any unforseen calamity, or if their republic in Africa should fall, to which, as being masters of the sea, they could easily retire, to secure themselves and families; more especially as the region was unknown to other nations.

Aristotle, who lived and wrote about 350 B. C., continues Calmet, in his books of wonderful things, speaking of this island, says, the magistrates of Carthage having observed that many of their citizens who had undertaken the voyage thither had not returned, prohibited, therefore, under the penalty of capital punishment, any farther emigration, and ordered those who had remained there to return to their country, fearing that as soon as the affair should be known, other nations would endeavor to establish there a peaceable commerce.

But there is an account of another voyage into the Atlantic, spoken of by Calmet, which was *anterior* to the preceding, and is attributed to Hercules, who by Galleo, (a writer of the sixteenth century, the same whose books and opinions about the Copernican system of astronomy were condemned by the Popish council, in sixteen hundred thirty-four,) is ranked as contemporary with Moses, who lived nearly 1600 B. C. This Hercules, the strong man of antiquity, according to heathen mythology, was a great captain, and leading character, chief of the Canaanites, who fled from Palestine, from the wars of Joshua, and went to Africa, settling as is supposed on the western coast of that country. This same Hercules is supposed to have circumnavigated the globe, and is spoken of as having so done by Diodorus, and that he founded the city of *Lecta* in *Septimania*, but no writer has pointed out its situation America may have been that country, especially as Hercules made voyages into the Atlantic between Africa and the continent of America to the south.

Calmet, in his commentary on the Jugurthine war, states in the history of the kingdom of Numidia, written in the Punic language, that he had read an African account or tradition of the arrival in that country of Hercules, with an army of Medes, Persians and Armenians. These soldiers, he says, married Lybian women, who were black, and that their language imperceptibly degenerated from its original purity, and in process of time the name of Medes and Arminians became changed to that of *Maurucii* or *Moors*.

There is a strong probability that the Romans and Carthaginians, even 300 years before Christ, were well acquainted with the existence of this country, obtained by these early navigators, Hercules, Votan, the Carthaginians and Phœnicians: hence, as we have argued, in various parts of this work, the tokens of the presence of the Greeks, Romans, Persians and Carthaginians, appear in many parts of the continent.

This opinion is believed by many of the early Spanish writers, who have written on the subject of the first population of this country, and have concluded, from the strongest evidence, that the Carthaginians, a people who were powerful some hundreds of years before Christ, and who were the eternal enemies of the Romans, have had much to do in colonizing America, as well also as the ancient Tyrians, who before they had become amalgamated with the Tyrians, were Hivites, one of the nations who peopled ancient Canaan.

Further Remarks on the Subject of Human Complexions.

As to the curious subject of the different complexions of man, I consider, says Dr. Mitchill, the human family under three divisions:

1st. The *tawny* man, comprehending the Tartars, Malays, Chinese, the American Indians, of every tribe, Lascars, and other people of the same cast and breed.

2d. The *white* man, inhabiting the countries of Asia and Europe, situated north of the Mediterranean sea; and, in the course of his adventures, settling all over the world: among whom I reckon the Greenlanders, and the Esquimaux nations.

3d. The *black* man, whose proper residence is in the regions south of the Mediterranean, particularly towards the interior of Africa. The people of Papua and Van Dieman's Land, seem to be of this class.

It is generally supposed, and by many able and ingenious men, that *external* physical causes, and combination of circumstances, which they call *climate*, have wrought all these changes in the human form and complexion. I do not, however, think them capable of explaining the differences which exist among the nations, on this principle. There is an *internal* physical *cause* of the greatest moment, which has scarcely been mentioned. This is the generative influence. If by the *act* of modelling the constitution in the *embryo* and fœtus, a predisposition to gout, madness, scrofula, and consumption may be engendered, we may *rationally* conclude, with the sagacious d'Azara, that the *procreative* power may *also* shape the natures, tinge the skin, and give other peculiarities to the form of man.—(*Am. Antq.* p. 335.)

This idea of the three original complexions, black, tawny and white, we have supposed was realized in the person of Noah's three sons, Shem, Ham and Japheth: and although Mr. Mitchill has not fixed on a starting place, he has, nevertheless, admitted the principle, and has referred the cause of complexion and shape to the procreative and generative act, excluding totally any influence which climate or food may be supposed to have, as has been contended by many; which, so far as we are able to understand his meaning, is referring the complexions of the human race immediately to the arbitrary act of God. To this doctrine we most cordially subscribe, because it is so simple and natural, the very way in which the great Creator works. First fixing the *principles* of nature, as gravitation and motion, which keep the worlds in their courses. Were it not for these, all would stand still and nature would die. Fire, in its endless variations, breathes through all matter, expands the leaves of all forests, and adorns them with all flowers, gives motion to the air, which, in that motion, is called the winds of heaven. Fire gives liquescency to the waters of the globe; were it not for this, all fluids that now move over the earth in rivers, brooks and springs, or oceans, or passes by subterranean channels through the earth, or circulates in the pores of trees and herbage, with the watery fluids of all animated life, would stand still, would congeal, would freeze to one universal mass of death.

Also, in the secret embryo of earth's productions, as in all vegetation, all animals, and all human beings, is fixed the principle of *variety*. Were it not for this, what vast confusion would ensue. If all human beings looked alike, and all human voices sounded alike, there would be an end to society, to social order, to the distinctions between friend and foe, relatives and strangers; conversation would be misapplied, identity at an end; subjects of investigation and research, arts and science, could have no objects to fix upon; such a state of things would be a fearful retrograde toward a state of insensibility and non-existence.

And is it not also as evident that God has fixed, as well the secret principle which produces complexion, as it appears in an unmixed state in the human subject, as that he has the other principles just rehearsed, and equally as arbitrarily. Vegetation mixes, and in this way gives varieties in form, color and flavor, not strictly original. Also the original complexions in their pure state, of black, tawny and white, have also by mixtures produced their varieties, but at the outset, in the embryo, there must be a first predisposing principle to each of these complexions, fixed on a more permanent basis than that of food and climate; or else food and climate, after these had made a white race of men, or a tawny race, black, might be expected in due time, if moved to a climate favoring, to change them all back again, as at first; but this is contrary to all experience on the subject, in all ages and climates of the earth. Therefore, we fix on the idea of a first principle, placed in the generative powers of the sons of Noah, from whom their several progenies derived the black, the red or tawny, and the white, in all the simplicity and beauty of *natural* operations.

This curious subject, with the amount of argument on both sides of the question, (that is, whether human complexions are produced by food and climate, or are original,) is in a masterly manner attended to, in the American edition of the New Edinburgh Encyclopedia, vol. 6. In that work it is shown that climate, in hundreds of instances, which respect the complexions of *all* the nations known on the globe, are found unchangeable. In the torrid climes, both the white and the black, with all the intermediate shades between the two extremes, are found, as also the black with curled hair in the northern regions, in many countries of the old world.

"As, therefore, the dark complexioned varieties of mankind are found near the poles; as people of the *same* complexion are found over the *whole* continent of America, under all its various climates; as there are numerous instances of comparative fairness of complexion under the heat of a burning climate; as radical differences of complexion are found in the *same* regions, and even among the same people; and as there are *numerous* instances where the original complexion has remained permanent, notwithstanding it has been exposed to a change of climate for centuries; it may fairly be inferred, that the characteristic complexions of the different varieties of the human race are *not* the result of climate."—(*Encylopedia*, as above, p. 670.)

Further Remarks respecting Human Complexion, with other Interesting Subjects.

In another communication, which in part was on the same subject, though addressed to the secretary of the American Antiquarian society, Dr. Mitchell says: "In that memoir, (alluding to the one addressed to De Witt Clinton,) I maintained the doctrine that there were but three original varieties of the human race, the tawny man, the white man and the black; a division which I am pleased to observe, the incomparable author of the *Animal Kingdom* has adopted in France.

The former of these seems to have occupied, in the earliest days, the plain watered by the Euphrates and the Tigris, while the white Arab, as he has sometimes been called, was found in the regions north of the Mediterranean sea, and the sable Arab, or negro, inhabited to the south of that expanse of water.

Of the brown or tawny variety, are the eastern Asiatics, and western Americans, divisible into two great stocks, or genealogies; first, those in high latitudes, whom I call Tartars; and, second, those who inhabit low or southern latitudes, whom I consider as Malays. I am convinced that terms *Tartar* and *Malay*, for the present purposes of reasoning, are equally applicable to the two great continents; and that, with the exception of the negro colonies in Papua, and a few other places, the islanders in the Pacific are Malays.

My observations led me, several years ago, to the conclusion that the two great continents Asia and America, were peopled by similar races of men; and that America, as well as Asia, had its Tartars in the north, and its Malays in the south. America has had her Scythians, her Alans, and her Huns; but there has been no historian to record their formidable migrations, and their barbarous achievements; how little of past events do we know.

The comparison of the language spoken by these Asiatic and American nations, colonies and tribes, respectively, was begun by our learned fellow citizen, the late Dr. B. S. Barton. The work has been continued by the Adelangs and Vater, distinguished philologists of Germany. Their profound inquiry into the structure of language and the elements of speech, embraces a more correct and condensed body of information concerning the original tongues of the two Americas, than was ever compiled and arranged before. Their *Mithridates*, a book on languages, surpasses all similar performances that have ever been achieved by man.

One of my intelligent correspondents, who has surveyed with his own eyes the region watered by the Ohio, worte me very lately a letter containing the following paragraph:

"I have adopted your theory respecting the Malays, Polynesians and Alleghanians. This last nation, so called by the *Lenni-lenapi*, or primitive stock of our hunting Indians, was that which inhabited the United States, before the Tartar tribes came and destroyed them, and who erected the mounds, works, fortifications and temples of the western country. This historical fact is now proved beyond a doubt, by the traditions of the *Lenni-lenapi* Indian, published by Heckewelder, in the work issued by the Philosophical Society of Philadelphia. I may add, that Mr. Clifford, of Lexington, Kentucky, has proved another identity between the Alleghanians and Mexicans, by ascertaining that many supposed fortifications were temples, particularly that of Circleville in Ohio, where human sacrifices were one of their rites. He has discovered their similarity with the ancient Mexican temples, described by Humboldt, and has examined the bones of victims in heaps, the shells used in sacred rites, as in India, and the idol of baked clay, consisting of three heads."

This opinion of human sacrifices was fully confirmed by the testimony of Mr. Manuel Liea, during the summer of 1818. He, on his return from the trading posts on the Upper Missouri, informed his fellow citizens at St. Louis, that the Wolf tribe of the Pawnee Indians yet followed the custom of immolating human victims. He purchased a Spanish prisoner, a boy about ten years old, whom they intended to offer as a sacrifice to the Great Star; and they did put to death, by transfixing on a sharp pole, as an offering to the object of their adoration, the child of a Paddo woman, who being a captive herself, and devoted to that sanguinary and horrible death, made her escape on horseback, leaving her new born offspring behind. The triad, or trinity of heads, (*see the plate*) instantly brings to mind a similar article, figured by the Indians of Asia, and described by Mr. Maurice in his *Oriental Researches*.

I received, a short time since, directly from Mexico, several pieces of cloth, painted in the manner that historians have often represented. I find the material in not a single instance to be cotton, as has been usually affirmed. There is not a thread indicating the use of the spinning wheel, nor an intertexture showing that the loom or shuttle was employed. In strictness, therefore, there is neither cotton nor cloth in the manufacture. The fabrics, on the contrary, are uniformly composed of pounded bark, probably of the mulberry tree, and resembles the bark cloths prepared to this day, in the Friendly and Society islands, in the Pacific ocean, as nearly as one piece of linen, or one blanket of wool resembles another.

I derive this conclusion from a comparison of the several sorts of goods. They have been examined together by several excellent judges. For, at a meeting of the New-York Literary and Philosophical society, in February, 1819, I laid these specimens of bark cloth, with their respective colorings and paintings, from Mexico, Otaheite and Tongataboo, upon the table, for the examination of the members. All were satisfied that there was a most striking similitude among the several articles. Not only the fabric but the colors, and the materials of which they apparently consisted, as well as the probable manner of putting them on, seemed to me strong proofs of the sameness of origin, in the different tribes of a people working in the same way, and retaining a sameness in their arts of making a thing, which answers the purpose of paper, of cloth and a material for writing and painting upon.

Soon after the arrival of these rolls from New-Spain, filled with hieroglyphics, and imitative characters, I received a visit from three *natives* of South America, born at St. Blas, just beyond the isthmus of Darien, near the equator. They were of the Malay race, by their physiognomy, form, and general appearance. Their dark brown skins, their thin beards, the long black, straight hair of their heads, their small hands and feet, and their delicate frame of body, all concur to mark their near resemblance to the Australasians; while the want of high cheek bones, and little eyes, placed wide apart, distinguished them sufficiently from the Tartars. Other similtudes exist. The history of M. de la Salle's last expedition, and discoveries in North America, is contained in the second volume of his Travels. "After travelling over plains, and sometimes across torrents, we arrived in the midst of a very extraordinary nation, called the Biscatonges, to whom we gave the name of weepers, in regard that upon the first approach of strangers, all these people, men as well as women, usually fell a weeping most bitterly.

That which is yet more remarkable, and perhaps very reasonable in that custom, is that they weep much more at the birth of their children, than at their death; because the latter is esteemed only by them as it were a journey or voyage, from whence they may return after the expiration of a certain time; but they look upon their nativity as an inlet into an ocean of dangers and misfortunes. Compare this with a passage in the Terpsichore of Herodotus, who flourished about 450 years before Christ, chap. 4th, where, in describing the Thracians, he observes, "that the Trausi have a general uniformity with the rest of the Thracians, (a branch of the most ancient Greeks.) On the birth of a child, it is placed in the midst of a circle of its relations, who lament aloud the evils which, as a human being, he must necessarily undergo, all of which supposed evils, they particularly enumerate to the child, though it understands it not."—*(Beloe's Translation.)*

To find a custom among one of the Indian nations, in America, which so strikingly agrees with that of the Thracian, a branch of the most ancient Greek people, who existed many hundred years before Christ, is very extraordinary, and would seem to justify a belief that we have the descendants of the Greeks in our western forests; which also argues that the ancestors of the tribe having this curious custom, came early to America, or they could not have so perfectly retained this practice, in their wanderings over Asia, who would have inevitably lost their ancient manners, by amalgamations. We have before shown, in this work, that Greeks visited South America, in the time of Alexander the great, who for aught that can be objected, may have left a colony, and the *Biscatongues* may be their descendants.

"There is an opinion among the Seneca nation of the Iroquois confederacy, to this day, that eclipses of the sun and moon are caused by a Manitau, or bad Spirit, who mischievously intercepts the light intended to be shed upon the earth and its inhabitants. Upon such occasions, the greatest solicitude exists. All the individuals of the tribe feel a strong desire to drive away the demon, and to remove thereby the impediment to the transmission of luminous rays. For this purpose, they go forth, and by crying, shouting, drumming, and the firing of guns, endeavor to frighten him, and they never fail in their object, for by courage and perseverance, they infallibly drive him off. His retreat is succeeded by a return of the obstructed light. Something of the same sort is practised among the Chippeways, when an eclipse happens. The belief among them is, that there is a battle between the sun and moon, which intercepts the light. Their great object, therefore, is to stop the fighting, and to separate the combatants. They think these ends can be accomplished by withdrawing the attention of the contending parties from each other, and diverting it to the Chippeways themselves. They accordingly fill the air with noise and outcry. Such sounds are sure to attract the attention of the warring powers. Their philosophers have the satisfaction of knowing that the strife never lasted long after their clamor and noisy operations began. Being thus induced to be peaceful, the sun and moon separate and light is restored to the Chippeways.

Now it is reported, on the authority of one of the Jesuit fathers of the French mission in India, that a certain tribe or people, whom he visited there, ascribed eclipses to the presence of a great dragon. This creature, by the interposition of his huge body, obstructed the passage of the light to our world; they were persuaded they could drive him away by terrifying sounds, in which they were always successful, as the dragon soon retired in great alarm, when the eclipses immediately terminated.

The manner of depositing the bodies of distinguished persons after death, is remarkable. Among the tribes inhabiting the banks of the Columbia river, which empties into the Pacific ocean, in latitude 47 degrees north, and in some of those which live near the waters of the Missouri, the dead body of a great man is neither consumed by fire, nor buried in the earth, but it is placed in his canoe, with his articles of dress, ornament, war, and hunting, and suspended in the canoe, between two trees, to putrify in the open air. The custom of exposing bodies to decomposition above ground, in the *Morais*, or places of deposite, for the dead, among the Polynesians, will immediately occur to every reader of the voyages made within the last half century, through the Pacific ocean for the purposes of discovery.

Cannibalism in America.

THE practice of cannibalism exists in full force, in the Fejee islands. A particular and faithful account of it is contained in the 14th volume of the Medical Repository, chaps. 209, and 215. The history of the five Indian nations dependent upon the government of New-York, by Dr. Colden, page 185—6, shows that the ferocious and vindictive spirit of the conqueror led him occasionally to feast upon his captive. The Ottawas having taken an Iroquois prisoner, made a soup of his flesh. The like has been repeatedly done since, on select occasions, by other tribes. Governor Cass, of Michigan, informed me, that among the Miamis, there was a standing committee, consisting of seven warriors, whose business it was to perform the man eating required by public authority. The last of their cannibal feasts was on the body of a white man, of Kentucky, about forty years ago. The appointment of the committee to eat human flesh, has since that time, gradually become obsolete; but the oldest and last member of this cannibal society is well remembered, and died only a few years ago.

A very circumstancial description of a cannibal feast, where a soup was made of the body of an Englishman, at Michilimackinack, about the year 1760, is given by Alexander Henry, Esq., in his book of travels through Canada and the Indian territories. In that work it is stated that man eating was then, and always had been, practised among the Indian nations, on returning from war, or on overcoming their enemies, for the purpose of giving them courage to attack, and resolution to die."—(*Medical Repository*, vol. 14, pp. 261, 262.)

As extraordinary as this may appear, we are informed by Baron Humboldt, in his personal narrative, that " in Egypt, in the 13th century, five or six hundred years ago, the habit of eating human flesh pervaded all classes of society. Extraordinary snares were spread, for physicians in particular. They were called to attend persons who pretended to be sick, but who were only hungry, and it was not in order to be consulted, but devoured."

Situated west, northwest and southwest of North America, in the Pacific ocean, are a vast number of islands, scattered over all that immense body of water, extending in groups quite across to China, along the whole Asiatic coast. The general character of these islanders is similar, though somewhat diversified in language, in complexion are much the same, which is copper, with the exception only of now and then people of the African descent, and those of the Japan islands, who are white.

By examining Morse, we find them in the practice of sacrificing human beings, and also of devouring them, as we find the savages of America were accustomed to do from time immemorial; having but recently suspended the appalling custom.

From this similarity, an account of which, however, might be extended in detail to a vast amount, existing between these islanders, and the disinterred remains of the exterminated race, who, as it is supposed, built most of the works of the west, it is inferred they are the same. Their complexion and manners agree, at the present time, with the people of these islands; we mean those of the Malay race, yet remaining in South America, in their native state of society.

Also the natives of the Caribbean islands, in the Caribbean sea, which is the same with the gulf of Mexico, only this sea is at the southern extremity of the gulf, are of the same race, who, in their migrations from the Pacific ocean, have peopled many parts of the South and North American continent, the remains of whom are found on those islands, as well as among the unsubdued nations in the woods of South America.

It is doubtless a fact, that the earliest tribes who separated from the immediate regions about Ararat, passed onward to the east, across the countries now called Persia, Bucharia, and the Chinese empire, till they reached the sea, or Pacific ocean, opposite the American continent.

From thence, in process of time, on account of an increase of population, they left the main continent, in search of the islands, and passing from one group to another, till all those islands became peopled, and until they reached even the western coast of not only South but North America.

At the same time, tribes from the same region of Ararat, travelled westward, passing over all Europe and southward, filling the regions of Africa, and the islands in the Atlantic ocean opposite the coasts of South and North America, till they also reached the main land, meeting their fellows, after having each of them circumambulated half of the earth.

And having started from the regions of Ararat and the tower of Babel, with languages differing one from another, and having also in process of time, acquired habits arising from differences of circumstances, mostly dissimilar one from the other, wars for the mastery the most dreadful must have ensued, each viewing the others as intruders, from whence they knew not. This is evident from the tradions of the inhabitants of the two Americas; some tribes pointing to the east, others to the west, and others again to the north, as the way from whence their ancestors came. According to Clavigero, the naturalist, the ancestors of the nations which peopled Anahuac, now called New-Spain, might have passed from the northern countries of Europe, (as Norway,) to the northern parts of America, on the coast of Labrador, which is called British America and Canada; also from the most eastern parts of Asia to the most western parts of America. This conclusion is founded on the constant and general tradition of those nations, which unanimously say, that their ancestors came into Anahuac, or New-Spain, from the countries of the north and northwest. This tradition is confirmed by the remains of many ancient edifices, built by those people in their migrations. In a journey made by the Spaniards in 1606, more than two hundred years since, from New-Mexico to the river which they call Tizan, six hundred miles from Anahuac towards the northwest, they found there some large edifices, and met with some Indians who spoke the Mexican language, and who told them that a few day's journey from that river towards the north, was the kingdom of Tolan, and many other inhabited places, from whence the Mexicans migrated. In fact, the whole population of Anahuac have usually affirmed, that towards the north were the kingdoms and provinces of Tolan, Aztalan, Capallan, and several others, which are all Mexican names, now so designated; but were we to trace these names to their origin, they would be found to be of Mongol or Mogul origin, from Asia. Boturini, or Bouterone, a learned antiquarian of Paris, of the 17th century, says, that in the ancient paintings of the Taltecas, a nation of Mexico, or more anciently called Anahuac, was represented the migrations of their ancestors through Asia, and the northern countries of America, until they established themselves in the country of Tolan. (*Morse*, p. 618.)

This river Tizan is, unquestionably, the river Columbia, which belongs to the territory owned by the United States, bordering on the coast of the Pacific, in latitude 47 degrees north; which from Anahuac, in Mexico, is about that distance (600 miles) and this river being the only one of much size emptying into the sea on that side of the Rocky mountains, between the latitude of Mexico and the latitude of the mouth of the Columbia, is the reason why that river, may, almost with certainty, be supposed the very Indian Tizan. But still farther north, several days' journey, were the kingdoms and provinces of Tolan, Aztalan, and Capallan, which were probably in the latitude with the northern parts of the United States's lands west of the Rocky mountains, and filling all the regions east as far as the head waters of the great western rivers; thence down those streams, peopling the vast alluvials in Indiana, Missouri, Illinois, Northwestern Territory, Ohio, Kentucky, Mississippi, and so on to the gulf of Mexico.

Although those kingdoms and provinces spoken of by the natives of Tizan, to these Spanish adventurers, had many hundred years before been vacated of their population and grandeur; yet it was natural for them to retain the tradition of their numbers and extent: and to speak of them as then existing, which, as to latitude and location, was true, although in a state of ruin, like the edifices at the Tizan, or Columbia.

In an address delivered at New-York, before the College of Physicians, by Dr. Mitchill, which relates to the migrations of Malays, Tartars and Scandinavians, we have the following: "A late German writer, professor Vater, has published, at Leipsig, a book on the population of America. He lays great stress on the tongues spoken by the aborigines, and dwells considerably upon the unity pervading the whole of them, from Chili to the remotest district of North America, whether of Greenland, Chippewa, Delaware, Natick, Totuaka, Cora or Mexico. Though ever so singular and diversified, nevertheless the same peculiarity obtains among them all, which cannot be accidental, viz: the whole sagacity of that people from whom the construction of the American languages and the gradual invention of their grammatical forms is derived, has, as it were, selected one object, and over this diffused such an abundance of forms, that one is astonished; while only the most able philologist, or grammarian of languages, by assiduous study, can obtain a general view thereof.

"In substance, the author (prof. Vater) says, that through various times and circumstances, this peculiar character is preserved. Such unity, such direction, or tendency, compels us to place the origin in a remote period, when one original tribe or people existed, whose ingenuity and judgment enabled them to excogitate or invent such intricate formations of language as could not be effaced by thousands of years, nor by the influence of zones and climates.

"Mr. Vater has published a large work, entitled *Mithridates*, in which he has given an extensive comparison of all the Asiatic, African and American languages, to a much greater extent than was done by our distinguished fellow citizen, Dr. Barton, of Philadelphia, professor of natural history. Mr. Vater concludes by expressing his desire to unravel the mysteries which relate to the new and old continents; at least to contribute the contents of his volume towards the commencement of a structure, which, out of the ruins of dilacerated human tribes, seeks materials for an union of the whole human race in one origin; which some have disputed, notwithstanding the plain statement of the Bible on that subject, which is a book entitled to the term *antiquity*, paramount to all other records now in existence on the earth.

"What this original and radical language was, has very lately been the subject of inquiry by the learned Mr. Mathieu, of Nancy, in France. The Chevalier Valentine, of the order of St. Michael, renewed by Louis XVIII, informs me that this gentleman has examined Mr. Winthrop's description of the curious characters inscribed upon the rock at Dighton, Massachusetts, as published in the Transactions of the Boston Academy of Arts and Sciences. He thinks them hieroglyphics, which he can interpret and explain, and ascribes them to the inhabitants of the ancient Atlantic island of Plato, called by him Atalantis. Mr. Mathieu not only professes to give the sense of the inscription, but also to prove that the tongues spoken by the Mexicans, Peruvians, and other occidental or western people, as well as the Greek itself, with all its dialects, and ramifications, were but derivations from the language of the primitive Atalantians of the island of Plato."—(*See page* 80 &c.)

Ancient Languages of the first Inhabitants of America.

First Letter to Mr. Champollion, on the Graphic Systems of America, and the Glyphs of Otolum or Palenque, in Central America.

BY C. S. RAFINESQUE.

You have become celebrated by decyphering, at last, the glyphs and characters of the ancient Egyptians, which all your learned predecessors had deemed a riddle, and pronounced impossible to read. You first announced your discovery in a letter. I am going to follow your footsteps on another continent, and a theme equally obscure; to none but yourself can I address with more propriety, letters on a subject so much alike in purpose and importance, and so similar to your own labors.

I shall not enter, at present, into any very elaborate discussion. I shall merely detail, in a concise manner, the object and result of my inquiries, so as to assert my claim to a discovery of some importance in a philological and historical point of view; which was announced as early as 1828, in some journals, (three letters to Mr. McCulloch on the American nations,) but not properly illustrated. Their full development would require a volume, like that of yours on the Egyptian antiquities, and may follow this perhaps at some future time.

It may be needful to prefix the following principles as guides to my researches, or results of my inquiries:

1. America has been the land of false systems; all those made in Europe on it, are more or less vain and erroneous.

2. The Americans were equal in antiquity, civilization and sciences, to the nations of Africa and Europe; like them the children of the Asiatic nations.

3. It is false that no American nations had systems of writing, glyphs and letters. Several had various modes of perpetuating ideas.

4. There were several such graphic systems in America, to express ideas, all of which find equivalents in the east continent.

5. They may be arranged in twelve series, proceeding from the most simple to the most complex.

1st Series.—Pictured symbols or glyphs of the *Toltecas, Aztecas,*

Huaztecas Skeres, Panos, &c. Similar to the first symbols of the Chinese, invented by Tien-hoang, before the flood, and earliest Egyptian glyphs.

2d. Series.—Outlines of figures, or abridged symbols and glyphs, expressing words or ideas, used by almost all the nations of North and South America, even the most rude. Similar to the second kind of Egyptian symbols, and the *tortoise letters* brought to China by the *Longma*, (dragon and horse,) nation of barbarous horsemen, under *Sui-gin*.

3d Series.—Quipos, or knots on strings, used by the Peruvians, and several other South American nations. Similar to the third kind of Chinese glyphs, introduced under *Yong-ching*, and used also by many nations of Africa.

4th Series.—Wampums, or strings of shells and beads, used by many nations of North America. Similar to those used by some ancient or rude nations in all the parts of the world, as tokens of ideas.

5th Series.—Runic glyphs, or marks and notches on twigs or lines, used by several nations of North America. Consimilar to the runic glyphs of the Celtic and Teutonic nations.

6th Series.—Runic marks and dots, or graphic symbols, not on strings nor lines, but in rows; expressing words or ideas; used by the ancient nations of North America and Mexico, the *Talegas, Aztecas, Natchez, Powhatans, Tuscaroras*, &c, and also the *Muhizcas*, of South America. Similar to the ancient symbols of the *Etruscans, Egyptians, Celts*, &c., and the *Ho-tu* of the Chinese, invented by *Tsang-hi*, called also the *Ko-teu-chu letters*, which were in use in China, till 827 before our era.

7th Series.—Alphabetical symbols, expressing syllables or sounds, not words, but grouped, and the groups disposed in rows; such is the graphic system of the monuments of Otolum, near Palenque, the American Thebes. Consimilar to the groups of alphabetical symbols used by the ancient *Lybians, Egyptians, Persians*, and also the last graphic system of the Chinese, called *Ventze*, invented by *Sse-hoang*.

8th Series.—Cursive symbols, in groups, and the groups in parallel rows, derived from the last, (which are chiefly monumental,) and used in the manuscripts of the *Mayans, Guatamalans*, &c. Consimilar to the actual cursive Chinese, some demotic Egyptian, and many modifications of ancient graphic alphabets, grouping the letters or syllables.

9*th Series.*—Syllabic letters, expressing syllables, not simple sounds, and disposed in rows. Such is the late syllabic alphabet of the *Cherokis*, and many graphic inscriptions found in North and South America. Similar to the syllabic alphabets of Asia, Africa and Polynesia.

10*th Series.*—Alphabets or graphic letters, expressing simple sounds, and disposed in rows. Found in many inscriptions, medals and coins in North and South America, and lately introduced every where by the European colonists. Similar to the alphabets of Asia, Africa and Europe.

11*th Series.*—Abreviations, or letters standing for whole words, or part of a glyph and graphic delineation, standing and expressing the whole. Used by almost all the writing nations of North and South America, as well as Asia, Europe and Africa.

12*th Series.*—Numeric system of graphic signs, to express numbers All the various kinds of signs, such as dots, lines, strokes, circles, glyphs, letters, &c., used by some nations of North and South America, as well as in the eastern continent.

In my next letter I shall chiefly illustrate the 7th and 8th series so as to decypher and explain one of the most curious and least known of the American modes of expressing and perpetuating ideas. I shall give a figure of a sample of those monumental symbols, with comparative figures of two alphabets of Africa, the nearest related to them, and where the elements may be traced, which are grouped in those glyphs.

[The characters here presented are the glyphs alluded to by this author, formed from the combinations of the African and American letters, shown and treated upon page 118 of this work. For an account of those glyphs, see pages 122, 123 and 124.]

At the first glance, the most cursory observer is impressed with the idea of their likeness to the Chinese glyphs, which, in the languages in which they were or are in use, is equivalent to the combination of *our* letters when grouped so as to spell words, and show that America, in its *earliest* history, was not without its literati, and means of improvement by the use of letters, but was lost by means of revolutions as once was the fate of the Roman empire.

We have glanced at the following circumstance before, on page 241: we hope the reader will excuse its repetition, as we wish in this place to give the entire remarks of the author on this most interesting subject, the letters and glyphs of America.]

"Some years ago, the *Society of Geography*, of Paris, offered a large premium for a voyage to Guatamala, and a new survey of the antiquities of Yucatan and Chiapa, chiefly those fifteen miles from Palenque, which are wrongly called by that name. I have restored to them the true name of Otolum, which is yet the name of the stream running through the ruins. I should have been inclined to undertake this voyage and exploration myself, if the civil discords of the country did not forbid it. My attention was drawn forcibly to this subject as soon as the account of those ruins, surveyed by Captain Del Rio, as early as 1787, but withheld from the public eye by Spain, was published in 1822, in English.

This account, which partly describes the ruins of a stone city 75 miles in circuit, (length 32 English miles, greatest breadth 12 miles,) full of palaces, monuments, statues, and inscriptions: one of the earliest seats of American civilization, about equal to Thebes of Egypt, as well calculated to inspire me with hopes that they would throw a great light over American history, when more properly examined.

I have been disappointed in finding that no traveller has dared to penetrate again to that recondite place, and illustrate all the ruins, monuments, with the languages yet spoken all around. The Society of Geography has received many additional accounts, derived from documents preserved in Mexico; but they have not been deemed worthy of the reward offered for a new survey, and have not even been published. The same has happened with *Tiahuanaco*, in Bolivia, South America, another mass of ancient ruins, and mine of historical knowledge, which no late traveller has visited or described.

Being therefore without hope of any speedy accession to our knowledge of those places, I have been compelled to work upon the materials now extant; which have happily enabled me to do a great deal, notwithstanding all their defects, and throw some light on that part of the history of America.

C. S. RAFINESQUE.

Philadelphia, January, 1832.

The Atlantic Nations of America.

The ocean separating Europe and Africa from America is yet called the Atlantic ocean, our littoral states are called the Atlantic states. The Atlantes of North Africa, who gave their name to the Atlas mountains, and whose descendants exist there as yet under the names of *Taurics, Berbers, Shelluh, Showiah, &c.*, were one of the primitive nations of both continents. They came to America soon after the flood, if not before, colonised and named the ocean, and the islands in it, as well as America, which was called the *Great Atlantis*, or rather *Atala*, meaning the first, or main land. This name is preserved in Hindu traditions. The Atlantes were not the only primitive colonists of America, but they were the most conspicuous and civilized. Their true name was Atalans. They may have been the founders of Otolum, and many other ancient cities. Their descendants *exist to this day in America*, under the names of *Talas* or *Tarascas, Atalalas, Matalans, Talegawis, Otalis* or *Tsulukis, Talahuicas, Chontalas* or *Tsendalas, &c.*, from Carolina to Guatamala.

When Columbus discovered again America, he and the earliest explorers were struck with the similarity between many American tribes and the *Guanches* of the Canary islands, remains of the Oceanic Atlantes, in features, manners and speech. Whether the *Haytians, Cubans* and *Aruacs*, were genuine Atlantes, is rather doubtful, because their language is more akin to the Pelagic than the Atlantic. But three at least out of the twenty-five original nations of America above enumerated, may safely be deemed children of the Atlantes. They are the ninth or Otalis, the tenth or Atalans, and the fourteenth or Chontals.

This could be proved in many ways, and by their languages compared with those of their African brethren, *Taurics, Guanches*, &c. after a separation of several thousand years. But the proofs would fill a volume.

Our actual *Cherokis*, and akin tribes, are the children of the first branch, named *Otalis*. This was their original name. Adair, only 100 years ago, says that the genuine or upland Cherokis were called Otalis, which name meant mountaineers, as in Africa. They call themselves now *Tsulukis*. Our name of *Cherokis* is derived from the word *Chelakis*, name of a tribe. They have not the sound of *r* in their speech. Only one tribe substitutes *r* to *l*. The interesting history of this nation shall deserve our attention hereafter. The *Chontal* branch or nation will come under notice in investigating the antiquities of Otolum or Palenque. It remains here to survey the genuine branch of ATALANS; eldest, perhaps, of the American Atlantes.

Among this, the best known, (and yet hardly known,) are the *Tarascas* of Michuacan, in West Mexico; the brave nation that first asserted the late Mexican independence. Their true name is *Tala;* and *Tala-s-ca,* meaning *Tala-self-the,* or, in our idiom, *the very self Tala.* They have no *r* in their speech, and this name was changed by the Othmis and Mexicans into *Tarascas*.—(*See grammar of their language by Basalenque, Mexico,* 1714.)

From this interesting little work, some other account from Vater, and the Spanish writers, we learn something of their language, which is yet spoken, and may be thoroughly studied. We also learn that they formed a powerful and civilized kingdom, independent of Mexico, at the Spanish invasion, which became the ally of the Spaniards, but was by them subdued by treachery and infamous conduct. But we learn very little of their previous history; and the little known is buried in untranslated Spanish books. It is by their language that we can hope to trace their origin and most remote history. *Languages do not lie,* says Horne Tooke. They reveal what time has buried in oblivion.

We shall therefore give some account of it, that the learned or curious may study its affinities. So far as we have done so already, we have been struck with its evident analogy with the Atlantic, Coptic, Pelagic, Greek, Latin and Italian languages of Africa and Europe, both in words and structure, in spite of a separation of some thousand years. This language is rich, beautiful and highly complex. It amalgamates particles to modify words, as in the Italian. The verbs have fifteen modifications, as in Italian, or nearly so; they can be compounded, as in Greek. It admits of all the Greek rhetorical figures. The plural is formed by *x*. It has nearly all the European vocal sounds, except *f* and *r*; also no *gn* and no *ll*; but it has three sibillant, *ts*, *tz* and *tzh*.

The analogies with the Italian are striking in the following phrases, and some even appear with the Saxon English.

English.	Tala.	Italian.	English.	Tala.	Italian.
1 Thou	Thu	Tu	1 I	Hi	Io
2 Was (wast)	Esca	Sei (fosti)	2 Was	Esca	Sie (fui)
3 Thou who	Thuqui	Tu che	3 I who	Hiquinini	Io che
4 Spoke	Vandahaca	Favelasti	4 Loved	Pamphzahaca	Amai

English.	Tala.	Italian.
1 Is not	Noxas	Non e
2 So wise	Mimixcti	Amico (savio)
3 As I	Isqui hi	Com'io

The following vocabulary of 85 words gives a fair sample of the language. The affinities with the Pelagic and its children, Greek, Latin, Etruscan and Italian, are marked by the letter *p*; those with the Atlantic dialects of Africa, with the letter *a*. They amount to 50 out of 85 with the Pelagic, or 60 per cent of analogy; and to 33 out of 65 with the Atlantic, or 51 per cent. These are striking facts, deserving attention, in spite of the unbelief of some ignorant or lazy philosophers or historians, who neglect or disbelieve these evident proofs. The sixteen English affinities are marked by an arterisk. The orthography is, of course Spanish.

English.	Tala.	English.	Tala.
Water	Ama, ma, *a. p.*	Land*	Haca, eche, andatze, *a. p*
Fire	Pa, vepo, tani, *a. p.*	Thine	Thuicheveri
Stone	Tzacapu, zampzin, *a. p.*	You	Thucha
	Cuiri, *a.*	Yours	Thuchaveri
Men	Puecha, *p.*	We	Hucha
	Marin, *p.*	Ours	Huchaveri
Dog	Vichu, *a.*	This	I, *p.*
Mountain*	Vata, *a.*	These	Ix
Star	Hosqua	That	Inde, ima
Day	Vina, *p.*	Mine, own	Huchevi
Night	Ahchiuri, tzire	Be	E, *a. p.*

English.	Tala.	English.	Tala.
Heaven*	Parini, avandu, a. p.	To be	Eni, a. p.
House*	O, chao, p. a.	I am	Ehaca, a. p.
Father,*	Tata, a. p.	Is*	Esti, a. p.
Mother,	Nana, p.	Was	Esca, a. p.
Hand, arm,	Cu, xu, a.	Place,* earth	Can, haca, a. p.
Foot	Du, a.	King	Irecha, a. p.
Head	Tsi, p.	Kingdom	Arikeve, p.
Mouth*	Mu, a. p.	Name	Acan, Guriqua
Beard	Hapu, p.	Fish	Mechoa, p.
End, tail	Yara, p.	City*	Fatziza, p.
One	Mah	Deer	Taximaroa
Alone	Mahco	Festival	Metotes, p.
Ten	Xam, p.	To give	Inspeni
Much	Cani, a.	To write	Carani, p.
Priest*	Amberi, p. quinametin	To say	Harani, p.
God	Tucapacha, a.	To hold	Uhcamani
Just	Casipeti	To wash	Hopo
Good	Ambaqueti,	To think	Hangue, p.
Wise, friend	Mimi, p. a.	To take	Piran, p.
Little	Caxeti	To come	Hurani, p. Tiro
Tree	Emba, ches, a. p.	Food	Caro, aqua, p. a.
Bark	Chucari, p.	Drink	Itsima, a.
Leaf	Zahcuri	Handsome	Tzitzis, a.
Bread	Curinda, a.	Living	Tzipeti, p.
Color*	Chara, p.	To live	Tzipeni
Plain	Pe, p.	Singer	Pireti, p,
Sand	Cutza	To sing	Pireni
Peak	Phurequa, p.	Not*	Noxas, p. a.
Evil	Sismaraqui, himboo	Like,* as	Isqui, p.
Boat	Xu, a.	Love	Pampza, p.
Self*	S, p.	Speech	Vanda, p.
I, me*	Hi, p. a	Who, whom	Qui, p.
Myself	His, p. a.	The	Ca
Thou*	Thu, p.		

Primitive Origin of the English Language.

BY C. S. RAFINESQUE.

The best work on the philosophy and affinities of the English language, is, at present, the introduction, by Noah Webster, to his great dictionary. Yet although he has taken enlarged views of the subject, and by far surpassed every predecessor, he has left much to do to those future philologists and philosophers who may be inclined to pursue the subject still farther: not having traced the English language to its primitive sources, nor through all its variations and anomalies.

But no very speedy addition to this knowledge is likely to be produced, since Mr. Webster has stated, in a letter inserted in the Genesee Farmer of March, 1832, (written to vindicate some of his improvements in orthography,) that no one has been found in America or England able to review his introduction! although many have been applied to! But I was not one of those consulted, few knowing of my researches in languages, else I could have done ample justice to the subject and Mr. Webster.

It is not now a review of his labors that I undertake, but merely an inquiry into the primitive origin of our language, extracted from my manuscript philosophy of the English, French and Italian languages, compared with all the other languages or dialects of the whole world, not less than 3000 in number.

The modern English has really only one immediate parent. The old English, such as it was spoken and written in England, between the years 1000 and 1500, lasting about five hundred years, which is the usual duration of fluctuating languages. Our actual English is a natural deviation or dialect of it, begun between 1475 and 1525, and gradually improved and polished under two different forms, the written English and the spoken English, which are as different from each other as the English from the French. These two forms have received great accession by the increase of knowledge, and borrowing from many akin languages words unknown to the old English. They are both subject yet to the fluctuations of orthography and pronunciation, which gradually modify them again.

The old English existed probably also under these two forms, and had several contemporaneous dialects, as the modern English, of which the Yorkshire and Scotch dialects are most striking in Europe, while Guyana, Creole and West-India Creole, are the most remarkable in America. Another dialect, filled with Bengali and Hindostani words, is also forming in the East-Indies.

A complete comparison of the old and modern English has not yet been given. A few striking examples will here be inserted as a specimen of disparity.

Written. Old English.	Written. Mod. English.	Written. Old English.	Written. Mod. English.
Londe	Lande	See	Sea
Sterre	Star	Benethen	Beneath
Erthe	Earth	Hewyn	Heaven
Yle	Island	Hedde	Head

As late as the year 1555, we find the English language very different from the actual, at least in orthography; for instance,

Eng. of 1555.	Writ. Mod. Eng.	Eng. of 1555.	Writ. Mod. Eng.
Preste	Priest	Fyer	Fire
Euyll	Evil	Howse	House
Youe	You		

This old English is supposed to have sprung from the amalgamation of three languages: British-Celtic, Anglo-Saxon and Norman-French, between the years 1000 and 1200. This has been well proved by many, and I take it for granted.

But the successive parents and the genealogies of the Celtic, Saxon and Norman, are not so well understood. Yet through their successive and gradual dialects springing from each other, are to be traced the anomalies and ffinities of all the modern languages of western Europe.

By this investigation it is found that these three parents of the English, instead of being remote and distinct languages, were themselves brothers, sprung from a common primitive source, having undergone fluctuations and changes every 500 or 1000 years. For instance, the Latin of the time of Romulus, was quite a different language from that spoken in the time of Augustus, although this was the child of the former, this of the Ausonian, &c.

The following table will illustrate this fact, and the subsequent remarks prove it.

I. Old English sprung partly from the British-Celtic.

2d Step. British Celtic of Great Britain, sprung from the Celtic of West Europe.

3d Step. This Celtic from the Cumric or Kimran of Europe.

4th Step. The Cumric from the Gomerian of Western Asia.

5th Step. The Gomerian from the Yavana of Central Asia.

6th Step. The Yavana was a dialect of the Sanscrit.

II. The Old English partly sprung from the Anglo-Saxon of Britain.

2d Step. The Anglo-Saxon sprung from Saxon or Sacacenas of Germany.

3d Step. The Saxon from the Teutonic or Gothic of Europe.

4th Step. The Teutonic from the Getic of East Europe.

5th Step. The Getic from the Tiras or Tharaca of West Asia. (Thracians of the Greeks.)

6th Step. The Tiras from the Cutic or Saca of Central Asia, called Scythian by the Greeks.

7th Step. The Saca was a branch of the Sanscrit.

III. Old English partly sprung from the Norman-French.

2d Step. The Norman French was sprung from the Romanic of France.

3d Step. The Romanic from the Celtic, Teutonic and Roman Latin.

4th Step. Roman Latin from the Latin of Romulus.

5th Step. The Latin from the Ausonian of Italy.

6th Step. The Ausonian from the Pelagic of Greece and West Asia.

7th Step. The Pelagic from the Palangsha or Pali of Central Asia.

8th Step. The Pali was a branch of the Sanscrit.

Thus we see all the sources of the English language concentrating by gradual steps into the Sanscrit, one of the oldest languages of Central Asia, which has spread its branches all over the globe. Being the original language of that race of men, fathers of the Hindus, Persians, Europeans and Polynesians.

All the affinities between English and Sanscrit, are direct and striking, notwithstanding many deviations, and the lapse of ages. While those between the English and other primitive languages, such as Chinese, Mongol, Arabic, Hebrew, Coptic, Berber, &c., are much less in number and importance; being probably derived from the natural primitive analogy of those languages with the Sanscrit itself, when all the languages in Asia were intimately connected.

Many authors have studied and unfolded the English analogies with many languages; but few if any have ever stated their numerical amount. Unless this is done we can never ascertain the relative amount of mutual affinities. My numerical rule affords a very easy mode to calculate this amount without much trouble.

Thus, to find the amount of affinities between English and Latin, let us take ten important words at random in each.

Writ. Eng.	*Latin.*	*Writ. Eng.*	*Latin.*
Woman	Femina	One	Unum
††Water	Aqua	††House	Domus
†Earth	Terra	†Moon	Luna
†God	Deus	Star	Aster
††Soul	Anima	††Good	Bonus

We thereby find three affinities in ten, or 30 per cent; as many analogies or semi-affinities, marked †, equal to 15 per cent more; and four words, or 40 per cent, have no affinities. This will probably be found a fair average of the mutual rate in the old English, but the modern has received so many Latin synonyms as to exceed perhaps this rate.

Of these analogies it is remarkable that most are not direct from the Latin, or even through the French; but are of Saxon origin, which had them with the Latin previously.

Thus the affinities between the English and Greek or Russian are derived through the Pelagic and Thracian, unless lately adopted.

Boxhorn and Lipsius first noticed the great affinities of words and grammar between the Persian and German dialects. Twenty-five German writers have written on this. But Weston, in a very rare work, printed at Calcutta, in 1816, on the conformity of the English and European languages with the Persian, has much enlarged the subject, and has given as many as 480 consimilar words between Persian and Latin, Greek, English, Gothic, and Celtic: but he has not stated the numerical amount of these affinities. All this is not surprising, since the Iranians or Persians were also a branch of Hindus, and this language a child of the Zend, a dialect of the Sanscrit. Hammer has found as many a 560 affinities between German and Persian.

But the late work of Col. Kennedy, *Researches on the Origin and Affinity of the principal Languages of Asia and Europe*, London, 1828, 4to., is the most important, as directly concerning this investigation; notwithstanding that he has ventured on several gratuitous assertions, and has many omissions of consequence.

Kennedy states that the Sanscrit has 2500 verbal roots, but only 566 have distinct meanings; while each admitting of 25 suffixes, they form 60,000 words, and as they are susceptible of 958 increments, as many as 1,395,000 words may be said to exist in this wonderful language.

Yet out of these 2500 roots, as many as 900 are found by Kennedy in the Persian and European languages, although the Greek has only 2200 roots, and the Latin 2400. Of these 900 affinities

 330 are found in the Greek,
 319 in Latin,
 265 in Persian,
 262 in Geman,
 251 in English,
 527 in Greek or Latin,
 181 in both German and English,
  31 in all the five languages.

This is something positive and numerical; but unfortunately not definite, and partly erroneous, as will be proved presently from the English. Kennedy denies affinities between the Celtic and Sanscrit; but the very words he has offered as examples, (only 100,) offer many evident affinities. His opinion that the Hindus and Egyptians came from the Babylonians, is very improbable. It was from the high table land of Central Asia that all the old nations came.

The 251 English affinities may be seen in Kennedy, as well as the 339 Latin, which are mostly found now also in English through the words derived from the Latin. These two united would be 590 or more already than the 566 separate meanings of the Sanscrit roots. But Kennedy has by no means exhausted the Sanscrit etymologies of the English. Although I have no English Sanscrit dictionary at hand, yet I have many Sanscrit vocabularies, where I find many words omitted by Kennedy. And what is not found in the Sanscrit itself, is found in its eastern children, the modern languages of Hindostan.

Among my vocabularies, the most important is one made by myself, of the principal words of the old Sanscrit, met with and explained in the laws of Menu translated by Jones. In these old and often obsolete words are found the most striking affinities, of which I here give the greater part.

English, Written.	Old Sanscrit of Menu.	English, Written.	Old Sanscrit of Menu.
Mother	Mara	Beetle	Blatta
Mind	Men	Penny	Pana
Mankind	Manavah	Gas	Akasa
Era	Antara	Father	Vasus
Hour	Hora	Play	Waya
Virtuous	Verta	Malice (sin)	Mala
Antique	Arti	Patriarch	Patri
Middle	Medhya	Eyes	Eshas
Teacher	Acharya	Right	Rita
Bos (master)	Bhos	Phantom	Vantasa
Before	Purva	Wood	Venu
Wind	Pavana	Me, mine	Man
Deity	Daitya	Animate	Mahat
Mouth	Muc'ha	Spirit	Eshetra

Being twenty-eight derived words out of eighty-four of this old vocabulary, 33 per cent.

Another very singular vocabulary I have extracted from the transactions of the Literary Society of Bombay, and Erskine's account of the ancient Mahabad religion of Balk from the book Desatir. Some words are given there of the language of the Mahabad empire, the primitive Iran, which appears to be a very early dialect of the Sanscrit and Zend. Out of thirty words twelve have analogies to the English, equal to 40 per cent.

English, Written.	Mahabad of Iran.	English, Written.	Mahabad of Iran.
Father	Fiter	Middle	Mad
End	Antan	Sky	Kas
Course	Kur (time)	Royal	Raka (king)
Nigh	Unim	Ignite	Agai (fire)
Amicably	Mitr (friend)	Man	Minhush
Globe	Gul	Donation	Datisu

I could add here at least 250 to the 251 of Kennedy, if it were not too tedious and long. But I can safely vouch that all the 566 radical roots of peculiar meaning, forming the base of the Sanscrit, are to be found in the English roots, or if a few are lacking it is merely owing to some having become obsolete through the lapse of nearly 5000 years, when the Yavanas, Sacas and Pallis separated from their Hindu brethren, and the revolution of six or seven successive dialects formed by each, till they met again in the English.

Kennedy has even some obsolete English and Scotch words, now out of use, which are derived from the Sanscrit.

This inquiry is not merely useful to unfold the origin and revolutions of our language; but it applies more or less to all the languages of Europe; which were formed in a similar way by dialects of former languages. Since every dialect becomes a language whenever it is widely spread and cultivated by a polished nation. Thus the French, Italian, Spanish, Portuguese, Romanic and Valaquian are now become languages, with new dialects of their own, although they are in fact mere dialects of the Latin and Celtic.

The physical conformation and features of all the European and Hindu nations are well known to agree, and naturalists consider them as a common race. The historical traditions of these nations confirm the philological and physical evidence. All the European nations came from the east or the west of the Imaus table land of Asia, the seat of the ancient Hindu empires of Balk, Cashmir and Iran. The order of time in which the Asiatic nations entered Europe to colonize it was as follows:

1. or most ancient. *Esquas* or *Oscans* or *Iberians* or *Cantabrians*.
2. *Gomarians* or *Cumras* or *Celts* or *Gaels*.
3. *Getes* or *Goths* or *Scutans* or *Scythians*.
4. *Finns* or *Laps* or *Sames*.
5. *Tiras* or *Thracians* or *Illyrians* or *Slaves*.
6. *Pallis* or *Pelasgians* or *Hellenes* or *Greeks*.

The settlement in Europe of these last is so remote as to be involved in obscurity. But their geographical positions, traditions and languages prove their relative antiquity. The Greek language is one of those that has been most permament, having lasted 2500 years, from Homer's time to the Turkish conquest. Yet it sprung from the Pelagic and has given birth to the Romanic or modern Greek dialects.

Colonies of the Danes in America.

But besides the evidences that the Malay, Australasia and Polynesian tribes of the Pacific islands, have, in remote ages, peopled America, from the west; coming, first of all, from the Asiatic shores of that ocean; and also from the east, peopling the island Atalantis, (equally early, as we believe,) once situated between America and Europe, and from this to the continent; yet there is another class of antiquities, or race of population, which, says Dr. Mitchill, deserves particularly to be noticed. "These are the emigrants from Lapland, Norway, and Finland in Europe," who, before the tenth century, settled themselves in Greenland, and passed over to Labrador. It is recorded that these adventurers settled themselves in a country which they called Vinland."

Our learned regent, Gov. De Witt Clinton, says Dr. Mitchill, who has out-done Governeur Colden, by writing the most full and able history of the Iroquois, or Five Nations, of New-York, mentioned to me his *belief* that a part of the old forts and other antiquities at Onondaga, about Auburn, and the adjacent country, were of Danish character.

"I was at once penetrated by the justice of his remark; an additional window of light was suddenly opened to my view on this subject. I perceived at once, with the Rev. Van Troil, that the European emigrants had passed, during the horrible commotions of the ninth and tenth century, to Iceland.—(*See History of England.*)

The Rev. Mr. Crantz had informed me, in his important book, how they went to Greenland. I thought I could trace the people of Scandinavia to the banks of the St. Lawrence; I supposed my friends had seen the Punic inscriptions made by them here and there, in the places where they visited. Madoc, prince of Wales, and his Cambrian followers, appeared, to my recollection, among these bands of adventurers. And thus the northern lands of North America were visited by the hyperborean tribes from the northwestermost climates of Europe; and the northwestern climes of North America had received inhabitants of the same race from the northeastern regions of Asia.

The Danes, Fins or Germans, and Welchmen, performing their migrations gradually to the southwest, seem to have penetrated to the country situated in the south of lake Ontario, which would be in the states of New-York and Pennsylvania, and to have fortified themselves there; where the Tartars, or Samoieds, travelling by slow degrees from Alaska, on the Pacific, to the southeast, finally found them.

In their course these Asian colonists probably exterminated the Malays, who had penetrated along the Ohio and its streams, or drove them to caverns abounding in saltpetre and copperas, in Kentucky and Tennessee; where their bodies, accompanied with cloths and ornaments of their peculiar manufacture, have been repeatedly disinterred and examined by the members of the American Antiquarian Society.

Having achieved this conquest, the Tartars and their descendants had probably a much harder task to perform. This was to subdue the more ferocious and warlike European colonists, who had intrenched and fortified themselves in the country, after the arrival of the Tartars, or Indians as they are now called, in the particular parts they had settled themselves in, along the region of the Atlantic.

In Pompey, Onondaga county, are the remains, or outlines, of a town, including more than 500 acres. It appeared protected by three circular or eliptical forts, eight miles distant from each other; placed in such relative positions as to form a triangle round about the town, at those distances.

It is thought, from appearances, that this strong hold was stormed and taken on the line of the north side. In Camillus, in the same county, are the remains of two forts, one covering about three acres, on a very high hill; it had gateways, one opening to the east and the other to the west, toward a spring, some rods from the works. Its shape is elliptical; it has a wall, in some places ten feet high, with a deep ditch.

Not far from this is another, exactly like it, only half as large. There are many of these ancient works hereabouts; one in Scipio, two near Auburn, three near Canandaigua, and several between the Seneca and Cayuga lakes. A number of such fortifications and burial places have also been discovered in Ridgeway, or the southern shore of lake Ontario.

There is evidence enough that long and bloody wars were waged among the inhabitants, in which the Scandinavians, or Esquimaux as they are now called, seem to have been overpowered and destroyed in New-York. The survivors of the defeat and ruin retreated to Labrador, a country lying between Hudson's bay and the Atlantic; in latitude 50 and 60 degrees north, where they have remained, secure from further pursuit.

From the known ferocity of the ancient Scandinavians, who with other Europeans of ancient times we suppose to be the authors of the vast works about the region of Onondaga, dreadful wars, with infinite butcheries, must have crimsoned every hill and dale of this now happy country.

In corroboration of this opinion, we give the following, which is an extract from remarks made on the ancient customs of the Scandinavians, by Adam Clarke, in a volume entitled *Clarke's Discovery*, p. 145.

1st. *Odin*, or *Woden*, their supreme god, is there termed the terrible or severe deity, the father of slaughter, who carries desolation and fire; the tumultuous and roaring deity; the giver of courage and victory; he who marks out who shall perish in battle; the shedder of the blood of man. From him is the fourth day of our week, denominated Wodnesday, or Wednesday.

2d. *Frigga*, or *Frega*: she was his consort, called also *Ferorthe*, mother Earth. She was the goddess of love and debauchery—the northern Venus. She was also a warrior, and divided the souls of the slain with her husband Odin. From her we have our Friday, or Freya's day; as on that day she was peculiarly worshipped, as was Odin on Wednesday.

3d. *Thor*, the god of winds and tempests, thunder and lightning. He was the especial object of worship in Norway, Iceland, and consequently in the Zetland isles. From him we have the name of our fifth day, Thor's day, or Thursday.

4th. *Tri*, the god who protects houses. His day of worship was called Tyrsday, or Tiiesday, whence our Tuesday. As to our first and second day, Sunday and Monday, they derived their names from the sun and the moon, to whose worship ancient idolaters had consecrated them.

From this we learn that they had a knowledge of a small cycle of time, called a week, of seven days, and must have been derived in some way from the ancient Hebrew Scriptures, as here we have the first intimation of this division of time. But among the Mexicans no trait of a cycle of seven days is found, says Humboldt; which we consider an additional evidence that the first people who found their way to these regions, called North and South America, left Asia at a period anterior at least to the time of Moses; which was about 1600 years before Christ.

But we continue the quotation, "All who die in battle go to Vall-palla, Odin's palace, where they amuse themselves by going through their martial exercises; then cutting each other to pieces; afterwards, all the parts healing, they sit down to their feasts, where they quaff beer out of the sculls of those whom they had slain in battle, and whose blood they had before drank out of the same skulls, when they had slain them.

The Scandinavians offered different kinds of sacrifices, but especially human; and from these they drew their auguries, by the velocity with which the blood flowed when they cut their throats, and from the appearance of the intestines, and especially the heart. It was a custom in Denmark to offer annually, in January, a sacrifice of ninety-nine cocks, ninety-nine dogs, ninety-nine horses, and ninety-nine men; besides other human sacrifices," on various occasions.

Such being the fact, it is fairly presumable that as the Danes, Scandinavians, and Lapponiac nations, found their way from the north of Europe to Iceland, Greenland and Labrador; and from thence about the regions of the western lakes, especially Ontario; that the terrific worship of the Celtic gods, has been practised in America, at least in the state of New-York. And it is not impossible but this custom may have pervaded the whole continent, for the name of one of these very gods, namely Odin, is found among the South Americans, and the tops of the pyramids may have been the altars of sacrifice.

"We have already fixed the attention of the reader," says Baron Humboldt, "on Votan, or Wodan, an American, who seems to be a member of the same family with the Woads, or Odins, of the Goths, and nations of the Celtic origin."

The same names, he says, are celebrated in India, Scandinavia, and Mexico, all of which is, by tradition, believed to point to none other than to Noah and his sons. For, according to the traditions of the Mexicans, as collected by Bishop Francis Nunez de la Vega, their Wodan was grandson to that illustrious old man, who, at the time of the great deluge, was saved on a raft, with his family. He was also at the building of the great edifice, and co-operated with the builder, which had been undertaken by men to reach the skies. The execution of this rash project was interrupted; each family receiving from that time a different language; when the Great Spirit, or Teatl, ordered Wodan to go and people the country of Anahuac, which is in America.

"Think, (says Dr. Mitchill,) what a memorable spot is our Onondaga, where men of the Malay race, from the southwest, and of the Tartar blood from the northwest, and of the Gothic stock from the northeast, have successfully contended for the supremacy and rule, and which may be considered as having been possessed by each long enough before" Columbus was born, or the navigating of the western ocean thought of by Europeans.

"John de Laet, a Flemish writer, says that Modoc, one of the sons of Prince Owen Gynnith, being disgusted with the civil wars which broke out between his brothers, after the death of their father, fitted out several vessels, and having provided them with every thing necessary for a long voyage, went in quest of new lands to the westward of Ireland. There he discovered very fertile countries," where he settled; and it is very probable Onondaga, and the country along the St. Lawrence, and around lakes Ontario and Erie, were the regions of their improvements.—*(Carver, p. 108.)*

"We learn from the historian Charlevoix, that the Eries, an indigenous nation of the Malay race, who formerly inhabited the lands south of lake Erie, where the western district of Pennsylvania and the state of Ohio now are. And Lewis Evens, a former resident of the city of New-York, has shown us in his map of the Middle Colonies, that the hunting grounds of the Iroquois extended over that very region. The Iroquois were of the Tartar stock and they converted the country of the exterminated Eries or Malays into a range for the wild beasts of the west, and a region for their own hunters."

He says, the Scandinavians emigrated about the tenth century of the Christian era, if not earlier; and that they may be considered as not only having discovered this continent, but to have explored its northern climes to a great extent, and also to have peopled them.

In the fourteenth township, fourth range of the Holland Company's lands in the state of New-York, near the Ridge road leading from Buffalo to Niagara falls, is an ancient fort, situated in a large swamp; it covers about five acres of ground; large trees are standing upon it. The earth which forms this fort was evidently brought from a distance, as that the soil of the marsh is quite of another kind, wet and miry, while the site of the fort is dry gravel and loam. The site of this fortification is singular, unless we suppose it to have been a last resort or hiding place from an enemy.

The distance to the margin of the marsh is about half a mile, where large quantities of human bones have been found, on opening the earth, of an extraordinary size: the thigh bones, about two inches longer than a common sized man's: the jaw or chin bone will cover a large man's face: the skull bones are of an enormous thickness: the breast and hip bones are also very large. On being exposed to the air they soon moulder away, which denotes the great length of time since their interment. The disorderly manner in which these bones were found to lie, being crosswise, commixed and mingled with every trait of confusion, show them to have been deposited by a conquering enemy, and not by friends, who would have laid them, as the custom of all nations always has been in a more deferential mode.

There was no appearance of a bullet having been the instrument of their destruction, the evidence of which would have been broken limbs. Smaller works of the same kind abound in the country about lake Ontario, but the one of which we have just spoken is the most remarkable. This work, it is likely, was a last effort of the Scandinavians.

North of the mountain, or great slope toward the lake, there are no remains of ancient works or tumuli, which strongly argues, that the mountain or ridgeway once was the southern boundary or shore of lake Ontario: The waters having receded from three to seven miles from its ancient shore, nearly the whole length of the lake, occasioned by some strange convulsion in nature, redeeming much of the lands of the west from the water that had covered it from the time of the deluge.

The following is the opinion of Morse, the geographer, on the curious subject of the original inhabitants or population of America. He says, " without detailing the numerous opinions of philosophers, respecting the original population of this continent, he will, in few words, state the result of his own inquiries on the subject, and the facts from which the result is deduced.

"The Greenlanders and Esquimaux," which are one in origin,

"were emigrants from the northwest of Europe," which is Norway and Lapland. A colony of Norwegians was planted in Iceland, in 874, which is almost a thousand years ago. Greenland, which is separated from the American continent only by Davis' strait, which, in several places, is of no great width, was settled by Eric Rufus, a young Norwegian, in 982; and before the 11th century, churches were founded and a bishopric erected, at Grade, the capital of the settlement.

Soon after this, Bairn, an Icelandic navigator, by accident, discovered land to the west of Greenland. This land received the name of Vineland. It was settled by a colony of Norwegians in 1002, and from the description given of its situation and productions, must have been Labrador, which is on the American continent, or Newfoundland, which is but a little way from the continent, separated by the narrow strait of Bellisle, at the north end of the gulf of St. Lawrence, a river of Canada. Vineland was west of Greenland, and not very far to the south of it. It also produced grape vines spontaneously. Mr. Elis, in his voyage to Hudson's bay, informs us that the vine grows spontaneously at Labrador, and compares the fruit of it to the currants of the Levant.

Several missionaries of the Moravians, prompted by a zeal for propagating Christianity, settled in Greenland; from whom we learn that the Esquimaux perfectly resemble the natives of the two countries, and have intercourse with one another; that a few sailors, who had acquired the knowledge of a few Greenland words, reported, that these were understood by the Esquimaux; that at length a Moravian missionary, well acquainted with the language of Greenland, having visited the country of the Esquimaux, found to his astonishment that they spoke the same language with the Greenlanders;" which of course was the same with the language of Iceland, and also of Norway, which is in Europe, lying along on the coast of the Atlantic; as that the first colony of Iceland was from Norway, and from Iceland a first colony settled in Greenland, from thence to Labrodor, which is the continent; showing that the language of the Esquimaux is that of the ancient *Norse* of Europe, derived from the more ancient Celtic nations, who were derived from the descendants of Japheth, the son of Noah; from which we perceive that both from country and lineal descent, the present inhabitants are brothers to the Esquimaux (Indians, as they are improperly called) who also are white, and not copper colored, like the red men, or common Indians, who are of the Tartar stock.

The missionry, found, " that there was abundant evidence of their being of the same race, and he was accordingly received and entertained by them as a friend and brother." These facts prove the settlement of Greenland by an Icelandic colony, and the consanguinity of the Greenlanders and Esquimaux.

Iceland is only about one thousand miles west from Norway, in Europe, with more than twenty islands between; so that there is no difficulty in the way of this history to render it improbable that the early navigators from Norway may have easily found Iceland, and colonized it.

" The enterprize, skill in navigation, even without the compass, and roving habits, possessed by these early navigators, renders it highly probable also, that at some period more remote than the 10th century, they had pursued the same route to Greenland, and planted colonies there, which is but six hundred miles west of Iceland. Their descendants the present Greenlanders and Esquimaux, retaining somewhat of the enterprize of their ancestors, have always preserved a communication with each other, by crossing and recrossing Davis's strait. The distance of ocean betweeen America and Europe on the east, or America and China on the west, is no objection to the passage of navigators, either from design or stress of weather; as that Coxe, in his *Russian Discoveries*, mentions that several Kamschadale vessels, in 1745, were driven out to sea, and forced, by stress of weather, to take shelter among the Aleutian islands, in the Pacific, a distance of several hundred miles; and also Captain Cook, in one of his voyages, found some natives of one of the Islands of the same ocean, in their war canoes, six hundred miles from land."—(*Morse.*)

In the year 1789, Captain Bligh was sent out under the direction of the government of England, to the Friendly Islands, in the Pacific, in quest of the bread fruit plant, with the view of planting it in the West Indies.

But having got into the Pacific ocean, his crew mutined, and put him, with eighteen of his men, on board of a boat of but thirty-two feet in length, with one hundred and fifty pounds of bread, twenty-eight gallons of water, twenty pounds of pork, three bottles of wine and fifteen quarts of rum. With this scanty provision he was turned adrift in the open sea, when the vessel sailed, and left them to their fate. Captain Bligh then sailed for the island of Tofoa, but being resisted by the islanders with stones, and threatened with death, was compelled to steer from mere recollection, (for he was acquainted with those parts of that ocean,) for a port in the East Indies called Tima, belonging to the Dutch. He had been with the noted Captain Cook, in his voyages. The reason the natives pelted them with stones as they attempted to land, was because they perceived them to be without arms. This voyage, however, they performed in forty-six days, suffering in a most incredible manner, a distance of *four thousand miles*, losing but one man, who was killed by the stones of the savages, in attempting to get clear from the shore of an island, where they had landed to look for water.

"In 1797, the slaves of a ship from the coast of Africa, having risen on the crew, twelve of the latter leaped into a boat, and made their escape. On the thirty-eighth day three still survived, and drifted ashore at Barbadoes, in the West Indies.

In 1799, six men in a boat from St. Helena, lost their course, and nearly a month after, five of them surviving, reached the coast of South America, a distance of two thousand seven hundred and sixty miles."—(*Thomas' Travels*, p. 283.)

"If we consider in what an early age navigation was practised, and consequently how soon after that era America would receive inhabitants within its torrid zone, it will appear probable that the Mexicans were a great nation before either the Tartars or Esquimaux arrived on the northern part of this continent."

Navigation was indeed commenced at an early age, by the Egyptians and Phœnicians, probably more than sixteen hundred years before the time of Christ, (*See Morse's Chronology*,) and doubtless, from time to time, as in later ages, arrivals, either from design or from being driven to sea by storm, took place, so that Egyptians, Phœnicians, and individuals of other nations of that age, unquestionably found their way to South America, and also to the southern parts of North America, from the east, and also from west, across the Pacific, in shipping.

But we entertain the opinion, that even sooner than this, the woods of the Americas had received inhabitants, as we have before endeavored to show in this work, at a time when there was more land, either in the form of islands in groups, or in bodies, approaching to that of continents, situated both in the Pacific and Atlantic oceans; but especially that of Atalantis, once in the Atlantic between America and the coast of Gibraltar.

In the remarks of Carver on this subject, through the interior parts of Northwestern America, we have the following:—"Many of the ancients are supposed to have known that this quarter of the globe not only existed, but also that it was inhabited."

Plato, who wrote about 500 B. C., in his book entitled *Timaeus*, has asserted that beyond the island which he calls *Atalantis*, as learned from the Egyptian priests, and which, according to his description was situated in the Western ocean, opposite, as we have before said, to the strait of Gibraltar, there were a great number of other islands, and behind those a vast continent.

If some have affected to treat the tradition of the existence of this island as a chimera, we would ask, how should the priests be able to tell us, that behind that island, farther west, was a vast continent, which proves to be true, for that continent is America; or rather, as a continent is spoken of by Plato at all, lying west of Europe, we are of the opinion that this fact should carry conviction that the island also existed, as well as the continent; and why not Atalantis? If Plato knew of the one did he not of the other?

If the Egyptian priests had told Plato that anciently there existed a certain island, with a continent on the west of it, and the strait of Gibraltar on the east of it, and it was found, in succeeding ages, that neither the strait nor the continent were ever known to exist, it would be, indeed, clearly inferred, that neither was the island known to them. But as the strait does exist, and the western continent also, is it very absurd to suppose that Atalantis was indeed situated between these two facts, or parts of the earth now known to all the world?

Carver says that Oviedo, a celebrated Spanish author, the same who became the friend of Columbus, whom he accompanied on his second voyage to the new world, has made no scruple to affirm, that the Antilles are the famous Hesperides, so often mentioned by the poets, which are at length restored to the king of Spain, the descendants of king Hesperus, who lived upwards of three thousand years ago, and from whom these islands received their name.

De Laet, a Flemish writer, says it is related by Pliny the elder, one of the most learned of the ancient Roman writers, who was born twenty-three years after the time of Christ, and left behind him no less than thirty-seven volumes on natural history, and some other writers, that on many of the islands on the western coast of Africa, particularly on the Canaries, some ancient edifices were seen; even called ancient by Pliny, a term which would throw the time of their erection back to a period perhaps five or six hundred years before Christ.

"From this it is highly probable," says Mr. Carver, that the inhabitants, having deserted those edifices, even in the time of Pliny, may have passed over to South America, the passage being neither long nor difficult. This migration, according to the calculation of those authors, must have taken place more than 200 years before the Christian era, at a time when the people of Spain were much troubled by the Carthaginians, and might have retired to the Antilles, by the way of the western isles, which were exactly half way in their voyage to South America."

Emanuel de Morez, a Portuguese, in his *History of Brazil*, a province of South America, asserts that America has been wholly peopled by the Carthaginians and *Israelites*. He brings, as a proof of this assertion, the discoveries the former are known to have made, at a great distance beyond the western coast of Africa. The farther progress of which being put a stop to by the Senate of Carthage, some hundred years before Christ, those who happened to be then in the newly discovered countries, being cut off from all communications with their countrymen, and destitute of many necessaries of life, fell into a state of barbarism.

George de Horn, a learned Dutchman, who has written on the subject of the first peopling of America, maintains that the first founders of the colonies of this country were Scythians, who were much more ancient than the Tartars, but were derived from the Scythians; as the term Tartar is but of recent date when compared with the far more ancient appellation of Scythian, the descendants of Shem, the great progenitor of the Jews.

He also believes that the Phœnicians and Carthaginians afterwards got footing in America, by crossing the Atlantic, and likewise the Chinese, by way of the Pacific. These Phœnician and Carthaginian migrations he supposes to have been before the time of Solomon, king of Israel, who flourished a thousand years before Christ.

Mr. Thomas, of Auburn, in his volume entitled *Travels through the Western Country,* has devoted some twenty pages to the subject of the ancient inhabitants of America, with ability evidencing an enlarged degree of acquaintance with it. He says explicitly, on page 288, that " the Phœnicians were early acquainted with those shores," believes " that vessels, sailing out of the Mediterranean, may have been wrecked on the American shores; also colonies from the west of Europe, and from Africa, in the same way. Supposes that Egyptians and Syrians settled in Mexico: the former the authors of the pyramids of South America, and that the Syrians are the same with the Jews; wanting nothing to complete this fact but the rite of circumcision. Says the Greeks were the only, or first people who practised raising tumuli around the urns which contained the ashes of their heroes."

And, as we know, tumuli are in abundance in the west, raised over the ashes, as we suppose, of their heroes, should we not infer that the practice was borrowed from that people? This would prove some of them, at least, originally from about the Mediterranean.

But, notwithstanding our agreement with this writer, that many nations, the Greeks, the Egyptians, the Syrians, the Phœnicians, Carthaginians, Europeans, Romans, Asiatics, Scythians and Tartars, have, in different eras of time, contributed to the peopling of America; yet we believe, with the celebrated naturalist, Dr. Mitchill, that the ancestors of the people known by the appellation of the Malays, now peopling the islands of the Pacific, were nearly among the first who set foot on the coasts of America. And that the people who settled in the islands of the Atlantic, and especially that of Atalantis, now no more, immediately after the dispersion, were they who, first of all, and the Malay second, filled all America with their descendants in the first ages.

But in process of time, as the arts came on, navigation, with or without the compass, was practised, if not as systematically as at the present time, yet with nearly as wide a range; and as convulsions in the earth, such as divided one part of it from another, as in the days of Peleg, removing islands, changing the shape of continents, and separating the inhabitants of distant places from each other, by destroying the land or islands between, so that when shipping, whether large or small, as in the time of the Phœnicians, and Tyrians of king Solomon, the Greeks and Romans came to navigate the seas, America was found, visited and colonized anew. In this way we account for the introduction of the arts among the more ancient inhabitants whom they found there; which arts are clearly spoken of in the traditions of the Mexicans, who tell us of white and bearded men, as related by Humboldt, who came from the sun, (as they supposed the Spaniards did,) changed or reduced the wandering millions of the woods to order and government, introduced among them the art of agriculture, a knowledge of metals, with that of architecture; so that when Columbus discovered America, it was filled with cities, towns, cultivated fields and countries; palaces, aqueducts, and roads, and highways of the nations, equal with, if not exceeding, in some respects, even the people of the Roman countries, before the time of Christ.

But as learning, and a knowledge of the shape of the earth, in the times of the nations we have spoken of above, was not in general use among men; and from incessant wars and revolutions of nations, what discoveries may have been made, were lost to mankind; so that some of the very countries once known, have in later ages been discovered over again:

We will produce one instance of a discovery which has been lost—the land of Ophir—where the Tyrian fleets went for gold, in the days of Solomon. Where is it? The most learned do not know—cannot agree. It is lost as to identity. Some think it in Africa; some in the islands of the South Atlantic, and some in South America; and although it is, wherever it may be, undoubtedly an inhabited country, yet as to certainty about its location, it is unknown.

Ancient Chronology of the Onguys or Iroquois Indians.
BY DAVID CUSICK.

In the traditions of the Tuscaroras, published by Cusick in 1827, few dates are found; but these few are, nevertheless, precious for history.

A small volume has been printed this year by the Sunday School Union, on the history of the Delaware and Iroquois Indians, in which their joint traditions are totally neglected, as usual with our actual book makers.

Although Cusick's dates may be vague and doubtful, they deserve attention, and they shall be noticed here.

Anterior to any date the Eagwehoewe, (pronounced *Yaguyhohuy*) meaning real people, dwelt north of the lakes, and formed only one nation. After many years a body of them settled on the river Kanawag, now the St. Lawrence, and after a long time a foreign people came by sea and settled south of the lake.

1st. date. Towards 2500 winters before Columbus' discovery of America, or 1008 years before our era, total overthrow of the Towancas, nations of giants come from the north, by the king of the Onguys, Donhtonha and the hero Yatatan.

2d. Three hundred winters after, or 708 before our era, the northern nations form a confederacy, appoint a king, who goes to visit the great Emperor of the Golden city, south of the lakes; but afterwards quarrels arise, and a war of 100 years with this empire of the south, long civil wars in the north, &c. A body of people escaped in the mountain of Oswego, &c.

3d. 1500 years before Columbus, or in the year 8 of our era, Tarenyawagon, the first legislator leads his people out of the mountains to the river Yenonatateh, now Mohawk, where six tribes form an alliance called the Long-house, Agoneaseah. Afterwards reduced to five, the sixth spreading west and south. The Kautanoh since Tuscarora, came from this. Some went as far as the Onauweyoka, now Mississippi.

4th. In 108 the Konearawyeneh, or Flying Heads, invade the Five Nations.

5th. In 242 the Shakanahih, or Stone Giants, a branch of the western tribe, become cannibals, return and desolate the country; but they are overthrown and driven north by Tarenyawagon II.

6th. Towards 350 Tarenyawagon III., defeats other foes, called Snakes.

7th. In 492 Atoarho I., king of the Onondagas, quells civil wars, begins a dynasty ruling over all the Five Nations, till Atoarho IX., who ruled yet in 1142. Events are since referred to their reigns.

8th. Under Atotarho II., a Tarenyawagon IV., appears to help him to destroy Oyalk-guhoer, or the Big-bear.

9th. Under Atotarho III., a tyrant, Sohnanrowah, arises on the Kaunaseh, now Susquehannah river, which makes war on the Sahwanug.

10th. In 602, under Atatarho IV., the Towancas, now Mississaugers, cede to the Senecas the lands east of the River Niagara, who settle on it.

11th. Under Atotarho V., war between the Senecas and Otawahs of Sandusky.

12th. Towards 852 under Atotarho VI., the Senecas reach the Ohio river, compel the Otawahs to sue for peace.

13th. Atotarho VII. sent embassies to the west, the Kentakeh nation dwelt south of the Ohio, the Chipiwas on the Mississippi.

14th. Towards 1042, under Atotarho VIII., war with the Towancas, and a foreign stranger visits the Tuscaroras of Neuse river, who are divided into three tribes, and at war with the Nanticokes and Totalis.

15th. In 1143, under Atotarho IX., first civil war between the Erians of lake Erie, sprung from the Senecas, and the Five Nations.

Here end these traditions.

C. S. RAFINESQUE.

The foregoing is a curious trait of the ancient history of the wars and revolutions which have transpired in America.

It would appear that at the time of the overthrow of the Tawancas, 1008 years before Christ, called in the tradition a nation of giants, that it was about the time the temple of Solomon was finished; showing clearly that as they had become powerful in this country they had settled here at a very early period, probably about the time of Abraham, within three hundred and forty years of the flood.

The hero who conquered them was called *Yatatan*, king of the Onguys, names which refer them, as to origin, to the ancient Scythians of Asia.

Three hundred winters after this, or 708 years before Christ, about the time of the commencement of the Roman empire by Romulus, the northern nations form a grand confedracy and appoint a king, who went on a visit to the great emperor of the Golden city, south of the western lakes.

Were we to conjecture where this Golden city was situated, we should say on the Mississippi, where the Missouri forms a junction with that river, at or near St. Louis, as at this place and around its precincts are the remains of an immense population. This is likely the city to which the seven persons who were cast away on the island Estotiland, as before related, were carried to; being far to the southwest from that island, supposed to be Newfoundland,—St. Louis being in that direction.

This visit of *Yatatan* to the Golden city, it appears, was the occasion of a civil war of one hundred years, which ended in the ruin of the Golden city. A body of the citizens escaping, fled far to the east, and hid themselves in the mountains of Oswego, along the southern shores of lake Ontario, where they remained about seven hundred years, till a great leader arose among them, called Tarenyawagon, who led them to settle on the Mohawk; this was eight years after the birth of Christ.

These refugees from the Golden city, had now multiplied so that they had become several nations, whence the grand confederacy of six nations was formed. Upon these, a nation called Flying Heads made war but were unsuccessful; also, in 242 years after Christ, a nation called Stone Giants, made an attempt to destroy them but failed. They were successful in other wars against the Snake Indians, a more western tribe.

About the time of the commencement of Mahomet's career in 602, a great tyrant arose on the Susquehannah river, who waged war with surrounding nations, from which it appears, that while in Africa, Europe, and Asia, revolution succeeded revolution, empires rising on the ruins of empires, that in America the same scenes were acting on as great a scale; cultivated regions, populous cities and towns, were reduced to a wilderness, as in the other continents.

Evidence that a Nation of Africans, the Descendants of Ham, now inhabit a District of South America.

BY C. S. RAFINESQUE.

The Yarura nation of the Oronoco regions, (also called Jarura, Jaros, Worrow, Guarau, &c.) is one of the darkest and ugliest in South America, some tribes of it are quite black like negroes and are called monkeys. They are widely spread from Guyana to Choco. The following 35 words of their language collected from Chili, Hervas and Vater have enabled me to trace their origin to Africa.

¶God	Conmeh Anderh	¶Man	Pumeh
¶Heaven	Andeh	Woman	Ibi
Earth	Dabu, Dahu	Father	Aya
Water	Uy, Uvi	Mother	Aini
River	Nicua	Head	Pachu
¶Sun and day	Doh	Eyes	Yondeh
Moon	Goppeh	¶Nose	Nappeh
Star	Boeboe	Tongue	Topeno
Fire	Condeh	Feet	Tao
Soul	Yuaneh	Evil	Chatandra
Wood	Yuay	Being	Abechin, conom
Plain	Chiri	Our	Ibba
¶Bread	Tarab, Tambeh	Will	Ea
Name	Kuen	Power	Beh
Give	Yero	1	Canameh
Come	Manatedi	2	Noeni
Mayze	Pueh	¶3	Tarani

Those marked ¶ or 7 out of 34 have some analogy with the English, equal to 19 per cent.

The language of the Gahunas, negroes of Choco and Popayan has 50 per cent analogy with the Yarura, since out of 8 words to be compared, 4 are similar.

God	Conomeh Y	Copamo G		One	Canameh	Amba
Man	Pumeh	Mehora		Two	Noeni	Numi

While the Ashanty or Fanty, negro language widely spread in West Africa has 40 per cent of affinity with the Yarura or six words similar in fifteen comparable.

Earth	Dabu Y	Dade	Father	Aya	Aga
Mother	Aini	Mina	Eyes	Yondeh	Ineweh
Woman	Ibi	Bis	Water	Uy	Uyaba

This is the maximum in Africa. But the language of the Papuas of New Guinea in Polynesia has 50 per cent of Anology, or six words out of twelve, which is the maximum with the Asiatic and Polynesic negroes.

Man	Puneh Y / Mehora G	Ameneh P	One	Canameh / Amba G	Amboher
Woman	Ibi	Bienib	Water	Uy	Uar
Mother	Aini	Nana	Evil	Chatandra	Tarada

It may have happened that the Gahunas came from the Papuas, through the Pacific; but the Yaruras from the Ashantis, through the Atlantic: yet have been once two branches of a single black nation.

"In support of the doctrine that the three sons of Noah were red, black and white, we bring the tradition of the *Marabous*, the priests of the most ancient race of Africans, which says, that after the death of Noah, his *three* sons, one of whom was white, the second tawny or red, the third black, agreed to divide his property fairly; which consisted of gold and silver, vestments of silk, linen and wool, horses, cattle, camels, dromedaries, sheep and goats, arms, furniture, corn, and other provisions, besides tobacco and pipes.

"Having spent the greater part of the day in assorting these different things, the three sons were obliged to defer the partition of the goods till the next morning. They therefore smoked a friendly pipe together, and then retired to rest, each in his own tent.

"After some hours sleep, the *white* brother awoke before the other two, being moved by avarice, arose and seized the gold and silver, together with the precious stones, and most beautiful vestments, and having loaded the best camels with them, pursued his way to that country which his white posterity have ever since inhabited.

"The Moor, or tawny brother, awaking soon afterwards, with the same intentions, and being surprised that he had been anticipated by his white brother, secured in great haste the remainder of the horses, oxen and camels, and retired to another part of the world, leaving only some coarse vestments of cotton, pipes and tobacco, millet, rice, and a few other things of but small value.

"The last lot of stuff fell to the share of the black son, the laziest of the three brothers, who took up his pipe with a melancholy air, and while he sat smoking in a pensive mood, swore to be revenged."—(*Anquetil's Universal History*, vol. 6, p. 117, 118.)

We have inserted this tradition, not because we think it circumstantially true, with respect to the goods, &c., but because we find in it this *one* important trait, viz., the origin of human complexions, in the family of Noah: and if the tradition is supposed altogether a fiction, we would ask, how came these Africans the most degraded and ignorant of the human race—by so important a trait of ancient history—as that such a man, with three sons, ever existed, from whom the three races were descended, if it were not so?

Disappearance of many Ancient Lakes of the West, and of the Formation of Seacoal.

This description of American antiquities is more captivating than the accounts already given; because, to know that the millions of mankind, with their multifarious works, covering the vales of all our rivers, many of which were once the bottoms of immense lakes, and where the tops of the tallest forests peer to the skies, or where the towering spires of many a Christian temple makes glad the heart of civilized man, and where the smoking chimnies of his wide spread habitations now are,—*once* sported the lake serpent, and the finny tribes, as birds passing in scaly waves along the horizon.

We look to the soil where graze the peaceful flock; to the fields where wave a thousand harvests; to the air above, where play the wings of innumerable fowls; and to the road where the sound of passing wheels denotes the course of men: and say, can this be so? Was all this space once the home of the waves? Where eels and shell fish once congregated in their houses of mud, is now fixed the foundation of many a stately mansion, the dwelling of man: Such the mutation of matter, and the change of habitation!

We forbear to ramble farther in this field of fancy, which opens before us with such immensity of prospect, to give an account of the disappearance of lakes supposed to have existed in the west. To do this, we shall avail ourselves of the opinions of several distinguished authors, as Volney, in his travels in America; Schoolcraft, in his travels in the central parts of the valley of the Mississippi; and Professor Beck, in his Gazetteer of Illinois and Missouri, &c.

We commence with the gifted and highly classical writer, C. F Volney; who, although we do not subscribe to his notions of theology, yet as a naturalist, we esteem him of the highest class, and his statements, with his deductions, to be worthy of attention.

He commences by saying, that in the structure of the mountains of the United States, exists a fact more strikingly apparent than in any other part of the world, which must singularly have increased the action, and varied the movements of the waters. If we attentively examine the land, or even the maps of this country, we must perceive that the principal chains or ridges of the Alleghanies, Blue-ridge, &c., all run in a transverse or cross direction, to the course of all the great rivers; and that these rivers have been forced to rupture their mounds or barriers, and break through these ridges, in order to make their way to the sea, from the bosoms of the valleys.

This is evident in the Potomac, Susquehannah, Delaware and James rivers, and others, where they issue from the confines of the mountains, to enter the lower country.

But the example which most attracted his attention on the spot, was that of the Potomac, three miles below the mouth of the Shenandoa. He was coming from Fredericktown, about twenty miles distant, and travelling from the southeast towards the northwest, through a woody country, with gentle ascents and descents. After he had crossed one ridge, pretty distinctly marked, though by no means steep, he began to see before him, eleven or twelve miles westward, the chain of the Blue-ridge, resembling a lofty rampart, covered with forests, and having a breach through it from top to bottom.

He again descended into the undulating wood country, which separated him from it; and at length, on approaching it, he found himself at the foot of this great mountainous rampart, which he had to cross, and ascertained to be about 350 yards high, or 120 rods, (nearly half a mile,) deep.

On emerging from the wood, he had a full view of this tremendous breach, which he judged to be about 1200 yards wide, or 225 rods, which is about three-fourths of a mile. Through the bottom of this breach ran the Potomac, leaving on its left a passable bank or slope, and on the right washing the foot of the breach. On both sides of the chasm, from top to bottom, many trees were then growing among the rocks, and in part concealed the place of the rupture: but about two-thirds of the way up, on the right side of the river, a large perpendicular space remains quite bare, and displays plainly the traces and scars of the ancient land, or natural wall, which once dammed up this river, formed of grey quartz, which the victorious river has overthrown, rolling its fragments a considerable distance down its course. Some large blocks that have resisted its force, still remain as testimonials of the convulsion.

The bed of this river, at this place, is rugged, with fixed rocks, which are, however, gradually wearing away. Its rapid waters boil and foam through these obstacles, which, for a distance of two miles form very dangerous falls or rapids. From the height of the mountain, on each side of the river, and from attending circumstances, the rapids below the gap and the narrows, for several miles above the immediate place of rupture, are sufficient evidence that at this place was originally a mountain dam to the river; consequently a lake above must have been the effect, with falls of the most magnificent description, which had thundered in their descent from the time of Noah's flood, till the rupture of the ridge took place.

At the end of three miles, he came to the confluence of the river Shenandoa, which issued out suddenly from the steep mountain of the Blue-ridge. This river is but about one third as wide as the Potomac; having, like that river, also broken through a part of the same ridge.

He says, the more he considered this spot and its circumstances, the more he was confirmed in the belief, that formerly the chain of the Blue-ridge, in its entire state, completely denied the Potomac a passage onward; and that then all the waters of the upper part of the river having no issue, formed several considerable lakes. The numerous transverse chains that succeed each other beyond Fort Cumberland, could not fail to occasion several more west of North mountain.

"On the other hand, all the valley of the Shenandoa and Conigocheague, must have been the basin of a single lake, extending from Staunton to Chambersburgh; and as the level of the hills, even those from which these two rivers derive their source, is much below the chains of the Blue-ridge and North mountain, it is evident that this lake must have been bounded at first only by the general line of the summit of these two great chains; so that in the earliest ages it must have spread, like them, toward the south, as far as the great Alleghanies."

At that period, the two upper branches of James river, equally bounded by the Blue-ridge, would have swelled it with all their waters; while toward the north, the general level of the lake, finding no obstacles, must have spread itself between the Blue-ridge and the chain of Kittatinny, not only to the Susquehannah and Schuylkill, but beyond the Schuylkill, and even the Delaware.

Then all the lower country, lying between the Blue-ridge and the sea, had only smaller streams, furnished by the eastern declivities of that ridge, and the overflowing of the lake, pouring from its summit over the brow of the ridge; in many places forming cascades of beauty, which marked the scenery of primeval landscape, immediately after the deluge.

"In consequence, the river there being less, and the land generally more flat, the ridge of talc granite must have stopped the waters, and formed marshy lakes. The sea must have come up to the vicinity of this ridge, and there occasioned other marshes of the same kind, as the Dismal swamp, near Norfolk;" being partly in the states of Virginia and North Carolina. "And if the reader recollect, the stratum of black mud mingled with osier and trees, which is found every where in boring on the coast, he will see in it a proof of the truth of this hypothesis."

But when the great embankment gave away, by the weight of the waters above, or by attrition, convulsion, or whatever may have been the cause of their rupture, the rush of the waters brought from above, all that stratum of earth now lying on the top of these subterranean trees, osiers and mud above noticed.

"This operation must have been so much the easier, as Blue-ridge in general is not a homogeneous mass crystalized in vast strata, but a heap of detached blocks, of different magnitudes, mixed with vegetable mould, easily diffusable in water; it is in fact a wall, the stones of which are imbedded in clay; and as its declivities are very steep, it frequently happens that thaws and heavy rains, by carrying away the earth, deprive the masses of stones of their support, and then the fall of one or more of these, occasions very considerable stone slips or avalanches, which continue sometimes for several hours.

"From this circumstance, the falls from the lake must have acted with the more effect and rapidity. Their first attempts have left traces in those gaps with which the line of summits is indented from space to space, or from ridge to ridge. It may be clearly perceived on the spot, that these places were the first drains of the surplus waters subsequently abandoned for others, where the work of demolition was more easy.

"It is obvious that the lakes flowing off must have changed the whole face of the lower country. By this were brought down all these earths of a secondary formation, that compose the present plain. The ridge of talcky granite, pressed by more frequent and voluminous inundations, gave way in several points, and its marshes added their mud to the black mud of the shore, which, at present, we find buried under the alluvial earth, afterward brought down by the enlarged rivers."

In the valley between the Blue-ridge and North mountain, the changes that took place were conformable to the mode in which the water flowed off. Several breaches having, at once or in succession, given a passage to the streams of water now called James, Potomac, Susquehannah, Schuylkill and Delaware, their general and common reservoir was divided into as many distinct lakes, separated by the risings of the ground that exceeded this level. Each of these lakes had its particular drain, and this drain being at length worn down to the lowest level, the land was left completely uncovered.

This must have occurred earlier with James, Susquehannah, and Delaware, because their basins are more elevated, and it must have happened more recently with the Potomac, for the opposite reason, its basin being the deepest of all."

How far the Delaware then extended, the reflux of its waters toward the east, he could not ascertain; however, it appears its basin was bounded by the ridge that accompanies its left bank, and which is the apparent continuation of the Blue-ridge, and North mountain. It is probable that its basin has always been separate from that of the Hudson, as it is certain that the Hudson has always had a distinct basin, the limit and mound of which were above West-Point, at the place called the Highlands, commencing immediately below Newburgh.

At this place on the western shore of the Hudson, the ancient bed or course of that river can be traced in a southwestern direction, to where it once united with the waters of the Delaware, and thus they travelled to the sea, in company, whereas the former has, subsequently sought to travel alone disembouging its flood into the sea at an entire and distant point of the compass. The ancient bed, however, is much higher than its present one, as the country over which it travels, plainly shows, favoring greatly the supposition of the lake, which had its foot against this range of mountains.

To every one who views this spot, it seems incontestible, that the transverse chain bearing the name of the Highlands, was formerly a bar to the course of the entire river, and kept its waters at a considerable height; and considering that the tide flows as far as ten miles above Albany, is the proof that the level above the ridge, was a lake which reached as far as to the rapids on Fort Edward.

At that time, therefore, the Cohoes, or falls of the Mohawk, did not appear, and till this lake was drained off through the gap at West-Point, the sound of those falls was not heard.

The existence of this lake explains the cause of the alluvials, petrified shells, and strata of schist and clay, mentioned by Dr. Mitchill, and proves the justice of the opinions of this judicious observer, respecting the stationary presence of waters in ages past, along the valley of many of the American rivers. These ancient lakes, now drained by the rupture of their mounds, explains another appearance which is observed in the valley of such rivers as are supposed to have been once lakes, as the Tennessee, the Kentucky, the Mississippi, the Kanhaway, and the Ohio. This appearance is the several stages or flats observed on the banks of these rivers, and most of the rivers of America, as if the water once was higher than at subsequent periods, and by some means were drained off more; so that the volume of water fell lower when a new mark of embankment would be formed, marking the original heights of the shores of these rivers.

In none is this appearance more perceptible than the Ohio, at the place called Cincinnati, or Fort Washington; here the original or first bank is nearly fifty feet high, and runs along parallel with the river, at the distance of about seventy-five rods. The high floods sometimes even now overflow this first level.

At other places the banks are marked, not with so high an ancient shore, but then the lowness of the country, in such places, admitted the spread of the waters to the foot of the hills of nature. When we examine the arrangement of these flats, which are presented in the form of stages along this river, we remain convinced that even the most elevated part of the plain, or highest level about Cincinnati, has been once the seat of waters, and even the primitive bed of the river, which appears to have had three different periods of decline, till it has sunken to its present bed or place of its current.

The first of the periods was the time when the transverse ridges of the hills, yet entire, barred up the course of the Ohio, and acting as mounds to it, kept the water level with their summits. All the country within this level was then one immense lake, or marsh of stagnant water. In lapse of time, and from the periodical action of the floods, occasioned by the annual melting of the snows, some feeble parts of the mound were worn away by the water.

One of the gaps having at length given away to the current, the whole effort of the waters was collected in that point, which soon hollowed out for itself a greater depth, and thus sunk the lake several yards. The first operation uncovered the upper or first level on which the waters had stood, from the time of the subsiding of the deluge, till the first rupture took place.

From the appearance of the shores of the river, it seems to have maintained its position after the first draining some length of time, so as distinctly to mark the position of the waters when a second draining took place, because the waters had, by their action, removed whatever may have opposed the first attempt to break down their mound or barrier.

The third and last rent of the barrier took place at length, when the fall of the water became more furious, being now more concentrated, scooped out for itself a narrower and deeper channel, which in its present bed, leaving all the immense alluvial regions of the Ohio bare, and exposed to the rays of the sun.

It is probable that the Ohio has been obstructed at more places than one, from Pittsburgh to the rapids of Louisville, as that below Silver creek, about five miles from the rapids of the Ohio, and towards Galliopolis and the Scioto, several transverse chains of mountains exist, very capable of answering this purpose. Volney says it was not till his return from Fort Vincent, on the Wabash, that he was struck with the disposition of a chain of hills below Silver creek.

This ridge crosses the basin of the Ohio from north to south, and has obliged the river to change its direction from the east towards the west, to seek an issue, which in fact it finds at the confluence of Salt river; and it may even be said that it required the copious and rapid waters of this river and its numerous branches, to force the mound that opposed its way at this place.

The steep declivity of these ridges requires about a quarter of an hour to descend it by the way of the road, though it is good and commodious, and by comparison with other hills around, he conceived the perpendicular height to be about 400 feet, or 25 rods. The summit of those hills, when Volney visited them, was too thickly covered with wood for the lateral course of the chain to be seen; but, so far as he could ascertain, perceived that it runs very far north and south, and closes the basin of the Ohio throughout its whole breadth.

This basin, viewed from the summit of this range, exhibits the appearance and form of a lake so strongly, that the idea of the ancient existence of one here is indubitable.

Other circumstances tend to confirm this idea, for he observed from this chain to White river, eight miles from Fort Vincent, that the country is interspersed with a number of ridges, many of them steep, and even lofty. They are particularly so beyond Blue-ridge, and on both banks of White river, and their direction is every where such, that they meet the Ohio transversely.

On the other hand, he found at Louisville that the south or Kentucky bank of the river, corresponding to them, had similar ridges; so that in this part is a succession of ridges, capable of opposing powerful obstacles to the waters. It is not till lower down the river that the country becomes flat, and the ample savannahs of the Wabash and Green rivers commence, which extending to the Mississippi, exclude every idea of any other mound or barrier to the waters on that side of the river.

There is another fact in favor of these western rivers having been, in many places, lakes, found in this country; and is noticed as a great singularity. In Kentucky, all the rivers of that country flow more slowly near their sources than at their mouths; which is directly the reverse of what takes place in most rivers of other parts of the world; whence it is inferred that the upper bed of the rivers of Kentucky is a flat country, and that the lower bed, at the entrances of the vale of the Ohio, is a descending slope.

Now this perfectly accords with the idea of an ancient lake; for at the time when this lake extended to the foot of the Alleghanies, its bottom, particularly towards its mouth, must have been nearly smooth and level, its surface being broken by no action of the waters; but when the mounds or hills, which confined this tranquil body of water were broken down, the soil, laid bare, began to be furrowed and cut into sluices by its drains; and when at length the current became concentrated in the vale of the Ohio, and demolished its dyke more rapidly, the soil of this vale washed away with violence, leaving a vast channel, the slopes of which occasioned the waters of the plain to flow to it more quickly; and hence this current, which, notwithstanding the alterations that have been going on ever since, have continued more rapid to the present day.

Admitting, then, that the Ohio has been barred up, either by the chain of Silver creek, or any other contiguous to it, a lake of great extent must have been the result. From Pittsburgh the ground slopes so gently that the river, when low, does not run two miles an hour; which indicates a fall of four inches to the mile.

The whole distance from Pittsburgh to the rapids of Louisville, following all the windings of the river, does not exceed 600 miles. From these data, we have a difference of level amounting to 200 feet; which does not exceed the elevation of the ranges of hills supposed to have once dammed up the Ohio river at that place. Such a mound could check the waters and turn them back as far as to Pittsburgh.

Such having been the fact, what an immense space of the western country must have lain under water, from the subsiding of the flood till this mound was broken down. This is made apparent by the spring freshets of the Ohio, at the present time, which rising only to the height of fifty feet, keeps back the water of the Great Miami, as far as Grenville, a distance of seventy miles up the country to the north, where it occasions a stagnation of that river, and even an inundation of its shores to a great extent.

In the vernal inundations, the north branch of the Great Miami forms but one with the south branch; the space between becomes one body of water.

"The south branch runs into lake Erie, and is sometimes called St. Mary's river. The carrying place, or portage between the heads of these two rivers is but three miles, and in high water the space can be passed over in a boat, from the one which runs into the Ohio, to the other which runs into lake Erie."

This Mr. Volney states to have been the fact, as witnessed by himself on the spot, in the year 1796; so near are all these waters on a level with each other. He says that, during the year 1792, a mercantile house at Fort Detroit, which is at the head of lake Erie, despatched two canoes, which passed immediately, without carrying, from the river Huron, running into lake Erie, to Grand river, which runs into lake Michigan, by the waters overflowing at the head of each of these rivers. The Muskingum, which runs into the Ohio, also communicates, by means of its sources, and of small lakes, with the waters of the river Cayahoga, which flows into lake Erie.

From all these facts united, it follows that the surface of the level country between lake Erie and the Ohio, cannot exceed the level of the flat next to the waters of the Ohio more than 100 feet, nor that of the second flat or level, which is the general surface of the country, more than seventy feet; consequently a mound or range of mountain, of 200 feet, at Silver creek, 600 miles down the Ohio from Pittsburgh, would have been sufficient to keep back its waters, not only as far as lake Erie, but even to spread them from the last slopes of the Alleghanies, to the north of lake Superior.

But whatever elevation we allow this natural mound, or if we suppose there were several in different places, keeping back the water in succession, the existence of sedentary waters in this western country, and ancient lakes, such as we have pointed out between Blue-ridge and North mountain, is not the less an incontrovertible fact, as must appear to every one who contemplates the country; and this fact explains, in a simple and satisfactory manner, a number of local circumstances, which, on the other hand, serve as proofs of the fact.

For instance, these ancient lakes explain why, in every part of the basin of the Ohio, the land is always levelled in horizontal beds of different heights; why these beds are placed in the order of their specific gravity; and why we find in various places the remains of trees, of osier, and of other plants. They also happily and naturally account for the formation of the immense beds of seacoal found in the western country, in certain situations and particular districts.

In fact, from the researches which the inhabitants have made, it appears that the principal seat of coal is above Pittsburgh, in the space between the Laurel mountain and the rivers Alleghany and Monongahela, where exists, almost throughout, a stratum, at the average depth of twelve and sixteen feet. This stratum is supported by the horizontal bed of calcareous stones, and covered with strata of schists and slate. It rises and falls with these on the hills and valleys, being thicker as it rises with the hills, but thinner in the vales.

On considering its local situation, we see it occupies the lower basin of the two rivers we have mentioned, and of their branches, the Yohogany and Kiskemanitaus, all of which flow through a nearly flat country, into the Ohio below Pittsburgh.

Now, on the hypothesis of the great lake of which we have spoken, this part will be found to have been originally the lower extremity of the lake, and the part where its being kept back would have occasioned still water. It is admitted by naturalists that coal is formed of heaps of trees carried away by rivers and floods, and afterwards covered with earth.

These heaps are not accumulated in the course of the stream, but in parts out of it, where they are left to their own weight; which becomes saturated with water, within a sufficient lapse of time, so as to increase their gravity sufficient to sink to the depths below.

"This process may be observed, even now, in many rivers of America, particularly in the Mississippi, which annually carries along with its current a great number of trees. Some of these trees are deposited in the bays and eddies, and there left in still water to sink; but the greater part reach the borders of the ocean, where the current being balanced by the tide, they are rendered stationary and buried under the mud and sand, by the double action of the stream of the river and the reflux of the sea.

"In the same manner, anciently, the rivers that flow from the Alleghany and Laurel mountains into the basin of the Ohio, finding, towards Pittsburgh, the dead waters and *tail* of the great lake, there deposited the trees and drift wood which they still carry away by thousands, when the frost breaks up, and the snows melt in the spring. These trees were accumulated in strata, level as the fluid that bore them; and the mound of the lakes sinking gradually, as we have before explained, its tail was likewise lowered by degrees, and the place of deposit changed as the lake receded; forming that vast bed which, in the lapse of ages, has been subsequently covered with earth and gravel, and acquired the mineral qualities of coal, the state in which we find it.

"Coal is found in several other parts of the United States, and always in circumstances analogous to those we have just described. In the year 1784, at the mouth of the rivulet Laminskicola, which runs into the Muskingum, the stratum of coal there took fire, and burnt for a whole year. This mine is a part of the mass of which we have been speaking; and almost all the great rivers that run into the Ohio, must have deposits of this kind in their flat and long levels, and in places of their eddies.

"The upper branches of the Potomac, above and to the left of Fort Cumberland, have been celebrated some years for their strata of coal embedded along the shores, so that boats can lie at their banks and load.

"Now this part of the country has every appearance of having been once a lake, produced by one or more of the numerous transverse ridges that bound the Potomac, above and below Fort Cumberland.

"In Virginia, the bed of James river rests on a very considerable bed of coal. At two or three places where shafts have been sunk, on its left bank, after digging a hundred and twenty feet through red clay, a bed of coal, about twenty-four feet thick, has been found, on an inclined stratum of granite. It is evident that at the rapids, lower down, where the course of the river is still checked, it was once completely obstructed: and then there must have been a standing water, and very probably a lake.

"The reader will observe, that wherever there is a rapid, a stagnation takes place in the sheet of water above, just as there is at a mill head; consequently the drifted trees must have accumulated there, and when the outlet of the lake had hollowed out for itself a gap, and sunk its level, the annual floods brought down with them and deposited the red clay now found there; as it is evident that this clay was brought from some other place, for the earth of such a quality belongs to the upper part of the course of the river, particularly to the ridge called Southwest.

"It is possible that veins or mines of coal, not adapted to this theory, may be mentioned or discovered on the coast of the Atlantic. But one or more such instances will not be sufficient to subvert this theory; for the whole of this coast, or all the land between the ocean and the Alleghanies, from the St. Lawrence to the West Indies, has been destroyed by earthquakes; the traces of which are every where to be seen, and these earthquakes have altered the arrangement of strata throughout the whole of this space."

This account, as given by Breckenridge, of the appearance of a portion of the country between two forks of a small branch of the Arkansas river favors this supposition.

"There is a tract of country," he says, "of about seventy-five miles square, in which nature has displayed a great variety of the most strange and whimsical vagaries. It is an assemblage of beautiful meadows, verdant ridges, and misshapen piles of red clay, thrown together in the utmost apparent confusion; yet affording the most pleasing harmonies, and presenting in every direction an endless variety of curious and interesting objects.

"After winding along for a few miles on the high ridges, you suddenly descend an almost perpendicular declivity of rocks and clay, into a series of level, fertile meadows, watered by some beautiful rivulets, and here and there adorned with shrubbery, cotton trees, elms and cedars.

"These natural meadows are divided by chains formed of red clay, and huge masses of gypsum, with here and there a pyramid of gravel. One might imagine himself surrounded by the ruins of some ancient city, and the plains to have been sunk by some convulsions of nature, more than a hundred feet below its former level, for some of the huge columns of red clay rise to the height of two hundred feet perpendicular, capped with rocks of gypsum." This is supposed to have been the work of an earthquake.

Thus far we have given the view of this great naturalist (Volney) respecting the existence of ancient lakes to the west, and of the formation of the strata of seacoal in those regions. If then it be allowed that timber being deposited deep in the earth, becomes the origin of that mineral, we discover at once the chief material which feeds the internal fires of the globe.

The earth, at the era of the great deluge being covered with an immensity of forests, more than it now presents, furnished the material, when sunk and plunged to the unknown depths of the then soft and pulpy globe, for exhaustless strata of seacoal.

This, by some means, having taken fire, continues to burn, and descending deeper and deeper, spreading farther and farther, till the conquerless element has even under sunk the ocean; from whence it frequently bursts forth in the very middle of the sea, accompanied with all the grandeur of display and phenomena of fire and water, mingled in unbounded warfare. This internal operation of fire feeding on the unctious minerals of the globe, among which, as chief, is seacoal, becomes the parent of many a new island, thrown up by the violence of that element.

We cannot but call to recollection in this place, the remarkable allusion of *Isaiah*, chap. xxx., 33, which is so phrased as almost induces a belief that he had reference to this very circumstance, that of the internal fires of the globe being fed by wood carbonated or turned to coal. "For Tophet is ordained of old. * *. He hath made it deep and large; the pile thereof is fire and *much wood;* the breath of the Lord, like a stream of brimstone doth kindle it."

Various accidents are supposeable by which seacoal may have, at first, taken fire, so as to commence the first volcano; and in its operations to have ignited other mineral substances, as sulphur, saltpetre, bitumen, and salts of various kinds. An instance of the ignition of seacoal by accident, is mentioned in Dr. Beck's Gazetteer, to have taken place on a tract of country called the *American Bottom*, situated between the Kaskaskia river and the mouth of the

Missouri. On this great alluvion, which embraces a body of land equal to five hundred square miles, seacoal abounds, and was first discovered in a very singular manner. In clearing the ground of its timber, a tree took fire which was standing and was dry, which communicated to the roots, but continued to burn much longer than was sufficient to exhaust the tree, roots and all.

But upon examination, it was found to have taken hold of a bed of coal, which continued to burn until the fire was smothered by the falling in of a large body of earth, which the fire had undermined by destroying the coal and causing a cavity. This is a volcano in miniature, and how long it might have continued its ravages with increased violence, is unknown, had it not have so opportunely been extinguished.

But this class of strata of that mineral lies, of necessity, much deeper in many places than any other of the kind, deposited since the flood, by the operation of rivers and lakes. If, as we have supposed in this volume, the earth, previous to the flood of Noah, had a greater land surface than at the present time, we find in this supposition a sufficiency of wood, the deposition of which being thrown into immense heaps by the whirls, waves and eddies of the waters, to make whole subterranean ranges of this coal equal in size to the largest and longest mountains of the globe.

These ranges, in many places, rise even above the ordinary surface of the land, having been bared, since the flood, by the violence of convulsions occasioned by both volcanic fires and the irruptions of bodies of water and incessant rains.

If those philosophers who affect to despise the writings of Moses, as found in the book of Genesis, who has given us an account of the deluge, would think of this fact, the origin of seacoal, they could not but subscribe to this *one* account at least, which that book has given of the flood.

The insignificant depositions of timber, occasioned by the drawing off of lakes, or change of water courses, since the flood, cannot be supposed to be in sufficient quantities to furnish the vast magazines of this mineral, compared with that of the universal flood. These strata of coal appearing too in such situations as to preclude all idea of their having been formed by the operation of water since the flood, so that we are driven, by indubitable deduction of fair and logical argument, to resort to *just such an occurrence as the deluge*, the account of which is given by Moses in the Scripture. So that if there were never an universal flood, as stated in the Bible, the ingenuity of sceptical philosophy would be sadly perplexed, as well as all others, to account for the deposition of wood enough to furnish all the mines of this article found over the whole earth, in its several locations, if wood be the origin of coal.

If another flood were to drown the world, its deposits of timber could not equal, by one half, the deposits of the Noachian deluge, on account of the land surface of the earth having, under the influence of that flood, been greatly diminished. If it be truly said in the Bible, that the earth *perished* by water, and also that the fountains of the great deep (subterranean seas,) were broken up, we arrive at the conclusion that there was more wood devoted to the purpose of coal creation, because there was, it is likely, double the quantity of dry land for the forest to grow upon.

Further, in proof that vegetables and wood are the prime origin of pitcoal, we give the remarks of J. Correa de Serra, in a paper read before the American Philosophical Society held at Philadelphia, 1815.

This gentleman, in speaking of his own examination of the remarkable fertility of a certain part of Kentucky, namely that of the Elk-horn tract, and of other parts of the west, says, "These western strata of earth contain imbedded in them an immense quantity of *marine* shells, and other organized bodies, belonging to the animal and vegetable kingdom. The *vegetable* remains in particular are in such astonishing abundance, that they form thick strata of *coals*, extending in some parts to hundreds of miles, keeping always nearly the same level, as it is particularly ascertained of that stratum of excellent coals, which is worked at Coal hill, opposite to Pittsburgh, across the Monongahela."

Again, further on in the same paper, and read at the same time, the writer says to the society, "Let us now remember the *unbounded* deposites of fossil vegetables which are found in this western region, the coal stratum of Pittsburgh for instance, extending for hundreds of miles. Let us also reflect on the *difference* of the alterations which vegetable bodies undergo, when decomposing, if imbedded between stony strata of a ponderous *solid* nature, or only covered by light permeable strata, or under a column of water. How different are these operations from their decomposition in the atmosphere! In the first case, the pressure of a solid stratum, the heat of a fermentation which cannot work but on itself, where *no principle* is lost, but all of them form *new* combinations, reduce the decomposed vegetable to the state of coals."—(*Transactions of the Phil. Society*, chap. xi., p. 174.)

But let it be observed, the author of the above remarks on the formation of coal, does not say that timber of the ancient forests of the earth, is the origin of coal, neither does he deny it; but believes that the marine forests, growing at the bottom of oceans, is the true origin, mingled with other marine substances, of the creation of sea or pitcoal. Accordingly, at all places where this mineral is found, the sea, in some former age of the earth, must have rested. America, therefore, at some unknown distance of ages, must have been, in many parts, beneath the sea. But of such an idea, we believe nothing, except at the time of Noah's flood. Lakes, however, as Volney contends, may have deposited the wood of forests in those parts of the west where coal is found.

Those places, therefore, where it is found too elevated to admit of this idea, we have only to recollect that they were strata of coal so created at the bottom of the lakes or seas, which have now shifted their situations, have been *hove up* by convulsions, occasioned by various agents acting in the bowels of the earth, as fire, air, galvanism and water.

It is said by those who have examined the immense coal bed at Pittsburgh, that the very kind of trees of which the coal was formed can be distinguished, as the beech, the maple, the birch, the ash, &c., lying in all directions through the whole stratum of the coal region.

Further Remarks on the Draining of the Western Country of its Ancient Lakes.

IN corroboration of the theory of Mr. Volney on this subject we give the brief remarks of that accurate and pleasing writer, Mr. Schoolcraft, well known to the reading class of the public. He says, while treating on the subject of the appearance of the two prints of human feet, in the limestone strata along the shore of the Mississippi, at St. Louis: "May we not suppose a barrier to have once existed across the lower part of the Mississippi, converting its immense valley into an interior sea, whose action was adequate to the production and deposition of calcareous strata. We do not consider such a supposition incompatible with the existence of *transition* rocks in this valley; the position of the latter being beneath the secondary. Are not the great northern lakes the remains of such an *ocean?* And did not the sudden demolition of this ancient barrier enable this powerful stream to carry its banks, as it has manifestly done, a hundred miles into the gulf of Mexico.

We think such an hypothesis much more probable, than that the every day deposits of this river should have that effect on the gulf. We have been acquainted with the mouths of the Mississippi for more than a century; and yet its several channels, to all appearance, are essentially the same as when first discovered.

Favoring the same position or theory, we give from Dr. Beck's Gazetteer, a quotation from Silliman's Journal, third volume, quoted by that author from Bringier on the Region of the Mississippi, who says that,

"Between White river and the Missouri, are three parallel porphyry ranges, running circularly from the west to the northeast. These three mountains are twenty-eight miles across, and seem to have been above water, when the whole country around was covered with an ocean."

At the foot of one of these ranges was found the tooth of some tremendous monster, supposed to be the mammoth, twice a large as any found at the Big-bone lick. An account of this creature, so far as we are able to give it, has already been done in this work; yet we feel it incumbent to insert a recent discovery respecting this monster, which we had not seen when those pages went to press. The account is as follows:

There were lately dug up, at Massillon, Starke county, Ohio, two large tusks, measuring each nine feet six inches in length, and eight inches diameter, being two feet in girth at the largest ends. The weight of one is as much as two men could lift. The outside covering is as firm and hard as ivory, but the inner parts were considerably decayed. They were found in a swamp, about two feet below the surface, and were similar to those found some time ago at Bone-lick, in Kentncky, the size of which animal, judging from the bones found, was not less than sixty feet in length, and twenty two in height, and twelve across the hips. Each tooth of the creature's mouth which was found, weighed eleven pounds.—(*Clearfield Banner.* 1832.)

This is, indeed, realizing the entire calculation made by Adam Clarke, the commentator, who tells, as before remarked, that having examined one toe of the creature supposed to be the mammoth, he found it of sufficient size and length to give, according to the rule of animal proportion, an animal at least sixty feet in length, twenty-five feet high.

It would seem that in nature, whether of animate or inanimate things, each has its giant. Of the materials composing the globe, the waters are the giant; among the continents, Asia; among fishes, the whale; among serpents, the great li-boa, of Africa; among quadrupeds, the mammoth; among birds, the condor; among men, the Patagonians; among trees, the banyan of the east; among herbs, the mustard of Palestine.

But among quadrupeds, the giant of that section of nature, it would appear, has become extinct; by what means is unknown—whether a change in the climate, a want of food—whether by disease or the arts of the ancient nations—all is locked in the fathomless depths of oblivion.

The animal, however, must have come down in its species, from the very outset of time, with all other animals. A male and female of this enormous beast must have been saved in the ark; but it is likely the Divine Providence directed a pair that were young, and therefore not as large and ferocious as such as were full grown would be. The finding of this animal in America, is, it would appear, incontrovertible evidence that the continent was, at some period, united with the old world at some place or places, as has been contended in this work; as so large an animal could neither have been brought hither by men, in any sort of craft hitherto known, except the ark; nor could they have swam so far, even if they were addicted to the water.

But to return to the subject of western lakes. How great a lapse of time took place from the subsiding of the flood of Noah, till the bursting away of the several barriers, is unknown. The emptying out of such vast bodies of water, as held an almost boundless region of the west in a state of complete submergency, must of necessity have raised the Atlantic, so as to envelope in its increase many a fair and level country along its coasts, both on this continent and those of Europe and Africa.

In such an emergency, all islands which were low on the surface, and not much elevated above the sea, must have been drowned, or parts of them, so that their hills, if any they had, would only be left, a sad and small memorial of their ancient domains.

It may have been, that the rush of these mighty waters from the west, flowing to the sea at once, down the channels of so many rivers, at first broke up and enveloped the land between the range of the West India islands and the shores of the gulf of Mexico. It is conjectured by naturalists, that the time was when those islands were in reality the Atlantic coast of the continent. *Some* convulsion, therefore, must have transpired to bring about so great a change.

If, as Schoolcraft has suggested, the Mississippi, in bursting down its barriers, drove the earthy matter which accompanied it in that occurrence a hundred miles into the sea, it may well be supposed that if all that space, now the gulf, was then a low tract of country, which is natural to suppose, as its shores are so now, that it was overwhelmed, while the higher parts of the coast, now the West India islands, are all that remains of that drowned country.

The gulf of Mexico is full of low islands, scarcely above the level of the sea, which have been, from the earliest history of that coast, the resort of pirates. Their peculiar situation in this respect, would favor the opinion, that the once low and level shores were, by the rush and overflowing of the waters, buried to a great extent in the country, leaving above water every eminence, which are now the islands of the gulf.

From an examination of the lakes Seneca, Cayuga and Erie, it is evident from their banks, that anciently the water stood in them ten and twelve feet higher than at present; these also, therefore, have been drained a second time, since those of which we have been speaking, of which these were once a part.

It is evident from the remarks of Breckenridge, which are the result of actual observations of that traveller, that there was formerly an outlet from lake Michigan to the Mississppi, by the way of the Illinois river, which heads near the southern end of that lake.

This is supported by the well known facts, that the waters of all the lakes drained by the St. Lawrence, have sunk many feet. The Illinois shows plainly the marks of having once conveyed a much greater body of water between its shores than at the present time.

All the western lakes, Superior, Michigan, Huron, lake of the Wooks, Erie, Seneca, Cayuga, and many lesser ones, are the mere remnants of the great inland fresh water sea which once existed in this region, and the time may come when all the lakes will be again drained off to the north by the way of the St. Lawrence, and to the south by other rivers, to the sea, adding a country of land freed in a measure from these waters, as great in extent as all the lakes put together.

It is believed by the most observing naturalists, that the falls of Niagara were once as low down the river as where Queenstown is situated, which is six or eight miles below the fall. If so, the time may come, and none can tell how soon, when the falls shall have worn through the stone ridge or precipice, over which the Niagara is precipitated, and coming to a softer barrier of mere earth, the power of the water would not be long in rending for itself a more level channel, extending to the foot of lake Erie, on an inclined plane of considerable steepness. One shock of an earthquake, such as happened in Virginia, in the vicinity of the coal mines, 1833, would probably fracture the falls of Niagara, so as to force the waters in its subterranean work, and undermine the falls.

This would affect lake Erie, causing an increased current in its waters, and the lowering of its bed, which would also have the same affect on lakes Michigan, Huron and Superior, with all the rest of a lesser magnitude, changing them from the character they now bear, which is that of lakes, to that of mere rivers, like the Ohio. In the mean time, Ontario would become enlarged, so as to rise, perhaps, to a level with the top of the falls, which is one hundred and fifty feet.

Lake Ontario is but about one hundred and fifty feet below the city of Utica, and Utica is four hundred feet above the valley of the Hudson river; consequently, deducting the hundred and fifty feet, which is the fall of land from the long level, as it is called, on which Utica stands, to the lake, there will be left two hundred and fifty feet elevation of lake Ontario above the vale of the Hudson

That lake, therefore, need to be raised but a little more than one hundred and fifty feet, when it would immediately inundate a greater part of the state of New-York, as well as a part of Upper and all of Lower Canada, till the waters should be carried off by the way of the several rivers now existing, on the easterly and southerly side of the lake, and by new channels; such catastrophe would most certainly cut for itself, in many directions, in its descent to the Atlantic.

But we trust such an occurrence may never take place; yet it is equally possible, as was the draining of the more ancient lakes of the west. And however secure the ancient inhabitants may have felt themselves, who had settled below the barriers, yet that inland sea suddenly took up its line of march, to wage war with, or to become united to, its counterpart, the Atlantic, and in its travel bore away the country, and the nations dwelling thereon.

It is scarcely to be doubted, but the same effects were experienced by the ancient inhabitants settled between the Euxine or Black sea and the Mediterranean, and the whole coast of that inland ocean, where its shores were skirted by low countries.

It is stated by Euclid, in a conversation that philosopher had with Anacharsis, of whom we have before spoken in this work, that the Black sea was once entirely surrounded by natural embankments, but that many rivers runing into it from Europe and Asia, at length overflowed its barriers, cutting for itself a deep channel, tore out the whole distance from its own shore to that of the Archipelago, a branch of the Mediterranean, which is something more than a hundred miles, now called the Bosphorus.

It is not impossible but from the rush of all these waters at once, into the Mediterranean, that at that time the isthmus which united Europe and Africa where now is situated the strait of Gibraltar, was then torn away. It is true that the ancients attributed this separation to the power of Hercules, which circumstance, though we do not believe in the strength of this hero, points out clearly that an isthmus once was there.

By examining the map of the Black sea, we find that beside the outlet of the Bosphorus, there is none other; so that previous to the time of that rupture it had no visible outlet. Some internal convulsions, therefore, must have taken place, so that its subterranean channels became obstructed, and caused it at once to overflow its lowest embankment, which it appears was toward the Archipelago, or the west.

The Caspian sea, in the same country, has no outlet, though many large rivers flow into it. If, therefore, this body of water, which is nearly 700 miles long, and nearly 300 wide, were to be deranged in its subterranean outlets, it would also soon overflow at its lowest points, which is also on its western side, at its southern end, and rushing on between the Georgian or Circassian and Taurus mountains, would plough for itself a channel to the Black sea.

From this view, the rupturing of the ancient embankments of lakes in Europe, Asia and America, it appears that the waters of the Atlantic are now, of necessity, much deeper than anciently; on which account many fair countries, and large islands, once thickly peopled, and covered with cities, towns and cultivated regions, lie now where sea monsters sport above them, while whole tracts of country once merged in other parts of the earth beneath the waters, have lifted hills and dales to the light and influence of the sun, and spread out the lap of happy countries, whereon whole nations of men now live, where once the wind drove onward the terrific billows.

Causes of the Disappearance of the Ancient Nations.

But what has finally become of these nations and where are their descendants, are questions, which, could they be answered, would be highly gratifying.

On opening a mound, below Wheeling on the Ohio, a few years since, a stone was found, having on it a *brand* exactly similar to the one commonly used by the Mxican nations, in marking their cattle and horses.

From this it is evident, that the ancient nations were not savages, or a trait of the *domestication* of animals would not be found in the country, they once inhabited. The head of the *Sustajases*, or Mexican hog, cut off square, was found in a saltpetre cave in Kentucky not long since by Dr. Brown. This circumstance is mentioned by Dr. Drake, in his *Picture of Cincinnati*. The nitre had preserved it. It had been deposited there by the ancient inhabitants where it must have lain for ages.

This animal is not found, it is said, north of the Mexican country, the north line of which, is about on the 40th degree of north latitude, and the presumption is that the inhabitants took these animals along with them in their migrations, until they finally settled in Mexico. Other animals, as the elk, the moose and the buffalo were doubtless domesticated by them, and used for agricultural purposes, as the ox, the horse, and various other animals are now in use among us.

The wild sheep of Oregon, Louisiana, California and the Rocky mountains, the same found in the north of Asia, may be remnants of the flocks of that animal, once domesticated all over these regions by those people, and used for food.

One means of their disappearance may have been the noxious effluvia which would inevitably arise from the bottoms of those vast bodies of water, which must have had a pestilential effect on the people settled around them. This position needs no elucidation, as it is known that the heat of the sun, in its action on swamps and marshy grounds, fills the region round them with a deathly scent, acting directly on the economy and constitution of the human subject, while animals of coarser habits escape.

Who has not experienced this on the sudden draining of stagnant waters, or even those of a mill pond. The reason is the filth settled at the bottoms of such places, becomes exposed by having the cover taken away, which was the waters, and the winds immediately wafting the deleterious vapors; the surrounding atmosphere becomes corrupted; disease follows, with death in its train.

But on the sudden draining of so great a body of water from such immense tracts of land, which had been accumulating filth, formed of decayed vegetation and animals, from the time of the deluge till their passage off at that time, the stench must have been beyond all conception dreadful.

Such was the fact on the subsiding of the waters of the Nile in Egypt, which, after having overflown the whole valley of that river about five hundred miles in length, and from fifteen to twenty-five in width, leaves an insufferable stench, and is the true origin of the plague, which sweeps to eternity annually its thousands in that country.

It is not, therefore, impossible, nor improbable, but by this very means, the ancient nations settled round these waters, may have, indeed, been exterminated; or if they were not exterminated, must have been exceedingly reduced in numbers, so as to induce the residue to flee from so dangerous a country, far to the south, or any where, from the effects of the dreadful effluvia, arising from the newly exposed chasms and gulfs.

Such, also, would be the effect on the present inhabitants, should the fall of Niagara at length undermine and wear down that strata of rock over which it now plunges, and drain the lakes of the west, the remnant of the greater bodies of water which once rested there. In the event of such a catastrophe, it would be natural that the waters should immediately flow into the head water channels of all the rivers northeast and south of lake Ontario, after coming on a level with the heads of the short streams passing into that lake on its easterly side.

The rivers running southeast and north from that part of lake Ontario, as high up as the village of Lyons, are a part of the Chemung, the Chenango, the Unadilla, the Susquehannah, the Delaware, the Mohawk, the Schoharie, the Au Sable, and the St. Lawrence, with all their smaller head water streams.

The vallies of these streams would become the drains of such a discharge of the western lakes, overwhelming and sweeping away all the works of men in those directions, as well as in many other directions, where the lowness of the country should be favorable to a rush of the waters, leaving isolated tracts of highlands, with the mountains as islands, till the work of submersion should be over.

All this, it is likely, will appear extremely visionary, but it should not be forgotten, that we have predicated it on the supposed demolition of Niagara falls, which is as likely to ensue, as that the barriers of the ancient lakes should have given away, where the respective falls of the rivers which issued from them, poured over their precipices.

Whoever will examine all the circumstances, says Volney, will clearly perceive, that at the place where the village of Queenstown now stands, the fall at first commenced, and that the river, by sawing down the bed of the rock, has hollowed out the chasm, and continued carrying back its breach, from age to age, till it has, at length, reached the spot where the cascade now is. There continues its secular labors with slow but incessant activity. The oldest inhabitants of the country remember having seen the cataract several paces beyond its present place. The frosts of winter have the effect continually of cracking the projecting parts of the strata, and the thaws of spring, with the increased powers of the augmented waters, loosen and tumble large blocks of the rock into the chasm below.

Dr. Barton, who examined the thickness of the stratum of stone, and estimates it at sixteen feet, believes it rests on that of blue schist, which he supposes forms the bed of the river, as well as the falls, up to the Erie. Some ages hence, if the river, continuing its untiring operations, may cease to find the calcareous rock that now checks it, and finding a softer strata, the fall will ultimately arrive at lake Erie; and then one of those great desications will take place, of which the valleys of the Potomac, Hudson and Ohio, afford instances in times past.

Lake Ontario formed by a Volcano,

THOUGH the northern parts of America have been known to us but about two centuries, yet this interval, short as it is in the annals of nature, has already, says Volney, been sufficient to convince us, by numerous examples, that earthquakes must have been frequent and violent here, in times past. And that they have been the principal cause of the derangements of which the Atlantic coast presents such general and striking marks.

To go back no farther than the year 1628, the time of the arrival of the first English settlers, and end with 1782, a lapse of 154 years, in which time there occurred no less than forty-five earthquakes. These were always preceded by a noise resembling that of a violent wind, or of a chimney on fire; they often threw down chimnies, sometimes even houses, and burst open doors and windows: suddenly dried up wells, and even several brooks and streams of water; imparting to the waters a turbid color, and the the fœtid smell of liver of sulphur, throwing up out of great chinks sand with a similar smell. The shocks of these earthquakes seemed to proceed from an internal focus, which raised the earth up from below, the principal line of which ran northeast and southwest, following the course of the river Merrimack, extending southward to the Potomac, and northward beyond the St. Lawrence, particularly affecting the direction of lake Ontario.

Respecting these earthquakes, Volney says, he was indebted to a work written by a Mr. Williams, from whose curious researches he had derived the most authentic records. But the language and phrases he employs are remarkable, says Mr. Volney, for the analogy they bear to local facts, noticed by himself, respecting the appearance of schists on the shores of lake Erie; and about the falls of Niagara; and by Dr. Barton, who supposed it to form the bed on which the rock of the falls rests.

He quotes him as follows:—" Did not that smell of liver sulphur, imparted to the water and sand vomited up from the bowels of the earth through great chinks, originate from the stratum of schist, which we found at Niagara, beneath the limestone, and which, when submitted to the action of fire, emits a strong smell of sulphur?"

It is true, says Volney, that this is but one of the elements of the substance mentioned, composing schist, but an accurate analysis might detect the other. This stratum of schist is found under the bed of the Hudson, and appears in many places in the states of New-York and Pennsylvania, among the sandstones and granites; and we have reason to presume that it exists round lake Ontario, and beneath lake Erie, and consequently that it forms one of the floors of the country, in which was the principal focus of the earthquakes mentioned by Mr. Williams.

The line of this focus running northwest and southeast, particularly affected the direction of the Atlantic to lake Ontario. This predilection is remarkable on account of the singular structure of this lake. The rest of the western lakes, notwithstanding their magnitude, have no great depth. Lake Erie no where exceeds a hundred or a hundred and thirty feet, and the bottom of lake Superior is visible in many places.

The Ontario, on the contrary, is in general very deep; that is to say, upwards of forty-five or fifty fathoms, three hundred feet, and so on; and in considerable extent no bottom could be found with a line of a hundred and ten fathoms, which is a fraction less than forty rods in depth.

This is the case in some places near its shores, and these circumstances pretty clearly indicate that the basin of this lake was once the crater of a volcano now extinct. This inference is confirmed by the volcanic productions already found on its borders, and no doubt the experienced eye will discover many more, by examining the form of the great *talus*, or slope, that surrounds this lake almost circularly, and announces in all parts, to the eye as well as to the understanding, that formerly the flat of Niagara extended almost as far as the middle of lake Ontario, where it was sunk and swallowed up by the action of a volcano, then in its vigor.

The existence of this subterranean fire, accords perfectly with the earthquakes mentioned by Williams, as above, and these two agents, which we find here united, while they confirm on the one hand, that of a grand subterranean focus, at an unknown depth, on the other, afford a happy and plausible explanation of the confusion of all the strata of the earth and stones, which occurs throughout the Atlantic coast. It explains, too, why the calcareous, and even granite strata there, are inclined in the horizon in angles of forty-five degrees and upward, even as far as eighty, almost perpendicular, or endwise, their fragments remaining in the vacuities formed by the vast explosions. To this fracture of the stratum of granite, are owing its little cascades; and this fact indicates that formerly the focus extended south beyond the Potomac, as also does this stratum. No doubt it communicated with that of the West India islands.

As favoring this supposition of Monsieur Volney, we recollect the dreadful earthquakes of 1811 and 1812, on the Mississippi, in the very neighborhood of the country supposed to have been the scenes of the effects of those early shocks, of probably the same internal cause, working now beneath the continent, and sooner or later may make again the northern parts of it its place of vengeance, instead of the more southerly, as among the Andes, and the Cordilleras of South America.

The earthquakes of 1811 and 1812 took place at New-Madrid, on the Mississippi, where its effects were dreadful, having thrown up vast heaps of earth, destroying the whole plain upon which that town was laid out. Houses, gardens, and the fields were swallowed up; many of the inhabitants were forced to flee, exposed to the horrors of the scenes passing around, and to the inclemencies of the storms, without shelter or protection. The earth rolled under their feet, like the waves of the sea. The shocks of this subterranean convulsion were felt two hundred miles around.

And, further, in evidence of the action of volcanic fires in the west of this country, we have the following, from Dr. Beck's Gazetteer of Illinois: " I visited Fort Clarke in 1820, and obtained a specimen of native copper in its vicinity. It weighed about two pounds, and is similar to that found on lake Superior, of which the following description was given at the mint of Utrecht, in the Netherlands, at the request of Dr. Eustis. From every appearance, that piece of copper seems to have been taken from a mass that had undergone fusion. The melting was, however, not an operation of art, but a natural effect, caused by a volcanic eruption.

" The stream of lava probably carried in its course the aforesaid body of copper, that formed into one collection as fast as it was heated enough to run from all parts of the mine. The united mass was, probably, borne in this manner to the place where it rested in the soil. Thus we see that even America, in its northern parts, as well as many parts of the old world, as it is called, has felt the shock of that engine, which is, comparatively speaking, boundless in power, capable of new modelling the face of whole tracts of country, in a few days, if not hours."

That many parts of the western country have once been the scene of the devastating power of volcanos, is also maintained by that distinguished philosopher, Rafinesque.—(*See Atlantic Journal*, No. 4, p. 138, 1832.

If by this agent water is thrown out from the bowels of the earth, so as to change the entire surface of large districts in many parts of the old world, why not in America, if the tokens of such operations are found here?

Volney was the first to call lake Ontario a volcano, and to notice our ancient mountain lakes, now dried up by eruptions or convulsions, each having a breach or water gap. I am induced to amplify his views, by deeming nearly all our lakes as so many volcanic outlets, which have not merely thrown water in later periods, but in more ancient periods have formed nearly all our secondary strata, by eruptions of muddy water, mud, clay, liquid coal, basalts, trap. This was when the ocean covered yet the land.

Submarine or oceanic volcanos exist as yet every where in the ocean, and their effects are known. They must of course be hollow outlets under water, that would become lakes if the ocean was dried up. We can form an idea of their large number and extent by the late but natural discovery, that all the Lagoon islands, and circular clusters of islands in the Atlantic, Pacific, and Indian oceans, are volcanic craters. This is now admitted, even in England; and the coral reef often crowning those clusters, are later superincumbent formations by insects. The Bahama islands in the Atlantic, the Maldives, near India, and the coral islands all over the Pacific, are the most striking of these singular volcanic clusters, nearly at a level with the ocean. Some of them are of immense extent, from sixty to one hundred and fifty miles in circuit, or even more.

Some circular bays and gulfs of the sea appear to be similar, differing by having only one breach. The bay of Naples is one also, an ancient crater, with islands in front.

The analogy between lakes and volcanic craters is obvious. Almost all fiery craters become lakes filled with water, when their igneous activity is spent.

All springs are smaller outlets of water, while the fumaroles and holes of igneous volcanos are small outlets of smoke, fire, air, gases, hot mud, &c. I can perceive no essential difference between them or any other eruptive basin, except in degree of caloric or kind of matter which they emit. They may both be quiescent or in activity. Springs vary as much as volcanos. We have few pure springs; they commonly hold mineral substances. They are cold, warm, hot, salt, bitter, saline, bituminous, limpid, colored, muddy; perpetual or periodical, flowing or spouting. Just like volcanic outlets.

Therefore volcanos are properly igneous springs, and springs or lakes are aqueous volcanos!

Under this view, we have no lack of volcanic outlets in North America, since one-half of it, the whole boreal portion, from New England and Labrador in the east, to North Oregon and Alaska in the west, and from lake Erie to the boreal ocean, is filled with them, being eminently a region of lakes and springs; covered with ten thousand lakes at least.

To these, as well as to the dry lakes of our mountains, the lime stone craters and sinks, may be traced as the original outlets of our last formations, in a liquid state, under the ocean, imbedding our fossils. The basaltic, trapic, and carbonic formations, have the same origin, since they are intermingled. But some kinds of sands and clays have been ejected since this continent became dry land. To trace all these formations to their sources, delineate their streams or banks, ascertain their ages and ravage on organized beings, will require time, assiduity, zeal, and accurate observations.

What connection there is between lakes or dry basins of primitive regions and their formations, is not well ascertained. Some are evidently the produce of crystalization; but others forming streams, veins, banks and ridges, may have been ejected in a fluid or soft state, before organic life had begun, and thus spread into their actual shapes. Many streams of primitive limestone, anthracite, wacke, grit, are probably so formed and expanded. Hollows in the primitive ocean must have been the outlets of these substances, now become lakes, after the land became dry.

The power which raises and ejects out of the bowels of the earth, watery, muddy and solid substances, either cold or inflamed, is one of the secrets of nature; but we know that such a power or cause exists, since we see it in operation. Water rises in lakes and springs much above the level of the ocean, while the Caspian sea is under that level. There is then no uniform level for water on the globe, nor uniform aerial pressure over them. Another cause operates within the bowels of the earth, to generate and expel liquid and solid substances—perhaps many causes and powers are combined there. Galvanism is probably one of the main agents. A living power of organic circulation, would explain many earthly phenomena.

Considering, therefore, the omnipotency of the two agents, fire and water, so created by Him who is *more* omnipotent, what changes of surface and of inhabitants may not have taken place in the western regions, as well as in the other parts of America.

We cannot close this subject better than by introducing an Arabian fable, styled the *Revolutions of Time.* The narrator is supposed to have lived three thousand years on the earth, and to have travelled much in the course of his life, and to have noted down the various changes which took place with respect to the surface of the globe in many places, and to have been conversant with the various generations of men that succeded each other.

This fable we consider illustrative of the antiquities of all countries, as well as of the changes which have most certainly taken place in our own, as it relates to surface and inhabitants. The name of the traveller was Khidr, and his story is as follows:

I was passing, say Khidr, a populous city, and I asked one of the inhabitants, "How long has this city been built?" But he said, "This city is an ancient city; we know not at what time it was built; neither we nor our fathers."

Then I passed by after five hundred years, and not a trace of the city was to be seen; but I found a man gathering herbs, and I asked him, "How long has this city been destroyed?" But he said, "The country has always been thus." And I said, "But there was a city here." Then he said, "We have seen no city here, nor have we heard of such from our fathers."

After five hundred years, I again passed that way, and found a lake, and met there a company of fishermen, and asked them, "When did this land become a lake?" And they said, "How can a man like you ask such a question? The place was never other than it is." "But heretofore (said I) it was dry land." And they said, "We never saw it so, nor heard of it from our fathers."

Then after five hundred years I returned, and behold, the lake was dried up; and I met a solitary man, and said to him, "When did this spot become dry land?" And he said "It was always thus." "But formerly, (said I,) it was a lake." And he said, "We never saw it, nor heard of it before."

And five hundred years afterwards I again passed by, and again found a populous and beautiful city, and finer than I had at first seen it; and I asked one of the inhabitants, "When was this city built?" And he said, "Truly it is an ancient place, and we know not the date of its building, neither we nor our fathers."

The human race has every where experienced terrible revolutions. Pestilence, wars and the convulsions of the globe, have annihilated the proudest works, and rendered vain the noblest efforts of man.

"Ask not the sage when and by whom were erected those lingering ruins of the west, the imperishable memorials of ages long since swallowed up in the ocean of time; ask not the wild Arab where may be found the owner of the superb palace, within whose broken walls he casts his tent; ask not the poor fisherman, as he spreads his nets, or the ploughman who whistles over the fields, where is Carthage?—where is Troy? of whose splendor historians and poets have so much boasted. Alas! they have vanished from the things that be, and have left but the melancholy lesson of the instability of the most stupendous labors of our race."

Remarks on Geology.

THE evidence that the globe has undergone many and dreadful convulsions, appears from its confused strata of rock, the undermost or primitive, called granite, appearing frequently above those of a secondary or later formation; yet by no means dare we come to the sacrilegious and all-astounding doctrine, arrived at by modern geologists. Which is, that many ages and revolutions of the globe had transpired before the creation of man: and also that *several* eras of creation had taken place, before *that* event, instead of *one*, as we are instructed in the Scriptures.

To show that such conclusions are arrived at by geologists, we quote the following from the pages of the Penny Magazine, a highly popular periodical, issued from the press in London, under the direction of several of the nobility of that country try of highly scientific character.—(See No. 70, for 1833, p. 178.)

"*Fossils*, by which is understood the petrified remains of animals, as their bones; also plants, shells, tortoises, fishes and vegetable remains, as timber, leaves, branches, ferns, mosses, &c., all of which are found in various parts embedded in rocks, clay, gravel, and other strata of the globe. These, found as they are, reveal to us the important and wonderful *fact*, that the author of nature had created different species of animals and plants at several successive and widely distant periods of time, and that many of those which existed in earlier ages of our globe, had become totally extinct *before* the creation of others of different characters in *later* periods, that prior to man being called into existence, innumerable species of living beings *had* covered the surface of the earth, for a *series* of ages.

"We farther learn, that a very great portion of those creatures of the later periods had become extinct, and had been replaced by others. When that great event, the creation of man, took place, the crust of the earth had already undergone numerous changes that appear to *us* to afford indisputable evidences of design ; to be evidences the *most* clear, of the establishment of an order of things adapted to the *predetermined* nature of that *more* perfect creature about to be sent as an inhabitant of the globe, to whom was to be given " dominion over the fishes of the sea, and over the fowls of the air, and over the cattle, and over *all* the earth."—(*Scripture. See Genesis.*)

"We are also taught by the study of fossils, that prior to the creation of man there had existed a totally different condition of our planet, in so far as regards the distribution of land and water, from that which now exists; that where there are now *continents* there must have been deep seas, and that extensive tracts of land must have occupied those parts of the globe *now* covered by the ocean."

Respecting this their opinion, however, we think that many of those appearances which indicate that once the waters of the ocean covered even the highest ranges of mountains, are to be accounted for from the fact, that the Noachian deluge surmounted fifteen cubits and upwards, the highest parts of the earth, and that *then* those deposits of marine shells, and bones of land and sea animals, took place.

As singular as it may appear, we announced to the reader that the authors of those opinions which go to establish the existence of an animal creation, and of its duration for many ages before the time of Adam, affect also to believe the Scriptures; as above it is seen that they quote from that book the circumstance of man's dominion over all animals, and over all the earth. If, therefore, they believe that book; how is it they go about to contradict the account it gives of the creation of the earth, as to the *time* expended in its creation, and as to the era *when* it was created.

They, that is, the geologists, say, that several ages had passed away *before* man was created, but Moses says that but *five* days had transpired, when on the sixth the man was created; and to fix the meaning of the terms *six days*, as to their *actual* amount of time, we have only to remember, that on that circumstance, "in six days God made the heavens and the earth," was predicated the seven days cycle of time, called a week, which, by Jewish and Christian nations have always been observed. The very *obligation* of working six days and of resting on the seventh, was founded on the fact, that in six days God made the heavens and earth, and rested on the seventh. How then can it be, that immense periods and ages of time had rolled away before the creation of man? If we believe the account as written under the direction of celestial inspiration, by what rule is six times twenty-four hours capable of being attenuated to the length of many ages or periods?

If the six days spoken of in the scripture, as being the foundation of the Sabbath, and of its observance are not *literally* so, then is the Sabbath founded in falsehood, and cannot be *morally* binding on any man since the world began : he, therefore, who can attack the ten commandments and drive one of them out of being, at a blow, cannot be supposed as filial to the scriptures, which give a circumstancial account, of the *time, duration,* and manner of the creation.

This geological, or stone argument, respecting the age of the earth is certainly preposterous, or the account in Genesis, of the creation, is a *fable*. We, therefore, consider their deductions, that is the authors of the remarks as above recited from the Penny Magazine, but a new and elaborate, yet covert mode of overturning the character of the Bible, and should be watched with a jealous eye, by the scientific, among those who do believe the scirptures.

The kinds of animals, according to John Mason Good, whose species seem now to be extinct, and whose remains are found embeded in the rock of the second formation, are not such as had *bones*, but mere worms, insects and shells of the sea, and certain kinds of vegetation, all of the lowest links in the scale of either animal or vegetable organization. This is important, to our views of this subject; because, *if* in this *second* stratum, which lies on the first or lowermost, or *primitive* rock, there are *no* remains of animals which either walked on the earth, or flew in the air, or swam in the sea, it goes far to disprove the theory of geologists respecting the passing away of several ages, before man was made ; as such kinds of fossils, are soon produced, and soon embeded.

But in the third formation of rock, of the kind denominated *flotez* or flat rock, of which there are several kinds, are found the fossil bones of large animals in great abundance, with those of vegetation also. The remains of all animals so discovered, are of the kinds well known, except in a few instances, as belonging to animals *not* extinct. In this very rock of the third and last formation, in its lowest parts, are found the remains of fishes, tortoises, and shells, though much mutilated, which circumstance goes very far in favor of *this* formation of stratum having been produced *since* the flood; its foundation being laid at that time; while the bones of land animals lie embedded above them, and after mingled.

Next above this are the alluvial deposits, containing fossils, which are found all over the globe, at certain places. In this are found the bones of the largest kinds of animals, some of which are unknown, but were *quadrupeds* of the largest magnitudes.

The same kinds, however, are found also imbedded in stone of the *third* class in local situations, and produced by local causes, as the sudden submergency of a certain place, by the disruption of a sea, lake, or rivers, involving the destruction of a great number of animals, both of land and water, which have in certain places been found.

Such are the fossils found in the composite rocks that fill up the great basin around Paris; the celebrated quarries of Alningen, on the Rhine, which, says Good, have been *erroneously* regarded of the same antiquity as Werner's universal formations of the kind found in the third class of rocks, as before specified.

Now as these remains consist in a good degree of animals *known*, it is an evidence that this very stratum has been formed since the flood; because the chief argument which supports the theory of several ages having passed away before the creation of Adam, rests on the strata of those ages containing altogether *unknown* animals, and these, nothing but worms and insects of the waters.

That the bones of large animals should be thus found in solid rocks of the third formation, and to have become such since the flood is not incredible; as nearly four thousand years have passed away since that era. And suppose the animals whose fossils are found in *local* situations, were involved by the disruption of the waters of some lake or inland sea, a thousand years *since* the flood; even then time enough has, long ago transpired, for the formation of *this* stratum.

If so, it is then a clear case, that such animals, both of land and water, as were killed by the flood may have contributed *solely* to the fossil formations, which are considered universal, and distinguished from those which are local and later.

The bones of those immense animals which by geologists are supposed to have inhabited the *earth* before the time of Adam, may be nothing more than sea animals, the species of which may, even now exist; for who will pretend to an acquaintance with all the inhabitants which feed on the pastures covering the bottom of the great deep? The bones of these were doubtless thrown over the earth by the flood, and mingled with those of land animals, and where the kind of earth favored the formation of rock, they are found, while others have crumbled to earth not so deposited.

We see no necessity of this dream about ages antecedent to the time of man's creation. The hypothesis is not called for, as time enough since that time has transpired, to produce all the appearances of the fossil kind belonging to geology.

But in all the excavations which have hitherto been made, and among all the fossil discoveries, the bones of man have not been found imbedded in rock of the third formation. But this is not to say they never will be found, in some future excavations. We should naturally expect to find this kind of fossil, as it is certain the earth was populous with men before the flood. This we learn from a remarkable passage to this effect, found in Genesis, several times repeated, at chap. vi., verses 11, 12 and 13. "The earth also was corrupt before God, and the earth was filled with violence. And God looked upon the earth, and behold it was corrupt. And God said unto Noah, the end of all flesh is come before me; for the earth is *filled* with violence." How, therefore, could this be, unless it was *filled* with inhabitants of our race.

If many parts of the earth which was dry land before the flood, is now ocean, it at once cuts off the opportunity of geological research in a great measure, and lessens the chance of finding fossil bones of the human subject. Again, all such of the race whose bones may have sunk down into the soft and miry earth, while covered by the flood, and did not chance to be covered by those kinds of stratum convertible into stone, would of course return to mould or earth, as it was, and therefore cannot be distinguished.

Now as strata of any kind are extremely rare, which contain the *bones* of animals, it is not very singular that they are not found, and the circumstance can never be used as a proof against the flood of Noah.

It is dangerous to inculcate opinions which go to overthrow the confidence men have in the Scriptures. The moment this is done, the *depraved* mind feels itself lightened of a monstrous burden. It is far better and more becoming us, that " God be true and every man a liar." The dreams of the geologist figures but poorly in competition with heaven about the origin of things, and the manner of creation.

Were the doctrine true, that several ages had transpired before the reputed time of the creation of Adam, in which the globe had been populous with animals, we only should ascertain that all that trouble was, so far as we are able to perceive, for nothing; as there could be no possible use in their existence, except to devour each other, and to return to earth as they were. The works of God are always presented to us, being complete from their foundation to their climax. But *man* being not among the number of his works at first on this hypothesis, shows thereby a lack of perfection, so far as concerns the operations of his hands, in the early and supposed ages of the planet.

The existence of the globe *even now*, with all its animals of land and sea, with all its phenomena of arrangement, could bring *no* praise, *no* glory to the Creator without a *man*, or some order of intelectual beings, who should be able to admire, and *to adore through* his works the author. Through *man* all animals praise God; but without *him* they are as though they had not been. To this view, even the Scriptures would seem to agree, and to speak of it much in the same way. (See Rev. v. 13.) " And every creature which is in heaven and *on* the earth, and under the earth, and such as are *in* the sea, and all that are in them, heard I saying, Blessing, honor glory and power be unto him that sitteth upon the throne and unto the Lamb for ever and ever." But without man, this voice, so far as creation is concerned, besides the man, could never have ascended, as there could have been no medium through which God could have received praise; no possible way, that his multifarious operations should in the least be appreciated, without such a being as man is, having a reasonable soul, and powers of perception suited to his station.

But if we believe the account as related by Moses, we perceive that *man* and animals were made at the same time, with the exception of but a few hours, so that this head of creation was not wanting in the very outset of time. But, on the contrary, if we suppose, with those of the geological school, that *more* time, immensely more, than has elapsed since the days of Adam, had passed away before; then are we met, at every turn, with this insuperable incongruity, of a creation *without* a head.

Resemblance of the Western Indians to the Ancient Greeks.

The reader will recollect we have shown on page 44, that the Greek fleet once moored on the coast of Brazil, in South America, said to be the fleet of Alexander the Great, and also the supposed Greek carving, or sculpture, in the cave on the Ohio river.—(See p. 140.)

In addition, we give from Mr. Volney's *View of America*, his comparison of the ancient Greek tribes with the tribes of the western Indians. He says, the limits of his work would not allow him to enter into all the minutiæ of this interesting subject; and therefore should content himself with saying, that the more deeply we examine the history and way of savage life, the more ideas we acquire that illustrate the nature of man in general, the gradual formation of societies, and the character and manners of the nations of antiquity.

While this author was among the Indians of the west, he was particularly struck with the analogy between the savages of North America and the so much vaunted *ancient* nations of Greece and Italy. In the Greeks of Homer, particularly in those of his Iliad, he found the customs and manners of the Iroquoiss, Delaware, and Miamis, strikingly exemplified. The tragedies of Sophocles and Euripides, paint almost literally the sentiments of the red men respecting necessity, fatality, the miseries of human life, and the rigor of blind destiny. But the piece most remarkable for variety, combination of features and resemblance, is the beginning of the history of Thucydides, in which he briefly traces the habits and way of life of the Greeks, before and after the Trojan war, up to the age in which he wrote. This fragment of their history appears so well adapted, that we are persuaded the reader will be pleased at having it laid before him, so that he can make the comparison for himself.

"It is certain that the region now known by the name of Greece was not formerly possessed by any fixed inhabitants, but was subject to frequent migrations, as constantly every distinct people or tribe yielded up their seats to the violence of a larger supervening number. For, as to commerce, there was none, and mutual fear prevented intercourse, both by land and sea; as then the only view of culture was barely to procure a penurious subsistence, as superfluous wealth was a thing unknown."

"Planting was not their employment, it being uncertain how soon an invader might come and dislodge them from their unfortified habitations; and as they thought they might every where find their daily support, they hesitated but little about shifting their habitations.. And for this reason they never flourished in the greatness of their cities, or any other circumstance of power. But the richest tracts of country were ever more particularly liable to this frequent change of inhabitants, such as that now called Thessaly and Bœotia, and Peloponesus chiefly, except Arcadia, and in general the most fertile parts of Greece. For the natural wealth of their soil, in particular districts, increased the power of some amongst them; that power raised civil dessension, which ended in their ruin, and at the same time exposed them the more to foreign attacks."

It was only the barrenness of the soil that preserved Attica through the longest space of time, quiet and undisturbed, in one uninterrupted series of possessors. One, and not the least convincing proof of this is, that other parts of Greece, because of the fluctuating condition of the inhabitants, could by no means, in their growth keep pace with Attica. The most powerful of those who were driven from the other parts of Greece, by war or sedition, betook themselves to the Athenians for secure refuge, and as they obtained the privilege of citizens, have constantly, from remote time, continued to enlarge that city with fresh accessions of inhabitants; insomuch, that, at last, Attica, being insufficient to support its numbers, they sent over colonies to Ionia.

The custom of wearing weapons, once prevailed all over Greece, as their houses had no manner of defence, as travelling was full of hazard, and their whole lives were passed in armour, like barbarians. A proof of this, is the continuance still, in some parts of Greece, of those manners which were once, with uniformity, common to all. The Athenians were the first who discontinued the custom of wearing their swords, and who passed from the savage life into more polite and elegant manners. Sparta is not closely built; the temples and public edifices by no means sumptuous, and the houses detached from each other, after the old mode of Greece.

In their war manners they resembled the Indians of America, for after a certain engagement they had with an enemy, and being victorious, they erected a trophy upon Leucinna, a promontory of Corcyra, and put to death all the prisoners they had taken, except one, who was a Corinthian.

The pretended golden age of those nations was nothing better than to wander naked in the forests of Hellas and Thessaly, living on herbs and acorns; by which we perceive that the ancient Greeks were truly savages of the same kind as those in America, and placed in nearly similar circumstances of climate, since Greece covered with forests, was then much colder than at present. Hence we infer, that the name of Pelasgian, believed to belong to one and the same people, wandering and dispersed about from the Crimea to the Alps, was only the generic appellation of the savage hordes of the first inhabitants, roaming in the same manner as the Hurons and Algonquins, or as the old Germans and Celts.

And we should presume, with reason, that colonies of foreigners, farther advanced in civilization, coming from the coasts of Asia, Phœnicia, and even Egypt, and settling on those of Greece and Latium, had nearly the same kind of intercourse with these aborigines; sometimes friendly, sometimes hostile; as the first English settlers in Virginia and New-England had with the American savages.

By these comparisons we should explain both the intermixture and disappearance of some of those nations, the manners and customs of those inhospitable times, when every stranger was an enemy, and every robber a hero; when there was no law but force, no virtue but bravery in war; when every tribe was a nation, and every assemblage of huts a metropolis.

In this period of anarchy and disorder, of savage life, we should see the origin of that character of pride and boasting, perfidiousness and cruelty, dissimulation and injustice, sedition and tyranny, that the Greeks display throughout the whole course of their history; we should perceive the source of those false ideas of virtue and glory, sanctioned by the poets and orators of those ferocious days; who have made war and its melancholy trophies, the loftiest aim of man's ambition, the most shining road to renown, and the most dazzling object of ambition to the ignorant and cheated multitude. And since the polished and civilized people of Christendom have made a point of imitating these nations, and consider their politics and morals, like their poetry and arts, the types of all perfection; it follows that our homage, our patronage, and veneration, are addressed to the manners and spirit of barbarous and savage times.

The grounds of comparison are so true, that the analogy reaches even to their philosophical and religious opinions; for all the principles of the stoic school of the Greeks are found in the practice of the American savages; and if any should lay hold of this circumstance to impute to the savages the merit of being philosophers, we retort the supposition, and say, we ought, on the contrary, to conclude, that a state of society, in which precepts so repugnant to human nature were invented for the purpose of rendering life supportable, must have been an order of things, and of government, not less miserable than the savage state. This opinion is supported by the whole history of these Grecian times, even in their most brilliant periods, and by the uninterrupted series of their own wars, seditions, massacres, and tyrannical proscriptions, down to the time of their subjugation by those other savages of Italy, called the *Romans;* who, in their character, politics, and aggrandizement, have a striking resemblance to the Six Nations.

With regard to religious notions, these do not form a regular system among the savages, because every individual in his independent state, makes himself a creed after his own fancy. If we may judge from the accounts of the historians of the first settlers, and those of late travellers in the northwest, it appears that the Indians compose their mythology in the following manner:

First: a Great Manitau, or superior being; who governs the earth and the æreal meteors, the visible whole of which constitutes the universe of a savage. This Great Manitau residing on high, without his having any clear idea where, rules the world, without giving himself much trouble; sends rain, wind, or fair weather, according to his fancy; sometimes makes a noise, which is the thunder, to amuse himself; concerns himself as little about the affairs of men as about those of other living beings that people the earth; does good, without taking any thought about it; suffers ill to be prepetrated without its disturbing his repose, and in the mean time, leaves the world to a destiny, or fatality, the laws of which are anterior, and paramount, to all things.

Under his command are subordinate Manitaus, or genii, innumerable, who people earth and air, preside over every thing that happens, and have each a separate employment. Of these genii, some are good; and these do all the good that takes place in nature; others are bad, and these occasion all the evil that happens to living beings.

It is to the latter chiefly, and almost exclusively, that the savages address their prayers, their propitiatory offerings, and what religious worship they have; the object of which is, to appease the malice of these Manitaus, as men appease the ill humor of morose, bad men. This fear of genii is one of their most habitual thought, and that by which they are most tormented. Their most intrepid warriors are, in this respect, no better than their women; a dream, a phantom seen at night in the woods, or a sinister cry, equally alarms their credulous, superstitious minds.

Their magicians, or, as we more properly call them, jugglers, pretend to very familiar intercourse with these genii; they are, however, greatly puzzled to explain their nature, form, and aspect. Not having our ideas of *pure spirit*, they suppose them to be composed of substances, yet light, volatile, and invisible, true shadows and manes, after the manner of the ancients. Sometimes they select some one of these genii, whom they suppose to reside in a tree, a serpent, a rock, a cataract, and this they make their fetih, or god, to which they resort, like the African. The notion of another life is a pretty general belief among the savages. They imagine that after death they shall go into another climate and country, where game and fish abound, where they can hunt without being fatigued, walk about without fear of an enemy, eat very fat meat, and live without care or trouble. The Indians of the north, place this climate toward the southwest, because the summer winds, and the most pleasing and genial temperature, come from that quarter.

This sketch of Indian manners, is supposed sufficient by Mr.

Volney, to prove that there is a real analogy between the mythological ideas of the Indians of North America and those of the Asiatic Tartars, as they have been described to us by the learned Russians, who have visited them not many years since.

The analogy between them and the nations of the Greeks, is equally evident. We discern the Great Manitau of the savages, in the Jupiter of the heroic ages, or their savage times; with this difference only, that the Manitau of the Americans, leads a melancholy, poor, and wearisome life, like themselves; while the Jupiter of Homer, and of Hesiod, displays all the magnificence of the court of Hecatompylean Thebes, the wonderful secrets of which have been disclosed to us in the present age. See the elegant work of Mr. Denon, on the high degree of taste, learning, and perfection, at which the arts had arrived in that Thebes, which was buried in the night of history, before Greece or Italy were known.

In the lesser Manitaus of the Indians, are equally evident the subordinate deities of Greece; the genii of the woods and fountains, and the demons honored with a similar superstitious worship.

The conclusion Volney draws from all this is, not that the Indians have derived their notions from Greece, but rather are derivable from Shamanism, or the Lamic system of Budda, which spread itself from Hindostan among all the savages of the old world, where it is found even to the extremities of Spain, Scotland, and Cimbrica.

Yet as traits of the Grecian nations are found, especially in South America, as in the discovery of the subterranean cavity of mason work, noticed on page 44, and in the cave on the Ohio, as noticed on page 143, it is not impossible, but that from the Greeks, sometime in this country before the Indians found their way here, they may have communicated their mythological notions to the more ancient inhabitants, from whom the Tartars, or our Indians, when they conquered or drove away that people, imbibed their opinions; as it is not without precedent, that the conquered have given to the conqueror their religion as well as their country.

Traits of Ancient Romans in America.

On pages 40 and 59 inclusive, of this work, we have ventured the conjecture, that the Romans colonized various parts of America. We still imagine such a conjecture by no means impossible, as tokens of their presence are evidently yet extant in the vale of Mexico. See page 269, where is an account of a temple, which was built and dedicated as sacred to the worship of the sun and moon.

The religions of nations furnish, it is presumed, the strongest possible evidence of origin. On this account, the temples of the sun and moon in Mexico, exactly answer to the same objects of devotion, worshipped by the ancient Romans.

That they are similar in both countries, we prove from Gibbon's Roman empire, page 233, vol. 1st, as follows:—The sun was worshipped at Emesa, by the Romans, under the name of *Elagabalus* or God, under the form of a black conical stone, which, it was universally believed, had fallen from heaven, on that sacred place.

This stone, we observe, was undoubtedly what is termed an ærolithis, a copious account of which is given by Dr. Adam Clarke, as being thrown out of the moon by the force of volcanic eruptions in that planet, which, as soon as they had passed out of the moon's attraction, fell immediately to the earth, being drawn hither by the stronger force of the centripetal power. A stone falling to the earth under such circumstances, was quite sufficient to challenge the adoration of the pagan nations as coming down from the gods, or from the sun, as a representative of that luminary.

Accordingly, this stone became deified, and was set up to be worshipped, as the sun's vicegerent among men. Gibbon says that to this protecting deity, the stone, Antonius, not without some reason, ascribed his elevation to the throne of the Roman empire. The triumph of this stone god over all the religions of the earth, was the great object of this emperor's zeal and vanity: and the appellation of *Elagabalus*, which he had bestowed on the ærolithis, was dearer to that emperor than all the titles of imperial greatness.

In a solemn procession through the streets of Rome, the way was strewed with gold dust; the black stone set in precious gems, was placed on a chariot drawn by six milk white horses, richly caparisoned. The pious emperor held the reins, and supported by his ministers, moved slowly, with his face toward the image, that he might perpetually enjoy the felicity of the divine presence.

In a magnificent temple, raised on the Palatine Mount, the sacrifices of the god Elagabalus were celebrated with every circumstance of cost and solemnity. The riches twines, the most extraordinary victims, and the rarest aromatics, were profusely consumed on his altar. Around him a chorus of Syrian damsels performed their lascivious dances to the sound of barbarian music, whilst the gravest personages of the state and army, clothed in long Phœnician tunics, officiated in the meanest functions, with affected zeal, and secret indignation.

To this temple, as to a common centre of religious worship, the imperial fanatic attempted to remove the Ancilia, the Palladium, and all the sacred pledges of the faith of Numa. A crowd of inferior deities attended in various stations, the majesty of the god of Emesa, Elagabalus.

But the court of this god was still imperfect, till a female of distinguished rank was admitted to his bed. Pallas had been first chosen for his consort; but as it was dreaded lest her warlike terrors might affright the soft delicacy of a Syrian deity, the *moon* adored by the Africans, under the name of Astarte, was deemed a more suitable companion for the sun. Her image, with the rich offerings of her temple as a marriage portion, was transported, with solemn pomp, from Carthage to Rome; and the day of these mystic nuptials was a general festival in the capital, and throughout the empire.

Here then, at Emesa, in Italy, the Romans worshipped the sun and moon; so did the Mexicans, with equal pomp and costliness, in the vale of Mexico. If, therefore, in the two countries, the same identical religion, having the same identical objects of worship, existed, it would seem, no great stretch of credulity, or exertion of fancy, to suppose them practised by the same people in either country.

The ancient Romans, or rather, the Romans after they had risen to great consequence, and had founded and built many cities, were remarkable in one particular, over and above all other particulars, and this was in the construction of a grand national road,

English miles in length. This national road issued from the Forum of Rome, traversed Italy, pervaded the provinces and terminated only by the frontiers of the empire, and was divided off into distinct miles, by a stone being set up at the termination of each, as in the present times.

The same was the case with the ancient people of South America, in the time of the Incas; who, as Humboldt informs us, had one grand road, which is even traceable at the present time, of a thousand leagues in length, running along on the high ground of the Cordilleras, and was paved with large flat stones the whole length.

In this very respect, that is, of paving their roads with large stones, the Romans and the South Americans were alike. For Gibbon says, that in the construction of the Roman national highway, they not only perforated mountains, raised bold arches over the broadest and most rapid streams, but paved it with large stones, and in some places even with granite.

In another respect they are alike; the Romans raised this road so as to be able to overlook the country as it was travelled; so also did the Americans, in choosing the high grounds of the Cordilleras to build it upon.

It would seem also, that in the very construction of their cities, towns, and palaces, as found scattered over many parts of South America, even along on the coast of the Pacific, according to Humboldt and more recent researches, they modelled them, in some sense, after the manner of the Romans; especially in the vastness of their capacity, or area which they occupied.

However, it is clear, that as the American architecture did not partake of the refinement of taste in the finish of their buildings, which characterise those of the Romans, that they, the former, are the elder of the two; and that the American nations in the persons of their ancestors, came from Africa, and about the country of the Mediterranean, in the very first age of their improvement, or departure from barbarism. From all this it cannot but be inferred, that the continent is indebted to that part of the old world for that class of inhabitants, who introduced among the first nations of the continent, the arts as found in practice by Columbus, when he landed on its shores.

With this view, we think there is light thrown on the curious subject of the Mexican tradition, with respect to the white and bearded men before spoken of in this volume; who, as they say, came among them from the rising sun, and became their legislators. And as the Romans were a maritime people, and had become refined long before the savages of the north of Europe, and made, according to Gibbon, prodigious voyages, they may have been the very people who colonized the island of Jesso and Japan, who were a white and bearded race, from whom, in another part of this work, we have supposed these Mexican legislators may have been derived. In either case there is no difficulty; the origin is the same.

We are firm in the belief that the Carthaginians, Phœnicians, Persians, Hindoos, Chinese, Japanese, Roman and Greek nations of antiquity, and others, have had more to do in the peopling of the wilds of America, as well also as the Europeans, after their civilization, than is generally supposed.

There was found among the nations of Mexico, another trait of character strongly resembling a Roman practice; and this was, that of single combat with deadly instruments, called the fight of the gladiators. This among the Romans was carried to so shameful and murderous a degree, that Commodus, one of their emperors, killed with his own hands, as a gladiator, seven hundred and thirty-five persons.

Of this emperor Gibbon says, that being elated with the praises of the multitude, which gradually extinguished the innate sense of shame, Commodus resolved to exhibit before the eyes of the Roman people, those exercises which till then he had decently confined within the walls of his palace, and to the presence of his favorites.

On the appointed day the various motives of flattery, fear, and curiosity, attracted to the amphitheatre an innumerable multitude of spectators; and some degree of applause was deservedly bestowed on the uncommon skill of the imperial performer. Whether he aimed at the head or heart of the animal, the wound was alike certain and mortal. With arrows whose points were shaped in the form of a crescent, Commodus often intercepted the rapid career, and cut asunder the long and bony neck of the ostrich. A panther was let loose, and the archer waited till he had leaped upon a trembling malefactor. In the same instant the shaft flew, the beast dropped dead, and the man remained unhurt. The dens of the amphitheatre disgorged at once a hundred lions; a hundred darts in succession, from the unerring hand of Commodus laid them dead as they ran raging around the arena.

Such, it appears, were the prowess and the sports of the ancient Romans, whose counterpart, as it respects this peculiar trait, the fight of the gladiator, was found among the Mexican usages of North America.

Again, when the Romans first got footing in the island of Britain they erected or laid the foundation of a town, which they named *Verulam*, which soon took the title and rank of a city. This town, according to their peculiar manner, was at first circumscribed by a wall, including about one hundred acres, the traits of which still appear.

These square inclosures are found in America, as treated upon in our account of the Roman squares, at or near Marietta; strengthening the belief that Roman colonies have, in former ages, settled in America.

Traits of White Nations in Georgia and Kentucky before Columbus's Time, and the Traditions of the Indians respecting them.

From the *American Journal of Sciences and the Arts*, we have a highly interesting description of the gold districts in Georgia and North Carolina, extending west even unto the state of Tennessee. In this Journal, gold is treated on as being extremely abundant, and from the situation of the veins, is far more eligible to the operations of the miner, than the gold mines of South America; these having, as is supposed, been greatly deranged in places, and buried deep by the operations of volcanos, while those in the states are still in their primitive state of formation.

Gold is found connected with various formations of slate, with red clay, and in the bottoms of streams, mingled with the sand and gravel. It is found with the heavy gravelly earth of the mountains, but most of all in the kind of rock called quartz, which is also mingled with slate. In North Carolina, on Valley river, gold is found in abundance, connected with the quartz rock, which also abounds with crystal, running in veins in every direction, in tissues from the size of a straw to that of a man's arm. The quartz is in great masses, very compact, and of a yellow golden hue, from the abundant presence of the metal. In the bottom of this river much deposited gold is found in strata.

It would appear, from the evidences yet remaining, that the ancient inhabitants were not insensible to the existence of the golden mines here, nor, of course, of its value; for, "in the vicinity were found the remains of ancient works; many shafts have been sunk by them in pursuit of the ore, and judging from the masses thrown up, one of them penetrated a quartz rock to a great depth, as about thirty feet still lies open to view.

There is also a deep and difficult cut across a very bold vein of this rock, in pursuit of metal, but it is now much filled up, having been used subsequently for an Indian burying ground. At this place, says the Journal, nothing short of the steel pickaxe, could have left the traces on the stone which are found here.

Not far from this place, have been found the remains of a small furnace, the walls of which had been formed of soap stone, so as to endure the heat without being fractured. In the county of Habersham, in Georgia, was lately dug out of the earth, at a place where the gold ore is found, a small vessel in the form of a skillet. It was fifteen feet under ground, made of a compound of *tin* and *copper*, with a trace of *iron*. The copper and tin in its composition, are undoubtedly the evidence of its antiquity. See the plate at letter G, where an exact fac simile of this vessel is engraved taken from the Journal of Science and Arts, conducted by professor Silliman.

Crucibles of earthen ware, and far better than those now in use, are frequently found by the miners. By actual experiment they are found to endure the heat three times as long as the Hessian crucibles, which are the best now in use. Bits of machinery, such as is necessary in elevating the ore from the depths, as used by the ancient nations, are also frequently found in the earth where those mines exist, which clearly shows those ancients acquainted with the minerals.

On the top of Yeona mountain, in the same region, still exist the remains of a stone wall, which exhibit the angles of a fortification, and guard the only accessible points of ascent to its summit. Timber in the Cherokee country, bearing marks of the axe, (not of stone,) have been taken up at the depth of ten feet below the surface. Indian tradition, says Mr. Silliman, gives no account of these remains. This article, which was found in the gold mine in Habersham county, formed of copper and tin, is in this respect, like the mining chisel described by Humboldt, on page 185 of this work. The timber found ten feet beneath the surface, in Georgia and North Carolina, bearing the marks of having been cut down and cut in two with axes of metal, are to be referred to the operations of the Europeans—the Danes, Welch, &c., of whom we have already spoken in several parts of this volume. We consider them the same with the authors of the stone walls which we have mentioned that were found in North Carolina, and also with the authors of the iron axes, found in a saltpetre cave, on the river Gasconade, far to the west, as mentioned in Beck's Gazetteer; and also the same with the authors of the stone buildings, a foundation of one of which is represented on the plate.—*(See Frontispiece.)*

It would appear from all this, that these Europeans had made extensive settlements in various places, extending over an immense range of this country, before they were cut off by the Indians; as we cannot suppose any other enemy capable of so dreadful and general a slaughter.

On the farm of a Mr. Richason, a highly respectable gentleman in Georgia, Habersham county, was opened one of the *first* gold mines discovered in the southern states. At this place a most singular discovery was also made, which was as follows:

This gentleman being desirous of examining the stone stratum, which formed the bed of a small river, had recourse to a dam, which he carried across the stream, and turned the whole of its water into a canal he had excavated in a direction favoring the descent of the stream; so that the bed where it had flowed was left dry. Now while digging and blasting the rocky bottom of this stream, he found, at a certain place, *three feet* below the surface, imbedded in the solid, compact rock, nearly a peck, or eight quarts of *flints*, which were elegantly wrought, for their adaptation to the *gun-lock*. Their form, however, in one respect, differs from the form of the flint suited to fire-arms *now* in use; and this difference consists in there being a groove across the head or thick end of the flint, showing that the chuck or jaws of the cock of the gun in which they were used, had a corresponding protuberance, so that the flint was held by what is called by joiners, a *dove-tail*, instead of a screw, as the gunlock is now manufactured.

The whole of these curious wrought flints were purchased by a gentleman, and carried to Milledgeville, Georgia, where he sold them as curiosities at a quarter of a dollar each.

In Europe, the invention of gunpowder, with the flint, took place in 1340, one hundred and fifty-two years before the discovery of America by Columbus, which was in 1492. It has been conjectured by some that these flints were lost by the *ancient Spaniards*, who were searching for the ancient city in America, called *El Dorado*, or the city of gold.

But this will not do, as it would show that gunpowder had been discovered by the Spaniards in Europe, which, if true, would have been known and ascribed to them instead of to Swartz the monk; unless we suppose that America had been found by the ancient Spaniards, long enough ago to have produced the formation of the rock three feet thick over the spot where they had been placed, or lost, by their last owner, which would throw the time of their being left there very far back.

We should, if we can give any plausible opinion at all on this subject, incline to ascribe their invention and use to Europeans of the Danish and Welsh description, who, we have shown, found this country, and settled in it as early as between the 9th and 10th centuries, which would give the stream nearly a thousand years to increase its stony deposits to the thickness of three feet, so that if by the upsetting of a boat as they were going up, down or across this stream, the flints were lost at the bottom of the water, and being encased in a bag, or basket, or any suitable vessel to hold them, is the reason why they were found in such compact order.

But if this supposition is at all plausible, it follows that the invention was *originated* in America; as it would have been known in Europe, if it had been found out there before those Europeans came to America. The *form* of the flint, as it respects the manner in which it was held by the chuck or lips of the lock, shows that the invention was but a new one. Whether the lock was an iron, copper, brass or wooden one, is unknown, or whether they had yet found out the adaptation of a gun barrel, is also unknown; but *some* mode of explosion, by the means of some sort of combustible matter, had doubtless been discovered, or the flint could have had no use.

That a perfect knowledge of this art was in their possession, we do not believe; as those *white* people, with the complete use and knowledge of guns, could never have been exterminated by the Indians or *natives* of the country. And that they were exterminated by the Indians, we prove from their tradition, which relates, that in the southern states, but particularly that of Kentucky, had been once settled by white people, and that they had been exterminated by war.

In 1800, some Indians of the Sacs tribe were at St. Louis, who on hearing it said that Kentucky was inhabited by white people, expressed much astonishment that any person should live in Kentucky, as it had been a place where much blood was shed, and that it was filled with the *manes* or souls of the butchered white inhabitants, a people who had arts among them unknown to the Indians. Even the *word* Kentucky, the name of the chief river of the state, signifies *river* of blood.—(J. H. McCulloch's *Researches in America,* p. 210 to 213.)

To these people we should think the flints discovered as above belonged, and that the use of powder, or of some explosive material or other, by which, either through a tube of iron, copper, or wood, a bullet or arrows were discharged, with deadly effect, as we can see no other use to which the flints could have been appropriated.

It is said that the ancient Phœnicians first discovered the art of manufacturing tools from the union of copper and tin, the same of which this skillet is found to be formed; and that of the Phœnicians, the Greeks and Romans, learned the art, who it is likely communicated the same to the ancient Britons; and from these, in process of time, the Danes, the Welch, the Scotch, and the Norwegians, and brought it with them to the wilds of America. Or if we reject this, we may refer the working of those mines of gold, not to the Malays, Polynesian, and Australasian tribes; but rather to the more enlightened nations of Egypt, Phœnicia, Greece, Rome, Media, Persia, Germany, all of whom, as we believe, have from time to time—from era to era—furnished emigrants to this country.

In evidence, in part, of this belief, we refer the reader to such parts of this volume as attempt to make this appear, and especially to page 116; where an account of the Phœnician characters, as having been discovered in America, is mentioned. But how the article of copper, the skillet of which we have spoken, and is engraved on the plate, and how the timber, which bears the mark of the axe, found buried in various places in North Carolina, came to be buried so deep, is a question of no small moment.

Surely the natural increase of earth, by the decay of vegetables, and forests, could never have buried them thus deep; their position would rather argue that they have been submerged by the sudden rush of waters. As favoring this opinion, we notice, that the mountain ranges here are such as cross the rivers flowing from the west, which pass off to the sea, through North Carolina, South Carolina, and Georgia. See the map of those states, when at once this appears to be the real formation and course of the mountains.

One of these ranges is denominated the Yeona range; which gives off three separate sections; one in Tennessee, one in western North Carolina, and one in Georgia, all running along the western ends of these states, which lie along the Atlantic. The Blue ridge and the Wuaka mountains approach each other, and form jointly the separation of the E. from the W. waters. As this range continues from the west; another range, not less formidable, approaches from the north. These are the Waldus ridge, and Cumberland mountains, which unite themselves with the former; where this union takes place, it is called Lookout mountain. At this point of intersection, where the union of immense mountains on either side, formed a barrier to the streams which flowed from fifty thousand square miles of country, the waters broke through.

The evidence at this place, of the war of the elements, is the admiration of all who pass the broken mountain, through what is called the suck, on boiling chaldron, near the confines of the state of Tennessee. At this place, the vast accumulation of waters, it is evident, broke through, and deluged the country below, toward the sea, overwhelming whatever settlements the Danes, or other people of the old world, may have made there, especially along the lowest grounds, till the waters were drained to the Atlantic. This position easily accounts for the appearances of such articles as have been disinterred, with that of timber, from the depths mentioned in the Journal of Science. Such a circumstance may have gone far to weaken the prowess of those nations. So that the survivors dwelling on the highest grounds, could not recover their numbers, their order, their state of defence and security, against the Indians farther west, who it is likely watched all opportunities to destroy them.

Finally, from all we can gather on this momentous subject, we are compelled, from the overwhelming amount of evidence to admit that mighty nations, with almost unbounded empire, with various degrees of improvement, have occupied the continent, and that, as in the old world, empire has succeeded empire, rising one out of the other, from the jarring interests of the unwieldy and ferocious mass: So also in this.

And, also, that convulsion has succeeded convulsion, deluge succeeded deluge, breaking down mountains, the barriers of rivers, deranging and destroying the ancient surface till it has, at length, assumed a settled and more permanent state of things, where the millions of the present race now inhabit.

But the majestic, yet fearful work of change and revolution, is doubtless going on in *other worlds* or planets as well as this, for wherever is the principle of life and motion, whether it belongs to organized and animated nature, or to the elements of which the earth is composed, the operation of revolution can but be going forward.

It is believed and asserted by astronomers, as their opinion, obtained from telescopic observation, that the moon, the satelite of the earth is a globe in *ruins*, or if not so, it at least is frequently much convulsed, by the operations of volcanic fires. Its surface as seen through the glasses, is found extremely mountainous, presenting an infinite variety of pointed mountains, overhanging ranges of ledge and precipice, with vales and flat regions embosomed between; consequently a great number of rivers, creeks, lakes and small seas must divide the land of this globe into a vast number of tracts of country, which are doubtless filled with animals, consequently, with rational beings in the form of men as ourselves, for we can conceive of none other, as fitted to preside over its animals. The same we believe of all the stars of heaven.

In exact accordance with this doctrine of change, as it respects the removal of entire worlds; the scriptures are full of allusions to such a catastrophe yet to take place. And why should it not? as he who *made* the worlds, also dictated the composition of that book, and can therefore be supposed as able to signify, beforehand, the great change which awaits our earth, as is plainly found recorded in it, and *that* change to be effected by the agency of fire, as is supposed to operate in the moon.

That fires *do* convulse that planet, is shown from the ærolithis, or hot stones frequently thrown through the moon's atmosphere, from its surface or interior by the force or power of volcanos, which have in a hundred instances, fallen to our earth, of different magnitudes, in different ages of the world, which among the ancient nations, was supposed to be cast down from the gods as objects of adoration, and their representatives.

But whatever changes are observed to be in *progress* either in our globe, or its companion the moon, may also be supposed to succeed and be in progression with other worlds, planets or fixed stars, both as to the revolution of their surfaces, and their final extinction from the firmament, where they are now situated is concerned.

In that *most* philosophical work, the bible, yet by some but little thought of, are prophetical accounts of the final ruin of this earth, by the agency of fire, the same element by which all animal or vegetable life are sustained and perpetuated, one of the *brightest* proofs of the power and wisdom of God afforded in the *material* universe, but the destruction contemplated is only to cause room and opportunity for a grander display, of the adaptation of another order of things, suited to such beings as have passed through the *incipient* degrees of the infancy of an intellectual state, and shall be found by him who is the judge of all virtue, worthy to be installed in those exalted degrees of reasonable and tremendous angelic powers.

We will just recount some of those predictions: see 2d Peter chap. iii. verse 7. "But the heavens and the *earth*, which are *now*, are kept in store, reserved unto fire, against the day of judgment." And at the 10th verse, "The heavens *shall* pass away with a great noise, and the elements shall melt with *heat*: the *earth* also, and the *works* that are therein *shall* be burnt up."

Much more relative to the *same* point is found in the same book, which to corroborate by occurrences in the great field of the astronomical or planetary heavens, we give the following from Good's *Book of Nature*, a work whose praise is found in the laboratory of philosophical truth, p. 33. "*First Lecture on matter and the material world.*"

"But worlds, and systems of worlds, are not only perpetually creating," by the hand of God, "but are also perpetually diminishing and disappearing. It is an extraordinary *fact*, that within the period of the last century, not less than *thirteen stars*, in different constellations, none below the sixth magnitude, seem totally to have perished; *forty* to have changed their magnitude, by becoming either much larger or much smaller; and *ten* new stars to have supplied the places of those that are lost. *Some* of these changes may perhaps be accounted for, by supposing a *motion* in the solar, or sidereal systems, by which the relative *positions* of several of the heavenly bodies have varied. But this explanation, though it may apply to several of the cases, will by no means apply to all of them. In *many* instances it is *unquestionable* that the stars [or suns] themselves, the supposed habitations of other kinds or orders of intelligent beings, together with the different planets by which it is probable they were surrounded, and to which they may have given light, and productive seasons, as the sun gives light and fruitfulness to our earth, have utterly vanished, and the spots which they occupied in the heavens have become blanks."

But there are other instances of the disappearance of stars from the heavens: 125 years B. C., it is recorded by Hipparchus that an extraordinary luminary appeared suddenly in the firmament, but disappeard in the course of a few years.

In 389 A. D., a star blazed forth near Aquilae, remained three weeks shining as bright as Venus, and then was seen no more. Tycho Brahe mentions the sudden appearance of a star as large and bright as Sirius, in the constellation Caseiopeia, and for a while was visible even at mid-day, but in the course of the year began to fade away, exhibiting all the signs of conflagration, and disappeared in March 1574. Instances of the kind are mentioned by Sir John Herschel, one in particular which was situated in the head of the constellation Swan in 1670.

Such is the demonstration of change and revolution in the immensity of God's words, which *no* doubt is agreeable to the beauty and harmony of the whole, proceeding on principles too deep, too abstruse for human research to penetrate.

Therefore, in addition to all the changes which the earth has undergone, from general or local causes, it is yet to pass through another still more wonderful; and whether the matter of which it is now composed will assume some other form, and be adapted to *other* states of being, or shall utterly vanish, and be annihilated, is unknown, yet it appears no less than thirteen of the heavenly bodies have passed away but a little while since, as shown above, Says Mr. Good, "what has thus befallen other systems will assuredly befall our own.

Description of Mount Ararat, on which the Ark rested.

NOTWITHSTANDING the remarks respecting Mount Ararat, on the first page of this work, we give the following additional account, from the recent travels of Sir Robert Ker Porter, which cannot but be highly interesting; as his account respects its actual appearance, having examined it himself, in 1820.

"On leaving our halting place, where we had rested for the night a fuller view of the great plain of Ararat gradually expanded before us, and the *mountain* itself in all its majesty, began to tower to the very canopy of heaven. We now took a descending position due east over a stoney and difficult road; which carried us for more than ten wersts, (or eight miles) through several close and rocky defiles, till we reached a small Mahometan village on the side of the Mosschian hills, where we again halted for the night. On the morning of the 17th, we set forth over a road as bad as that of the day before, in a direction southeast, and gradually descending from a great height through a very extended slopeing country towards the immense plain of Ararat.

As the vale opened beneath us in our descent my whole attention became absorbed in the view before me. A vast plain peopled with countless villages, and the *subordinate* range of *mountains* skirting the *base* of the awful monument of the antediluvian world, I seemed to stand on a stupendous brink in the history of man, uniting the two races of men before and after the flood. But it was not till we had arrived upon the flat plain that I beheld Ararat in all its amplitude of grandeur. From the spot where I stood it appeared as if the hugest mountains of the world had been piled upon each other to form this sublime immensity of earth, rock and snow. The icy peaks of its double heads rose majestically into the clear and cloudless heavens, from which the suns rays were reflected in an ocean of light glaring around its summits. This stage of the view united the utmost pionts of the grandeur of plain and inaccessable mountain height. The inhabitants dwelling on the plain, around this mountain, all unite in reverencing it as the haven of the great ship which preserved the father of mankind from the waters of the deluge. The height of Ararat has never yet been satisfactorily measured; but the best measurments of it was taken by Montieth of the Madras engineers, from the spot where Porter viewed it to the highest point of the loftiest head, and was found to be fifty-five thousand yards, which is full five miles and a half perpendicular altitude. At the distance of about a half mile from the highest peak, there ascends another horn or point of the mountain, but not as high as the former. In order to produce those two peaks, the mountain, a great distance up, is divided. Between these two points on the narrow vale it is believed the Ark rested, as it was impossible that it could have rested on either of the inaccessible points, which have never been trodden by the foot of man, being perpetually covered with snow and ice, while the plain around is covered with verdure in its season.

On the eastern side of this mountain the slope is gentle, so far up as to where it divides into the fingers; but on the other sides is very steep jagged and precipitous giving off branches in a confused and broken manner, stretching off after the general range of the mountains of Armenia.

This peculiar form must have favored the descent of the family of Noah into the plains below where he first commenced the cultivation of the vine, and it is likely of other plants calculated to produce food.

From all appearances, this tremendous mountain is the product of internal fires, which it is likely were in operation before the flood, as no traditions of the inhabitants speak of its having been a volcano since that time.

The descending portion of the country, which bounds the great plain being partly round the base of Ararat, favors this supposition, as well also as the nature of the strata which forms the mountains giving evidence, by the vast quantities of eruptive matter that here burnt, one of the volcanic fires of the antediluvian world."—(*Porter's Travels*, vol. 1, pp. 181—185.)